POVERTY, INEQUALITY AND UNEMPLOYMENT IN INDIA

Professor K.N. PRASAD received his education under Patna University during 1939-49 and at Cambridge University during 1956-60 from where he earned his Ph.D. Degree.

Dr Prasad taught in Patna University from 1949 to 1989. He became university Professor of Economics 1964. He headed the Economics Department of Patna College and Patna University during 1954-1989 and was Vice Chancellor of Patna University twice.

Professor Prasad is the author of 25 books, and 125 papers, several of them having been published in periodicals of international repute. He was associated with many universities and institutions in their various activities. Apart from the important positions he has held in the academic and administrative bodies of Patna University and other universities, he has served also on many State-level and a few national-level committees and commissions. He is a widely travelled man.

Since December 1989, Professor Prasad is Member (Economics, Industry and Employment) Bihar State Planning Board. He is also at present Member, Second Irrigation Commission of Bihar.

POVERTY, INEQUALITY AND UNEMPLOYMENT IN INDIA

(Incorporating Their Regional/ Inter-State Dimensions)

K.N. PRASAD
Member
Bihar State Planning Board, Patna

CONCEPT PUBLISHING COMPANY, NEW DELHI 110059

ISBN 81-7022-459-4

First Published 1993

Published and Printed by
Ashok Kumar Mittal
Concept Publishing Company
A/15-16, Commercial Block, Mohan Garden
NEW DELHI-110059 (India)

Lasertypeset by
Microtech Advance Printing Systems (Pvt.) Ltd.
H-13, Bali Nagar,
NEW DELHI-110015

To

Those of My Highly Telented Contemporaries who could not Achieve Much in Life having been denied Mental Peace and Quiet, on the One Hand and the Necessary Facilities, Support and Opportunity, on the Other

PREFACE

"Bear Wealth, Poverty will Bear itself."
"Money is like muck, not good, except it be spread?."

We have heard for long of the Third World. We have also heard of the Poverty of Nations (in Myrdal's *Asian Drama*). Ever since the early 1950s one of the most fertile fields in Economics has been the subject of underdevelopment of the vast majority of the countries in the world. Underdevelopment, Backwardness and Poverty have been interchangeable terms in the economic literature. In explaining poverty, unemployment has occupied a prominent place. At times poverty and unemployment have tended to shade into each other. But both analytically and operationally their separate entities have had their due justification.

In India, with the inauguration of the planning era, poverty and unemployment have been considered negative aspects of development. Inequality has been decried more than poverty and unemployment right from the beginning, and, more so, after the acceptance of the notion of the Socialistic Pattern of Society. Poverty, inequality and unemployment have figured consistently and prominently in all the plans. Poverty alleviation, of course, preceded systematic unemployment eradication. But the interdependence of the two types of programmes has always been recognized, so has been the need to dovetail them. For some time past there have been vociferous demands and solemn promises for a constitutional guarantee of the right to work, and, in the interval, around the common man's right to his basic minimum needs.

But Poverty, Inequality and Unemployment have been among those applied topics that have aroused considerable interest in teaching, research and examinations even before the achievement of Independence. Naoroji, Gokhale, Tilak, Gandhi, Nehru, J.P., Lohia, and others have reflected and written a lot on these problems.

Colleges and university departments teach and discuss these

themes and register candidates for research degrees who choose particular areas to work on. At every level of examination we have questions set on these topics.

An outcrop of books on these topics exists in the market—some very good, some good, and some not so good — some of these approach the problems from the national angle and completely ignore the inter-State variations, disparities or imbalances in respect of them. Others investigate the problems chiefly from the angle of individual States, and in the process forget to highlight the regional dimensions, as also underplay their aggregative, macro-economic aspects. These limited angles lower the value of such works. Then, we have books which concern themselves wholly with the topical issues and the current situations in these spheres and fail to realise the significance of setting problems in their proper perspective. Lastly, we have books which are straight commentaries on field studies and abound with tables. These may be of immense use and interest to people of those pockets which are investigated but those outside them may find them irrelevant to their purpose.

Poverty, Inequality and Unemployment in India seeks to optimize the merits of the existing works and to steer clear of their shortcomings. Balance or Measure is its hallmark. Theory goes hand in hand with practice. Applications do not remain mere reproductions as attempts are made to reach the soul of the data and to deduce meaningful conclusions from them. Words and statistics are used in a balanced and coherent manner.

My four decades of teaching experience in the university has provided me with some ability to judge the amount, the form and the manner in which the results of the current researches have to be accepted and purveyed to the readers.

I would now like to explain, in brief, *how this volume originated.* During 1967-68 was published my *The Economics of a Backward Region in a Backward Economy: A Case Study of Bihar in relation to other States of India*, in two volumes. It was very well received. It was reviewed favourably in several journals at home and abroad. The book became popular in a very short time and was used and quoted extensively. But in some years it became out of stock. In so far as it could not be reprinted without being thoroughly revised and updated, which had to be an enormous task, and since I was busy writing other books, one after another, this task could not be undertaken until my retirement from the Patna University Service in January 1989.

In 1983 appeared my *Problems of Indian Economic Development*, which contained seven chapters on topics of inter-State interest and nine chapters on the Bihar economy. This book also sold out in about three years.

In February 1989 when I resumed working on this book, I realised that the 1967-68 volumes would have to be rewritten in six to eight volumes, instead of two, so as to be in a position to embody information up to date. Further, each volume would have to be complete in itself, a separate book by itself. The book in your hands is therefore one such volume. Although it has its umbilical card with as well as its roots essentially in the old book, it is in its present form an altogether different and self-contained book. Not a single page in it has anything in common with the earlier one.

As far as the nature and content of the study is concerned, it is not directed at interregional imbalances *per se* but at interregional imbalances in Indian economic development. For this patent reason the relevant chapters begin with or contain discussions on both economic development and the Indian economy. In most cases the references to inter-State disparities are the inevitable parts of the general discussions or are, in the Marshallian terminology, *the leading species of a large genus*. The aim and object of this study is to distil the experience of the four decades of planning in the country and in its 17 major States.

It would be futile for me to try to point out here what is almost universal knowledge — that in my discussions of the economy-wide problems, the interregional and intraregional disparities and divergencies do not often get duly emphasised and are ordinarily assumed away. This entails confusion, besides diluting and distorting the validity and efficacy of the policy recommendations that are made.

In this volume the inter-State differences in poverty, inequality and unemployment since the inauguration of five-year planning in this country have been identified and indicated and fully accounted for. In examining every problem in its varied aspects the relative positions of the 17 major States have been evaluated both quantitatively (as far as possible) and qualitatively.

It has been my earnest endeavour to extend the analysis in this revised and enlarged volume much beyond what is incorporated in the literature on the subject available at present (in my own city, which is, by and large, a bookless place and elsewhere, as far as it could be within the reach of my utterly limited resources, without any aid at any time from any quarter whatsoever.

I have designed this new volume to be a succinct and coherent piece of research. With this end in view every possible effort has been made by me to render this work really good and useful and of very wide general interest for all concerned. However, only the reader would be in a position to tell how far I have succeeded in my fresh endeavour.

Let me say something about the States studied in these volumes. The Indian Union comprises 25 States and 7 Union Territories. Of these, 17 States—Andhra Pradesh, Assam, Bihar, Gujarat, Haryana, Himachal Pradesh, Jammu and Kashmir, Karnataka, Kerala, Madhya Pradesh, Maharashtra, Orissa, Punjab, Rajasthan, Tamil Nadu, Uttar Pradesh and West Bengal—are the building blocks of my work in this volume.

I have taken the liberty of calling these 17 States major States in spite of the fact that Himachal Pradesh and Jammu and Kashmir are not major States. For fiscal transfers from the Centre these two States are classified as Special-category States and the remaining 15 States are classified as Non-Special-category States.

The regional classification of the States in India varies with different authors. I have grouped them in five regions or zones, namely, the Northern Region comprising Haryana, Himachal Pradesh, Jammu and Kashmir, Punjab and Rajasthan; the Eastern Region comprising Assam, Bihar, Orissa and West Bengal; the Central Region comprising Madhya Pradesh and Uttar Pradesh; the Western Region comprising Gujarat and Maharashtra; and finally, the Southern Region comprising Andhra Pradesh, Karnataka, Kerala and Tamil Nadu.

Andhra Pradesh came into being on October 1, 1953, composed of the Telugu-speaking areas. Telengana was added to it in 1956. With the bifurcation of the bilingual State of Bombay, Gujarat State was formed on May 1, 1960. Consequent upon reorganisation of Punjab, Haryana State was created on November 1, 1966. Himachal Pradesh became a full-fledged State on January 25, 1971. United Mysore State was created in 1956; in 1973 it was renomenclatured as Karnataka. Kerala, an amalgam of Travancore-Cochin State and Malabar, came into existence on November 1, 1956.

Madhya Pradesh State was formed on November 1, 1956, out of Madhya Bharat, Vindhya Pradesh and the Central Provinces.

Maharashtra State came out of the reorganisation of Bombay on May 1, 1960, with parts of Hyderabad and Madhya Pradesh. The PEPSU was merged with Punjab in 1956. Reorganised Punjab came into being on November 1, 1966. Rajasthan took its present form on November 1, 1956. On January 14, 1969, Madras changed its name to Tamil Nadu.

In my study, which purports to be comparative, in relation to time, the States and the regions/zones, the emphasis rests on the percentage shares, period-wise, of the States and the regions/zones rather than on the absolute figures of out-put, income, employment, population, poverty, inequality, unemployment, etc. In spite of this it has been our foremost endeavour to give both absolute and percentage figures, except where the tables have tended to become unwieldy. Comments made on parts of the entire period generally transcend them and extend to the entire period. The sum – totals of absolute figures of the 17 States studied here do not add up to the all-India totals because some other States and all Union Territories have not been included in my study. Similarly, the percentage shares of the 17 States do not add up to 100, the reason being the same.

Capacity to predict requires quantitative rather than qualitative knowledge. In natural sciences the transition from the qualitative to the quantitative is easy and inevitable but in social sciences it is either impossible or bestrewn with peril and difficulty. The issues in which we are interested call for the specification of the direction of the net outcome of influences operating on the country as a whole and State-wise—the influence of one variable on another. The specification of this direction demands a specification of the magnitudes and the signs of the influences. For such issues all that economic theory can do is to specify some measurable quantity on which the outcome would depend in a decisive manner. To determine the outcome in any particular case, however, it is necessary to measure the quantity. Such measurement need not involve a statistical process but it always requires a detailed specification of the environment to which economic theory is to be applied and which economic theory cannot furnish itself. Quantitative comparisons of alternative situations are not always practicable. Hence, considerable reliance has to be placed on judgement and intuition for indicating the more significant aspects of the problem.

In our case the predictive value of the data used and the conclusions arrived at is limited. The data used here are to be relied upon more for indicating the direction of change (i.e., their qualitative value) than for indicating the magnitude of change (i.e., their quantitative value). But an ostensible drawback of the qualitative methodology consists in the fact that the ranks are not weighted according to the relative importance of the characteristics.

Notwithstanding the shortcomings of the data system employed by us, we can safely assert here that for the sake of policy formulation its conceptual purity and reliability is less open to question.

It would bear no repetition to state here that our subject of study has its roots in macroeconomics and locational theory. It is addressed, in the main, to the determination of the levels of output, income and employment in the country as a whole as well as the 17 major States, their sectoral compositions, their rates of growth, their levels of productivity, poverty and unemployment, degrees of inequality, and so forth. The States are open in the sense that commodities and factors of production move more or less freely across their borders. There are, in general, no trade restrictions and no barriers to migration among them. Given these preconditions, the comparative cost advantages of certain States lead to the establishment in them of particular basic activities for serving primarily outside markets, whereas their local markets are catered to by other producers. Levels of demand (governed by income and elasticity factor) determine how far these basic activities would expand through the working of the multiplier, having a certain value. The supply-side factors (comprising output, income, employment, inter-regional trade, government sector revenue and expenditure, etc.) affect the competitive postures of the 17 States and hence the value of the multiplier. Parallels from one State to another are useful in such a context only up to a point. But they cannot provide the complete answer to any particular question because a State has to work out its own inner potentialities by a process of experimentation, i.e., trial-and-error.

For our study we have used data compiled from different sources: Government of India, State Governments, Planning Commission, State Planning Boards, Reserve Bank of India, Centre for Monitoring of Indian Economy, private institutions and institutes, private persons, etc. In so far as there were discrepancies in the data on certain items they had to be used with due care. Each table gives at its bottom the sources of the data contained in it. The data were taken from their respective sources in two forms—directly and after necessary processing. On the whole, the second form predominates. The Five-Year Plans proved rich quarries for general information. My own old works have supplied me consistently with valuable information for the earlier years.

My study had to encounter a number of problems and difficulties. One was the glaring lack of data in certain areas. In these areas the information available was extremely meagre and as such did not throw sufficient light on the issues concerned. In certain cases where I had data, I found that they were not relevant to the problem at issue, or, alternatively, they had gaps in them, with the result that they did not quite suit my purpose. This difficulty was confronted more at the State level and less at the national level. Both aggregation and disaggregation of the data posed problems on this account. Also, the data could not be juxtaposed in such cases and hence could not be analysed. More importantly, time series studies proved impossible to carry out in most cases. Data were available for some years but not for all years. Cross-sectional studies could have been conducted but they would not have been worthwhile. Another difficulty facing my study was that while data were available for some States for particular years, they were not available for all the 17 major States and not for even those few particular years.

The data drawn from different sources were based on different conceptualisations and different definitions of the terms used, on different assumptions, on different methods of estimation, with different base years, etc. Comparability of the data and the estimates made was impaired by one or more or all of these factors. In some cases the data available or the estimates made on the basis of those data looked totally absurd, incompatible and irreconcilable. The estimates made could be reliable only in the proportions in which the data on which they were based were reliable. Even the Union Government's, more particularly the State Governments', publications of successive years were beset with discrepancies and presented data which contradicted themselves. Nothing but confusion resulted from this. These data had to be distilled and processed before they could be used. They had, however, to be presented despite their limitations because if this was not done, even a rough and ready idea of that aspect of the problems could not have been formed and complete ignorance would have prevailed. This explains why in some areas of my study data in crude and rudimentary forms have been used, of course, after due conditioning, processing and chiselling, with a pinch of salt, so to say. Estimates based on such data were at best approximate. In consequence, where the data were only partially reliable, conclusions, theories and predictions derived from them could not be wholly accurate, and had, as a matter of fact, to be used with due caution and commonsense. How accurate one's conclusions and hence one's predictions could be hinged fundamentally on whether or not the ground on which the analysis had been installed was firm or not, and the ground could be firm only if the data and other information that one used were adequate and dependable.

The prevailing rot in our contemporary society is sickening enough to fill any right-thinking man's heart with grave concern for its future. Therefore, the remedy lies in an overhaul of the total, and not in just tinkering with the marginal, conditions. Considering this, I have preferred the eugenic to the genetic view of the problems in this reconstructed and expanded volume.

In this volumes have not, therefore, attempted to present a conspectus listing categorically the policy suggestions made by me. They lie diffused over different chapters. The only plausible reason for this is my strong belief that any such endeavour would necessitate further research for testing some of the premises and hypotheses. But I do not have the requisite resources for undertaking this nor can I hope that I would obtain any assistance from any agency by approaching them inasmuch as I do not fulfil the other extraneous conditions which have become more important in decision-making in the last few decades. Such was my sad experience in the past as well when I felt like an idiot while trying to comply with the queries of the great experts who sermonised from their pulpits and who wore inclined more to reject outright than to accept my proposed projects with helpful suggestions.

Likewise, there was room in this volume for application of more statistical tools with a view to broadening the base of analysis and interpretation but that could not have been done without some assistance from outside. For this I did not the necessary finance. As a result, this volume had to be a one-man project from beginning to end on account of this constraint. Bulk of my savings has been invested in the preparation of this volume.

The role of data is critical to the accuracy and usefulness of the predictions based on the statistical methods. In order to apply economic analysis to real-life situations, appropriate statistical measurements must replace the mathematical symbols. To obtain these measurements statistical techniques have to be used in the compilation and interpretation of economic data. This is a task which is beyond the capacity and competence of one single man.

The economist is a trustee of the people. As an official adviser he may be called upon to make fiduciary value judgements. He may be tempted to search for an economic formula or simpliciter, even if it can never be a panacea or cure-all for our economic ills. Such a search now-a-days presumes team work, and not a lone-wolf type work, for its success and hence availability of the necessary research facilities. Persons of more or less equal academic background are apt to produce works of different qualities because they have to work in different environments and because some receive whereas others do not receive technical and financial support from the agencies meant for it. Thus even in this area one is struck by inter-regional imbalances of great magnitudes. After all, discrimination is not a one-area practice in our country but rather a multi-area operation.

As already indicated above, this book is the product of my own "effort and sacrifice" from beginning to end. I have not taken any advantage in any form from my present position as Member (Economics, etc.) of the Bihar State Planning Board or Second Bihar Irrigation Commission. Whenever I required some recent data, not otherwise handy, I sought the help of my research student, Mr. Krishna Kumar. He brought to me the data from the reading-room of the A.N. Sinha Institute, Patna. Being a retired teacher, I was not entitled to the use of the libraries of Patna College (to which I had donated by personal library prior to my superannuation from the Patna University Service); University Department of Economics, Patna University; etc. Only two persons, Mr B.P. Mishra and Dr. U.M. Thakur of the Patna University library helped me with some books by borrowing them in their own names. Mr A.K. Sinha of the BITCO spared the CMIE publications on request in advance on a few occasions for my use. Mr. Dayalu Shankar, Joint Director (Evaluation), State Planning Board – an able and helpful man – arranged for my use unofficially, the old volumes of the *Statistical Abstract of India* from the library of the Directorate of Statistics as well as furnished to me some statistical information which I needed at times through his Assistant Statistical Officer, Mr Udaya Shankar Kakaudwar, another helpful man in the Board. But for their help, I, who have been without any technical or research assistance, would have gone without even that little support. Dr. D.R. Pendse (Tata Services Ltd.), the SAIL, Development Commissioner for Small-Scale Industries, Development Commissioner for Handlooms, Chairman, Khadi and Village Industries Commission, Director General C.S.O., and Chairman, IDBI, were kind enough to send some of their useful publications to me on request. My brother-in-law, Mr. S.K. Soni, helped me in obtaining some institutional publications through Mr. T.N. Bhasin and Mr. A. Sharma, his younger colleagues. Mr. Bimla Nanda Bissell, Information Officer, World Bank, New Delhi Branch, gave me some publications of the Bank. Parts of this volume were written during my stay in Delhi with my sister-in-law, Mrs Indra Kapoor, and her husband, Mr Mohinder Kapoor, and parts with my elder son, Sanjiv Verma, in NOIDA, and his wife, Meena. Sanjiv also acted as a link between me and my publisher. Mr. S.N. Mishra, who has by now become as good as a member of my family, typed most of the tables in this book as well as some portions of its text. Mr Jaya Shankar Mishra, Manoj, Diwakar and Rakesh who live with me in the outhouse were also helpful in some way or other. To crown all, my wife, Mrs Usha Prasad, in spite of her adverse health, extended to me her usual help in the preparation of this work at various stages in a gamut of ways. At a later stage, my old student Dr (Mrs) Indira Dutta and her husband Mr Dutta, resident in Delhi helped me in continuing my contact with my publisher. Dr D.M. Diwakar also took similar pains. All these persons deserve my thanks.

Before I conclude, I would like to make it clear to all concerned that all the *opinions and views* expressed by me in this volume are genuinely and strictly my own and have nothing to do with those of the institutions I am serving at present.

"A good life is the only religion".
"Debt is the worst poverty".

At Science College Compound
Patna-800005
September 12, 1992

K.N. PRASAD

CONTENTS

PART III: A Critique of the Recent Debates

LIST OF TABLES

THE PROLOGUE

Poverty, inequality and unemployment are the negative aspects of economic development. The First Five-Year Plan considered mass poverty and unemployment to be two associated phenomena. Its authors wrote, "The urge to economic and social change under present conditions comes from the fact of poverty and of inequalities in income, wealth and opportunity." The First Plan desired to throw open to the people new opportunities for a richer and more varied life. It stood for the abolition of want. It emphasised "the need to raise the standards of living of the poorer sections of the community". In its opinion, development lay in increased availability of supplies of material goods and in the realisation of full employment and attainment of economic equity and social justice. It was convinced that the elimination of poverty could not obviously be achieved merely by redistributing the existing wealth. It suggested that the potential resources available to the community should be utilised more effectively. It observed unequivocally that the steps to augment production were not on all fours with the steps to remove the existing inequalities and hence separate steps were needed. In its view, economic equality and social justice had any meaning only when the production potential of the community was substantially stepped up.

The drafters of the First Plan deemed unemployment to be at once an economic and a social problem involving human values. They thought that the capability of economic development to bring about a rise in the standards of living of the average citizen, and in the level of employment as well as a fall in the inequalities of income and wealth was not infinite but limited.

The First Plan expressed its preference for economic and social stability but not at the expense of economic and social change needed for economic progress. For it economic progress consisted in the attainment of the three accepted objectives of planning —maximum production, full employment and economic equality. But it was only through a balanced stress on all the three objectives that development could proceed.

The Approach Paper on the Eighth Plan speaks of distortions and dilutions and failures of planning in the past. It also points to the high levels of unemployment and underemployment and their rising levels in some regions. It refers to the progressive decline of employment in the traditional crafts and industries. It painfully notes that over-all employment has grown at a slower rate than the labour force. It underscores the failure of organised industries, despite growth of output, to provide additional employment opportunities on account of inroads into the traditional labour-intensive lines of production made by the more capital-intensive techniques.

The authors of the Approach Paper comment on the disparities between different social groups, between wage labourers and property owners, workers in organised and unorganised sectors which have been accentuated, according to their information. Similarly, the disparities between per head agricultural income and per head non-agricultural income have widened. The dichotomy between rural and urban areas has become more articulate.

The framers of the Approach Paper express concern for the guarantee of the right to work, or to provide employment opportunities to all, and to ensure everybody access to adequate means of livelihood. They also show concern for the high average rate of inflation that hits the common man hard, for the expansion of a parallel economy, and for the danger of the debt trap faced at present by the nation on account of more than doubling of its foreign indebtedness and the fact that debt-service ratio is as high as 28 per cent of its current receipts.

The authors of the Approach Paper allude to the near stagnation in the per capita availability of most basic consumer goods relative to the growth of goods and services which figure prominently in the consumption by the relatively well-to-do and largely urban segments. They are critical of the maldistribution of income, which has been caused and intensified by policies towards imports of technology and components, and fiscal measures, which together have encouraged the growth of certain consumption patterns which are not acceptable to the fair-minded from any point of view — economic, social and political. Maldistribution of wealth has stimulated the growth of production of elitist consumer goods.

The Approach Paper recognises the urgent need to remove the causes of discontent and unrest by attacking unemployment, illiteracy, ill-health and the decline in the living conditions of the poor and vulnerable sections of society. It comes to grips with the equal need to create not merely a just social order but also an order that is perceived to be just. Only on this basis can the foundations of peace be laid and the integrity and self-confidence of society restored.

The Approach Paper wants the development strategy to be reoriented in such a way that it gives primacy to the immediate and urgent needs of the poor, such that everyone is enabled to have adequate employment, afford at least the minimum desirable package of food, clothing and shelter, and have access to education, health, child care and other related services.

The architects of the Approach Paper lament that even after four decades of planning the task of ensuring employment and even a minimum standard of living to everybody remains unfulfilled. They, therefore, call for more direct measures to bring about a more even distribution of income across space and between classes. According to them, the attainment of the above-mentioned basic tasks must be the central concern of the development strategy and processes during the 1990s, the decade in front of us. See Ch. 20 for later developments in the approach.

PART I

THE POVERTY AND INEQUALITY QUESTION(S)

1

THEORIES EXPLAINING INDIAN POVERTY AND INEQUALITY

Poverty is generally sought to be denoted, rather crudely, by per capita real income. This does not fully describe the grimness, abjectness or abysmalness of poverty. Poverty stands for lack of money income, its insufficiency to ensure the minimum requirements of life. Of late, poverty has been identified with certain unsatisfactory results, e.g. low expectation of life, a low rate of literacy, a high infantile mortality rate – measures or indicators of the quality of life which are physical, concrete or objective. Some authorities have suggested a poverty-weighted index, expressed as a weighted average of the increase in real per capita income of various quintile groups.

From the definition of poverty proceeds the concept of Poverty Line, which is defined in absolute terms. Those people or that percentage of a population is stated to be below the Poverty Line the individual or family income of which is not adequate to ensure them the minimum requirements of life (e.g. nutrition, clothing and shelter) or, more conservatively, only food, a socially decent life being the ultimate goal. In the short run, the common man must be entitled to a minimum calorie intake to keep the body and soul together, i.e., to guarantee him bare survival.

One observable feature of the Poverty Line concept that has become patent is its non-rigid character. It is flexible and shifts through and over time. It keeps rising as prices rise or as average income per capita rises or is planned to rise in real terms. To illustrate, in 1986 (details of the earlier years are adduced later on in this chapter) the Poverty Line in India was redrawn at Rs 6,400 per annum. Families below this line were further sub-divided. Those earning less than Rs 3,500 a year (the earlier criterion) were called the hard-core cases and were slated to receive greater attention in the direct poverty-alleviation programmes. About seven million families fell in this category.

The Poverty Line concept has immense operational significance because it necessitates focusing of the development policy on those below the Poverty Line. At the field or ground level, the household or family is taken as the unit of policy. Besides, the programme is largely target group-based or oriented.

As per evolution of the concept in India so far, those below the Poverty Line are to be ensured a minimum income necessary for leading life at the subsistence level, for enjoying the minimum necessities of life, for leading a minimum standard of living, or for enjoying a basic minimum level of consumption. The norm of minimum calorie consumption is the hall-mark, the most notable feature of the Indian notion of the Poverty Line. The average income, monthly or annual, per capita, or per household comprising a certain (average) number, say, five members, sufficient to guarantee that minimum calorie consumption must be made available to the unit in question through provision of assets (chiefly milch cattle, sewing machines, spinning *charkhas*, weaving *karghas,* rice-pounding *dhenkis,* oil-pressing *kolhus*, etc.) and working capital. This takes after the principle of pump-priming, or a once-over measure.

While discussing the theories explaining poverty, we should at least in analysis guard ourselves against the pitfall of mixing them with those concerned with either the aggravation or the persistence of poverty, notwithstanding the fact that there cannot be a hard and fast dividing line in reality.

The extent of poverty turns inversely on average per capita income and directly on the degree of inequality of income distribution.

Let us enumerate here the theories expounding the causes of Indian poverty:

A. Theories in Terms of Low Income and Earning

(a) Whether the marginalised 40 per cent comprising the bottom quintiles eat better or not depends on the level of their income or earning, which at present is low. Casual, uncertain, low productivity activities keep their incomes down. The total purchasing power commanded by them in the market, and their entitlement in it is small, primarily due to want of employment. The terms at which they can exchange their ownership into commodities and services they wish to acquire are unfavourable to them. This, in effect, is the collapse of exchange entitlement. Bulk of the purchasing power is concentrated in the hands of the wealthy land-owners and factory-owners, who are fewer in number.

(b) The income-getting power of every section of a community is governed by the internal and external influences (the latter represent the economic relations of the people with foreigners). The former concern (i) the productive system and its development which embraces capital accumulation and the entire set of incentives and disincentives, (ii) nature of the people especially moral qualities of the commercial sort, (iii) the material environment—physical surroundings, climatic influences and the infrastructure, and (iv) the stock of current ideas, that is, knowledge or technology.

(c) The disadvantaged groups like the small and marginal farmers, the Scheduled Castes and Scheduled Tribes which are the prime source of supply of agricultural labour, the backward classes, rural artisans, fishermen, etc., are the social groups with maximum concentration of poverty in them.

(d) Unplanned or semi-planned, inefficient and inadequate production. The poor have no regular or full-time jobs. They have instead very low-paid jobs. The real price of labour is low. Labour is insufficiently rewarded. It gets a wage that is less in value than its marginal product. It is thus exploited. This is class exploitation. Archaic production relations prevail in many segments of production. The wages paid in them cannot maintain life and efficiency. The earnings in the low-paid jobs are low, but even those who are self-employed do not earn much and their share in national product has tended to decline with the passage of time.

(e) The poor man's earning is low because his net worth is low. His net worth depends on his education and health or on possession of livestock and/or house to live in. The few skills that he has are not all that relevant. So he finds scraping a living most difficult.

(f) For about two centuries India had been subjected to colonial oppression with its attendant loot and drain of wealth out of the country. Poverty became an integral part of the life of an average Indian.

(g) In a managed economy, where we have an amalgam of market and non-market solutions, there arises from time to time a disequilibrium in terms of trade between agriculture and non-agriculture. That too compounds the given poverty.

(h) The above is in its quintessence the interlocking vicious circle explanation. The vicious circles hold down the teeming millions who are poor — at the minimum subsistence level — and make poverty and low levels of living self-perpetuating. To break them we would need a massive dose of outside capital culminating in the *Big Push.*

B. Theories in Terms of Growth Process and Rate of Growth

(a) The poor in India stay poor because the growth process has proved ineffective. The trickle-down effect has been ineffective in improving the living levels of the poor.

(b) Ingrained in the growth process there is nothing to guarantee that it would not be biased in favour of the relatively rich. To illustrate, the top five per cent of the cultivators corner most of the development gains. A one per cent increase in rural per capita expenditure results in 1.72 per cent increase in per capita expenditure of this top five per cent of the peasants, and 1.58 per cent increase in the per capita expenditure of the top ten per cent of them.

(c) That is to say, the growth process cannot overcome relative poverty.

(d) Instead it increases absolute poverty. It centres at the top, which is at the cost of those at the bottom. With wealth increasing, absolute misery multiplies. This is the digest of the saying "poverty in the midst of plenty".

(e) For abolishing poverty the growth process is an extremely time-consuming process. It would need ages to purge poverty out of the country but the masses cannot afford to have the patience to wait that long.

(f) The rate of growth is too low owing to the lack of capital and smallness or limitedness of the resource-base. The immensity of the task and the inadequacy of the growth rate are in sharp contrast today. The extremely low growth rate is incapable of making a dent on poverty. To break the vicious circle of poverty or to lift the economy from the low-level equilibrium trap a very high growth rate is essential. In order to pull the bottom 40 per cent up the poverty threshold not only the growth rate has to be fast but it has also to be accompanied by a decline in distribution inequality, i.e., a direct attack on poverty cannot be avoided.

(g) The pressure for an immediate distribution of the benefits or fruits of growth prevents the growth rate from gathering momentum. People have to stint themselves more and more, consume less and less, save more and more currently, if the economy is sought to be lifted by its own bootstraps or shoestrings, that is, by tightening its own belt. But this cannot be done as it conflicts with the risen expectations of the people. To resolve the conflict, the growth rate has to be lowered, or, alternatively, the objective of self-reliance has to be compromised with resort to foreign capital.

(h) The foregoing boils down to asserting that the reasons for poverty are in conformity with the reasons for backwardness which has often been typified by "a syndrome of poverty" or underdevelopment — underdevelopment is a euphuism for poverty.

C. The Low Productivity Explanation

(a) Mass poverty in India owes itself to low (labour) productivity levels, which are self-feeding. These are due to a general dearth and an inefficient use of the key factors of production, e.g. natural resources, capital and knowledge in relation to the supply of manpower, so much so that where two can do, three or four are employed. Productivity levels are also low because the poor classes have not so far been properly cared for. The state had no concern for them for ages. In consequence, the social rate of return from them was nil.

Productivity of labour is low everywhere — in agriculture, in cottage production, in the formal and informal urban sectors, and so on. Poor health, inadequate nutrition and little formal education are bars to productivity.

(b) The poor have either no instruments of production or if they have any, they have very low levels of productivity when operated upon, being primitive and absolute.

(c) Productivity is a function of technology. Stagnant or

slow-changing technology or its tardy diffusion and adoption and adaptation keep average productivity low, with the result that income grows less than proportionally with applications of fresh doses of labour and capital to the existing land. Measures will have to be taken to step up the productivity of both the wage-employed and self-employed persons, particularly of the former because, with the passage of time, work ethic or culture among them has tended to decline. Security of employment instead of having on incentive effect has had a disincentive one on the productivity of those employed in the government sector.

D. The Structural Explanation

(a) One stream of thought in India maintains that in the course of time much structural change has taken place in India. In several occupations the erstwhile engaged persons had to be displaced from their old posts. In general, the poor sections were the sections to be affected most and to be hit hard. Their standard of living suffered a serious setback. The faster the speed of the structural change was in an occupation, the harder the blow was in its intensity.

(b) Another strand of thought has believed that there has scarcely taken place any structural change in India. Thereby hangs the real explanation of Indian poverty. Because of predominance of agricultural population in total population and hence of primary production, where productivity has been relatively lower, poverty has not only been the lot of those engaged in agriculture and activities allied to it but poverty has also tended to persist because of the static and stagnant character of the rural economy. Motion has been there (a static economy in motion), for the laws of motion are inexorable and universal but the dead-wood and deadweight elements have had such a retarding influence on it that the net motion was low and slow and could not weed them out and free the system from their clutches.

(c) The preceding ultimately resolves itself into an explanation of India's rural poverty. As a matter of fact, diagnosing Indian poverty is, in essence and in effect, diagnosing India's rural poverty, which forms the hard core of India's over-all poverty.

Rural poverty is not attributable to the preponderantly agrarian make-up of the rural economy *per se* (because there are preponderantly agrarian economies that are as productive and efficient and hence rich as preponderantly industrial economies), but rather to the intra-sectoral institutional biases and inter-sectoral imbalances (in sum, the much-maligned urban bias of the Indian planners, as insinuated by Lipton). Even urban poverty is summarily dismissed as a mere overflow of rural poverty. Solve rural poverty and urban poverty would be solved automatically is the slogan.

E. The Unemployment Explanation

(a) This explanation is an offshoot of a deduction from the Income Explanation (see A above). Unemployment and underemployment constitute a paramount cause of Indian poverty. The link between poverty and unemployment stands in the limelight. Earning of the poor folk is not for all the year round; it is concentrated in certain seasons or months or even weeks so that in other seasons unemployment is the only alternative facing the poor. The lack of purchasing power is due to the failure of the poor to find productive employment on a year-round basis. Their earnings are low not only because of the low-productivity openings in which they find employment but also because of underemployment in the absence of alternative avenues, and demand for their products and hence a limited market for them, or due to the non-supply of inputs and credit in requisite amounts and at proper time, and so forth. In many families there is hardly any bread-winner and a dole or relief is the only solution in such cases.

(b) In so far as one man can support a number of persons poverty which is of the order of 40 per cent of total population is more rampant than unemployment and underemployment which would in the worst cases not exceed 25 or 30 per cent. Unemployment is a causative factor in poverty but the two are associative factors in certain pockets and classes of the country. In relation to the growth process and the growth rate the two stand to each other in a very kindred and intimate, and an almost identical, relationship. They have a good many factors as their common causes. There is also some common ground between their remedies.

F. The Population Factor

(a) Excessive population is a cause of poverty as well as of its persistence or perpetuation, besides of its accentuation or intensification. Chronic, cumulative poverty corroborates the Malthusian trap. The ever-rising numbers press on the given means of subsistence. Real wages fall off in rural areas. The share-croppers, agricultural labourers and artisans become worse off. The major portion of the rise in average income is neutralised by rapid population growth, even if the pace at which food supply increases is faster than the pace at which population increases. The rise in the people's standard of living is, therefore, marginal. It is the individual family, not the individual, which bears the brunt of this endemic phenomenon in our country. Improvident fertility, the reckless procreation without heed of the future, failure of employment to rise at the rate required to absorb the new additions to the labour force and to clear the backlog of unemployment is reflected in the continuously swelling army/reservoir of the poor and the unemployed. The "tragic grandeur", Myint's choice phrase, of this Malthusian drama is symbolised, as already stated above, by the teeming millions that are poor and unemployed and are hence struggling to survive somehow or other at the minimum subsistence level. Poverty and unemployment interact — poverty intensifies unemployment, whereas unemployment lies at the root of the poverty of many people. Furthermore, poverty and overpopulation sustain each other. Low levels of living can be a cardinal factor in restricting the freedom of parents to choose a desired, ideal or optimum size of family. Poverty accompanied by low animal protein consumption leads not to depopulation but instead to overpopulation. Whether we deploy the Malthusian thesis focusing on food supply per head of population or the Leibensteinian theory pinpointing the low-level equilibrium trap, the end result is the same: The Population Factor is a dissipator or swamper of the gain in per capita income and hence of the redressal of poverty to that degree.

(b) However, the causation between excessive population growth and grinding poverty in India is not a direct and simple one; other factors, social and cultural, are involved in it.

G. Non-economic Factors

(a) Among social arrangements for production responsible for poverty we should include disadvantage and disabilities suffered by particular social groups on account primarily of the accidents (places, also, but secondarily) of birth which have accumulated over the long years. In addition to the inequality suffered on the social plane by many people, another inequality encountered by them has been in the sphere of employment. Opportunity for employment became the privilege of the upper castes like the opportunity for higher and professional education which was monopolised by them. Education, employment and status became the tripod which was integral to our society for long. This was challenged only recently and sought to be rectified by means of positive discrimination (Table 1.1). But this therapy is at present beset with a potent abuse: what is meant for a group of castes is tending to be blatantly usurped by the leaders of the politically most dominant and most represented caste for the benefits of the members of that caste along with extraordinary zeal, vehemence, vengeance and aggressiveness. Economic forwardisation of the backwards has in practice come to denote economic forwardisation of the politically most vocal and most powerful backward caste — the group has dissolved into the caste, though not without sowing the seeds of another war, an inter-caste war within an earmarked social group as this has caused much frustration and disillusionment and bad spleen among the other backward castes. In the past 5 to 7 per cent of the 17 to 20 per cent upper castes had, by turn, the lion's share of all opportunities – social, political, cultural and economic – to themselves, now the same 5 to 7 or 10 to 11 per cent of the 52 to 60 per cent middle castes have these to themselves. History has repeated itself in this area also. It appears as if constancy is the law even in this realm. In politics morality cannot be a perfect cube, for no one is really above board to successfully challenge such inequities. Only if we had some leaders who were acceptable to both "forward" and "backward" groups alike or, at least in the short run either to the "forward" or to "backward" group as a whole, things would definitely look up but, unfortunately, at present we have only "caste" leaders unexcelled in their bigotry.

TABLE 1.1: Representation of scheduled castes and scheduled tribes in Central Government services

Group	Number of Employees	Scheduled Castes	Percentage of Scheduled Castes to Total	Scheduled Tribes	Percentage of Schedued Tribes to Total
A	61176	5204	8.51	1373	2.24
B	86018	10021	11.65	1720	2.00
C	2224212	330330	14.85	100425	4.52
D (Excluding Sweepers)	1092715	223045	20.41	70583	6.46
Total	3464021	568600	18.24	174101	4.98
*All-India Services**					
IAS	4702	533	11.12	269	5.72
IPS	2514	282	11.21	124	4.93

* As on January 1, 1988.

Source: Government of India, *India 1990.*

Note: Article 335 of the Constitution provides that the claims of the members of Scheduled Castes and Scheduled Tribes shall be taken into consideration, consistent with maintenance of efficiency of administration in making appointments to posts and services in connection with the affairs of the Union or the States. Article 16(4) permits reservation in favour of citizens of backward classes who may not be adequately represented in services. In pursuance of these provisions the Government has made reservations for the Scheduled Castes and Scheduled Tribes in services under its control.

For the Scheduled Castes, reservation is 15 per cent of the vacancies for which recruitment is made by open competition on an all-India basis and 16 per cent of the vacancies to which recruitment is made on an all-India basis other than by open competition. For the Scheduled Tribes, reservation is 7.5 per cent in both cases. Reservation in direct recruitment to Groups C and D posts which normally attract candidates from one locality or region is fixed in proportion to the population of the Scheduled Castes and Scheduled Tribes in the respective States/Union Territories.

Contd.

(b) Exploitation of the poor tenants by their landlords who deny them security of tenure and charge exorbitant rents. The abject poverty of the share-croppers and temporary tenants cannot be eradicated without comprehensive tenancy reform, which would raise the share-croppers and temporary tenants to the status of occupancy tenants.

Note Contd.

Reservation is also made at 15 per cent of the vacancies for the Scheduled Castes and 7.5 per cent for the Scheduled Tribes in promotions on the result of competitive examinations limited to departmental candidates in Groups B, C and D and in promotion by selection in Groups B, C and D and to the lowest rung of Group A in grades or services to which direct recruitment, if any, does not exceed 7.5 per cent. Reservation has been provided for the Scheduled Tribes in promotion on the basis of seniority, subject to fitness in Groups A, B, C and D posts in grades or services to which direct recruitment, if any, does not exceed 7.5 per cent in promotion by selection within Group A to posts carrying a maximum salary of Rs. 5,700 (revised scale 4500-5700) per month or less, Scheduled Caste and Tribe officers who are senior enough to be in the zone of consideration for promotion and are within the number of vacancies for which the select list has to be drawn, are included in that list provided they are not considered unfit for promotion.

During the period from June to August, 1989, a special drive was launched to fill up the huge number of vacancies for ST/SC in various Central Ministries/departments and public sector undertakings. Another drive, initiated in June, 1990, was expected to be completed by October, 1990.

The State Governments have also framed rules under the powers given to them by Item 41 of the State List of the Seventh Schedule to the Constitution for reservation of posts for these classes and have taken steps to increase their representation in State services. Reservation in State Government services, however, is under the exclusive jurisdiction of the State Governments.

The matter pertaining to 27 per cent reservation of the Central jobs for the 52 per cent population constituted by the other backward classes in Indian society is still undecided. 4.5 per cent of the Central Class I and 14 per cent of the Central Class II jobs had gone to these classes. The Central Goverment jobs added up to one per cent of the total employment in the country. A rough idea of concentration on of government employment in certain classes or castes is given in the *Economic & Political Weekly*, dated 29.9.90 To adduce some figures: In 1981, Brahmins were 48 per cent of the Lok Sabha, 36 per cent of the Rajya Sabha, 50 per cent of Governors and Lt. Governors, 54 per cent of Secretaries to the former, 53 per cent of Union secretaries, 70 per cent of private secretaries to ministers, 62 per cent of joint and additional secretaries, 51 per cent of vice-chancellors, 56 per cent of the Supreme Court judges, 50per cent of High Court judges and additional judges, 41 per cent of the ambassadors and 57 per cent of chief executives of State Public Undertakings.

The small producers are exploited by middlemen and moneylenders, which fact calls for state action. The inputs and services and reliefs meant for the weaker sections are diverted and misappropriated by the well-to-do sections. The poor do not have their due share in the public grants system. The cooperative system has not benefited them in proportion to their number and need. The credit policies of the public sector banking and non-banking financial institutions have discriminated against small producers. The growth and expansion of the public sector has not altered the situation in favour of the poor, who have also been ignored by an inefficient and corrupt administration. No part of the system seems to be informed by social purpose.

(c) For long the poor in India have suffered in silence, in a spirit of resignation, accepting their poverty as an act of God, as their bad *Karma*. Their value system has borne the injustices perpetrated upon them by the system, the iniquitous policies of their rulers and the disintegration suffered by their community life, which are sociological facts with an in-built normative aspect. The personal characteristics of the poor, their habits, their life-style, their living conditions all of which created an atmosphere which has motivated them into drinking and drug-taking, gambling, prostitution, etc., and what not.

(d) Demographic characteristics of the population have also influenced poverty by influencing income distribution in a modern society.

H. Factors Aggravating and Perpetuating Poverty

(a) Fall in production, especially agricultural, and among agricultural production, production of foodgrains, which has aggravated the misery of the poor.

(b) Constant inflation has eroded the real worth of the limited earnings of the poor and worsened their economic plight.

(c) Physical deterioration in the environment caused by the poor (who have exploited the natural resources to which they have had access) has boomeranged on them and exacerbated their poverty.

(d) Poverty has persisted because of the economic and technical dualism, the process of cumulative causation and the vicious circle of poverty (which is broken after a long struggle).

I. The Inequality of Distribution of Income

(a) The social arrangements for distribution like those for production and exchange have great significance in explaining poverty and inequality. But here we are concerned with structural, inequalities, not of the productive but, of the distributional system. We are interested in class as well as personal distribution of income and wealth. Apart from under-production and inefficient production, inequitable distribution of income, that is, mal-distribution, has immediate relevance to our instant problem. The two interact and accentuate the adverse effects of each other.

(b) Inequalities exist in various forms: (i) in income distribution, (ii) in property (means of production, assets, or wealth) ownership, (iii) in opportunity for education, specially higher and professional, (iv) in opportunity for employment [in most cases (iii) is meaningless without (iv)], and (v) consumption of public and private goods and services.

(c) Poverty has to do a great deal with skewed income distribution. Inter-class inequality in income distribution has widened in the past three decades. The investment-oriented growth strategy has been specially at fault for this. The condition of the bottom 20 per cent has deteriorated, and that of the next 20 per cent stagnated. The lowest 20 per cent of the rural and urban households have claimed nearly 70 per cent of the total household income. The highest 20 per cent of them have claimed nearly half of it. This is inequality of income between the rich and the poor.

(d) Inequality of income between rural and urban areas that had increased during 1951-69 slightly decreased during 1970–80. So that the urban poor's lot does not suffer further the informal sector in urban areas should be formalized through small credits on easy terms and on-the-job training. Inequality of income between the employed and the unemployed has further increased with the increasing volume of unemployment and the country appears to have been divided into two nations, one inhabitated by the employed and the other by the unemployed, and the latter having been obliged to serve as a colony to the former. This polarisation has to be arrested, and the Eighth Plan has to prove itself equal to the ordeal.

(e) Inflation by its nature aggravates inequality. It cuts into the earnings of the poor class and leads to a set-back in its economic condition. The Government's failure to check the increase in the prices of essential articles of mass consumption has added to the suffering and privation of the weaker sections. It is necessary, therefore, that consumption of core items should be stabilised by stabilising their prices.

(f) Inequality in investment in human capital, particularly in professional training and competence, is a principal determinant of income inequality in the wage-employed or self-employed sections of society. In India the low levels of literacy and education and skills have accounted for the limited spread of the new technology more than the deficiency of capital supply. The quality of human capital would be a significant determinant of the degree inequality in earned incomes in the coming years.

(g) Some inequality has been built into the growth process itself whereby the rich have become richer and the poor poorer, relatively, of course. The gains of development have not been equitably shared. They have gone proportionally more to those already at the top or to those in the next decile who have moved up in the scale or ladder. The benefits of extended and improved social services like education and health have flowed largely to the better-to-do individuals and families. The poor have had a very small share in the welfare services provided by the state, if at all.

(h) Income inequality has increased because incomes from property (non-wage incomes like interest, rent and profits and dividends) have risen by higher percentages than incomes from labour (wages and salaries and other benefits flowing to employees), as would appear from Table 1.2 which covers a period of 14 years from 1971-72 to 1984-85. Growth has upset the ratios in which the various kinds of income have been shared, bringing about an improvement in some respects and a deterioration in other respects. During the period wage income has increased by three per cent, and non-wage income by 2.7 per cent. In other words, the wage: non-wage income or earned: unearned income ratio has improved. Real wages of the working class rose but slightly and at a rate lower than that at which the national product rose. The self-employed sector suffered a set-back, while the wage-employed sector gained by comparison. Between the private and public sectors, the latter spent relatively more on the wages and salaries of its employees than the former, as indicated in Table 1.3.*

(i) Of the current income, 77 to 79 per cent is consumed by all sections of the people. The rich consume less than the poor.

---

* Consider the new system of pension under which those who have been members of legislature for a very brief period draw a sumptuous pension, while in the services the salaried classes have to put in a minimum number of years of service to qualify for a pension of lower sum in a large number of cases. What does this signify in terms of an equitable sharing of economic opportunity between those who are the architects of laws and those who are supposed to abide by them? And all this is taking place in a poor country. In the past few years the people's representatives have done nothing to deserve this unprecedented improvement in the terms and conditions of their membership of the legislative bodies. On the contrary, things have taken an adverse turn in most spheres, aggravating the people's daily plight. In this context a letter published in *Times of India*, Patna, dated September 9, 1992 and reproduced below would prove of immense interest.

Politicians' Perks

Sir, — Whether it is good or bad, the truth is that almost all political parties are agreed today at least on one point, which is raising the perks and monetary emoluments of the representatives to the maximum extent, as also those of the freedom-fighters (who could not have the wages of their sacrifice in their minds when they participated in the freedom movement) and attaining an all-India parity in this regard. This plunder of the public resources by the people's representatives is so organised that anyone who dissents is bound to be routed at the hustings (A.K. Roy is an example).

Were we to project the trend of this, we would say that in the next stage the people's representatives would have allotted to themselves the surplus land under the ceiling legislation yet to be redistributed. In the third stage, they will have other assets of the nation and the states apportioned among themselves. As for the award of life-long pension, anyone who has taken the oath of the House would become entitled to it (one day's presence would suffice) and if there is at any time stringency of funds, the government servants would be asked to wait for their salary while the people's representatives are paid their bills forthwith.

In fact, this world was made for the Haves, not for the Have-nots. Politics is any day the most flourishing industry of India.

— Rakesh Kumar, Research Student, Science College, Patna-5.

Consumption expenditure on the basic physiological needs is a far larger percentage of the current income in the case of the poor. Still in our country it has been estimated that the rich class has been spending six times more on foodgrains than the poor classes. In rural areas consumption expenditure is concentrated in the top 20 per cent of the population which accounts for approximately 40 per cent, as against just 22 per cent accounted for by the bottom 40 per cent of the population. In urban areas the top 20 per cent account for about 42 per cent of total consumer outlay, whereas the bottom 40 per cent account for just 20 per cent of it. For the marginal rate of saving to be continuously rising the marginal rate of consumption has had to be continuously falling. This was tantamount to a curtailment of current consumption, or a rise in it at a rate far slower than the rate of rise in current production. In a word, inequality in consumption has tended to increase. The miserable consumption of the poor is ascribable, in part, to the ostentatious consumption and extravagant living of the rich. The rich have directed their earned and unearned (unaccounted) incomes into non-priority areas (luxurious consumption, and palatial residential buildings and for speculative gains in sale and purchase of urban land).

TABLE 1.2: Distribution of factor incomes at current prices

(*in Percentage*)

	1971-72	1984-85
Compensation of employees (i.e., wages, salaries, etc.)	39.2	42.2.
Interest	5.6	8.6
Rent	5.2	3.5
Profits and dividends	4.6	6.0
Income of self-employed persons, etc.	45.4	39.7
Total	100.0	100.0

Source: Tata Services Ltd., *Statistical Outline of India*, 1989-90.

Needed all along has been a less uneven distribution of income as well as a less uneven class consumption. Income is redistributed directly by income-tax and transfer payments. The latter play an insignificant part in India. The tax system is tilted more to the proportional than the progressive method. Progressive taxation has proved to be a clumsy instrument, blunted by widespread tax evasion and the origin and growth of the parallel economy.

TABLE 1.3: Distribution of factor incomes in organised segments of private and public sectors : 1984-85

(In Percentage)

Kind of Income	Private Sector	Public Sector
Compensation of employees, etc.	21.19	46.81
Interest	5.78	8.50
Rent	0.68	1.10
Profits and dividends	7.43	8.51
Total	35.08 (Rs. 23235 crores)	64.92 (Rs. 43016 crores)
Total	Rs. 66,251 crores	

Source: Tata Services Ltd., *Statistical Outline of India*, 1989-90.

The upper-income groups would oppose measures calculated to redistribute consumption more than they would oppose measures aimed at redistribution of money income because the former have a damaging effect on incentives, savings and investment.

Assistance can be given to the poor in cash or the social consumption goods can be redistributed among them. In the first alternative the poor choose how to allocate the purchasing power they have been given. Fiscal and administrative burdens are involved in this. In the second alternative the task of allocation rests with the public authority. Bias may vitiate the choice of articles to be produced. The first alternative bristles with the difficulty of identifying the poor, which is not confronted in the second alternative.

(j) What goods and services would be produced and in what amounts is determined in an unplanned economy by how the incomes flowing from sale and investment of services of agents of production are spent, that is, production is governed by distribution. If distribution of income is unequal, the production pattern would be lop-sided. Income and hence demand governs supply in a free market economy.

In a planned economy both production and distribution are regulated in part by the state and are left free in part to the unseen operation of the anonymous, blind market forces of demand and supply.

Existence and persistence of income inequalities in India have distorted the production structure. The share of wage goods in the total supply has fallen relatively to that of non-wage goods in it. Also, the supply of wage goods has grown at a pace slower than that at which the supply of non-wage goods has grown. Increased production of consumer durables and of elite goods, in particular, is the outcome. This is indicative of misdirection of investment. Short of a ceiling on the living standards for the affluent, there could not be a floor to the living standards for all. At the same time, those who have low levels of living must be made to partake increasingly of the social consumption goods and services by giving them priority in their allocation and by enhancing their access to these amenities of life. Education and medical services would probably have a larger influence on income distribution in the coming years than several public policies designed and directed to altering the distribution pattern in the economy.

(k) In our country income inequality has been aggravated by (i) a lop-sided production pattern, (ii) technical and economic dualism, (iii) market imperfections like growth of monoploid and oligopolistic elements, (iv) risen public debt servicing charges on the part of the state, (v) anti-social income transfers encompassing black money (a parallel economy) which is growing at the rate of Rs. 90 million per hour – several million worth of foreign exchange being lost annually through illicit transfers, etc., (vi) shifts stemming from the policies of subsidisation (import subsidy, export subsidy, investment subsidy, fertilizer subsidy, electricity subsidy, food subsidy, etc.) – provision of commodities and services at subsidised prices, the import licensing policy, and (vii) unpredictable and indeterminate responses of different classes in India to change and growth. To exemplify, the banking sector has been helping the richer households in the main. In the early 1980s households with assets of less than Rs. 10,000 were getting 67 to 90 per cent of their credit from money-lenders, while those with assets of value of "above Rs. 5,00,000" were getting 95 per cent of their credits from the institutional sources.

J. Inequality in the Distribution of Wealth

(a) Income is derived from property, from the degree of its utilisation, and from the price of the unit services of property. Distribution of property influences distribution of income substantially.

(b) Distribution of wealth, education and skills, and employment opportunities may tend towards gross concentration of economic power.

(c) At the low levels of income the institution of private property and the law of inheritance may be the causes of poverty. Also, at the top of the income scale, income from property may be of greater moment. Distribution of property is given by inheritance and personal savings.

(d) This problem has three aspects: ownership of property, control of property and use of property. Property is means of production: Land, capital or investment goods, human capital, and other material assets – even man's own labour power, his pair of hands, his back. It is owned and operated both privately and publicly. Sometimes there arises joint control and ownership of property.

(e) In the Third World land is inequitably shared; so are other instruments of production like irrigation water, fuel from the common wood, common grazing pasture, and similar other community assets. The poor have no control over the income-earning assets.

(f) Wealth, which is the fountain-head of economic power, is concentrated in India. A wide variation is found between the top and the bottom tenths of the population. This concentration is on the increase in rural as well as urban areas. To give an illustration, six per cent of the top urban households own around 72 per cent of the total urban land . Over 72 per cent of the profits earned in industry are explained by monopoly power and control.

Monopoly capital has grown. Private monopolies have grown in many segments of the economy. The industrial and import licensing policies have helped the growth of private monopolies over all these years.

The maldistribution of assets has resulted in the maldistribution of economic power. Factors which control the distribution and uses of resources have spilled from the economic to the wider purview of social life.

(g) Concludingly, poverty and inequality are related intimately to each other. The deprivation aspect of poverty is interconnected with the inequality question. The number of the poor is a very crude measure of inequality. A higher level of inequality tends to be associated with a higher level of poverty, and conversely.

2

INDIAN POVERTY AND INEQUALITY IN RETROSPECT

Poverty, unemployment and inequality in India are the known facts of life. On a broad level, India's development economics is closely connected with the solution of these basic problems. The bulk of the people live so close to the margin of poverty that poverty is their very culture. Germane to the culture of development is the end of the poverty culture.

Inequality refers to relative poverty. Under it we have the few well-to-do juxtaposed against the many ill-to-do. There is inequality of incomes, of wealth, of consumer expenditure, of opportunity, and all the rest.

In 1952-53 the top five per cent claimed 14 per cent of national income; in 1956-57 the figure was 17.5 per cent. The top 10 per cent claimed 24 per cent of national income in 1952-53 and 25 per cent in 1956-57. The bottom 20 per cent claimed 7.5 per cent of national income in 1952-53 and eight per cent in 1953-54 and 8.5 per cent in 1956-57.

In 1955-56 nearly 72 per cent of the population below per capita income of Rs. 255 at current prices accounted for 49 per cent of national income. About 28 per cent of it above this average accounted for 51 per cent of national income. Twenty-five per cent of it remained content with a measley 9.5 per cent of national income. The top 10 per cent of it accounted for 34 per cent of national income.

In 1960-61 the percentage of population below the poverty line was 55.4. In 1964-65 around 47.5 per cent of the disposable income went to the top 20 per cent, while the bottom 20 per cent got a meagre 7.5 per cent or even less.

During the 1960s, the income, generally, was concentrated at the top and in urban areas. The estimated average annual income of the topmost decile was approximately 18 times that of the lowest decile in the urban sector, whereas for the rural sector it was about 10 times.

In 1975-76 the lowest 20 per cent of all households, rural as well as urban, accounted for 7 per cent of the total household income, while the highest 20 per cent accounted for 49.4 per cent of the aggregate household income.

Inter-State income disparities disclosed a small decline during the 1950s but increased during the 1960s and the early 1970s.

There is ample evidence of growth of monopoly capital in India. The total assets of the top 51 giant companies in the private sector rose by 36 per cent per year from Rs. 1,000 crores in 1960-61 to Rs. 11,683 crores in 1983-84.

Monopoly trends have become stronger. The grip of big business on the economy is now tighter in spite of the controls. In 1963-64, 75 big business houses controlled 44 per cent of the paid-up capital of all non-government and non-banking companies. They controlled Rs. 2,606 crores worth of capital. In 1983 each one of the 20 big business houses controlled Rs. 292 crores or more worth of capital assets, totalling Rs. 5840 crores. The Tatas accounted for Rs. 2,672 crores, the Birlas Rs. 2,831 crores — showing six to eight times rise in less than two decades.

Over 72 per cent of the profits earned in industrial enterprises is accounted for by monopoly power and inflation.

The gains of development in the past four decades have not been shared equitably by all sections of the population, rural and urban. Inter-class inequalities have widened over these decades. The investment-oriented growth strategy has accentuated inequality. A higher level of inequality has tended to be associated with a higher level of poverty. In the short run an employment-oriented growth strategy can be a corrective of increased inequality but in the long term removal of absolute poverty alone would lower relative income disparities.

Per capita monthly consumer expenditure is taken as an index of poverty and inequality. In 1952, in rural areas, per capita monthly consumer expenditure was Rs. 27.81. Of this, Rs. 16.65 was spent on food. Of that, Rs. 9.63 was spent on grains, Rs. 3.92 on milk and milk products, Re. 0.15 on meat, fish and eggs, Rs. 0.83 on sugar, and Re. 0.45 on edible oils. The non-food items claimed Rs. 11.16. The inter- State position is depicted in Table 2.1.

TABLE 2.1: State-wise per capita per month consumer expenditure in rural areas 1952

State	(Rupees)
Assam	24.24 (3)
Bihar	24.03 (4)
Madhya Pradesh	16.40 (8)
Maharashtra (including Gujarat)	19.32 (6)
Orissa	15.02 (9)
Punjab (including Haryana)	31.96 (1)
Tamil Nadu	18.28 (7)
Uttar Pradesh	23.45 (5)
West Bengal	28.10 (2)
All-India	27.81

Source:(1) K.N. Prasad, *Economics of a Backward Region in a Backward Economy : A Case Study of Bihar in relation to other States*, Vol. I, Scientific Book Agency, Calcutta, 1966.
(2) *NSS Report Nos. 311 & 319.*

Note: Figures in brackets indicate the ranks of the States.

The All-India and inter-State situations in 1957-58 are contained in Table 2.2. Both table are self-explanatory.

TABLE 2.2: State-wise per capita expenditure (total, rural and urban) (1957-58)

State	Per Capita Current Expenditure	Per Capita Personal Expenditure at Current Prices (Rs.)
Andhra Pradesh	246.2 (9)	222.6 (10)
Assam	352.5 (1)	321.7 (2)
Bihar	238.1 (11)	220.1 (11)
Jammu & Kashmir	NA	286.5 (4)
Karnataka	278.6 (5)	256.2 (6)
Kerala	242.0 (10)	219.5 (12)
Madhya Pradesh	267.3 (7)	242.8 (7)
Maharashtra	273.1 (6)	236.0 (8)
Orissa	195.8 (13)	180.0 (14)
Punjab	352.4 (2)	327.1 (1)
Rajasthan	325.2 (3)	294.7 (3)
Tamil Nadu	237.1 (12)	208.6 (13)
Uttar Pradesh	247.5 (8)	226.1 (9)
West Bengal	321.8 (4)	272.9 (5)
All-India	270.7	243.3

Source: K. N. Prasad, *The Economics of a Backward Region in a Backward Economy : A Case Study of Bihar in relation to other States*, Vol. II.

Note: Figures in brackets indicate the ranks of the States.

Table 2.3 gives the pattern of inequality in per capita consumption by fractile groups for rural and urban areas in 1967-68. It suggests that in rural areas per capita consumption of the poorest decile of the population comprising the destitutes, disabled persons, pensioners and others was roughly 35 per cent of the average in rural areas and about 28 per cent of it in urban areas. These people were not fully in the mainstream of economic activity. The remaining 90 per cent of the population benefited directly from the growth in production and employment. The lowest decile of all households shared 3.2 per cent of the total private consumption of the country as a whole, while the highest decile claimed 23.9 per cent of the aggregate.

TABLE 2.3: Estimates of the share of different fractile groups in total consumption: 1967-68

Fractile Group	Rural	Urban	Combined
0 - 5	1.48	1.14	1.33
5 - 10	2.02	1.64	1.86
10 - 20	5.01	4.25	4.69
20 - 30	6.08	5.35	5.76
30 - 40	7.09	6.42	6.81
40 - 50	8.13	7.57	7.91
50 - 60	9.29	8.88	9.13
60 - 70	10.68	10.74	10.60
70 - 80	12.46	12.59	12.52
80 - 90	15.15	15.90	15.48
90 - 95	9.37	10.24	9.74
95 - 100	13.24	15.55	14.17
Total Population	100.00	100.00	100.00

Source: *National Sample Survey* (22nd Round), July, 1967—June, 1968, based on a sample of 15,800 rural and 8,600 urban households.

In 1968-69, at current prices, average per capita per annum private consumption expenditure came to Rs. 488 for all-India. At 1972-73 prices, minimum private consumption needed a monthly expenditure of Rs. 40.60 in 1974-75. The positions in 1977-78 and 1983, all-India and State-wise, are shown in Table 2.4.

Food items claimed nearly two-thirds of the expenditure in rural areas and three-fifths of it in urban areas.

Per capita final consumption expenditure was Rs. 1,677 in 1986-87 at 1970-71 prices and Rs. 1,709 at 1980-81 prices.

TABLE 2.4: State-wise monthly per capita consumer expenditure at current prices

(Rupees)

State	1977-78		1983	
	Rural	Urban	Rural	Urban
Andhra Pradesh	69.7	93.2	115.4	153.5
Assam	59.0	94.4	113.0	154.0
Bihar	57.4	83.1	93.8	138.5
Gujarat	70.3	100.9	122.7	163.6
Haryana	92.4	100.4	151.8	186.9
Himachal Pradesh	81.4	123.0	150.8	258.6
Jammu & Kashmir	72.9	88.4	129.3	155.3
Karnataka	64.9	87.6	116.8	166.3
Kerala	74.2	82.7	145.2	176.4
Madhya Pradesh	60.0	90.9	100.5	144.9
Maharashtra	76.9	110.3	110.4	184.4
Orissa	52.5	87.0	98.8	151.4
Punjab	114.4	121.7	170.5	185.2
Rajasthan	108.7	95.7	127.0	159.9
Tamil Nadu	63.3	86.1	112.2	163.7
Uttar Pradesh	67.3	82.5	104.5	135.5
West Bengal	59.3	97.1	104.6	170.0
All-India	68.9	96.2	112.4	164.0

Source: NSS Reports No. 311 & No.319.

Note: Per capita per year final consumption expenditure at 1970-71 prices was Rs. 488 in 1960-61, Rs. 522 in 1970-71, Rs. 603 in 1980-81 and Rs. 650 in 1984-85.

At 1979-80 prices, total private consumption expenditure was Rs. 75,033 crores in 1979-80, and Rs. 94,386 crores in 1984-85 and would be Rs. 1,53,745 crores in 1994-95, as estimated. The share of the bottom 30 per cent of the population in national income was 13.7 per cent in 1979-80 and 16.7 per cent in 1984-85 and would be 17.3 per cent in 1994-95. Per capita annual consumption expenditure for total population was Rs. 1,147 in 1979-80 and Rs. 1,316 in 1984-85 and would be Rs. 1,824 in 1994-95. For the bottom 30 per cent of the population the corresponding figures were Rs. 523 and Rs. 734 and would be Rs. 1,051. In 1984-85 per capita consumption expenditure grew at the rate of 2.79 per cent.

It is postulated that private consumption expenditure would be less if the share of domestic capital formation, public consumption and exports was higher.

Coming to the estimation of the population percentages below the well-defined Poverty Line, we can point out (by avoiding repetition) that the norm is fixed at a daily per capita calorie intake of 2,400 units in rural areas and 2,100 units in urban areas. For 1960-61 Dandekar and Rath had assumed that Rs. 180 per person per year consumer expenditure assured that intake in rural areas and Rs. 270 in urban areas. On the basis of these two criteria the percentage of population below the Poverty Line was 40 in rural areas and 50 in urban areas. Data for 1964-65 and for 1967-68 were estimated by other economists, such as Wadhva, (Table 2.5) and Mukherjee, Bhattacharya and Chatterjee (Table 2.6). These data indicate a rising poverty curve.

TABLE 2.5: Percentage of rural people below minimum level of living defined as Rs. 15 per month at 1960-61 prices

(Rupees)

State	1960-61	1964-65	1967-68
Andhra Pradesh	47.41	34.47	38.19 — 51.19
Assam	13.78	9.77	21.32 — 31.93
Bihar	37.64	42.80	61.29
Gujarat	25.01	27.66	34.70 — 48.06
Haryana	—	10.24	28.62
Jammu & Kashmir	20.57	14.63	20.90
Kerala	56.72	50.44	57.31
Madhya Pradesh	47.16	46.32	60.59 — 68.73
Maharashtra	40.14	47.02	44.51 — 56.71
Mysore	34.20	48.99	47.62 — 57.02
Orissa	68.88	62.04	63.84 — 72.02
Punjab	13.56	15.95	32.92
Rajasthan	33.50	24.73	37.07 — 46.96
Tamil Nadu	46.45	n.a.	51.98
Uttar Pradesh	39.47	41.61	60.84
West Bengal	22.14	50.19	61.24
All-India	38.03	44.57	53.02

Source: C.D. Wadhva, *Some Problems of India's Economic Policy,* 2nd ed.

In 1968-69 two celebrated economists, Bardhan and Minhas, reviewed the poverty situation in the country. Bardhan adopted Rs. 180 for rural areas and Rs. 216 for urban areas as per person per annum consumer expenditure capable of guaranteeing a living outside the poverty bondage. On these criteria 54 per cent of the rural population and 41 per cent of the urban population were below the Poverty Line. Minhas took a minimum level of living as the measuring-rod of poverty and calculated that the absolute number of the poor had not altered significantly during 1950-51 to 1967-68,

TABLE 2.6: The poverty situation during the 1960s

State	Per Capita Total Annual Consumption Expenditure (Rs.)		Total Calorie Equivalent of Daily Diet		Percentage of Population Rural/Urban) laying below the Minimum Consumption Level		Monthly Per Capita Expenditure Class in which a Diet with 2,250 Calories is reached* (Rs.)		Percentage of Population below the Poverty line		Density of the Poor*
	Rural	Urban	Rural	Urban	Rural	Urban	Rural	Urban	1960-61	1967-68	
Andhra Pradesh	236	273	2,355	2,436	62.41	58.11	18-21	21-24	47	39	11.4
Assam	233	271	2,260	2,213	47.67	23.37	18-21	21-24	14	21 to 32	1.4
Bihar	169	238	2,198	2,365	37.38	41.28	13-15	18-21	38	61 to 71	10.8
Gujarat	164	315	2,222	2,187	19.09	50.50	13-15	24-28	25 to 37	48	8.6
Jammu & Kashmir	165	239	2,380	2,250	13.69	42.30	13-15	18-21	8	12	—
Kerala	464	617	3,007	2,672	90.75	88.89	34-43	43-55	42	49	13.9
Madhya Pradesh	147	271	2,475	2,568	25.79	51.62	11-13	21-24	36 to 47	61	13.5
Maharashtra	238	370	2,303	2,226	61.04	58.18	18-21	28-34	40	56	8.6
Karnataka	172	275	2,238	2,273	26.92	57.39	13-15	21-24	34	48	10.9
Orissa	167	310	2,342	2,293	43.88	35.57	13-15	24-28	56	64	14.9
Punjab (including Haryana	165	271	2,402	2,128	13.98	52.09	13-15	21-24	18	28 to 32	3.4
Rajasthan	120	202	2,495	2,343	13.29	21.84	8-11	15-18	33	37	10.4
Tamil Nadu	235	374	2,321	2,196	55.19	70.78	18-21	28-34	51	59	9.1
Uttar Pradesh	146	220	2,237	2,294	18.13	37.65	11-13	15-18	39	61	12.4
West Bengal	199	374	2,233	2,313	44.09	48.53	15-18	28-34	22 to 42	61 to 74	4.0
All-India	170	274	2,194	2,159	30.92	46.50	13-15	21-24	38	53	—
Total	—	—	—	—	38.00	54.00	—	—	—	—	—

Source: (1) V.M. Dandekar and N. Rath, *Poverty in India*, Bombay, 1971.
(2) M. Mukherjee, M. Bhattacharya and G.S. Chatterjee's paper in *Commerce*, August 14, 1972 for figures in cols. (10) to (12).
* Relate to the 1960s.

Note: In 1963-64 per capita per month consumption expenditure of Rs. 0-15 denoted rural poverty and of Rs. 0-24 urban poverty.

except that there were variations in it in response to the state of the harvests — the number of the poor tapered off during good harvests and shot up during droughts.

For 1968-69 two alternative tests were used—P Test and H Test – for fixing the Poverty Line at a specified per capita per annum income. But they gave strange results. The seven States which suffered from worst poverty were: Uttar Pradesh, Orissa, Madhya Pradesh, Kerala, Rajasthan, Tamil Nadu and Gujarat. But Bihar was not amongst such States.

Between 1960-61 and 1967-68 the percentage of rural population below the bare minimum level of living went up by 40 per cent. The percentage nearly trebled in West Bengal and more than doubled in Punjab and Haryana. It went up by more than 40 per cent in Assam, Bihar, Gujarat, Mysore and Uttar Pradesh. The percentage remained unchanged in Andhra Pradesh, Jammu and Kashmir and Kerala. No State suffered a significant fall.

As would appear from Table 2.7, there were "rings of poverty" concentrated around "a solid core of destitution" in the country during the 1960s.

The Planning Commission made its own estimates of the people below the Poverty Line separately for rural and urban areas by using Rs. 77 as per capita per person consumption expenditure at 1979-80 prices[1] for being above the Poverty Line in rural areas and Rs. 88 for the same purpose in urban areas. Its findings were that in 1972-73, 54.09 per cent people, in 1977-78, 50.82 per cent people, and in 1983-84, 40.4 per cent people in rural areas were below the Poverty Line. For urban areas the corresponding figures were 41.2, 38.2 and 28.1 per cent. For rural and urban areas combined the figures were 51.5, 48.3 and 37.4 per cent respectively. The absolute numbers (in millions) were: 244.2, 253.1 and 221.5 respectively for rural areas, and 47.3, 53.7 and 49.5 respectively for urban areas. For both areas they were 291.5, 306.8 and 271.0 in that order. Table 2.8 embodies State-wise data on these lines.

The Janata Government in its Sixth (Draft) Plan had underestimated the percentage of population below the Poverty Line at 30.

For the Sixth Plan for a family of five the poverty line was drawn at Rs. 3,500 a year, that is, Rs. 700 per month per person – the mid-point of the monthly per capita expenditure class having a daily calorie intake of 2400 per person in rural areas and 2100 per person

TABLE 2.7: Destitution in India during the 1960s

State	Severe Destitution		Destitution							Poverty			Total Population (million) (1963-64	Per capita monthly expenditure (Rs.) (1963-64) (million)	Population below poverty line (1971) (million)	Per cent of population below poverty line
	Population (million)	Per cent	Rural			Urban									
			Population ('000s)	No. of destitutes ('000s)	Per cent	Population ('000s)	No. of destitutes ('000)	Per cent	Total Per cent	Population (million)	Per cent				
1	2	3	4	5	6	7	8	9	10	11	12	13	14	15	16
Andhra Pradesh	5.9	15.5	31,197	7,993	25.62	6,648	2,055	30.91	26.55	15.8	41.8	37.8	22.03	17.9	42.3
Assam	0.2	1.5	11,763	460	3.91	966	—	—	3.91	1.1	9.0	12.7	27.96	6.2	40.6
Bihar	6.5	13.3	45,044	10,103	22.43	4,083	1,369	33.54	23.35	17.4	35.3	49.1	22.02	27.0	49.4
Gujarat	2.4	11.0	16,382	2,947	17.99	5,802	930	16.03	17.48	6.9	31.2	22.2	25.39	8.5	33.3
Jammu &													2.4	25.6	
Kashmir	0.1	2.4	3,075	172	5.59	623	109	17.46	7.60	0.6	15.4	3.7	28.52	2.0	44.6
Kerala	3.7	18.8	15,263	4,335	28.40	2,737	1,132	41.35	30.37	8.0	44.4	18.0	21.41	7.8	37.9
Madhya Pradesh	5.4	15.7	29,496	7,106	24.09	4,956	1,617	32.62	25.32	12.8	37.1	34.5	24.31	18.0	44.9
Tamil Nadu	4.4	12.4	25,775	4,464	19.26	9,569	2,372	24.79	20.76	12.4	34.9	35.3	25.38	16.1	40.4
Maharashtra	5.2	12.3	30,253	6,982	23.08	12,117	2,689	22.19	22.83	15.2	35.9	42.4	26.16	16.2	33.5
Mysore (Karnataka)	4.2	16.8	19,410	5,012	25.82	5,661	2,361	41.71	29.41	11.0	44.0	25.1	21.66	11.7	41.3
Orissa	3.3	18.0	17,371	4,911	28.27	1,138	271	23.77	27.99	7.6	40.8	18.5	20.11	13.4	64.7
Punjab (including Haryana)	1.9	8.8	17,485	2,072	11.85	4,462	1,112	24.92	14.51	4.8	22.1	21.9	29.81	2.7	20.8
														(excluding Haryana)	
Rajasthan	2.9	13.2	18,103	3,818	21.09	3,561	1,024	28.75	22.35	7.4	34.2	21.7	24.68	11.3	45.6
Uttar Pradesh	13.3	17.0	67,969	16,904	24.87	10,016	3,898	38.92	26.67	30.4	39.1	78.0	22.32	38.6	44.8
West Bengal	2.2	5.9	28,216	3,657	12.96	9,299	1,294	13.96	13.21	8.5	22.9	37.5	28.13	15.0	34.9
All-India	61.7	13.2	3,82,020	81,783	21.41	84,880	22,647	26.68	22.37	161.6	34.6	466.9	24.25	218.3	41.2

Source: (1) for columns (2) to (14) Da Costa's article in A. J. Fonseca, *Challenge of Poverty in India*, Delhi, 1971.
(2) for columns (15) and (16) FICCI, *Planning for Results*, New Delhi, 1972. Those who do not consume 2,250 calories a day are taken to be below the line.

Note: Per capita per month consumer expenditure of Rs. 0-11 denoted severe rural destitution and of Rs. 0-15 denoted severe urban destitution.

TABLE 2.8: Population below poverty line : Statewise (1977-78 and 1983-84)

(Percentage)

State	Rural		Urban		Total		Percentage of Agricultural Labourers to Total Main Workers (1981)	Monthly Per Capita consumer Expenditure in Rural Areas (1983)
	1977-78	1983-84	1977-78	1983-84	1977-78	1983-84		
1	2	3	4	5	6	7	8	9
Andhra Pradesh	45.4	38.7	37.2	29.5	43.6	36.4(7)	56.68(1)	115.4(9)
Assam	48.5	23.8	36.5	21.6	47.3	23.5(13)	NA	113.0(11)
Bihar	57.8	51.4	44.8	37.0	56.3	49.5(1)	35.44(2)	93.8(17)
Gujarat	43.1	27.6	29.8	17.3	38.9	24.3(12)	22.82(11)	122.7(7)
Haryana	23.2	15.2	32.5	16.9	25.2	15.6(15)	16.40(12)	151.8(2)
Himachal Pradesh	27.8	14.0	17.2	8.0	27.0	13.5(17)	NA	150.8(3)
Jammu & Kashmir	31.7	16.4	40.5	15.8	18.4	16.3(14)	NA	129.3(5)
Karnataka	53.2	38.5	44.6	29.2	50.8	35.0(8)	26.66(7)	116.8(8)
Kerala	47.4	26.1	53.2	30.1	48.4	26.8(11)	28.19(4)	145.2(4)
Madhya Pradesh	61.6	50.3	46.9	31.3	58.9	46.2(2)	24.17(9)	100.5(15)
Maharashtra	60.4	41.5	41.4	23.3	50.6	34.9(9)	26.79(6)	110.4(12)
Orissa	67.9	44.8	41.8	29.3	65.1	42.8(4)	27.65(5)	98.8(16)
Punjab	13.1	10.9	25.6	21.0	16.4	13.8(10)	22.83(10)	170.5(1)
Rajasthan	33.5	36.6	33.9	26.1	33.6	34.3(10)	7.37(14)	127.0(16)
Tamil Nadu	56.3	44.1	45.3	30.9	52.8	39.6(5)	31.45(3)	112.2(10)
Uttar Pradesh	49.8	46.5	49.2	40.3	49.7	45.3(3)	16.32(13)	104.5(14)
West Bengal	58.3	43.8	34.5	26.5	52.2	39.2(6)	24.81(8)	104.6(13)
All-India	51,2	40.4	38.2	28.1	48.3	37.4	25.16	112.4

Source: (1) Reply to Unstarred Question No. 1969, Rajya Sabha, March 12, 1987.
(2) Bihar State Planning Board, *Selected Plan Statistics*, 1986.

Note: Figures in brackets indicate the Ranks of the States.

in urban areas. At 1979-80 prices, the mid-points were Rs. 76 in rural areas and Rs. 88 in urban areas. On this basis nearly 50 per cent of the population in India lived below the Poverty Line.

Sundaram and Tendulkar have attempted a finer classification of the rural poor according to the nature of households. The agricultural labour households are embedded in extreme poverty and have maximum concentration of rural poverty (see Table 2.9).

TABLE 2.9: Category-wise incidence of rural poverty (based on the NSS data)

Household type	Percentage of all households	Incidence of poverty	Percentage of total poor
Self-employed in agricultural occupation	46.1	30.0	35.0
Self-employed in non-agricultural occupation	10.6	38.1	10.2
Agricultural labour households	29.9	58.8	42.3
Other labour households	6.9	38.5	6.7
Other rural households	6.5	23.5	3.8

Source: K. Sundaram and S. D. Tendulkar, *Economic and Political Weekly*, November 5-12, 1983.

In retrospect, the percentage of population below the Poverty Line fell from 55.1 in 1960-61 to 51.5 in 1972-73, to 48.3 in 1977-78, to 41.5 in 1981-82, and to 37.4 in 1983-84. But when these percentages are reduced to absolute numbers, we find an increase from nearly 242 million in 1960-61 to 282 million in 1972-73 but then a fall to 273 million in 1977-78, and then again a rise to 284 million in 1981-82 but again a decline to 271 million approximately in 1983-84 (see Table 2.10) as the total number of the poor in India.

In 1983-84 Orissa, Madhya Pradesh, Bihar, Uttar Pradesh, West Bengal and Maharashtra disclosed poverty levels above the national average of 40 per cent. The two agriculturally most prosperous States, viz., Punjab and Haryana, and Kerala, which received maximum investment funds from the non-resident Indians, registered lowest poverty levels. As Hanumantha Rao's study bears out (see Table 2.11), a high negative correlation exists between rise in average rural consumption expenditure and poverty. This lends support to the general theory that poverty-alleviation programmes that help to improve average rural consumption expenditure have a direct impact and make a dent on poverty. Poverty among the Scheduled Castes and Scheduled Tribes lessened between 1977-78 and 1983-84 on account of the differential treatment meted out to them. The percentage of poverty among the former came down to 50.9 from 63.2 and among the latter to 57.1 from 71.4. This was a real achievement.

TABLE 2.10: Number and percentage of population below the poverty line (1983-84)

State	Total Number (in lakhs)	As Percentage to Total
Andhra Pradesh	205.1	7.5(6)
Assam	49.8	1.8(13)
Bihar	365.5	13.5(2)
Gujarat	87.6	3.2(11)
Haryana	21.7	0.8(15)
Himachal Pradesh	6.1	0.2(17)
Jammu & Kashmir	10.3	0.4(16)
Karnataka	137.6	5.1(8)
Kerala	71.5	2.6(12)
Madhya Pradesh	254.9	9.4(3)
Maharashtra	232.0	8.5(4)
Orissa	118.1	4.3(10)
Punjab	24.4	0.9(14)
Rajasthan	126.2	4.6(9)
Tamil Nadu	200.2	7.4(7)
Uttar Pradesh	530.6	19.6(1)
West Bengal	225.1	8.3(5)
All-India	2710.0*	100.0

Source: *First Report of the Ninth Finance Commission for 1989-90.*
Note: Figures in brackets indicate the ranks of the States.
* Percentage of population below the Poverty Line in India was 55.4 in 1961-61, 51.5 in 1972-73, 41.5 in 1981-82 and 36.9 (provisional estimate) in 1984-85.

In 1985, whereas per capita GNP in U.S. dollars was 250 in India, that for the poorest 40 per cent in the country was 101.4. A mere 16.2 per cent of total GNP accrued to the poorest 40 per cent of all households.

TABLE 2.11: State-wise analysis of rural poverty in India

Region/State	Rural 1977-78 Per cent	Poverty 1983-84 Per cent	Percentage of decline	Average rural consumption per capita 1977-78 (Rs.)	Expenditure per capita on poverty alleviation during the period (Rs.)
Eastern & Central Region					
Orissa	67.9	44.8	34.1	69.9	8.0
Madhya Pradesh	1.6	50.3	18.4	68.6	8.4
West Bengal	58.3	43.8	24.8	69.6	4.9
Bihar	57.8	51.4	11.2	69.0	6.6
Uttar Pradesh	49.8	46.5	6.6	69.5	9.0
Rajasthan	33.5	36.6	9.4	69.7	11.4
Average	54.5	46.6	14.5	69.2	7.8
Southern Region					
Tamil Nadu	56.3	44.1	21.6	68.8	12.1
Karnataka	53.2	37.5	29.5	70.2	9.0
Kerala	47.4	26.1	45.0	76.2	10.1
Andhra Pradesh	45.5	38.7	14.9	72.3	11.6
Western & Northern Region					
Maharashtra	60.4	41.5	31.2	71.9	6.7
Gujarat	43.1	27.6	35.9	78.4	10.4
Haryana	23.2	15.1	34.5	80.8	17.4
Punjab	13.1	10.9	13.1	81.7	31.2
Average	44.8	30.3	32.4	74.5	9.4
All-India	51.1	40.4	21.1	70.9	8.8

Source: Hanumantha Rao, *Economic and Political Weekly*, 1985-86.

In 1985-86 the number of people in India below the Poverty Line was 272.7 million. Of these, 80 per cent, that is, 222 million were in rural areas, comprising 39.9 per cent of the entire rural population, and 50.7 million were in urban areas, being 27.7 per cent of the total urban population. In brief, in India 36.9 per cent of the whole population was below the Poverty Line. Evidently, the percentages of those below the Poverty Line had come down as compared to those in the previous years. But the absolute number of the poor had risen from one bench-mark year of study to another.

The NSS data for 1987-88 place the percentage of the population below the Poverty Line at 29.2. In that year even the worst drought affected States like Gujarat and Rajasthan had a few percentage points knocked out of their poverty line figures.

As Tables 2.12 and 2.13 reveal, three-fourths of India's poor are concentrated in the eastern and central regions. The western region has done much better than other regions in the eradication of poverty. The north-western regions can claim the national trophy for its performance in poverty-alleviation programmes. On the contrary, in the eastern region very large proportions of the total population cannot enjoy any quality of life, if viewed in its strictest, ideal sense.

In 1988, 39 per cent of the Indian population was below the Poverty Line. This meant an absolute figure of 307 million people. Of these, 252 million who were in rural areas were below the minimum subsistence level. Of them, 124 million were by far the worst of all. One-third of the urban population, numbering 70 million, was below the Poverty Line — 33 million of them were ultra-poor.

Around that year one to two per cent of the Indian population got less than 33 per cent of its calorie needs. Another six to eight per cent got 35 to 50 per cent of its calorie requirements. Yet another 35 to 50 per cent got 50 to 75 per cent of the recommended calorie intake. Undernutrition was the lot of 42 to 60 per cent of the population. The remaining 40 to 58 per cent who were more fortunate could not be said to have attained perfection in this regard.

TABLE 2.12: Estimates of the poor in India region

Region/State	Percentage of population below the poverty Line		
	1970	1983	1988
Southern Region			
Andhra Pradesh, Karnataka, Kerala and Tamil Nadu	61.0	46.2	43.2
Eastern Region			
Bihar, Orissa, West Bengal and Assam	61.8	57.3	51.3
Central Region			
Madhya Pradesh, Rajasthan, and Uttar Pradesh	46.9	40.2	37.2
Western Region			
Maharashtra and Gujarat	46.1	38.2	34.9
Northern Region			
Punjab, Haryana, and Himachal Pradesh	12.6	9.8	9.3

Source: The World Bank Report, 1989.

TABLE 2.13: Estimates of the very poor in India

Region	Incidence of Dire Poverty-Destitution-Very Poor by Relation As percentage of the population		
	1970	1983	1988
Southern Region	29.3	25.8	26.1
Eastern Region	26.7	29.4	31.7
Central Region	25.9	27.1	27.0
Western Region	1.2	1.1	1.0
North-Western Region	less than 1.0	less than 1.0	less than 1.0

Source: The World Bank Report, 1989.

The poor are not a homogeneous group; there are gradations of the poor. According to an estimate, in 1990 an expenditure of Rs. 107 to Rs. 110 a month in rural areas could assure a food packet yielding 2,400 calories. In urban areas the amount of money required was Rs. 122 a month to assure a food packet yielding 2,100 calories needed by an adult there to subsist. Those whose earning/income fell below these minimum limits were dubbed as poor. There were, in 1990, 300 million to 400 million people in India who were poor. The measure used for this purpose was bare subsistence or survival. Here food was to man what fodder was to animal, the sole motive-power.

A little above that stood the satisfaction of the basic minimum needs. In 1990, Rs. 127 a month was required in rural areas and Rs. 149 a month in urban areas to assure their fulfilment. In the IRDP formerly Rs. 3,500 per year was taken as the expenditure necessary for lifting a poor household from under the Poverty Line to a position above it. By 1990 this sum had risen to Rs. 6,400 per annum.

The very poor today are those people who spend less than Rs. 70 a month.

The destitutes are very, very poor. They spend less than Rs. 60 a month. They form the bottom 10 per cent of society — nearly 50 to 60 million. They are the people best qualified for social security.

Households falling in the yearly consumer expenditure class of Re. 1 to Rs. 1,225 are composed of the destitutes and those falling in the yearly consumer expenditure class of Rs. 2,266 to Rs. 3,500 constitute the very, very poor. The former are the poorest and the most deprived section of our community.

A new class of the poor, *ultra-poor,* is defined by Kakwani and Subharao as people belonging to those households whose per capita consumption per month is below Rs. 40. They include those persons whose physical personal maintenance is unstable.

Implied in the Poverty Line concept is the fact that the estimates of the gap between the present consumption and the desired consumption of an average India varies from 17 to 28 per cent. The extent of hunger or undernutrition is to be measured by the difference between the actual level of consumption and the desirable level of consumption according to the nutritional norms.

Nearly 22 per cent of the our total population is below the ideal minimum consumption level. The idle poor are the largest chunk of this. Malnutrition today cripples six out of every 10 children the country has.

Indian poverty is an accumulated deposit of the past many decades. It is generally low-end poverty. Although in the course of years the percentage of the people below the Poverty Line has fallen, yet their absolute number has risen as we have seen above. However, even this is some achievement inasmuch as 55 per cent to 60 per cent of the new additions to the aggregate population have gone above the Poverty Line. The distribution of the benefits of development was sufficiently wide so as to reach 40 to 45 per cent of the newly born, in spite of the fact that it rendered many of the rich richer in the process. As a result of the poverty-alleviation programmes, the rural poor have become more dependent on the state and bartered for it a substantial part of self-help. All the same, the IRDP has fostered a sense of competitiveness and aspiration among the hitherto deprived sections of our society. Whatever poverty there is (its estimate varying with the criterion employed), it is a distinct social reality, intimately linked as it is with the agrarian tensions that have reared their head almost simultaneously. Marginalisation of those below a certain threshold has proceeded hand in hand with the uplift of particular income fractiles, although the vicious circle of poverty is not yet totally broken.

For a while we propose to anticipate Table 3.4. There we attempt to illustrate the dictum that a higher per capita State's Domestic Product (SDP) is generally associated with a lower percentage of population below the Poverty Line. In 1975-76/1977-78 an exact relationship existed between the two in the case of Punjab; a close one in the case of Andhra Pradesh, Assam, Bihar, Gujarat, Haryana and Himachal Pradesh; a distant one in the case of Karnataka, Madhya Pradesh, Orissa, Rajasthan, Tamil Nadu, Uttar Pradesh and West Bengal; and absence of any relationship in the case of Jammu

& Kashmir and Maharashtra.

Continuing the argument in the foregoing paragraph, we find that in 1983-84 the richest State, namely, Punjab, had the lowest percentage of population below the Poverty Line. The level of per capita SDP and the percentage of population below the Poverty Line were very closely related in the case of Punjab, Bihar and Uttar Pradesh; more or less closely related in the case of Gujarat, Haryana, Karnataka, Rajasthan and Tamil Nadu; but not closely related in the case of other States.

The nexus between rise in per capita income and fall in percentage of population below the Poverty Line is not direct because the former is not uniform in all the expenditure classes.

Were per capita income a reliable index of the level of development and the relative prosperity of a State, then it should have varied inversely with the absolute poverty ratio. But this is not so in the case of India. To cxemplify, while per capita SDP of Karnataka was nominally higher than the all-India per capita income, percentage of people below the Poverty Level in 1987-88 also was definitely above the national percentage/average. Thus both were unsatisfactory statistical measures so far as Karnataka is concerned.

But despite everything that is said for and against it, the level of per capita SDP is the only best indicator so far available of the level of economic development of a region. Most economic and non-economic variables are mirrored in it. It is the average of all averages.

Low resource base, underemployment and overt/open unemployment and low productivity largely account for Indian poverty. Dualism, cumulative causation processes and population pressure are actually obstacles to the growth of per capita income and the alleviation of poverty. The curse of poverty has been a joint product of a traditional society, a static economy and the colonial rule for about 200 years.

So far it has not been possible to make a major impression on poverty because of the inadequate rate of growth of the economy, uneven distribution of income and consumption as well as a high rate of growth of population.

The poverty problem has become excruciatingly formidable owing to the slow growth of the commodity sector (primary and secondary activities). The joint family system which furnished to the jobless a modicum of social security against unemployment has rapidly declined. Very low incomes are found among families relying almost entirely upon monetised transactions as well as among those who are essentially self-sufficient. The poor are forced to take up low-paid jobs instead of waiting endlessly for something better to come along.

It is high time we shifted our attention to **inter-State disparities in poverty.** On so doing we would find that nothing very precise of certain can be asserted about the regional pattern of poverty in India because no two studies include and exclude exactly the same States or the same number of States. The ranking order of the States within the broad groups varies from study to study and from period to period. No two authors agree on the extent of poverty in the various States or on the extent to which the problem has worsened or improved within a certain period. A State which scores high on an inequality index sometimes scores low in terms of number of the poor below the Poverty Line. But a State like Bihar remains the poorest of all States on every possible count, to quote Chaudhary.

The dimension of the poverty problem as well as the absolute number of the poor in India varies from State to State. In other words, the incidence of abject and abysmal Indian poverty is not uniform all over the country. A very large chunk of the grindingly poor is concentrated in a few distinctly discernible regions where the over-all pace of economic growth has not been fast enough to make an appreciable dent on the problem.

The cost of subsistence living varies between different States and between rural and urban areas of each separate State. So does the level of per capita consumer expenditure as it is and as is necessary to ensure a minimum living. This is due partly to differences in prices and due partly to differences in consumer preferences in the sense that consumers in some States seem to attach a higher priority to food than those in some other States.

About 72 per cent of the total poverty-ridden population and nearly 66 per cent of the total pool of unemployment have been concentrated in seven States, viz., Bihar, Uttar Pradesh, West Bengal, Madhya Pradesh, Maharashtra, Tamil Nadu and Andhra Pradesh. For all its much-vaunted prosperity Maharashtra has a very high percentage of its people below the Poverty Line. This reminds us of Henry George, who through identification and separation explains the coexistence of poverty with progress, the greatest enigma of our time. "Widespread destitution is found in the midst of the greatest abundance. The contrast between the House of Have and House of Want" got sharper with progress.

The agriculturally prosperous States such as Punjab and Haryana have the lowest percentages of their population below the Poverty Line (which can be construed to mean that more than industrial progress, agricultural progress is a sure solvent of poverty, the nub of which is rural poverty). The industrially advanced States such as West Bengal, Tamil Nadu and Maharashtra have very high percentages of poor population. The States, such as Bihar, Orissa and Madhya Pradesh, which are backward both agriculturally and industrially, come in between.

TABLE 2.14: Size of holdings

State	Average Size of Holdings (Hectares)			Average size of operational holdings in 1985-86 (Hectares)
	1970-71	1980-81	Percentage Change in 1980-81 over 1970-71	
1	2	3	4	5
Andhra Pradesh	2.51	1.87	(-) 25.5	2.34
Assam	1.47	1.36	(-) 7.5	NA
Bihar	1.50	0.99	(-) 3.4	1.11
Gujarat	4.11	3.45	(-) 16.0	3.71
Haryana	3.77	3.52	(-) 6.7	3.58
Himachal Pradesh	1.53	1.54	(+) 0.7	NA
Jammu & Kashmir	0.94	0.99	(+) 5.3	—
Karnataka	3.20	2.73	(-) 14.7	2.98
Kerala	0.57	0.43	(-) 24.6	0.49
Madhya Pradesh	4.00	3.42	(-) 15.5	3.58
Maharashtra	4.28	2.95	(-) 31.1	3.66
Orissa	1.89	1.59	(-) 15.9	1.60
Punjab	2.89	3.79	(+)31.1	2.74
Rajasthan	5.46	4.44	(-) 18.7	4.65
Tamil Nadu	1.45	1.08	(+) 5.9	1.23
Uttar Pradesh	1.16	1.01	(-) 13.0	1.05
West Bengal	1.20	0.94	(-) 21.7	0.99
All-India	2.30	1.82	(-) 20.9	—

Source: Centre for Monitoring Indian Economy, *Basic Statistics Relating to the Indian Economy,* Vol. 2, *States,* September, 1985.

Note: Although marginal and small holdings up to two hectares account for 75 per cent of total holdings, the area operated by them is just 26 per cent. Consequently, about three-fourths of the operated area is encompassed by semi-medium, medium and large holdings that can be termed economic holdings. Unless the marginal and small farmers are provided alternative, non-agricultural, employment or are employed in the remaining categories of farms through their risen crop intensity, the chances of their ceasing to be poor are extremely remote.

One reason why the percentage of poor population is far higher than the national average in the eastern region of India is that the land holdings in it are of very small size (see Table 2.14) and are fragmented too. Besides, low-wage pockets predominate more in this region than in the northern region, serving as an impetus to those intending to migrate.

TABLE 2.15: State-wise distribution of agricultural labourers and monthly per capita consumer expenditure in rural areas

State	Percentage of agricul-tural labou-rers to Total population in the State (1981)	Relative shares in total popu-lation of agricultural labourers (1981) (per cent)	Relative shares in SC & ST populations* (1981) (per cent)	Weighted (combined) relative shares (3) + (4) (per cent)	Monthly per capita rural consumer expendit-ture (1983) (Rs)
(1)	(2)	(3)	(4)	(5)	(6)
Andhra Pradesh	36.8(1)	14.8(1)	7.0(5)	10.9(3)	115.4(9)
Assam	—	0.9(15)	2.1(12)	1.5(14)	113.0(11)
Bihar	35.5(2)	13.1(2)	10.0(3)	11.6(2)	93.8(17)
Gujarat	22.6(10)	4.4(9)	4.6(10)	4.5(10)	122.7(7)
Haryana	16.1(12)	1.0(14)	1.5(14)	1.3(15)	151.8(2)
Himachal Pradesh	2.7(16)	0.07(17)	0.8(15)	0.4(16)	150.8(3)
Jammu & Kashmir	3.5(15)	0.1(16)	0.3(16)	0.2(17)	129.3(5)
Karnataka	26.8(6)	6.5(8)	4.6(10)	5.6(8)	116.8(8)
Kerala	28.2(4)	3.4(11)	1.7(13)	2.6(12)	145.2(4)
Madhya Pradesh	24.2(9)	8.6(6)	12.2(2)	10.4(4)	100.5(15)
Maharashtra	26.6(7)	11.5(3)	6.4(6)	9.0(5)	110.4(12)
Orissa	27.7(8)	4.2(10)	6.1(8)	5.2(9)	98.8(16)
Punjab	122.2(11)	1.9(12)	2.8(11)	2.4(13)	170.5(1)
Rajasthan	7.3(14)	1.3(13)	6.3(7)	3.8(11)	127.0(6)
Tamil Nadu	31.7(3)	10.7(4)	5.9(9)	8.3(6)	112.2(10)
Uttar Pradesh	16.0(13)	9.2(5)	14.9(1)	12.2(1)	104.2(14)
West Bengal	25.2(8)	6.9(7)	9.5(4)	8.2(7)	104.6(13)
All-India	25.0	100.0	100.0	100.0	112.4

Source: (1) *Census of India*, 1981; (2) *NSS Report No. 319;* (3) *Second Report of the Ninth Finance Commission*, 1989.

Notes: Figures in brackets indicate the ranks of the States.

* A large percentage of agricultural labourers is claimed by the Scheduled Castes.

States with higher percentages of rural labour are generally also the States with larger percentages of their rural population living below the minimum consumption level (the Poverty Line determinant). Table 2.15 casts light on this facet of the problem.

Poverty is most acute in areas which have a heavy pressure of population or in which productivity is low because of the scanty development of local resources, and there is lack of continuous work.

In many areas on account of the pranks of the monsoon those living at the margin of subsistence go down below it every three or four years.

It is odd that the prevalence of disparities in living standards as between the States has never been the most potent factor in social and political tension in the country, except in a very limited number of cases. Other extraneous considerations—outsiders exploiting the local people and depriving them of employment opportunities, etc.—have, of course, had their part to play in inciting the trouble. But more of this later.

It is suggested that the poor regions should shelter behind a Poverty Curtain[2] and make use of their potential productive resources to meet their basic needs. The rich regions should share their prosperity with the poor regions so that there takes place a balanced development of all regions in the country.

A reference to the **consumption pattern** of the people is a necessary part of the study of the problem of poverty in both its theoretical and applied aspects. In 1950-51 more than half of India's national income was utilised for consumer expenditure on food alone. Per capita per day consumption of foodgrains was 395 g in 1960-61, 445 g in 1970-71, 454 g in 1980-81, 472 g in 1986-87 and 441 g in 1987-88. Per capita availability of foodgrains has stagnated around 171.8 kg per year. Tables 2.16 and 2.17 reveal disparities in consumer expenditures on cereals and foodgrains in 1964-65 and 1970-71, respectively, specially marked with regard to their distribution as between different expenditure groups. The richest class's expenditure on foodgrains continued to be about six times that of the poorest class.

Table 2.18 gives average annual growth rates of per capita availability of some selected consumer goods during 1961—88. That the consumption pattern for particular sections of society is now qualitatively worse cannot be denied if reliance is placed on this table. This has to be seen against the background of rise at the rate of three to four per cent per annum of the output of cereals, as contrasted with the stagnation or decline of the output of pulses, the prime source of nutrition to the weaker and more vulnerable sections of our society.

TABLE 2.16: State-wise per capita consumption expenditure on cereals for a 30-day period in rural and urban areas

State/Union Territories	All-Classes 1964-65		All-Classes 1970-71	
	Rural	Urban	Rural	Urban
Andhra Pradesh	11.68	9.46	14.50	13.59
Assam	11.88	10.37	18.84	17.68
Bihar	13.52	10.96	16.90	16.39
Gujarat	9.83	8.35	11.71	10.66
Haryana	10.49	7.92	13.53	10.67
Jammu & Kashmir	11.11	7.20	16.61	9.95
Kerala	7.57	7.79	10.49	10.13
Madhya Pradesh	10.80	8.58	13.66	11.87
Maharashtra	10.00	7.09	11.98	10.25
Mysore	11.63	9.16	14.25	13.22
Orissa	10.59	10.24	15.59	15.73
Punjab	8.99	7.56	11.60	10.50
Rajasthan	11.37	7.95	10.76	10.87
Tamil Nadu	10.63	9.23	13.03	11.63
Uttar Pradesh	11.40	7.93	12.69	11.19
West Bengal	11.46	8.88	16.88	14.07
Union Territories	10.73	7.53	15.92	11.11
All-India	11.15	8.53	13.98	12.05
Coefficient of Variation	11.57 per cent	13.25 per cent	11.16 per cent	13.53 per cent

Source: NSS 19th Round, July, 1964, to June, 1965; and 25th Round, July, 1970, to June, 1971.

Sugar is a large item of personal consumption, accounting for about five per cent of private consumption expenditure. The 7.7 per cent weight assigned to sugar products in the wholesale price index signifies its volatile, sensitive role.

Differences in consumers' expenditure on foodgrains between any two categories of States are caused by differences in quantity and differences in prices. We have low-priced States such as Orissa and Madhya Pradesh. Rigid equality in foodgrains consumption is not essential because of differences in dietary habits between States and between different groups of people in one and the same State.

TABLE 2.17: State-wise per capita consumption expenditure on foodgrains for a period of 30-day in rural and urban areas

State/Union Territories	All-Classes 1964-65		All-Classes 1970-71	
	Rural	Urban	Rural	Urban
Andhra Pradesh	12.69	10.59	15.57	15.05
Assam	13.13	12.01	20.05	19.42
Bihar	16.44	13.04	19.12	18.75
Gujarat	11.31	10.06	13.34	12.79
Haryana	12.35	8.99	16.07	12.41
Jammu & Kashmir	12.06	8.07	17.95	11.03
Kerala	8.78	8.61	12.72	11.61
Madhya Pradesh	12.87	10.47	15.56	14.21
Maharashtra	11.60	8.74	13.67	12.41
Mysore	12.87	10.62	15.61	15.06
Orissa	11.38	11.63	16.35	17.30
Punjab	10.28	8.72	13.19	12.12
Rajasthan	12.88	9.08	12.09	12.37
Tamil Nadu	11.68	10.56	14.07	13.06
Uttar Pradesh	14.31	9.71	15.27	13.44
West Bengal	12.27	10.06	17.72	15.49
Union Territories	12.04	8.96	17.49	12.91
All-India	15.87	10.00	15.70	13.88
Coefficient of Variation	24.64%	13.10%	14.14%	17.15%

Source: NSS 19th and 25th Rounds.

TABLE 2.18: Average annual growth rates of per capita availability of some selected consumer goods (1961-1988)

Item	Growth Rates
Cereals	1.23
Pulses	− 0.91
Cotton cloth	− 0.20
Man-made fabrics	0.08
Edible oils	0.10
Vanaspati	0.02
Coffee	− 0.61
Tea	5.90
Sugar	0.23
Electricity	0.75

Source : Economic Survey, 1986 & 1988.

The NSS 44th Round report has demonstrated that consumption of *jowar* and *bajra* was nil in Bihar and Orissa, but was maximum in Maharashtra. Per person consumption of rice and wheat taken together was quite high in the poorer States. In Gujarat and Haryana average monthly per capita expenditure on milk and milk products was more than that on cereals.

Our claim to self-sufficiency attained in 1977-78 may prove illusory any time if our rain-gods are displeased with us — self-sufficiency measured crudely by the substitution of food imports by domestic production. Between 1947 and 1985 the Government imported huge amounts of foodgrains from abroad, except in five years, i.e., 1972, 1978, 1979, 1980 and 1985. Some statistical information on imports and exports of food items since 1984-85 is contained in Table 2.19.

TABLE 2.19: Exports of farm products and imports of food articles

($ Million)

Year/Period	Exports of Farm Products
1980-81 to 1984-85	3008
1985-86	3109
1986-87 to 1989-90	3261

	Imports of food Articles			
	Cereals & cereal preparations	Edible oils	Sugar	Pulses
1984-85	204	799	81	85
1985-86	90	612	342	154
1986-87	68	496	175	183
1987-88	51	748	149	212
1988-89	436	502	—	264
1989-90	227	127	58	137

Source: RBI, *Occasional Papers*, December, 1989.

In order that the problem is immune to ambivalence food output must further be stabilised and strengthened, for on it is predicated the trinity of per capita farm income, standard of living of people inhabiting rural areas and nutritional level of the urban poor. These three are tied to one another in cross or co-effects. While employment generation may influence the last two and impart a general buoyancy to the economy, it would soon peter out if it is not supported by a rise in food output, and hence its impact eroded and swamped away acutely by price spirals. This is why some economists (for instance, Ahluwalia) postulate an inverse relationship between rural poverty and per capita output for rural population. On the opposite side of the fence are economists like Narain who establish a positive relationship between rural poverty and prices. A meeting – point is constituted by such economists are Griffin and Ghose who mark off a strong positive relationship between rural poverty and time after accounting for fluctuations in prices and per capita farm, especially food, output.

The common man is accustomed to evaluate the success of planning in terms of availability to him of essential goods and services at prices within his reach. But in our country per capita availability of wage-goods means of subsistence has increased at the snail's pace of 0.37 per cent per annum during 1950-76, 1.24 per cent per annum during 1950-64 and 0.17 per cent per annum during 1964-76. Per capita per annum consumption of cloth was 15 metres in 1960-61, 15.6 metres in 1970-71, 14.7 metres in 1980-81, 15 metres in 1986-87 and 14.7 metres in 1987-88. Per capita domestic consumption of electricity was 3.4 kWh in 1960-61, 7.0 kWh in 1970-71, 13.5 kWh in 1980-81 and 25 kWh in 1986-87. In 1985-86 the number of refrigerators per lakh of households was 255.

To achieve a doubling of consumption not only has the production to be doubled but also its components. The First Five-Year Plan had made a forecast that doubling of per capita income would result in a little over 70 per cent rise in the consumption standards. For part of the rise in per capita income would be saving and investment.

In the course of four decades and in the wake of economic development, despite the fact that it has been slow and tardy, the old composition as well as complexion of economic classes has become transformed in different degrees in different States as has the composition and complexion of social classes along with it, though to a lesser extent.

Mohanty and George conclude that while not many who were rich a decade ago have fallen on bad days, those who have managed to come out of poverty have been quite many. The private consumption of the lower strata of the population, which are lucky to be in the hub of economic activity in whatever form, has since the 1980s begun growing *pari passu* with the growth of the private consumption of the community as a whole, whether as fast as or more or less faster than the latter cannot be precisely told, though one could hazard a guess. For making a perceptible impression it should grow faster and be upgraded with speed and despatch. The crying need of the hour is judicious, selective and effective curbs on consumption outlays by the well-off strata of society, particularly those on the inessential and non-functional items of their consumption. Riotous living and ostentatious consumption of the rich must be restrained. Short of this, the desired restructuring of demand in the economy would not be attained. The fiscal weapons can play their expected role in this *via* price manoeuvre, a path which produces less resentment. In policy, the accent has to be on the redistribution of consumption expenditure but in a manner that does not take a heavy toll of the potentialities of economic growth. In the absence of voluntary or involuntary checks upon the islands of prosperity no clear breakthrough in this sphere is conceivable in the near future.

As a corollary, social valuation of consumption at different points of time cannot and should not be overlooked. We could possibly construct a poverty-weighted index of social welfare. Measures to improve the quality of social justice would not succeed much or fast or stabilise unless preceded by measures to guarantee the fulfilment of the basic human needs to one and all by creating jobs and by adopting other kindred methods. The poor must begin to partake of the good life in order to know what it is like.

In India two States, namely, Andhra Pradesh and Tamil Nadu, which embarked on ambitious schemes of distribution of rice among the vulnerable sections of society free or at a subsidised price were, era long, alleged to have upset the traditional rice balance of their own as well as of their neighbouring States. Lest it be forgotten, let us note here that the schemes of social justice have a tendency to snowball.

Poverty today is related not to the notion of a minimum level of subsistence of a more or less fixed character based on physical needs but rather to the idea of relative poverty, which is wedded to the standard of living enjoyed by most people in the community at a specified time. Thus poverty is today expressed in terms of relative deprivation, which can only be cured by ensuring economic and social equality. Inequality thus becomes the cause of poverty. To abolish poverty we need the socialist doctrines of egalitarianism.

Resource allocation can be modified by the state through taxation and cash transfers rather than by the provision of goods and services unless there is some overriding reason for the latter. Economists like Stanford and Bernard recommend that the poor should be helped better by cash transfers rather than by the provision of free or below-cost services. But their advice is rejected by others, who hold that cash transfers would be insufficient in obviating poverty and reducing income inequality and suggest that services like education and health should be provided to all citizens as "a common badge of citizenship" by the state and only by the state. Cash grants may or may not be spent on the ends for which they are meant but in the case of income redistribution in kind there is no such risk. Moreover, redistribution in kind is easier to attain politically.[3]

NOTES

1. In 1979 the Planning Commission defined the poverty threshold or line as the per capita monthly expenditure of Rs. 49.09 in rural areas at 1973-74 rural prices. For 1983, Rs. 91 per person per month consumption expenditure was taken as the Poverty Line as fixed by Kakwani and Subharao.
2. This term refers to the existence of a large number of people living in glaring poverty below the Poverty Line, forming a curtain, as it were. Such poverty has to be dealt with at the deepest levels of ideological and institutional conflict.
3. On this read K.N. Prasad, *Problems of Economic Development in the Third World*, Ch. 9.

3

REGIONAL DIMENSIONS OF INDIAN POVERTY AND INEQUALITY

Attempts have been made from time to time to estimate the extent of poverty in the different States. In 1968-69 it was estimated at 66 per cent of the population in Bihar. Those with consumption expenditure below Rs. 20 per month at 1960-61 prices were said to be below the Poverty Line. The total number of people below the line was estimated at 37 million.

In 1973-74 the percentage of population in Bihar below the Poverty Line was 60.76, according to one estimate, and 58.00 according to another. At prices prevalent in that year, those with a per capita monthly expenditure of Rs. 51 or less were adjudged to be below the line. On the same criterion, in 1977-78, the percentage was 56.3. For 1983-84, the figure was 49.5 per cent. In 1988-89 those who subsisted on Rs. 107 (or, say, Rs. 110) or less per month were taken to be below the Poverty Line. Their number was estimated at 1.1 million, involving 0.22 million households, each household having, on an average, five members and less than Rs. 6,400 as its annual income. These formed 42 per cent of the total population. With per capita State's Domestic Product (SDP) and per capita consumption expenditure rising very slowly large numbers of people stayed poor and swelled the number of the poor in the State.

Table 3.1 presents data on the extent of poverty in 1977-78 and 1983-84 State-wise and gives it breakdown between rural and urban population. Bihar's position as the poorest State with the highest percentage of the poor is clear from this table.

A study made by Kakwani and Subharao shows that between 1977-78 and 1983 poverty decreased in all States, except Bihar, where it increased slightly. This contradicts the information contained in the preceding paragraph. According to these writers, the Poverty Line varies substantially across the States as well as over time (see Table

3.2). These variations are attributable entirely to those in prices. A higher Poverty Line is indicative of a more expensive State to live in.

An inverse relationship is generally posited between per capita income and the extent of poverty. This is a subject that calls for careful examination. This is attempted in the following pages.

TABLE 3.1: Extent of poverty

State	Percentage of Population below the Poverty Line					
	Total		Rural		Urban	
	1977-78	1983-84	1977-78	1983-84	1977-78	1983-84
Andhra Pradesh	43.6(11)	36.4(7)	45.4(10)	38.7(8)	37.2(10)	29.2(7)
Assam	47.3(10)	23.5(13)	48.5(11)	23.8(13)	36.5(11)	21.6(12)
Bihar	56.3(13)	49.5(1)	57.8(5)	52.4(1)	44.8(5)	37.0(2)
Gujarat	38.9(12)	24.3(12)	43.1(12)	27.6(11)	29.8(15)	17.3(14)
Haryana	25.2(15)	15.6(15)	23.2(16)	15.2(15)	32.5(14)	16.9(15)
Himachal Pradesh	27.0(14)	13.5(17)	27.8(15)	14.0(16)	17.2(17)	8.0(17)
Jammu & Kashmir	18.4(16)	16.3(14)	31.7(14)	16.4(14)	40.5(9)	(15.8)(16)
Karnataka	50.8(6)	35.0(8)	53.2(7)	38.5(9)	44.6(6)	29.2(8)
Kerala	48.4(9)	26.8(11)	47.4(10)	26.1(12)	53.2(1)	30.1(5)
Madhya Pradesh	58.9(2)	46.2(2)	61.6(2)	50.3(2)	46.9(3)	31.1(3)
Maharashtra	50.6(7)	34.9(9)	60.4(3)	41.5(7)	41.4(8)	23.3(11)
Orissa	65.1(1)	42.8(4)	67.9(1)	44.8(4)	41.8(7)	29.3(6)
Punjab	16.4(17)	13.8(16)	13.1(17)	10.9(17)	25.6(16)	21.0(13)
Rajasthan	33.6(13)	34.3(10)	33.5(13)	36.6(10)	33.9(13)	26.1(10)
Tamil Nadu	52.8(4)	39.6(5)	56.3(6)	44.1(6)	45.3(4)	30.9(4)
Uttar Pradesh	49.7(8)	45.3(3)	49.8(8)	46.5(3)	49.2(2)	40.3(1)
West Bengal	52.2(5)	39.2(6)	58.3(4)	43.8(5)	34.5(12)	26.5(9)
All-India	48.3	37.4	51.2	40.4	38.2	28.1

Source: *Seventh Five-Year Plan*.
Note: Figures in brackets indicate the ranks of the States.

Often per capita income is taken to indicate the absolute level. A higher per capita income denotes a lower absolute level of poverty, and *vice versa*. But in this tenet the distribution of income is not taken into account, it is assumed to remain constant, which is erroneous. For as real per capita income rises, it is possible that the rich are getting richer or the poor are getting poorer. In other words, any distribution of income may accompany the increase in per capita income. In order to ascertain whether a rise in real per capita income has lowered the extent of absolute poverty we have to find out as to

TABLE 3.2: State-specific poverty lines for different NSS rounds

State	Poor				*Ultra Poor*			
	1972-73	1973-74	1977-78	1983	1972-73	1973-74	1977-78	1983
Andhra Pradesh	37	44	54	76	30	35	43	14.5
Assam	42	50	61	99	33	40	48	79
Bihar	44	62	63	104	35	50	50	83
Gujarat	44	48	56	85	35	38	44	68
Haryana	42	51	62	92	34	40	49	73
Karnataka	40	50	56	90	32	40	45	72
Kerala	41	52	59	100	33	41	47	80
Madhya Pradesh	40	51	57	85	32	41	46	68
Maharashtra	46	52	60	91	36	41	48	72
Orissa	37	48	52	94	29	38	42	75
Punjab	42	51	62	92	34	40	49	73
Rajasthan	38	49	56	78	30	39	45	62
Tamil Nadu	37	47	59	99	30	27	47	79
Uttar Pradesh	40	51	57	87	32	41	45	70
West Bengal	46	59	68	112	37	47	54	89
All-India	40	50	57	91	32	40	46	72

Source: *Economic and Political Weekly,* March 31, 1990.
Note: Households having per capita consumption 20 per cent below the Poverty Line were *ultra poor*.

what has happened to the share of the lower 60 per cent of the population. An increased per capita income *per se* does not guarantee a decline in the number of the absolute poor. Alongside of this, it has to be seen whether the distribution of income has become more or less unequal. This boils down to a question of character of economic growth and political and institutional organisation.

The secular rise in per capita income in the poorer States over the period has been at a rate much lower than in the richer States, and the inter-States differences in per capita income are now absolutely greater and probably also relatively greater than they were precedent to this period.

We have noted above that absolute poverty is measured in terms of a certain income (price deflated and hence real) level sufficient to provide adequate nutrition. The absolute number of people below a minimum level of real income may or may not diminish with an increase in per capita income. If it does, there in development, if it does not, there is no development. A substantial increase in population during the time of our study may cause the number of the absolute poor to rise or of those at the threshold to rise. Instead of the trickle-down of the benefits of economic growth in favour of the poor we may have the trickle-up of these benefits in favour of the non-poor, to borrow the words of Todaro.

But the pattern of income distribution is a function of the economic structure and economic system. The aggregate economic performance of a State also impinges on the extent of absolute poverty. An increased per capita income with an increased burden of unemployment in a household or increased indebtedness or increased unproductive, non-functional expenditure may not denote reduced absolute poverty. That is to say, not every the rise in production is conducive to poverty elimination—only the rise of that part of production which is really productive of welfare has this effect. It is in this sense that the composition of State Domestic Product becomes of considerable significance.

Let us look at Table 3.3 and Table 3.4. The State-wise extent of poverty for 1977-78 and 1983-84 is embodied in Table 3.3. It shows increase in per capita State Domestic Product (SDP) in 1983-84 over that in 1977-78 at both current and constant prices. The percentages of these increases State-wise are noted in Table 3.4. Against them are noted in the same table percentages of decrease in the extent of poverty State-wise. Except for Rajasthan where we have a negative correlation, in the case of all other States we have a positive one but this is not uniform in its character; it varies from 1 : 0.04 to 1 : 1.76, the all-India average ratio being 1 : 0.22. Out of the 17 States, in one State we have a negative ratio and in the remaining 16 we have ratios much below unity in value. On the whole, one per cent rise in SDP can strike one percentage point off the poverty percentage. This extremely low relationship between growth and poverty alleviation apart, increased reliance on the poverty-alleviation programmes involving enormous public expenditures during 1977-78 to 1983-84 has resulted in nearly 11 per cent decline in the all-India poverty extent. Transfers from larger incomes to smaller, provided they do not lead to a too serious reduction in SDP, lower the extent of poverty. Other things being equal, net poverty would be less, the larger the stream of SDP and higher the per capita SDP, the more equally the SDP is distributed among persons, the more steadily it grows, and the less are the aggregate disutilities that are sustained by its creation.

TABLE 3.3: Per capita State's Domestic Product

State	1977-78		1983-84	
	At Constant prices	At Current prices	At Constant prices	At Current Prices
Andhra Pradesh	418	1101	758	1994
Assam	272	866	586	1862
Bihar	252	735	454	1319
Gujarat	447	1341	921	2848
Haryana	491	1472	1087	3032
Himachal Pradesh	398	1154	768	2225
Jammu & Kashmir	335	986	673	1929
Karnataka	332	896	731	1970
Kerala	394	1182	608	1883
Madhya Pradesh	570	1628	614	1751
Maharashtra	277	799	1026	2961
Orissa	268	857	549	1757
Punjab	805	1991	1487	3678
Rajasthan	323	925	716	2025
Tamil Nadu	365	1031	657	1856
Uttar Pradesh	311	892	579	1661
West Bengal	662	1803	822	2237
All-India	388	1163	764	2288

Source: (1) *National Accounts Statistics;*
(2) Bihar State Planning Board, *Selected Plan Statistics*, 1986.

When a rise in per capita income does serious damage to natural resources, a cardinal governor of the survival system of a sizable chunk of the rural population, or to human behaviour, or to the interrelationship between the two, the decline in absolute poverty becomes dubious. In a number of States the establishment of infrastructural industrial plants by eroding the community rights of the natives in natural resources has aggravated their poverty.

TABLE 3.4: Interrelations of population and income growth

State	Percentage Increase in Per Capita SDP at Current Prices in 1983-84 over 1977-78	Percentage Increase in Per Capita SDP between 1977-78 and 1983-84 at Constant Prices	Percentage Decrease in Population below the Poverty Line between 1977-78 and 1983-84	Ratio between cl. (2) and cl. (4)
1	2	3	4	5
Andhra Pradesh	99(2)	44.8	7.2	1 : 0.16
Assam	95(3)	53.6	23.8	1 : 0.44
Bihar	80(10)	55.5	6.8	1 : 0.12
Gujarat	87(6)	50.3	14.6	1 : 0.29
Haryana	72(15)	54.8	9.6	1 : 0.17
Himachal Pradesh	87(5)	48.2	13.5	1 : 0.28
Jammu & Kashmir	NA	50.2	2.1	1 : 0.04
Karnataka	76(13)	54.6	15.8	1 : 0.28
Kerala	81(9)	35.2	11.6	1 : 0.33
Madhya Pradesh	89(4)	7.2	12.7	1 : 1.76
Maharashtra	78(12)	73.0	15.7	1 : 0.21
Orissa	108(1)	51.2	22.3	1 : 0.43
Punjab	65(16)	47.7	2.6	1 : 0.05
Rajasthan	87(7)	54.9	(—)0.7	(—)1 : 0.01
Tamil Nadu	82(8)	44.4	13.2	1 : 0.29
Uttar Pradesh	79(11)	46.3	4.4	1 : 0.09
West Bengal	73(14)	19.5	13.0	1 : 0.66
All-India	NA	49.2	10.9	1 : 0.22

Source: (1) Derived from Table 3.3.
(2) U.P. State Planning Institute, *Inter-State Disparities*, 1990.

Absolute poverty is located disproportionately in rural areas. Broadly, rural poverty is the hard core of Indian poverty. Urban poverty is far smaller in volume than rural poverty. The social and political tensions that urban poverty generates are much more acute than those generated by rural poverty. Within the urban economy the unorganised or informal sectors compare unfavourably with the organised or formal sectors so far as employment, income and living conditions are concerned.

The distributive measures make an impression not only on poverty but also on production/income growth via their *efficiency effect.* Poverty-oriented employment programmes, if productive, create assets as well as goods and thus public expenditures on these programmes have an *output effect* too. The two effects cannot easily be isolated because they are intertwined.

Indian poverty is a product of the total conjuncture – social, political, legal and economic, or, in brief, of social inequality and exploitation, on the one hand, and underdevelopment, on the other, as the Eighth Plan Approach Paper remarks. We have concentrations of the weaker sections of society such as the Scheduled Castes and Scheduled Tribes in particular States (Table 3.5). In these sections of our society which are disadvantaged, vulnerable, neglected, excluded and down-trodden poverty is almost insufferable. The social imbalances that obtain today owe their origin and growth largely to the interrelations and interactions of these sections with other sections and, in consequence, overshadow and intercept the impact of the various programmes and projects on poverty alleviation. Ten per cent of the State Plan in Bihar, known as the Component Plan, is meant for 10 million Scheduled Castes people in the State, whereas 25 per cent of the State Plan, called the Tribal Sub-Plan, is meant for 8.75 million Scheduled Tribes people in the State. Uttar Pradesh, West Bengal and Bihar have to bear the maximum burden on this account. Agricultural labourers generally belong to the Scheduled Castes and are either landless or have little land, mostly undeveloped. Furthermore, they suffer from serious social disabilities, infirmities and rigidities. The mega projects in irrigation, power and transport frequently disrupt the lives and the environment of work of the Scheduled Tribes. Relief and rehabilitation provided to them is often inadequate.

Absolute poverty is concentrated among the people engaged primarily in agriculture and kindred activities. For the target poverty groups we have generally to look to these sectors. The benefits from an over-all economic growth have percolated insufficiently to the poor who have their habitat in these sectors. It is these sectors that intensely dilute the relationship between economic growth and incidence of poverty. And there are patent reasons for that.

TABLE 3.5: State's shares in scheduled caste and scheduled tribe population

State	Percentage Share in Total Population of Scheduled Castes 1981	Percentage Share in Total Population of Scheduled Tribes 1981
Andhra Pradesh	7.60	6.15
Assam	NA	NA
Bihar	9.68	11.25
Gujarat	2.32	9.39
Haryana	2.35	—
Himachal Pradesh	1.00	0.38
Jammu & Kashmir	0.47	—
Karnataka	5.34	3.53
Madhya Pradesh	7.02	11.17
Orissa	3.69	11.45
Punjab	4.30	—
Rajasthan	5.57	8.10
Tamil Nadu	8.47	0.49
Uttar Pradesh	22.38	0.45
West Bengal	11.45	5.94
All-India	100.00	100.00

Source: Registrar-General of India.

The absolute numbers of people dependent on agriculture have grown faster than has agricultural output. But the percentage of total population engaged in agriculture has fallen marginally. To put it more rigorously, while both the percentage of population engaged in agriculture and the share of agriculture in Gross Domestic Product (GDP) have fallen, the rate of fall has been greater in the case of the latter than in the case of the former, with the result that the gap between per capita agricultural income and per capita non-agricultural income has widened. Tables 3.6 and 3.7 provide the necessary information on this subject. Table 3.8 brings out how agricultural income per head is much lower than industrial earning per head. In comparing the two we should not forget that agricultural income is, by and large, the product of self-employment, whereas industrial earning is mainly the outcome of wage-employment. From these tables the inter-State differences in the level of development can also be appreciated. The poorer States are in an unfavourable position when compared with the richer ones. Per worker output/income is a measure of productivity, whereas per capita income is an index of standard of living and hence of general economic welfare. Low productivity and poverty are related to each other causatively and associatively.

TABLE 3.6: Sectoral distribution of state domestic product at factor cost (at 1970-71 prices)

(Percentage)

State	Agricultural			Non-Agricultural		
	1970-71	1980-81	1986-87	1970-71	1980-81	1986-87
Andhra Pradesh	56.6(8)	47.4(7)	36.1(5)	43.4	52.6	63.9
Assam	61.4(15)	62.1(15)	44.9(12)	38.6	37.9	55.1
Bihar	58.0(10)	49.6(8)	44.6(11)	42.0	50.4	55.4
Gujarat	48.0(4)	37.5(3)	26.1(3)	52.0	62.5	73.9
Haryana	64.6(16)	51.9(12)	46.8(14)	35.4	48.1	53.2
Himachal Pradesh	57.0(9)	55.1(14)	40.1(8)	43.0	44.9	55.9
Jammu & Kashmir	56.5(7)	51.4(11)	42.4(10)	43.5	48.6	57.6
Karnataka	54.2(6)	44.5(6)	41.5(9)	45.8	55.5	58.5
Kerala	49.4(5)	40.2(4)	32.6(4)	50.6	59.8	67.4
Madhya Pradesh	59.7(12)	49.6(8)	38.2(6)	40.3	50.4	61.8
Maharashtra	28.4(1)	27.7(1)	17.2(1)	71.6	72.3	82.8
Orissa	65.5(17)	63.3(16)	57.6(16)	34.5	36.7	42.4
Punjab	58.3(11)	49.7(9)	52.8(15)	41.7	51.3	47.2
Rajasthan	61.0(14)	50.3(10)	46.5(13)	39.0	49.7	53.5
Tamil Nadu	39.3(2)	28.6(2)	19.9(2)	60.7	72.4	80.1
Uttar Pradesh	60.0(13)	54.4(13)	46.5(13)	40.0	45.6	53.5
West Bengal	43.5(3)	43.3(5)	39.6(7)	56.5	56.7	60.4
All-India	49.2	41.6	—	50.8	58.4	—

Source: (1) *National Accounts Statistics;*
(2) CMIE, *Basic Statistics Relating to the Indian Economy,* Vol. 2, *States,* 1985.

Note: Figures in brackets indicate the ranks of the States.

A striking fact displayed by Table 3.9 is that the rise in per capita factory wage income has been faster than that in per hectare yield of foodgrains. In addition, industrial wage earning has been stabler than agricultural income. The regional variations in agricultural incomes are more pronounced than those in industrial earnings/wages. Added to this is another remarkable fact, i.e., the regional variations in the rate of rise in industrial earnings/wages have been rather mild, and not violent like those in the case of rate of rise in foodgrain yields. The amplitude of fluctuations in the rate of growth too has been higher in the case of agriculture than in that of non-agriculture. In Table 3.9 we have taken factory earnings and yield of all foodgrains as a symbol respectively of non-agriculture and agriculture.

TABLE 3.7: Sectoral employment of main workers.

(Percentage)

State	Mainly Agricultural		Mainly Non-Agricultural	
	1971	1981	1971	1981
Bihar	82.26(14)	79.21(15)	17.74	20.79
Gujarat	65.60(8)	60.58(5)	34.40	39.42
Haryana	65.29(7)	61.37(6)	34.71	38.63
Maharashtra	64.87(6)	61.63(7)	35.13	38.37
Orissa	77.45(13)	47.65(2)	22.55	52.35
Punjab	62.67(5)	59.15(4)	37.33	40.85
Uttar Pradesh	77.38(12)	74.34(13)	22.62	25.66
West Bengal	58.43(3)	55.45(3)	41.57	44.55
Andhra Pradesh	70.11(11)	69.28(10)	29.89	30.72
Karnataka	66.12(9)	65.12(8)	33.88	34.88
Kerala	48.50(2)	41.37(1)	51.50	58.63
Madhya Pradesh	79.42(14)	76.27(14)	20.58	23.73
Rajasthan	24.23(1)	69.45(11)	75.77	30.45
Tamil Nadu	61.72(4)	70.85(12)	38.28	29.15
All-India	69.79(10)	66.69(9)	30.21	33.31

Source: Bihar State Planning Board, *Selected Plan Statistics*, 1986.
Note: Figures in brackets indicate the ranks of the States.

Finally, as we have noted earlier, the burden of dependency is on the high side in a number of States (including Bihar) and between 1971 and 1981 it had increased in several States, Bihar included. The extent of poverty corresponds more or less to the burden of dependency. In rural areas this burden is heavier.

In a predominantly agricultural country or State agricultural growth by itself tends to bring down the incidence of poverty, but whether it does so in a decisive degree or not is still unestablished. Studies by some economists, such as Mundel, demonstrate that the production performance of agriculture is not a decisive factor

TABLE 3.8: Per capita agricultural and manufacturing incomes

(In Rupees)

State	Per Capita Rural Income from Agriculture (Average : 1982-85) (Rs)	Income Generated (Net Value) Added in Agriculture Per Cultivator 1984-85 (Rs.)	Value of Agricultural Produce Per Hectare of Gross Cropped Area (1984-85) at 1980-81 Prices (Rs.)	Real Per Capita SDP in Manufacturing Sector (1984-85) (Rs.)	Per Capita Gross Factory Output (1984-85) (Rs.)	Net Value Added in Registered Working Factories (1984-85) Per Worker (Rs.)	Net Value Added in Registered Working Factories (1984-85) Per Capita (Rs.)
1	2	3	4	5	6	7	8
Andhra Pradesh	1093(6)	6160(7)	3098(7)	81(8)	1104(7)	25897(12)	250(10)
Assam	928(11)	NA	3598(5)	69(11)	614(14)	3794(7)	159(12)
Bihar	590(14)	4362(12)	3030(8)	63(12)	809(11)	42755(3)	151(13)
Gujarat	1210(5)	7466(5)	2728(11)	210(2)	3328(2)	38499(5)	581(2)
Haryana	1880(2)	12708(3)	2857(9)	157(5)	2351(4)	37848(6)	412(4)
Himachal Pradesh	NA	NA	2783(10)	NA	862(10)	62099(1)	316(6)
Jammu & Kashmir	NA	NA	NA	NA	450(16)	NA	NA
Karnataka	1074(8)	5976(9)	2426(13)	158(4)	1096(8)	34252(8)	261(8)
Kerala	933(10)	25730(1)	4747(1)	80(9)	958(9)	33871(9)	252(9)
Madhya Pradesh	905(12)	3659(14)	1771(15)	74(10)	958(9)	38641(4)	188(11)
Maharashtra	1239(3)	6630(6)	1934(14)	304(1)	3514(1)	51883(2)	702(1)
Orissa	1017(9)	6008(8)	2442(12)	21(14)	588(15)	22238(16)	83(16)
Punjab	2325(1)	17981(2)	3642(4)	166(3)	2375(3)	25522(13)	342(5)
Rajasthan	1222(4)	5157(10)	1097(16)	48(13)	763(12)	32058(11)	146(14)
Tamil Nadu	578(15)	4549(11)	3759(3)	152(6)	2189(5)	33682(10)	458(3)
Uttar Pradesh	869(13)	4357(13)	3276(6)	80(9)	732(13)	22875(15)	115(15)
West Bengal	1075(7)	10171(4)	4125(2)	117(7)	1485(6)	25382(14)	313(7)

Source: (1) P.C. Sarkar, *RBI Occasional Papers*, March, 1989.
(2) U.P. State Planning Institute, *Inter-State Disparities*, April, 1990.
(3) Tata Services Ltd., *Statistical Outline of India*, 1989-90.

Note: Figures in brackets indicate the ranks of the States.

TABLE 3.9: **Disparity in rates of growth of income in agriculture and non-agriculture.**

State	Per Capita Daily Earnings of Factory Workers (Rs.)			Yield of all Foodgrains Per Hectare (kgs.)		
	1971	1985	Increase (+) During the Period (Times)	1977-78	1985-86	Increase (+)/ Decrease (-) During the Period
1	2	3	4	5	6	7
Andhra Pradesh	7.02	31.12	4.4	943	1205	1.3
Assam	5.71	21.22	3.7	987	1003	1.0
Bihar	8.72	22.45	2.6	943	1157	1.2
Gujarat	9.30	30.19	3.2	865	748	(-) 1.1
Haryana	8.41	34.93	4.1	1276	1843	1.4
Himachal Pradesh	9.17	22.35	2.4	NA	NA	NA
Jammu & Kashmir	5.97	18.81	3.1	NA	NA	NA
Karnataka	8.66	NA	NA	1019	953	(-) 1.1
Kerala	7.03	29.80	4.2	1454	1650	1.1
Madhya Pradesh	9.63	36.68	3.8	699	759	1.1
Maharashtra	10.20	41.56	4.1	723	523	(-) 1.4
Orissa	9.09	37.89	4.2	832	920	1.1
Punjab	7.64	28.76	3.7	2400	3243	1.3
Rajasthan	8.11	34.47	4.2	591	531	(-) 1.1
Tamil Nadu	8.52	32.37	4.9	1429	1630	1.1
Uttar Pradesh	8.33	NA	NA	1093	1470	1.3
West Bengal	10.03	43.89	4.4	1363	1532	1.1
All-India	9.08	34.06	3.7	991	1142	1.1

Source: (1) *Indian Labour Journal*, March, 1989.
(2) Bihar State Planning Board, *Selected Plan Statistics*, 1986.

underlying the incidence or rural poverty, though improved performance does help to ameliorate it. To quote him, unless there are sufficiently strong offsetting forces at work, an increase in agricultural production would tend to increase real incomes of both poor cultivating households as well as rural labour households. Therefore, an over-all decline in the incidence of rural poverty could be expected with a rise in agricultural production per capita. This throws in bold relief the proposition put forth in the immediately preceding pages that productivity and poverty are inversely related.

TABLE 3.10 State-wise percentage shares in All-India production of rice and wheat

State	1977-78				1982-83				1985-86	
	Rice		Wheat		Rice		Wheat		Rice	Wheat
	A	P	A	P	A	P	A	P	A	P
Andhra Pradesh	8.82	10.06	—	—	9.50	16.31	—	—	11.6	—
Assam	5.59	4.33	—	—	6.09	5.55	—	—	4.2	0.3
Bihar	13.88	10.47	9.24	8.11	11.89	6.58	6.22	5.18	9.5	6.5
Gujarat	1.20	1.27	—	—	1.25	1.05	—	—	1.0	2.0
Haryana	0.91	1.83	6.37	9.04	1.29	2.74	7.42	10.22	2.2	10.8
Karnataka	2.72	4.33	—	—	2.84	4.43	—	—	3.6	0.3
Kerala	2.08	2.40	—	—	2.11	2.87	—	—	2.0	—
Madhya Pradesh	11.63	8.34	15.03	9.24	12.65	7.31	14.55	8.66	7.4	8.8
Maharashtra	3.72	4.45	5.66	3.03	3.93	4.19	4.41	1.88	2.2	1.5
Orissa	10.93	8.17	—	—	10.52	6.23	—	—	7.8	0.2
Punjab	0.82	5.30	12.19	20.91	3.49	8.92	13.19	21.60	9.0	23.6
Rajasthan	—	—	8.53	8.21	—	—	8.91	8.88	0.3	7.3
Tamil Nadu	6.62	11.20	—	—	4.60	7.09	—	—	8.8	—
Uttar Pradesh	11.98	9.16	31.01	29.95	13.12	1.89	35.50	35.96	12.4	35.3
West Bengal	13.43	14.25	—	—	12.86	10.64	—	—	13.4	1.6
All-India	100.0	100.0	100.0	100.0	100.0	100.0	100.0	100.0	100.0	100.0

Source: (1) Bihar State Planning Board, *Selected Plan Statistics*, 1986.
(2) *Indian Agriculture in Brief.*
A = Acreage.
P = Production.

Inquiries (for instance, one by Kakwani and Subharao) confirm the relationship between movement in foodgrains production and movement in poverty. The relationship is, of course, inverse. Table 3.10 depicts the distribution of foodgrains (total, rice and wheat) production in the major States of India in 1977-78 (for which year we have also estimates of poverty in the different States), 1982-83 (the year preceding 1983-84 for which also we have State-wise estimate of poverty) and 1985-86. These data tell a story different from that told by Table 3.4. Whereas Table 3.4 tells that the percentage of population below the Poverty Line in the major States (except Rajasthan) declined between 1977-78 and 1983-84, Table 3.10 tells that with increased shares in foodgrain production the percentage of the poor and their attendant misery must have diminished in Andhra Pradesh, Assam, Gujarat, Haryana, Kerala, Punjab, Rajasthan, Tamil Nadu, Uttar Pradesh and West Bengal in 1982-83, as compared to 1977-78, and similarly with decreased shares of Bihar, Karnataka, Maharashtra, and Orissa the percentage of the poor and their attendant misery must have risen during the same period. In 1985-86, as compared to 1982-83, the poverty problem must have become more acute in Andhra Pradesh, Assam, Gujarat, Karnataka, Kerala, Maharashtra and Rajasthan on account of the reduced shares of these States in the total foodgrain basket, and it must have become less acute in Bihar, Orissa, Punjab, Tamil Nadu, Uttar Pradesh and West Bengal because of their increased share in the total foodgrain kitty.

The rate of reduction in poverty incidence has been the lowest in agriculturally lagging regions. As many as 70 per cent of India's rural poor as well as ultra poor have been located geographically in States with low or moderate rates of agricultural growth with medium or high instability. The regions experiencing high or medium growth with low instability have accounted for only 27 per cent of the poor and 25 per cent of the ultra poor (See Table 3.11)

On the basis of foodgrain production per agriculturist (cultivators and agricultural workers combined) in 1977-78 and in 1982-83 it can be said that 1982-83 was a worse year compared to 1977-78 for the poor (See Table 3.12). With agricultural output fluctuating from year to year neither the intensity nor the extent of rural poverty was stable.

TABLE 3.11: Distribution of poor according to levels of growth and instability in foodgrain production

Category	State	Percentage of New Sown Area with Rainfall			Percentage of			Number of Agricultural Workers per 100 Hectares of Net Sown Area, 1980-83
		High (1,150mm and above)	Medium (750mm to 1,150 mm)	Low (up to 750mm)	Rural popula-tion, 1983	Poverty popula-tion 1983	Ultra poor	
1	2	3	4	5	6	7	8	9
High growth and low instability	Punjab, Jammu & Kashmir	5.3	20.5	74.2	3.2	0.9	NA	85
High growth and medium instability	Haryana, Uttar Pradesh	8.4	64.1	27.5	19.6	18.7	19.0	148
High growth and high instability	Gujarat	7.3	25.0	67.7	4.5	2.0	2.73	83
High growth and low instability	Andhra Pradesh, Himachal Pradesh	1.0	66.0	33.0	8.7	4.5	3.9	145
Medium growth and medium instability	Karnataka	9.4	24.3	66.3	5.1	4.4	4.6	95
Medium growth and high instability	Maharashtra, Orissa Rajasthan	25.0	24.1	50.9	17.6	17.6	16.7	87
Low growth and low instability	Assam, Kerala	100.0	Nil	Nil	7.5	5.4	6.5	173
Low growth and medium instability	Tamil Nadu, West Bengal	54.2	45.8	Nil	14.0	19.6	18.4	188
Low growth and high instability	Bihar, Madhya Pradesh	63.5	33.5	3.0	19.8	26.9	26.1	130
All categories	**All-India**	30.7	35.8	33.5	100.0	100.0		120

Source: *Economic and Political Weekly,* March 31, 1990.

TABLE 3.12: Per agriculturist foodgrains production

(In kg)

State	All Foodgrains 1977-78	1982-83	Increase(+)/ Decrease(-) in 1982-83 over 1977-78
Andhra Pradesh	943(9)	1274(4)	(+)331(2)
Assam	987(8)	1080(7)	(+) 93(6)
Bihar	943(9)	816(11)	(-)127(13)
Gujarat	865(10)	923(10)	(-) 58(8)
Haryana	1276(5)	1249(5)	(-) 27(11)
Karnataka	1019(7)	936(9)	(+) 83(7)
Kerala	1454(2)	1593(2)	(+)139(5)
Madhya Pradesh	699(13)	696(13)	(-) 3(10)
Maharashtra	723(12)	677(14)	(-) 46(12)
Orissa	832	730(12)	(-)102(14)
Punjab	2400(1)	2829(1)	(+)429(1)
Rajasthan	591(14)	651(15)	(+) 60(9)
Tamil Nadu	1429(3)	1245(6)	(-)184(15)
Uttar Pradesh	1093(6)	1322(3)	(+)229(4)
West Bengal	1363(4)	1043(8)	(+)320(3)
All-India	991	1041	(+) 50

Source: Bihar State Planning Board, *Selected Plan Statistics*, 1986.

Some salient features of rural poverty can be mentioned here. In the first place, the intensity of rural poverty varies as between classes. Secondly, the role of the poor in the rural social structure varies identically. Thirdly, the economic position of the poor also varies in the same manner. We have among the rural poor small farmers and agricultural labourers with land and without it. The duration of employment is a significant determinant of their poverty. More often than not, poverty goes hand in hand with unemployment. The two together with inequality are mutually inclusive. Wages paid and the method and form of their payment count a good deal. The relative economic position of the rural labour force in terms of real wage and working conditions is far worse than that of the urban labour force. Relations of rural workers with their landlords are personalised and profoundly influence the pattern of their life and its level. Rural indebtedness is a proximate cause of the interlinking of these relationships.

Income accrues to an individual either from his labour, physical or mental, or from his ownership of property/assets. In rural society land is the chief asset but, as Table 3.13 reveals, in relation to their population shares the shares of the poor States in total gross cropped area are low, and hence their land base is weak. Per capita net cultivated area is smaller. Average size of operational holdings is also smaller. A vast majority of the holdings are too small in size to support a family of five persons. The owners of these holdings subsist on very low earnings with little or no resources of their own for either land development or provision of the high-cost inputs needed for raising productivity or yield per hectare. Fragmentation of holdings and increased sale of land to the rich farmers have been the principal force behind the steady decline of the marginal farmers to the subsistance level and then to the status of the landless labourers. Efforts made to consolidate strips of land were thwarted by the ceiling legislation, the compulsions of the Green Revolution, and the government land redistribution policy, and fragmentation of holdings gathered momentum in spite of them. To illustrate, in 1981 out of the total of 75.77 lakh holdings, 64.34 per cent were tiny pieces of less than one hectare and 14.64 per cent were between one hectare and two. The large landholders having holdings of more than 10 hectares which accounted for less than two per cent of the aggregate number of holdings did not utilise their holdings effectively – nearly eight per cent of the total land that was cultivated remained uncultivated every year.

Absolute poverty affects women proportionately more. There are more women that men in the lowest end/fraction of the income scale. Among them we have those which compose households headed by themselves. Women generally work in occupations that exploit them by paying them less. Such occupations are agriculture and allied activities, construction trades, and the like.

Agricultural prices do not have a pointed correlation with the incidence of rural poverty insofar as they concern more who derive their current incomes from sales of the marketable surplus than those who are on the margin of self-sufficiency and in some way or other are dependent on earnings from sale of their manual labour to the former.

In considering the regional dimensions of poverty reference has to be made to the **rural-urban disparities**. Not only have the disparities between one part of the country and another, one class of society and another, one sector of the economy and another, and one gender and another become accentuated over the years, but also have

TABLE 3.13: State-wise land base

State	Net Area Sown as Percentage of Total Reported Area in the State 1982-83	Area Sown More than Once as Percentage of Net Area Sown in the State 1982-83	Percentage Share in the Total Cropped Area in the Country 1982-83	Percentage Share in Total Population of the country (1981)	Net Area Sown Per Head of Population in the State (sq. km.) (1981)	Per Capita Net Cultivated Area in 1985-86 (hectare)	Average Size of operational Holding 1985-86 (hectare)
1	2	3	4	5	6	7	8
Andhra Pradesh	40.2	15.7	7.4	7.81	0.0021	0.18	2.34
Assam	34.3	31.9	2.0	2.91	0.0013	0.12	NA
Bihar	47.7	16.5	5.6	10.21	0.0010	0.10	1.11
Gujarat	51.4	5.4	5.9	4.97	0.0027	0.26	3.71
Haryana	81.8	47.5	3.1	1.88	0.0027	0.25	3.58
Himachal Pradesh	18.3	67.7	0.5	0.62	NA	0.12	NA
Jammu & Kashmir	16.1	38.4	0.6	0.87	NA	NA	NA
Karnataka	54.4	7.7	6.4	5.42	0.0028	0.25	2.98
Kerala	11.4	31.3	1.6	3.71	0.0008	0.08	0.49
Madhya Pradesh	43.0	16.7	12.9	7.62	0.0036	0.34	3.58
Maharashtra	59.5	9.0	11.6	9.17	0.0029	0.26	3.66
Orissa	39.4	35.8	4.8	3.84	0.0022	0.22	1.60
Punjab	83.5	64.6	4.0	2.44	0.0025	0.23	2.74
Rajasthan	45.7	17.5	10.6	4.99	0.0046	0.40	4.65
Tamil Nadu	40.4	14.6	3.5	7.06	0.0011	0.11	1.23
Uttar Pradesh	58.0	43.4	14.3	16.21	0.0015	0.14	1.05
West Bengal	63.0	25.9	4.0	7.97	0.0009	0.09	0.99
All-India	46.6	21.8	100.00	100.0	—	—	—

Source: (1) Central Statistical Organisation, *Statistical Abstract of India*, 1985.
(2) Registrar-General of India, *Census of India*, 1981.

those between rural and urban areas, as indicated by the per capita level of income, per capita level of consumption, and per capita availability of social services and economic overheads. Statistics on inequality in consumer expenditure are presented State-wise in Table 3.14. Inasmuch as government expenditure on social overheads has had urban orientation rural-urban disparities in consumption, private and social, have become wider with the passage of time.

TABLE 3.14: Monthly per capita consumer expenditure

(Rupees)

State	1977-78		1983	
	Rural	Urban	Rural	Urban
Andhra Pradesh	69.7	93.2	115.4	153.5
Assam	59.0	94.4	113.0	154.0
Bihar	57.4	83.1	93.8	138.5
Gujarat	70.3	100.9	122.7	163.6
Haryana	92.4	100.4	151.8	186.9
Himachal Pradesh	81.4	123.0	150.8	258.6
Jammu & Kashmir	72.9	88.4	129.3	155.3
Karnataka	64.9	87.6	116.8	166.3
Kerala	74.2	82.7	145.2	176.4
Madhya Pradesh	60.0	90.9	100.5	144.9
Maharashtra	76.9	110.3	110.4	184.4
Orissa	52.5	87.0	98.8	151.4
Punjab	121.7	114.4	185.2	170.5
Rajasthan	108.7	95.7	127.0	159.9
Tamil Nadu	63.3	86.1	112.2	163.7
Uttar Pradesh	67.3	82.5	104.5	135.5
West Bengal	59.3	97.1	104.6	170.0
All-India	68.9	96.2	112.4	164.0

Source: *NSS Reports.*

As delineated by Rath, the predominately poverty-stricken regions are of four categories:

(1) The alluvial plains of eastern Uttar Pradesh, Bihar, Assam, Bengal, Orissa, coastal Andhra Pradesh and deltaic Tamil Nadu.

(2) The upland regions of central India, namely, Madhya Pradesh, Rajasthan, Gujarat, Maharashtra, Andhra Pradesh and Karnataka, where there is a significant tribal population in varying rural settings.

(3) The non-tribal upland regions, essentially agricultural, but with medium or low rainfall (and without large-scale irrigation

facility).

(4) The other mountainous regions and narrow strips.

In sum, mass poverty is concentrated in the eastern Indian States. Inequality aggravates poverty. In the poorer States 75 to 85 per cent of the total tangible wealth of all rural households is held by cultivators who form nearly 60 to 65 per cent of the rural population. About 10 to 15 per cent of the non-cultivating population holds hardly 5 to 10 per cent of the tangible rural wealth, and scarcely one to three per cent holds about 15 to 25 per cent of it. In rural areas approximately three-fourths of total assets are owned by the three to four deciles. The top 8 to 13 per cent own nearly 45 to 52 per cent of the total assets and the bottom 10 to 15 per cent own hardly anything. The bottom 30 to 35 per cent own just two to four per cent of the total assets. A rough idea of relative poverty can be formed on the basis of these data.

More concretely, the distribution of land is highly skewed in some regions. In such regions a few large holdings still exist amidst a sea of marginal and small holdings. To amplify, in Bihar the small and marginal farmers constitute around 80 per cent of the total number of farmers but they hold only around 40 per cent of the total cultivated area. The large and medium farmers are about 20 per cent but hold about 60 per cent of it. Only 6 per cent of the operational holdings are larger than five hectares and they comprise a greater land area than the total area operated in Punjab. Four lakh households with an average holding of 12 hectares owning and operating nearly 40 per cent of the total cultivated area dominate the Bihar economy and politics. The structural imbalance in landholding is an inhibiting factor in agricultural production in States such as Bihar.

We revert now to other measures of poverty like per capita consumption and consumption expenditure. Household consumption expenditure is an index of poverty (as it is of progress, of living standard and of welfare). Not only that there have arisen regional disparities in it but also they have tended to increase over time. The rate of growth in consumption per capita has been positively and significantly related to the growth rate in the Gini Index (see Tables 3.15 and 3.16). But the faster growth rate in consumption has tended to increase inequality. Inequality in per capita consumption has had wide variations across the States and over time. During 1977-78 average consumption grew slowly but consumption inequality fell in many States, and the reduction in the incidence of poverty was greater in magnitude than in the earlier period of high growth. Kakwani and Subharao conclude that the beneficial effects of growth on the incidence of poverty can be nullified by adverse movements in the inequality of consumption. The effect of growth and inequality on poverty reduction was generally low in States with low consumption per capita. Rise in average per capita personal consumption was slower than that in per capita consumption, with the result that inequality fell only insignificantly. Bihar had a negative trend in average consumption per capita — better in the second and subsequent periods than in the first. The poverty ratio became more responsive to the changes in mean income and income inequality in all States, except Bihar and West Bengal. While the poverty ratio grew monotonically from 8 per cent to 12 per cent between 1972-73 and 1983, the degree of inequality remained more or less at the same level during this period.

TABLE 3.15: Trends in average consumption per capita (real) by states (1972-1983)

(Rs. Per Month)

State	Per Capita Consumption at 1973-74 Prices				Annual Growth Rates at 1973-74 Prices		
	1972-73	1973-74	1977-78	1983	1973-74 Over 1972-73 Per Cent	1977-78 Over 1973-74 Per Cent	1983 Over 1977-83 Per Cent
Andhra Pradesh	53.8	58.3	65.1	75.9	8.4	2.8	2.8
Assam	50.2	52.0	49.2	57.4	−.6	−1.4	2.8
Bihar	46.8	45.2	45.9	45.3	−3.4	0.4	−0.2
Gujarat	58.8	56.8	3.3	72.6	−3.4	2.7	2.5
Haryana	83.5	71.8	75.1	83.0	−14.0	1.1	1.8
Karnataka	56.6	52.3	57.9	65.3	−7.4	2.6	2.2
Kerala	51.5	53.8	63.0	73.0	4.5	4.0	2.7
Madhya Pradesh	51.5	49.3	52.5	59.5	−4.3	1.6	2.3
Maharashtra	45.7	50.8	48.7	61.0	11.2	−1.0	4.2
Orissa	47.9	44.9	50.5	52.8	−6.3	3.0	0.8
Punjab	88.8	74.8	93.0	93.2	−15.8	5.6	0.0
Rajasthan	69.3	66.0	75.3	81.3	−4.8	3.44	1.4
Tamil Nadu	50.9	51.3	53.6	56.7	0.8	1.1	1.0
Uttar Pradesh	53.3	50.3	59.6	60.1	−5.6	4.3	0.2
West Bengal	42.0	40.6	43.6	46.9	−3.3	1.8	1.3
All-India	53.0	51.8	56.7	61.7	−2.3	2.3	1.5

Source: N. Kakwani and K. Subharao, article in *Economic and Political Weekly*, March, 31, 1990.

TABLE 3.16: State-wise patterns of inequality in consumption (1973-74 to 1983)

State	Gini Index				Theil's Measure			
	1972-73	1973-74	1977-78	1983	1972-73	1973-74	1977-78	1983
Andhra Pradesh	0.28	0.29	0.30	0.295	0.127	0.143	0.151	0.142
Assam	0.19	0.21	0.18	0.198	0.062	0.075	0.057	0.064
Bihar	0.29	0.28	0.26	0.260	0.141	0.128	0.112	0.109
Gujarat	0.31	0.24	0.29	0.260	0.127	0.094	0.136	0.105
Haryana	0.29	0.30	0.30	0.280	0.135	0.142	0.147	0.123
Karnataka	0.28	0.29	0.32	0.300	0.129	0.131	0.174	0.150
Kerala	0.31	0.32	0.36	0.330	0.163	0.167	0.212	0.189
Madhya Pradesh	0.31	0.29	0.34	0.300	0.159	0.137	0.188	0.143
Maharashtra	0.32	0.27	0.30	0.290	0.172	0.123	0.143	0.133
Orissa	0.32	0.27	0.31	0.270	0.162	0.117	0.153	0.119
Punjab	0.32	0.28	0.31	0.290	0.163	0.127	0.165	0.135
Rajasthan	0.32	0.28	0.33	0.340	0.170	0.131	0.184	0.196
Tamil Nadu	0.28	0.28	0.32	0.330	0.129	0.125	0.174	0.177
Uttar Pradesh	0.28	0.24	0.30	0.290	0.131	0.095	0.151	0.141
West Bengal	0.31	0.30	0.30	0.290	0.156	0.148	0.143	0.138

Source: *Economic and Political Weekly*, March 31, 1990.

The NSS reports furnish reasonably comparable time series data on the levels and distribution of household consumption expenditure in rural and urban areas. They give the relevant information for the country as a whole. They show how the top 30 per cent of our population accounts for over 50 per cent of the total income expenditure and demand for manufactured goods. With their help the effect of increase in per capita income on the extent of poverty can be investigated. We can recall here that Dandekar and Rath had used "a split minimum calorie intake" to measure the extent of poverty. On the other hand, Minhas had endeavoured to measure it in terms of the minimum per capita expenditure per annum sufficient to provide the critical minimum basket of goods. The Planning Commission, concept of the Poverty Line is in terms of minimum nutritional requirements — so many calories per person per day — separately for rural and urban areas, and then converted into a monthly per capita expenditure. The Seventh Finance Commission combined per capita monthly public expenditure on social services or amenities with per capita private consumption expenditure to arrive at the augmented Poverty Line. This was a modified State-specific norm.

We have stated above that, by and large, in any year foodgrain production in the States is a crucial determinant of their poverty in that year since the welfare of the majority of their people is indissolubly bound up with it. In Table 3.17 we give State-wise data of foodgrain production per person employed in agriculture as well as per head of population. In the received theory, the former is taken as a measure of the level of productivity or efficiency of labour, whereas the latter is taken as a measure of the level of welfare enjoyed by the population, assuming that the later figure is also coincidental with the quantity of foodgrain consumption per head of population.

TABLE 3.17 State-wise foodgrains production 1984-85

(In kg)

State	Foodgrain Pro-dction per Participant in Agriculture (Basis: 1981 Census Population)	Foodgrain Production Per Head of Population (Basis: 1981 Census Population)	Extent of Gap between (2) & (3)	Extent of Gap between (3) and Norm of 183 Kg Foodgrain Consumption per Person Per Year
1	2	3	4	5
Andhra Pradesh	621(15)	182(9)/164(7)	439(15)	(-)1(10)
Assam	NA	NA/125(12)	NA	NA
Bihar	639(13)	150(14)/132(10)	489(13)	(-)33(15)
Gujarat	809(10)	157(12)/63(15)	652(10)	(-)26(13)
Haryana	3118(3)	537(2)/454(2)	2581(3)	(+)404(2)
Himachal Pradesh	945(9)	230(7)/228(4)	715(9)	(+)47(8)
Jammu & Kashmir	1162(7)	213(8)/124(13)	849(8)	(+)30(9)
Karnataka	740(11)	177(10)/115(14)	563(11)	(-)6(11)
Kerala	455(16)	50(15)/41(16)	405(16)	(-)133(3)
Madhya Pradesh	8697(1)	254(4)/171(6)	8453(1)	(+)71(5)
Maharashtra	659(12)	157(12)/128(11)	502(12)	(-)26(13)
Orissa	1516(4)	247(5)/217(5)	1269(4)	(+)64(6)
Punjab	5727(2)	975(1)/902(1)	4752(2)	(+)792(1)
Rajasthan	1110(6)	233(6)/164(7)	877(7)	(+)50(7)
Tamil Nadu	630(14)	151(13)/138(9)	479(14)	(-)32(14)
Uttar Pradesh	1274(5)	277(3)/238(3)	997(5)	(+)84(4)
West Bengal	1109(8)	172(11)/159(8)	937(6)	(-)11(12)
		(All India :-/186)		

Source: *Statistical Abstract of India*, 1987.

Note: Figures in brackets indicate the ranks of the States.

In Col. 3 figures after bars are average for 1985-86 to 1987-88 taken from *Selected Indicators for Districts in Maharashtra and States in India 1987-88.*

The extent of the gap between the two is indicated in column 3 of Table 3.17.

Apart from these facts we have also the norm of foodgrain consumption equal to 183 kg per person per year. Viewed against this norm, we can arrive at the extent of foodgrain gap per person per year for different States. Although this extent cannot become an over-all index of the level of poverty in the States, whether more rich or more poor, in view of the existence of the territorial division of labour based on the age-old comparative cost or advantage principle, yet the pathetic position of the more backward states is far too prominent in the picture to await such comments or such indices.

Table 3.18 shows the estimate of the incidence of poverty lines for households with agriculture and non-agriculture for each State in 1977-78, as well as the share of each State in the 15 States' total of poverty households and all households. The incidence of poverty among the households in agriculture varied from around 9 per cent in Punjab to 64 per cent in West Bengal. In the case of non-agriculture it varied from around 12 per cent in Punjab and Rajasthan to 51 per cent in West Bengal. Generally, the incidence of poverty among the households in non-agriculture was higher in the States where it was higher for agriculture as well. The correlation coefficient between the two incidences of poverty in the two sectors in the 15 States in 1977-78 was 0.91. The incidence of poverty for non-agriculture was higher in Punjab and Haryana than that for agriculture, while in the rest of the States the latter was higher than the former. For agriculture in Bihar, Karnataka, Madhya Pradesh, Maharashtra, Orissa, Tamil Nadu and West Bengal, the share of poverty households was higher than that of total households. Thus, these States together accounted for about 67 per cent of the total poverty households with about 55 per cent of the total rural households. Similarly, for non-agriculture, six of them (Tamil Nadu being the only exception) accounted for about 52 per cent of the total poverty households with about 40 per cent of the total households.

Table 3.19 presents the incidence of poverty among households with non-agriculture as the principal occupation by different sectors for each major State for 1977-78. In eight States — Assam, Bihar, Haryana, Karnataka, Orissa, Punjab, Rajasthan and Tamil Nadu — construction reported the highest incidence of poverty in rural non-agriculture sector. Incidence of poverty was the highest for manufacturing in Madhya Pradesh and Kerala, while three States — Gujarat, Maharashtra and Uttar Pradesh — reported highest poverty incidence in mining and quarrying. The incidence of poverty was higher for manufacturing, as compared to those of transport and services in 12 out of the 15 States.

TABLE 3.18: Incidence of poverty and percentage shares of poverty households and all households for the households with principal industry 'Agriculture' and principal industry 'Non-agriculture' in rural areas: 1977-78.

State	Incidence of Poverty		Agriculture		Non-Agriculture	
	Agriculture	Non-Agriculture	Percentage Share in Poverty	Percentage Share in Total HHs	Percentage Share in Poverty HHs	Percentage Share in Total HHs
1	2	3	4	5	6	7
Andhra Pradesh	29.8	23.1	6.19	8.89	6.50	9.93
Assam	36.0	31.4	2.93	3.48	1.86	2.08
Bihar	53.2	49.6	15.11	12.13	13.83	9.84
Gujarat	31.3	17.7	3.32	4.53	1.66	3.31
Haryana	15.9	25.6	0.56	1.51	1.46	2.01
Karnataka	44.6	37.1	5.28	5.06	4.33	4.13
Kerala	38.5	33.1	2.75	3.05	7.18	7.64
Madhya Pradesh	49.4	38.0	10.93	9.45	4.94	4.58
Maharashtra	50.2	37.9	10.00	8.52	8.71	8.11
Orissa	60.5	48.4	7.33	5.17	5.84	4.26
Punjab	9.2	11.9	0.43	2.03	1.03	3.05
Rajasthan	22.8	11.6	2.47	4.63	2.68	4.67
Tamil Nadu	47.3	33.5	7.87	7.10	9.54	10.03
Uttar Pradesh	34.9	34.9	14.13	17.27	16.90	17.08
West Bengal	63.6	51.4	10.70	7.18	13.54	9.28
All-India	39.1	31.6	100.00*	100.00*	100.00*	100.00*

Source: *Economic and Political Weekly*, July 14, 1990.
Note: Poverty lines for estimating incidence of poverty are defined in the source cited.
HHs = Households.
* Total 15 States.

A comparison of Tables 3.18 and 3.19 shows that in six States—Bihar, Haryana, Kerala, Madhya Pradesh, Punjab and Uttar Pradesh—the incidence of poverty in manufacturing was higher than that of poverty in agriculture.

TABLE 3.19: Incidence of poverty among households with principal industry "Non-Agriculture" by principal industry (1977-78)

State	Mining and Quarrying	Manufacturing	Electricity, Gas and Water	Construction	Trade	Transport	Services	Others	Total Non-Agriculture
1	2	3	4	5	6	7	8	9	10
Andhra Pradesh	26.8	22.8	11.6	21.3	20.3	18.0	22.9	29.1	23.1
Assam	0.0	25.4	50.0	65.5	23.3	41.5	30.2	48.1	31.4
Bihar	39.8	54.6	31.7	66.0	47.8	42.2	46.7	50.4	49.6
Gujarat	59.6	19.8	15.8	21.4	15.2	14.3	15.1	11.8	17.7
Haryana	16.1	30.1	0.0	40.0	18.8	27.1	18.6	21.6	25.6
Karnataka	44.5	42.8	24.6	52.2	32.7	38.5	25.3	37.2	37.1
Kerala	35.4	43.6	22.9	30.1	28.3	32.2	22.0	43.1	33.1
Madhya Pradesh	32.1	51.5	0.0	43.7	33.8	41.5	27.5	35.9	38.0
Maharashtra	56.6	42.2	17.9	53.6	35.6	37.3	26.4	45.9	37.9
Orissa	59.5	52.0	30.8	72.1	53.6	38.2	43.0	42.8	48.4
Punjab	0.0	11.0	7..8	16.3	9.6	11.3	12.3	11.9	11.9
Rajasthan	26.0	22.0	13.5	31.2	20.0	12.2	12.4	19.1	11.6
Tamil Nadu	30.7	34.6	11.5	38.7	33.8	29.1	32.4	34.1	33.5
Uttar Pradesh	42.6	38.4	6.4	38.3	35.8	36.9	31.6	30.6	34.9
West Bengal	28.8	54.2	29.4	54.5	55.1	49.1	44.2	61.7	51.4
All-India	31.2	35.3	13.5	37.4	30.5	28.5	26.7	33.3	31.6

Source: *Economic and Political Weekly*, July 14, 1990.

A very rough idea of the concentration of income State-wise can be formed on the basis of Table 3.20, which supplies statistics on income-tax. Allowing for the fact that agricultural is the least taxed sector of the economy and the agriculturally leading States do not contribute much to income-tax as agricultural incomes in them are not subject to income-tax, the more developed States contribute much more to the income-tax pool than the less developed ones. Also obvious from Table 3.20 is the decline in the relative positions of today's less developed States over the period so far as their economic condition is concerned. In general, the States with larger shares in Central investments and services had fared much better than those with smaller shares in them. While there are a good many flaws of these computations that have to be guarded against, the difference between income *originating* in a State and income *accruing* to it is the greatest source of the complication and difficulty in reaching any cut and dried, unqualified conclusion or in making any prediction in this area of the economic problem faced by less developed States.

Having mentioned the income-tax shares of the States which roughly reflect their relative poverty or wealth levels, we would like to put to use the common saying "Rich People, Rich Governments" (and *vice versa*) with the aid of Table 3.21 which contains data on per capita State revenue, the States' own tax revenue as a percentage of their SDP, etc., and which goes to show how some of the poorest States have overdone themselves in tapping the publicly least objectionable method—the public borrowing method—to mobilise additional resources, in total disregard of the heavy burden of debt servicing innate in the method, which makes a little mockery of their additional resource mobilisation.

Investments in agriculture, industry, and infrastructure in the poorer States are very low both absolutely and relatively to their populations, besides as percentages of all-India totals. They have prevented the poorer States from breaking out of their low-level equilibrium trap and attaining a real break-through. Their per capita incomes have grown at rates slower than per capita incomes of the relatively better-off States. Their budgetary (non-Plan) and Plan outlays as percentages of aggregate national figures have been far less than those of the States richer than themselves. Thus, in Bihar Plan-wise the Plan outlay percentage was 3.45 per cent (First Plan), 4.07 per cent (Second Plan), 3.92 per cent (Third Plan), 3.30 per cent (Annual Plans), 3.36 per cent (Fourth Plan), 3.28 per cent (Fifth

TABLE 3.20: Percentage distribution of income tax (all categories)

State	Number of Assessees Percentage 1952-53	Number of Returns Percentage 1985-86	Increase in Number of Assessees/ Returns between 1952-53 and 1985-86 Times	Total Income Assessed Percentage 1952-53	Returned Income Percentage 1985-86	Increase in Returned/ Assessed Income between 1952-53 and 1985-86 (Times)	Income Tax including Tax deduced at source Percentage 1952-53	Tax Payable Percentage 1985-86	Increase in Tax Payable between 1952-53 and 1985-86 (Times)
1	2	3	4	5	6	7	8	9	10
Andhra Pradesh	2.0(8)	4.9(7)	1140(13)	1.8(7)	3.2(8)	354(5)	1.3(8)	1.8(8)	54(6)
Assam	1.3(11)	0.5(15)	1966(15)	1.1(10)	0.6(14)	10(13)	0.9(10)	0.5(10)	20(10)
Bihar	3.0(5)	3.1(10)	4731(7)	2.3(5)	1.4(11)	122(8)	1.8(5)	0.5(10)	12(12)
Gujarat	—	10.6(3)	—	—	7.1(4)	—	—	3.7(5)	—
Haryana	—	2.1(12)	—	—	1.2(12)	—	—	0.5(10)	—
Karnataka	2.0(8)	4.6(8)	9716(2)	1.6(9)	3.4(7)	423(4)	1.1(9)	2.8(6)	94(4)
Kerala	1.8(9)	1.3(13)	2963(9)	1.7(8)	1.1(13)	123(7)	1.5(7)	0.7(9)	20(10)
Madhya Pradesh	2.4(7)	2.8(11)	5068(6)	2.0(6)	1.7(9)	163(6)	1.6(6)	0.7(9)	19(11)
Maharashtra	34.2(1)	25.6(1)	3441(8)	36.5(1)	27.6(1)	150(1)	37.7(1)	28.6(1)	300(1)
Orissa	0.6(12)	0.7(14)	5568(5)	0.4(11)	0.4(15)	18(11)	0.3(12)	0.2(11)	25(9)
Punjab	2.8(6)	7.1(4)	10928(1)	1.8(7)	4.5(6)	494(3)	1.1(9)	2.5(7)	88(5)
Rajasthan	1.5(10)	3.2(9)	9669(3)	1.1(10)	1.6(10)	29(10)	0.8(11)	0.5(10)	26(8)
Tamil Nadu	10.3(3)	6.6(15)	2915(10)	10.4(3)	5.9(5)	113(9)	10.0(3)	5.5(4)	216(2)
Uttar Pradesh	8.6(4)	11.5(2)	6048(4)	6.1(4)	15.6(2)	509(2)	31.8(2)	19.3(3)	158(3)
West Bengal	18.0(2)	6.4(6)	1635(12)	25.9(2)	15.2(3)	12(12)	31.8(2)	21.7(2)	271(7)
All-India	100.0	100.0	4604	100.0	100.0	20	100.0	100.0	39

Source: (1) *Statistical Abstract of India 1951-53.*
(2) *Statistical Abstract of India 1987.*

Note: Figures in brackets indicate the ranks of the States.

Plan), 2.91 per cent (Sixth Plan) and 2.83 per cent (Seventh Plan). In 1987-88 the percentage of Bihar's total receipts to those of the country was 4.83 per cent and that of its total disbursements to those of the country was 4.19 per cent. The corresponding percentages for 1988-89 were 3.69 per cent and 3.50 per cent. Both items had gone down in percentage shares. The figures for 1989-90 were 6.78 per cent and 6.72 per cent respectively.

TABLE 3.21: Some characteristics of the States' revenue and debt position

State	Percentage Share in Total Income Tax as Assessed during 1985-86 to 1987-88 (Average)	State's Own Revenue as Percentage of the State's SDP (1986-87)	State's Per Capita Revenue (Tax plus Non-Tax, excluding share in Central Taxes) in 1985-86 (Rs.)	Percentage Share in Total Internal Public Debt (31.3.89)
Andhra Pradesh	4.4(7)	14.20(4)	398.22(7)	6.7(5)
Assam	1.1(12)	8.40	264.46(14)	3.4(14)
Bihar	2.4(10)	8.40(9)	165.81(16)	7.9(3)
Gujarat	11.2(2)	13.60(5)	429.82(5)	6.3(6)
Haryana	0.9(13)	14.60(2)	563.27(3)	2.3(16)
Himachal Pradesh	0.3(16)	—	805.75(1)	0.9(17)
Jammu & Kashmir	0.4(15)	—	—	2.7(15)
Karnataka	5.0(6)	14.70(1)	414.80(6)	4.4(11)
Kerala	3.1(9)	14.60(2)	333.41(9)	3.7(13)
Madhya Pradesh	3.3(8)	12.50(6)	317.55(10)	6.2(7)
Maharashtra	27.4(1)	14.20(4)	485.90(4)	9.9(2)
Orrisa	0.6(14)	8.40(9)	264.45(13)	4.0(12)
Punjab	3.1(9)	10.70(8)	571.39(2)	5.3(9)
Rajasthan	2.0(11)	10.90(7)	292.82(11)	6.1(8)
Tamil Nadu	9.5(9)	14.30(3)	371.54(8)	4.9(10)
Uttar Pradesh	5.4(5)	7.60(11)	188.77(15)	14.3(1)
West Bengal	7.7(4)	7.90(10)	275.88(12)	7.4(4)
All-India	100.00			100.00

Source: (1) Government of Bihar, Finance Department, *Memorandum to the Ninth Finance Commission*, 1988.
(2) *Ninth Finance Commission Report (Second)*, 1989.
(3) U.P. State Planning Institute, *Inter-State Disparities*, April 1990.
(4) *Economic and Political Weekly*, June 6, 1990

Note: Figures in brackets indicate the ranks of the States.

In consequence, the social overheads suffered most. To illustrate, in 1986-87 Bihar spent on education and related departments 5.71

per cent of the total amount spent on this head in the country. This was much lower in comparison with its percentage share in total population. Table 3.22 portrays the situation. In 1981 Bihar had 11.80 per cent of all the illiterates in the country, much higher than the proportion of population.

TABLE 3.22 Budgeted expenditure (revenue account) on education and related department (1986-87)

State	Budgeted expenditure (Rs. crores)			Per capita budgeted expenditure (Rs.)	percentage of expenditure on education to total budget
	Plan	Non-Plan	Total		
Andhra Pradesh	116.69	678.07	794.76	132.63	24.5
Assam	67.42	217.84	285.26	125.00	25.9
Bihar	62.33	437.59	499.92	63.03	25.4
Gujarat	112.47	476.15	588.62	153.17	25.4
Haryana	33.34	162.37	195.71	128.78	21.6
Himachal Pradesh	13.05	89.18	102.23	213.54	20.6
Jammu & Kashmir	24.30	95.60	119.90	175.15	19.1
Karnataka	32.48	490.61	523.09	124.04	23.0
Kerala	36.71	474.34	511.05	180.39	33.6
Madhya Pradesh	50.07	468.69	518.76	87.35	20.3
Maharashtra	70.18	895.57	965.75	135.79	21.2
Orissa	41.56	217.76	259.32	88.33	21.1
Punjab	19.66	264.49	284.15	150.57	24.7
Rajasthan	38.61	375.93	414.54	103.16	26.4
Tamil Nadu	119.52	531.41	650.93	121.87	26.6
Uttar Pradesh	117.86	794.98	912.84	72.75	22.1
West Bengal	107.68	585.67	693.35	112.97	26.2
All-India	1154.55	7599.61	8754.16	112.77	23.8

Source: *Selected Educational Statistics*, Department of Education, 1988.

Special anti-poverty policy measures/programmes have contributed suitably towards the achievement of their goal. Studies (by a number of economists) disclose that these programmes proved basically a sound policy response and succeeded in stepping up the income/consumption levels of the poor and the ultra poor as well as in lowering consumption inequality, specially in States with better rural administration. The IRDP (embracing TRYSEM and

DWCRA) has been the most effective of all the rural programmes so far (Tables 3.23 and 3.24). Funds for this programme were allocated on the criterion of population, and the percentage shares of the most populous States like Bihar and Uttar Pradesh in the total number of the poor and of the ultra poor were proportionate to their populations (Table 3.24). It is evident from the figures that there occurred shortfalls in certain respects of the IRDP in the poorer States like Bihar and Assam, when seen against the all-India averages. Employment was created marginally and the beneficiaries continued to be underemployed. The ultra poor were not in a position to take advantage of the programme.

TABLE 3.23: State-wise distribution of IRDP funds and the poor

State	Percentage Distribution		
	IRDP Expenditure 1988-89	Poor Population 1983	Ultra Poor Population 1983
Andhra Pradesh	8.6	5.01	3.9
Assam	1.7	3.24	2.1
Bihar	12.8	17.44	20.0
Gujarat	3.0	2.73	1.7
Haryana	1.6	0.86	0.6
Karnataka	4.5	4.56	4.6
Kerala	2.6	3.30	3.0
Madhya Pradesh	9.7	8.66	8.5
Maharashtra	8.0	7.95	7.5
Orissa	4.0	5.27	5.4
Punjab	1.6	0.77	0.5
Rajasthan	4.2	3.53	3.2
Tamil Nadu	7.2	7.32	8.2
Uttar Pradesh	21.3	18.23	18.3
West Bengal	9.0	11.12	12.7
All-India	100	100	100

Source: *Economic and Political Weekly*, March 31, 1990.

The assistance rendered per family was on the low side. This was so due to the difficulty in mobilising bank credit for the programme. The banks rejected applications for loans on a large scale, i.e., 26 to 27 per cent. They were reluctant to lend working capital on a regular basis to the poorest households even after they had proved their creditworthiness. This resulted in a fall in attaining the target. But more than the financial constraint, organisational inadequacy, lack of clarity in plan formulation and implementation, lack of proper monitoring, etc., limited the success of the programme.

It is suggested that the choice of assets to be provided should be properly dovetailed with the level and structure of demand in the region in question. In addition, supporting marketing networks should be simultaneously promoted.

TABLE 3.24: Measures of success of the IRDP

(In Percentage)

State	Eligible* Beneficiaries	Investments Intact**	Intact and No Credit Overdue	Eligible and Crossed Poverty Line***
1	2	3	4	5
Andhra Pradesh	68	76	34	9
Arunachal Pradesh	73	61	38	4
Assam	27	70	6	10
Bihar	76	85	18	3
Gujarat	78	88	43	4
Haryana	71	46	15	0
Himachal Pradesh	87	85	45	29
Jammu & Kashmir	97	80	50	19
Karnataka	85	64	26	4
Kerala	89	74	19	5
Madhya Pradesh	81	73	27	6
Maharashtra	83	69	30	10
Orissa	83	68	19	7
Punjab	30	77	57	18
Rajasthan	72	48	15	9
Tamil Nadu	83	63	28	3
Uttar Pradesh	54	79	41	5
West Bengal	46	97	23	8
All-India Average	70	73	29	7

Source: *Economic and Political Weekly,* March 31, 1990.

* Proportion of beneficiaries with pre-IRDP income, Rs 4,800.

** Proportion of IRDP investment that remained fully operational after two years.

*** Proportion of beneficiaries with pre-IRDP income, Rs 4,800 and post-IRDP income equal to Rs. 6,400 after two years in terms of currents prices.

Among the various programmes for the uplift of the poor, incorporating the employment and wage policies appropriate to their economic betterment, the 20-Point Programme has an important place. Announced on July 1, 1975, amidst the Emergency clamped upon the nation by the then Prime Minister but upheld, on principle, even by Jayaprakash Narayan from behind the bars, the 20-Point Programme was calculated to be chiefly a poverty-alleviation programme. It has been revised thrice since then—first, in January 1980; second, in January 1982; and third, in August 1986. It had made the rural employment programmes the central programme for rural development. Restructured in 1986, it remains the "cutting edge" of a five-year plan for the poor. It is committed to eradicating poverty, improving the quality of life and removing social and economic inequalities. It tries to ensure that the poverty-alleviation programmes reach all the poor in every village. It emphasises wage-employment programmes which have to be integrated with the programmes for area development and human resource development so that the national and community assets like school buildings, roads, tanks, fuel, fodder resources, etc., are created and recreated. Promotion of handlooms, handicrafts and other village and small industries, improvement of skills of the self-employed, revitalisation of the panchayats, cooperatives and local bodies are among the 20 points.

Table 3.25 presents information on the poverty-alleviation-oriented expenditure and employment programmes for the year 1988-89. Actual expenditure on the creation of assets was Rs. 3,240.80 crores. The total outlay on the 20-Point Programme was 14390.90 crores.

Tables 3.26 and 3.27 provide information on the poverty-alleviation-oriented approved annual plan for 1990-91. The Minimum Needs Programme (MNP) would involve an outlay of Rs. 3,453.78 crores. It would provide the poor with the basic social services so that they are empowered and a people's economy is installed.

Land reform in its dual sense, redistributive (the surplus land acquired by the State to be redistributed among the landless) and protective (in the sense of tenancy reform) is one of the leading points in the 20-Point Programme. Land measuring 29.9 lakh hectares was declared surplus. Possession of 24.86 lakh hectares of land was taken and 18.55 lakh hectares of land were distributed to 42 lakh landless agricultural labourers and other eligible persons. Similarly, a large part of an estimated 60 lakh hectares of waste, fallow and other classes of land which vested in the state were

TABLE 3.25: State-wise poverty-alleviation-oriented expenditure and employment programmes (in 1988-89)

State	Percentage of Population below the Poverty Line in 1983-84	Percentage Share in Total Number of Families assisted under IRDP	Percentage Share in Total Number of youth trained under TRYSEM	Percentage share in: Total Plan Expenditure including value of foodgrains in India on NREP	Percentage share in: Employment Generated under NREP	Percentage Share in: Total Plan Expenditure on RLEGP	Percentage Share in: Total Employment Generated under RLEGP	Percentage Share in (Under JEY): Total Expenditure (1989-90)	Percentage Share in (Under JEY): Total Outlay (1990-91)	Percentage Share in (Under JEY): Employment Generation (1989-90)	Percentage Share in (Under DPAP): Total Expenditure	Percentage Share in (Under DPAP): Sumtotal of Hectares improved	Percentage Share in Expenditure on Nutrition
1	2	3	4	5	6	7	8	9	10	11	12	13	14
Andhra Pradesh	36.4(7)	7.9(4)	6.1(8)	9.7(3)	8.6(5)	9.5(3)	9.8(4)	7.9(5)	7.2(6)	8.5(6)	13.5(2)	14.1(2)	1.5(12)
Assam	23.5(13)	1.6(13)	3.5(10)	1.3(12)	1.0(12)	1.2(13)	0.7(13)	0.9(12)	1.9(13)	0.6(12)	—	—	1.6(11)
Bihar	49.5(1)	12.5(2)	9.7(2)	12.5(2)	10.8(3)	16.7(2)	12.8(2)	13.9(2)	14.5(2)	10.8(3)	9.2(5)	4.4(9)	3.5(7)
Gujarat	24.3(12)	3.4(11)	6.6(6)	3.4(10)	3.3(11)	3.1(12)	2.8(11)	3.3(10)	3.1(11)	2.3(11)	7.9(6)	4.7(8)	20.2(2)
Haryana	15.6(15)	1.5(14)	0.8(14)	1.0(13)	0.5(14)	1.0(14)	0.5(15)	0.8(13)	0.7(14)	0.3(14)	1.5(13)	0.9(11)	2.3(8)
Himachal Pradesh	13.5(17)	0.6(16)	0.7(15)	0.6(15)	0.4(15)	0.4(16)	0.4(16)	0.4(16)	0.4(16)	0.4(13)	—	—	0.7(17)
Jammu & Kashmir	16.3(14)	0.7(15)	0.8(14)	1.5(11)	0.7(13)	0.5(15)	0.3(17)	0.5(15)	0.7(14)	0.4(13)	1.9(12)	1.2(12)	1.0(14)
Karnataka	35.0(8)	4.1(10)	2.6(12)	4.9(6)	5.8(7)	5.1(7)	7.4(7)	4.6(8)	4.5(10)	4.7(9)	11.0(4)	7.3(6)	16.1(3)

Contd.

TABLE 3.25 *Contd.*

1	2	3	4	5	6	7	8	9	10	11	12	13	14
Kerala	26.8(11)	2.3(12)	2.5(13)	4.4(8)	3.8(10)	3.2(11)	2.3(12)	2.8(11)	2.4(12)	2.7(10)	—	—	4.8(5)
Madhya Pradesh	46.2(3)	11.1(3)	6.8(5)	7.6(4)	9.8(4)	7.0(6)	8.4(6)	5.5(7)	10.0(3)	9.7(4)	7.5(5)	7.5(5)	3.9(6)
Maharashtra	34.9(9)	6.7(7)	6.6(6)	5.7(5)	6.6(6)	7.6(5)	8.8(5)	9.2(2)	7.6(5)	9.4(5)	13.8(1)	17.1(1)	1.9(10)
Orissa	42.8(4)	5.9(8)	7.4(3)	3.4(10)	4.5(9)	4.9(8)	6.4(8)	4.3(9)	4.9(8)	5.9(7)	4.9(9)	6.8(7)	1.2(13)
Punjab	13.8(16)	1.6(13)	3.2(11)	0.9(14)	0.5(14)	1.2(13)	0.6(14)	0.6(14)	0.6(15)	0.3(14)	—	—	1.0(15)
Rajasthan	34.3(10)	5.0(9)	7.2(4)	4.1(9)	5.5(8)	3.7(10)	4.0(9)	4.6(8)	4.8(9)	5.3(8)	4.6(11)	2.1(10)	0.9(16)
Tamil Nadu	39.6(5)	6.8(6)	6.3(7)	9.7(3)	11.1(2)	9.2(4)	11.1(3)	8.8(4)	6.5(7)	10.9(2)	5.0(8)	8.5(13)	23.1(1)
Uttar Pradesh	45.3(2)	18.2(1)	18.9(1)	22.3(1)	20.5(1)	19.3(1)	18.2(1)	23.3(1)	19.4(1)	19.5(1)	13.3(3)	14.1(2)	6.8(4)
West Bengal	39.2(6)	7.6(5)	5.8(9)	4.6(7)	3.8	4.6(9)	3.7(10)	6.6(6)	8.2(4)	5.9(7)	4.710	8.1(4)	2.2(9)
All-India	100.0 (3772212)	100.0	100.0 (227050)	100.0 (Rs. 901.83 crores)	100.0 (394.9 Man days)	100.0 (Rs. 669.37 crores	100.0 (296.5 million Man days)	100.0 (Rs. 2272.60 crores)	100.0 (Rs. 2613.13 crores)	100.0 (828.3 million)	100.0 (Rs. 95.25 crores)	100.0 (2855.53 hectares)	100.0 (Rs. 2563.2 million)

Source: Government of India, *Planning Commission Annual Plan 1990-91.*

Note: Figures in brackets indicate the ranks of the States.

The IRDP and allied programmes are:

(1) IRDP

(2) TRYSEM.

(3) DWCRA.

(4) Roads in tribal areas.

(5) CAPART (rural technology).

(6) NIRD.

(7) Others.

TABLE 3.26: Poverty-alleviation-oriented rural expenditure (1988-89).

Head of Expenditure	Expenditures by			
	Centre	States	Union Territories (Rs. crores)	Total
Rural Development	1625.90	1325.35	4.09	2982.34
Special Area Programmes	0.00	926.51	0.00	926.51
Social Services	3238.79	4452.77	360.96	8052.52
Rural Employment Centres	1131.88	669.28	0.00	1801.16
		Grand Total		11961.37

Source: *Annual Plan 1990-91,* Planning Commission.

Note: Total outlay in the Annual Plan comes to Rs. 48,069.83 crores. Hence, the outlay on the poverty-alleviation-oriented rural programmes amounted to nearly 24.88 per cent in 1988-89.

distributed to landless labourers and marginal farmers. About 200 lakh tenants got occupancy rights and came directly under the State.

Likewise, the IRDP seeks to make the equality of opportunity for employment a reality. The positive discrimination granted to the weaker sections in admission to the educational institutions is aimed at making the equality of opportunity for education a reality (except in the professional and technical lines in some States), while positive discrimination granted to them in employment removes the discrepancy between it and the equality of opportunity for employment. This is believed to be an epoch-making policy measure because in its absence many educated members of the weaker sections remained without jobs for a pretty long time consequent upon the unique position held and the great power exercised by the people coming of the forward sections of society and already in employment. Equality of opportunity for education for the backward sections was devoid of any real meaning and content without positive discrimination legitmatised by the State.

Eradication of inequality requires that the incomes accruing to individuals and households are influenced through fiscal policies, social security and welfare programmes, that income generation and its sharing are influenced through redistribution of wealth and productive assets and investment and technical choices and returns to the agent of production, and that monopolistic and restrictive and oligopolistic trades are controlled.

TABLE 3.27: State-wise poverty-alleviation-oriented approved annual plan 1990-91 outlays

(Rs in Crores)

State	Rural Development	Special Area Programmes	Social Services	Total (2) to (4)	As Percentage of All-States' Total Annual Plan Outlay	As Percentage of All-India Total Annual Plan Outlays	Number of the Poor (1983-84) (Million)	Ranking in Terms of Percentage of population below the Poverty Line (1983-84)	Ranking in Terms of Total population 1981
1	2	3	4	5	6	7	8	9	10
Andhra Pradesh	119.50	23.06	317.32	459.88	6.3(6)	3.8(6)	19.4(7)	(7)	(5)
Assam	33.65	2.70	163.01	199.36	2.7(12)	1.6(12)	4.6(13)	(13)	(13)
Bihar	189.48	12.77	297.71	499.96	6.8(4)	4.1(4)	34.6(2)	(1)	(2)
Gujarat	65.36	0.00	308.73	379.09	5.2(8)	3.1(8)	8.3(11)	(12)	(10)
Haryana	13.88	3.00	234.22	251.10	3.4(11)	2.1(10)	2.0(15)	(15)	(15)
Himachal Pradesh	11.26	0.00	113.51	124.51	1.7(14)	1.0(14)	0.6(17)	(17)	(17)
Jammu & Kashmir	13.33	27.67	207.66	248.66	3.4(11)	2.0(11)	0.9(16)	(14)	(16)

Contd.

TABLE 3.27 *Contd.*

1	2	3	4	5	6	7	8	9	10
Karnataka	91.35	40.00	239.40	370.75	5.1(9)	3.1(8)	12.9(8)	(8)	(8)
Kerala	44.25	1.10	119.88	165.23	2.2(13)	1.4(13)	6.8(12)	(11)	(12)
Madhya Pradesh	105.64	0.00	440.50	546.14	7.5(3)	4.5(3)	24.1(3)	(3)	(6)
Maharashtra	271.00	2.00	559.00	832.00	11.4(2)	6.9(2)	21.9(4)	(9)	(3)
Orissa	75.44	0.00	225.19	300.63	4.1(10)	2.5(9)	11.3(10)	(4)	(11)
Punjab	49.75	7.00	191.92	248.67	3.4(11)	2.0(11)	2.3(14)	(16)	(14)
Rajasthan	57.53	0.45	239.65	297.63	4.1(10)	2.5(9)	11.7(9)	(10)	(9)
Tamil Nadu	73.87	0.00	465.16	466.03	6.4(5)	3.9(5)	19.1(6)	(5)	(7)
Uttar Pradesh	249.44	20.16	698.70	968.30	13.3(1)	8.1(1)	50.2(1)	(2)	(1)
West Bengal	96.54	20.51	317.92	434.97	5.9(7)	3.6(7)	21.4(5)	(6)	(4)
All States	1633.33	182.26	5475.46	7291.05	100.00	—		—	—
All-India	21982.34	926.51	8052.52	11961.37	—	100.00	256.2	—	—

Source: Government of India, Planning Commission, *Annual Plan 1990-91.*
Note: Figures in brackets indicate the ranks of the States.

Vaidyanathan suggests a pooling of the allocations for the anti-poverty programmes and distributing the pool through the State Governments to the district administration in proportion to the volume of poverty and unemployment.

4

THE RURAL-URBAN DIVIDE IN INDIA

There has been for long much talk on the neglect of the rural sector in India. Critics and commentators have averred that the planned development in India has been urban-biased. They have alleged that food distribution and price policies have all favoured the urban consumers. They have insinuated that over the years the two sectors, rural and urban, have become highly differentiated in terms of economic and social status. In the words of L.K. Jha, concern over the plight of the poverty-stricken millions and the contrasts between the life-styles of rural and urban communities have given rise to discontent and a questioning of the whole thrust of planning, if not of planning itself.

Since Independence urbanisation has, on the one hand, added a new dimension to the poverty syndrome in the country-side, and, within the cities, on the other. The tensions between the rich and the poor in our big cities are mounting rapidly. Class segregation is on the increase. The poor are no longer wanted in the heart of big cities and in exclusively posh colonies, except for being drafted into manual work. They are being progressively thrown out of their rural habitat to build *shanty* colonies for themselves on the fringes of the cities. The cities need the poor as automations to keep the show going but are becoming increasingly intolerant of their existence as human beings. The city migrants come to have a different consumption pattern and hence a different volume of expenditure. By comparison with men in similar circumstances in rural areas these city denizens have a lower marginal propensity to save. They are apt to substitute superior for inferior grains. They eventually earn more and eat more and better, and whether they continue to live with their kith and kin or not, they certainly miss their rural fraternity and wear a cross of the clinging sense of ennui on their bosom.*

---

* On this see our *Problems of Indian Economic Development,* Chs. 12 and 23.

The crux of Indian poverty, though not its sum-total, is rural poverty because the rural base is very much imposing and marked. Its sheer magnitude overshadows its urban counterpart. The genesis of rural poverty is a complex set of relationships within rural society that controls distribution and uses of resources in it and spills over from the narrowly economic to the wider social life of the countryside.

Let us try to build up a kaleidoscopic picture, through the plan period, of this issue in its various ramifications and manifestations:

During 1953-54 to 1956-57 income distribution in the urban sector was more unequal than in the rural sector. The degree of inequality in the rural sector had declined and that in the urban sector risen.

Around 1960, the top 10 per cent of the urban households accounted for 42.4 per cent of national income, whereas the top 10 per cent of the rural households received 33.6 per cent of the rural income. In both sectors the share of the bottom 20 per cent was about 41 per cent.

TABLE 4.1: Distribution of household consumer expenditure

Category	1958-59	1961-62	1965-66	1970-71	1972-73	1977-78	1983
1	2	3	4	5	6	7	8
Rural							
Bottom 30 per cent	13.1	14.7	15.1	15.4	15.4	15.0	15.2
Middle 40 per cent	34.3	33.2	34.3	35.1	33.7	33.1	33.9
Top 30 per cent	52.6	52.1	50.6	49.5	50.9	51.9	50.9
Urban							
Bottom 30 per cent	13.2	12.9	13.6	13.7	13.8	13.6	13.9
Middle 40 per cent	31.7	31.4	31.9	31.8	31.9	32.4	32.8
Top 30 per cent	55.1	55.7	54.5	54.5	54.3	54.0	53.3

Source: (1) Sixth Five-Year Plan;
(2) NSS Report No. 319.

Between 1958-59 and 1983 rural-urban inequality increased, as judged by the share of the bottom 30 per cent households. For the rural sector in 1958-59 it was 13.1 and for the urban sector 13.2 per cent. In 1983 the respective figures were 15.2 and 13.9 per cent. In both cases there was a rise in the percentage but the gulf had widened from 0.1 per cent (in favour of the rural sector) to 1.3 per cent (in favour of the rural sector).

The distribution of land and other assets in the rural sector appears to have remained unaltered between 1961 and 1981 in the sense that the top 20 per cent of the rural households owned over 80 per cent of land and other assets, while the bottom 20 per cent had only four per cent of them.

What is the position at present? Studies lack unanimity of opinion on the estimates. Broadly, at the top three per cent rural households own nearly half of all agricultural land, while at the bottom 75 per cent of all rural households own just 10 per cent of it. The top 10 per cent of all rural households possess 56.23 per cent of total agricultural land and the bottom 70 per cent have a bare 13.8 per cent. About 10 per cent of the top rich farmers account for nearly 40 per cent of total rural household income.

Small and marginal farmers with less than two hectares form 70 per cent of all landholders. But the land they operate is hardly 24 per cent of total land. As against this, the holders with 2 to 10 hectares work 50 per cent of all land. The large holders with over 10 hectares comprise a very tiny fraction of all landholders at three per cent but they operate more than 26 per cent of all land.

Over the decades concentration in urban property has increased. The urban rich own almost the entire urban land and industrial assets. They are also the holders of the major part of black wealth and income (estimated at Rs. 50 to 60 thousand crores).

In the opening pages of the section on poverty and inequality in retrospect we have indicated the main trends in the growth of monopoly capital between 1960-61 and 1983-84, which is part and parcel of the urban wealth.

During 1953-54 to 956-57 income distribution in the urban sector was more unequal than in the rural sector. The degree of inequality in the rural sector had decreased and that in the urban sector increased.

In 1960 the situation was as follows: The top 10 per cent of the urban households accounted for 42.4 per cent of the national income. On the other hand, the top 10 per cent of the urban households received 33.6 per cent of the rural income. The share of the bottom 20 per cent in both sectors was 41 per cent.

In terms of assets the percentage of *poor rural households* was 30 per cent of all in 1961. This had risen to 35 per cent of all rural households in 1971. In 1961, in terms of assets, e.g. huts, some household goods and some livestock, *a poor rural household* had been defined as one with less than Rs. 1,000 worth of assets but in 1971 the worth of assets had risen to Rs. 2,500.

In 1975-76 the lowest 20 per cent of all rural and urban households accounted for 7 per cent of the total household income, while the highest 20 per cent accounted for 49.4 per cent of it.

The inequality in assets distribution became accentuated since the mid-1960s. The concentration of assets-holding has tended to increase. The concentration in asset ownership led to concentration of income and saving and to further concentration of assets.

At present about 10 per cent of the top rich farmers account for nearly 40 per cent of total rural household income.

In 1960-61, 6.38 per cent of the total rural population had per capita consumer expenditure of less than Rs. 8 a month; 11.95 per cent of less than Rs. 11 a month; 9.88 per cent of less than Rs. 13 a month; and 9.82 per cent of less than Rs. 15 a month. These four groups formed a little under 40 per cent of the rural population. In 1960-61 they lived on less than 50 paise per day per person.

During 1961-62 and 1963-64 in rural areas in case of individuals in each expenditure basket from Re. 0 to Rs. 15-18 per month there existed deficiencies in foodgrain consumption in terms of the minimum calorie requirements; the deficiency varying from 49 per cent at the lowest monthly expenditure level (Re. 0–8) to 11 per cent for the monthly expenditure level (Rs. 15-18). Of the total rural population of 355 million, 184 million (about 52 per cent of the total) were absolutely poor.

In 1960-61 the consumption expenditure of the 10 per cent of the urban population was 30 per cent higher than that of its rural counterpart. In 1967-68 it was only 10 per cent higher. The position of the urban population had deteriorated in relative terms.

In the early 1960s the individuals in rural and urban areas who lived near the Poverty Line consumed foodgrains in excess of the norm of foodgrains consumption, that is, 518 g per capita per day for rural and 432 g per capita per day for urban areas.

Between 1961-62 and 1963-64 deficiencies in foodgrains consumption existed in urban areas only for individuals in two expenditure groups, i.e. Re. 0-8 and Rs. 8-11 per month.

In 1967-68 half the urban population numbering 52 million was poor and its per capita per day consumption expenditure amounted to Re. 0.71. Twenty per cent of the rural population and 15 per cent of the urban population were among the poorest and had a per capita per day consumption expenditure of Re. 0.35 only.

The differential between the rural and the urban upper middle and richer classes increased only marginally in 1967-68, as compared to that in 1960-61.

The condition of the bottom 20 per cent of the rural population remained static between 1960-61 and 1967-68; that of the bottom 20 per cent of the urban population deteriorated. The condition of the next 20 per cent of urban population remained more or less stationary. The rural foodgrain consumption of the rural population in the consumption expenditure groups up to Rs. 40 per month was deficient by 20 to 51.4 per cent. Seventy per cent of the total population numbering 420 million remained below the Poverty Line.

Between 1960-61 and 1967-68 the nutritional deficiency in rural areas had widened considerably. Seventy per cent of the rural population was at the Poverty Level in 1967-68, as compared to 52 per cent in 1960-61.

During 1952-68, the bottom 10 per cent in rural areas consumed 10.51 seers of foodgrains per person per 30 days, whereas the top 10 per cent in rural areas consumed 26.03 seers of them per person per 30 days.

The levels of consumption of cereals generally rose with the levels of living and income. There were serious contrasts between the richer and the poorer sections of the rural population. When prices rose, those in the lowest income groups reduced their consumption of cereals, and conversely. The poorest section lived below the subsistence level. Consumption of rice and coarse cereals by the general rural population claimed 40 to 50 per cent of the total cereal basket. The share of wheat was less than one-third. Price rise aggravated the disparity in terms of per capita consumption between the richer and the poorer sections of the rural population.

During 1961-72 per capita private consumer expenditure in rural areas increased by less than 0.5 per cent per annum. Even this small gain was not equitably distributed among all sections of the population.

In their preface the authors of the Fourth Plan admitted increase in rural disparities partly owing to the very efforts made to move rapidly towards self-sufficiency in food and partly due to certain tardiness in the matter of implementing land reforms.

In 1971 the degree of consumption inequality in rural areas was less than that of inequality in land distribution. The per capita consumption of agricultural labourers was lower than that of the other groups of the rural population. But the inequalities were tangibly smaller. The per capita consumption of the non-agricultural class appeared to be slightly above the average, although the inequalities within this class were visibly larger.

In 1971-72, 28.8 per cent of the rural population and 32.6 per cent of the urban population suffered from either calorie or protein deficiency or from both, which was a cause for concern.

In 1973-74 the top 10 per cent of the population accounted for 23.5 per cent in aggregate consumption expenditure in rural areas and 26.1 per cent of it in urban areas. The lowest 20 per cent accounted for 9.5 per cent of total consumption in rural areas, while the highest 20 per cent accounted for 38 per cent of it in them. The corresponding figures for urban areas were 9.2 per cent and 40 per cent. In the combined case, income inequality was far more articulated than consumption inequality.

Around 1980 in metropolitan cities expenditure exceeded income in the lowest annual income group by 9 to 10 per cent, the highest outlay on food being 72 to 73 per cent of total expenditure.

The high rates of personal income and wealth have been a factor in propagating black income generation in the country which, in turn, has been buttressing the existing concentration of economic power.

Summing up, as compared to the rural incomes, the urban incomes have been more skewed.

A very illuminating study of the subject for the period 1970-71 to 1980-81 has been made by D. Mohanty and A. George. It would be our endeavour to reproduce here their main findings:

Agriculture and industry are the two major commodity-producing sectors of an economy. Most primary activity is concentrated in rural areas. The share of rural areas in the primary sector NDP dropped slightly from 95.8 per cent in 1970-71 to 93.6 per cent in 1980-81 owing largely to a declines in the rural share in fishing and mining and quarrying. The share of the rural sector in NDP originating in agriculture dropped from 96.9 per cent in 1970-71 to 95.2 per cent in 1980-81, thereby confirming the trend towards growing urbanisation. During the period import-dependence of agriculture increased.

The rural sector's share in NDP originating in secondary activities showed a notable increase from 30.9 per cent in 1970-71 to 35.2 per cent in 1980-81, primarily due to a rise in the share of rural manufacturing from 25.4 per cent to 31.8 per cent during the decade. The share of unregistered manufacturing in total manufacturing increased from 45.5 per cent in 1970-71 to 46.3 per cent in 1980-81. So far as the organised manufacturing segment is concerned, increase in real wages was highest during 1960-70 to 1970-80 in basic and capital goods industries, one reason being that wage bargaining capacity of the public sector employees was high.

The private sector in India has not experienced the crowding-out effect. The Government and private corporate business have financed declining proportions of their investment from out of their own savings. The spells of industrial slow-down have been marked by a number of contributory factors like slackening of rate of growth in real public sector investment, erratic growth in public sector investment, lags and delays in completion of projects and smallness of markets of industrial products.

Share of the rural sector in NDP originating in tertiary activities increased from 28.8 per cent in 1970-71 to 34 per cent in 1980-81 consequent upon commercialisation of agriculture and increased movements of people between rural and urban areas. Trade, hotels and restaurants recorded the highest increase from 18.2 per cent in 1970-71 to 30.3 per cent in 1980-81.

The per annum rate of growth in rural share during 1970-71 to 1980-81 in NDP originating in the secondary sector was 1.3 per cent and that in the tertiary sector 1.7 per cent, while the per annum rate of decline in NDP originating in the primary sector was 0.2 per cent. During the 1980s the share of the rural sector in agriculture was 95.2 per cent, and that in the tertiary sector 30.3 per cent.

The share of rural population as well as of workers has been diminishing over the Plans as a result of growing urbanisation.

The drop in the share of rural income during 1970-71 to 1988-89 has been less than the fall in the share of agriculture in NDP. This is indicative of the growing diversification of the rural economy.

The fall in the share of commodity-producing sectors in total rural income from 79.3 per cent during the Fourth Plan period to 72.6 per cent during the Seventh Plan period was compensated for by a rise in the share of essential infrastructure.

The relative importance of the primary sector, especially agriculture, in terms of its contribution to aggregate rural income tapered off from 63.7 per cent in the Fourth Plan period to 54.5 per cent during the Seventh Plan period — the share of the secondary sector increased from 11.1 per cent to 17.9 per cent during the same period as a sequel to increase in the share of manufacturing from seven per cent to 16.6 per cent and the share of the tertiary sector moved up from 16.6 per cent to 22.8 per cent during the same period.

The differential in the rate of growth of rural and urban incomes narrowed down during the Fourth and Seventh Plan periods. This provides a clue to the rise in consumption of sophisticated urban goods in rural areas.

Both rural and urban sectors seem to have contributed equally to the process of acceleration of economic growth during the 1980s.

The share of rural population in total population declined at an exponential rate of 0.5 per cent per annum during the first half of the 1980s and at 0.6 per cent per annum during the second half.

The average per capita urban NDP in real terms (at 1980-81 prices) declined from Rs. 2,945 in the Fourth Plan to Rs. 2,939 during the Fifth Plan but increased marginally to Rs. 3,019 during the Sixth Plan. As against this, the average per capita rural NDP in real terms showed a steady increase from Rs. 1,136 in the Fourth Plan to Rs. 1,318 during the Sixth Plan, with the result that the ratio of rural : urban income increased from 1.00: 2.59 in the Fourth Plan to 1.00 : 2.29 during the Sixth Plan. Per capita urban NDP increased to Rs. 3,344 in the Seventh Plan, the ratio of rural : urban per capita showed a further improvement to 1.00 : 2.27 (see Table 4.2). In sum, a narrowing down of the gap between urban and rural per capita incomes points to an increase in the rural sector's share in non-agricultural income.

An increase in per capita rural NDP may have been accompanied by increased inequality, particularly in the distribution of the benefits of the Green Revolution.

During the 1980s the income terms of trade within the rural sector had shifted in favour of the non-agricultural sectors. And the rural share of non-agricultural income had risen from 32.1 per cent in 1970-71 to 37.6 per cent in 1980-81.

Mohanty and George's thesis is that a decline in the income share of agriculture does not *per se* imply a deterioration in rural income.

Part of non-agricultural activity is located in rural areas. In the latter half of the 1980s non-agricultural income accounted for about one-half of rural income. The rural share of non-agricultural income increased from 37.6 per cent in 1980-81 to 42.8 per cent in 1988-89.

In 1987-88, 500 million out of 800 million Indian population purchased consumer durables — bicycles, portable radios, mechanical wrist watches, table fans, mopeds, motor-cycles, electric irons, sewing machines, moulded suit cases, TVs, stainless steel utensils, etc. Of the durables, 11 to 70 per cent went to rural areas.

TABLE 4.2: Per capita NDP at 1980-81 prices

(Rs.)

	Rural	Urban	All-India	Rural-to-Urban Ratio
Fourth Plan				
Average for the Plan (a)	1136	2945	1503	1.00 : 2.59
Terminal Year of the Plan (b)	1136	2871	1497	1.00 : 2.53
Fifth Plan				
(a)	1212	2939	1588	1.00 : 2.42
(b)	1286	3096	1692	1.00 : 2.41
Sixth Plan				
(a)	1318	3019	1727	1.00 : 2.29
(b)	1395	3120	1829	1.00 : 2.24
Seventh Plan				
(a)	1475	3344	1960	1.00 : 2.27
(b)	1619	3485	2112	1.00 : 2.16

Source: RBI, *Occasional Papers*, December 1989.
Note: Estimates for the Fourth and the Seventh Plans relate to the last and first four years of the Plans respectively.

During the 1970s workers moved more into secondary and tertiary sectors with the former becoming more attractive.

The rural working force was 82.3 per cent of total working force in 1970-71 and dropped to 79.7 per cent of it in 1980-81.

The proportion of non-agricultural workers in the rural working force increased from 15.6 per cent in 1970-71 to 17.4 per cent in 1980-81 because of the rise in the number of those engaged in the secondary sector.

The share of rural income in total NDP which declined from 62.8 per cent in 1970-71 to 58.6 per cent in 1980-81 stabilised around 58 per cent thereafter.

The stability in rural income during the 1980s despite indifferent performance of the agricultural sector, accounts to a large extent for the decline in the poverty ratio and the relative betterment and uplift of the rural sector. In the latter half of the 1980s non-agricultural income accounted for about one-half of rural income and provided the major impetus to the stability of rural income.

The ratio of rural-to-urban per capita income had slightly improved in favour of the rural sector from 1:2.4 in 1970-71 to 1:2.3 in 1980-81. Rural income became more dispersed during the 1980s and the rural share of non-agricultural income increased.

In 1987-88 per capita expenditure in urban areas was 63 per cent higher than the per capita expenditure in rural areas. In 1977-78 it had been 40 per cent higher. Sixty-four per cent of consumer expenditure was on food in rural areas and 56 per cent in urban.

To conclude, rural-urban income disparities were reduced to some extent during the 1980s, as compared with the position during the 1970s.

In cross-sectional studies like P.R. Brahamananda's it is stated that the gulf between urban organised labour and unorganised urban and rural labour further widened during 1984-89.

The diversification of income source has made rural consumption less vulnerable to periodic fluctuations in agriculture. But urban per capita income remains higher than rural per capita income. However, an average rural poor man is better off than an average urban poor person. The wage income of the former is higher. His fringe benefits have now a higher money value than before. His work preference has become more refined. Roughly, the poverty of the urban poor is more unbearable than that of the rural poor because of the peculiarities of the urban environment. In certain respects an average rural middle-class family is better-off than an average urban middle-class family. In rural areas the peak levels of per capita consumption and investment are found in families where barter and production for direct use account for 40 to 50 per cent of all economic transactions. The picture would be still different if non-cost elements were to be taken into consideration.

Those who shed tears for the villages, thinking they are the country's best heritage, point out how despite over four decades of planning thousands of them are still without supply of safe drinking water or even water of any kind, leave aside other amenities that go to constitute what is called "the quality of life". Table 4.3 depicts the rural situation in respect of infrastructure for the year 1977. Needless to say that public expenditure on social services like education, health

TABLE 4.3: Percentage distribution of villages by extent of availability of basic amenities in India in 1977

Amenities	Percentage of villages by distance group (km)					
	Within the village	1–2	3–5	6–10	11 and above	Total
I. *Transport and Communications*						
Railway station	1.20	4.79	12.35	16.27	65.39	100.00
Bus stop	17.91	22.35	28.71	18.84	12.19	100.00
Mettaled road	23.48	22.28	23.66	16.39	14.19	100.00
Post office	19.70	33.54	32.17	10.44	4.15	100.00
II. *Education*						
Primary School	63.88	26.24	7.52	1.67	0.69	100.00
Middle School	15.48	28.28	35.33	14.69	6.22	100.00
High/Higher Secondary School	5.37	15.55	31.17	25.36	22.56	100.00
III. *Basic Health and Medicalcare*						
Hospital (allopathic)	3.74	9.07	22.67	25.90	38.62	100.00
Dispensary (all types)	9.28	15.31	30.20	26.00	19.21	100.00
Primary Health Centre	2.98	9.00	22.61	27.76	37.65	100.00
IV. *Supporting facilities for agricultur and animal husbandry*						
Fertilizer depot	6.36	12.12	25.41	25.36	30.75	100.00
Seeds store	5.69	10.53	24.11	26.03	33.64	100.00
Veterinary dispensary	4.36	11.39	29.44	30.38	24.43	100.00
Repairs to agricultural implements	2.69	4.12	11.95	20.13	61.11	100.00
Warehousing and storage	3.81	4.39	12.52	18.62	60.66	100.00
V. *Marketing*						
Daily market	4.38	10.43	22.70	25.65	36.84	100.00
Heat	8.51	18.33	30.40	23.26	19.50	100.00
Fair price shop for grocery	16.53	18.52	23.73	17.80	23.42	100.00
VI. *Credit cooperating and banking*						
Credit/Cooperative	16.40	18.22	26.13	19.11	10.14	100.00
Bank	5.90	10.85	23.13	26.75	33.37	100.00
VII. *Drinkang water*						
(i) Summer season	92.61	6.34	0.83	0.16	0.06	100.00
(ii) Other seasons	93.54	5.62	0.67	0.15	0.02	100.00
VIII. *Electrification*						
Availability of electricity	33.36			66.64		100.00

Source: Central Statistical Organisation, *Economic Census 1977, Report on the Basic Amenities in Indian Villages.*

care, water supply, house sites for the rural poor, supplementary nutrition for the expectant mothers and school-going children coming of the disadvantaged and vulnerable sections of society, municipal services in urban areas, etc., brought about an uplift in the living standards of the general masses that was not reflected in the level and distribution of private consumption expenditure. The investments made in the successive Plans led to the creation of a network of infrastructure that somewhat mitigated the urban-rural differences in this regard.

To reiterate what we have stated above, the limited impact of the Plans on the well-being of the poor sections of the population, in rural areas or urban, is a consequence of the country's inability to restructure the distribution of assets among the various classes and to provide sufficient employment for the growing workforce.

Similarly, reduction of disparities in income and wealth is a matter which cannot be left to the free play of enlightened self-interest or the blind and inexorable market forces of demand and supply. In this crucial area purposive and active public action through positive as well as negative methods has been the centre-piece of the growth strategy in India. Quite a lot has been attempted in this country through the rural development programmes, through taxation of the rich and provision of employment of the poor, with the result that not an inappreciable percentage of 20 to 25 of the existing poor have been assisted to move from under the Poverty Line to points above it.

The **problem of urban property** calls for a multi-pronged strategy designed *inter alia* (i) to provide gainful, productive, viable employment to the unemployed, particularly women and youth, (ii) to raise the earnings of those already employed in the low-paid, blind-alley jobs, (iii) to step-up the productivity and earnings of those who are self-employed workers, and (iv) to improve the access of the urban poor to the basic amenities of life, such as education, health care, sanitation and safe drinking water.

As far as urban land is concerned, its social regulation is overdue. Urban property must be taxed (so should agricultural income). The improvement of public services in cities should not, however, be at the expense of the hitherto neglected rural areas. The urban poor should be organised in some form or the other. Voluntary associations have a role to play in this field. Among the urban poor we have the predominance of the rural migrants eagerly waiting for some employment or other in the informal sector, if not in the formal.

Over a wider canvas it is extremely difficult to attempt a comparative account of the economic condition in the rural and urban areas on account of unavailability of time-series data on the various aspects that are involved. Notwithstanding this, Tables 4.4 and 4.5 shed a good deal of light on them in their own limited way. Obviously, income per worker rose more in non-agriculture than in agriculture during 1950-51 to 1974-75 (see Table 4.4). The last column of Table 4.4 shows that rural wages have almost caught up with urban wages in a number of States, e.g. Haryana, Himachal Pradesh, Kerala, Punjab, Tamil Nadu and Uttar Pradesh.

TABLE 4.4: **Changes in income in agriculture and non-agriculture**

(in Rupees)

	Income Per Worker				Rise (Times) during the Period	
	1950-51		1974-75			
	At Current Prices	At Constant Prices	At Current Prices	At Constant Prices	At Current Prices	At Constant Prices
In Agriculture	283	319	1561	450	5.5	1.4
In Non-agriculture	619	668	4191	1589	6.7	2.4

Source: J.S. Uppal, *India's Economic Problems.*

Table 4.5 is a bold attempt, even as its statistics constitute its Achilles heel. It displays glaring inter-State disparity in each and every respect. Although manufacturing is not precisely equivalent to the organised industrial sector, yet this equivalence is assumed here for simplifying the study. Likewise, we have equated registered working factories with existing manufacturing units. We cannot be emphatic about our inferences because we do not know at what prices—constant or current—figures of produce/output/income have been estimated. So they are only rough and ready, or broad approximations. They have utility more in the ordinal than in the cardinal sense. The influence of technical advance on productivity remains indeterminate. The cropping pattern might have altered

TABLE 4.5: Rural-Urban imbalances during 1956-1986

STATE	VALUE OF AGRICULTURAL PRODUCE PER HECTARE OF GROSS CROPPED AREA (1984-86) (AT 1980-81 PRICES) (RS.)	VALUE OF AGRICULTURAL OUTPUT PER HECTARE (1960-61) (RS.)	INCREASE OF (2) OVER (3) (TIMES)	NET OUTPUT PER WORKER IN AGRICULTURE (1960-61) (RS.)	INCOME GENERATED (NET VALUE ADDED) IN AGRICULTURE PER CULTIVATOR IN 1984-85 (RS.)	INCREASE OF (6) OVER (5) (TIMES)	PER PERSON NET OUTPUT IN ORGANIZED MANUFACTURING (1960-61) (RS.)	PER WORKER NET VALUE ADDED IN REGISTERED FACTORIES (1985-86) (RS.)	INCREASE (+)/ DECREASE (-) OF (9) OVER (8) (TIMES)	PER CAPITA RURAL INCOME FROM AGRICULTURE (RS.)	AVERAGE PER CAPITA ANNUAL EARNINGS OF FACTORY WORKERS (RS.) 1961	AVERAGE PER CAPITA ANNUAL EARNINGS OF FACTORY WORKERS (RS.) 1985	INCREASE (TIMES) BETWEEN 1961 AND 1985	(13) DIVIDED BY (11) (TIMES)	AVERAGE PER CAPITA ANNUAL EARNING OF FACTORY WORKERS (1956) (RS.)	ANNUAL PER CAPITA INCOME OF AGRICULTURAL LABOURERS (1956-57) (RS.)	(16) OR DEVIDED BY (17) (TIMES) CAPTL.	AVERAGE PER CAPITA DAILY EARNING OF A FACTORY WORKERES (1985) (13) OF DEVIDED BY 365 (RS.)	AVERAGE DAILY WAGES OF AN AGRICULTURAL LABOURER CAPTL. (1984-85) (RS.)	(19) OR DIVIDED BY (20) (TIMES)
1	2	3	4	5	6	7	8	9	10	11	12	13	14	15	16	17	18	19	20	21
Andhra Pradesh	3098	465	6.6	365	6160	16.8	1387	1912	-1.4	1093	1149	8409	7.3	7.7	595	104.4	5.7	23.03	13.49	1.7
Assam	3598	916	3.9	620	—	—	3544	1358	-2.6	928	1599	10566	6.6	11.4	1526	185.9	8.2	28.94	18.43	1.6
Bihar	3030	461	6.5	302	4362	14.4	3508	3650	+1.04	590	1856	6880	3.7	11.6	1236	88.3	14.0	18.84	13.10	1.4
Gujarat	2728	378	7.2	578	7466	2.7	2987	3231	+1.08	1210	1702	3760	2.2	3.1	*	#	#	10.30	21.61	0.5
Haryana	2857	*	*	*	12708	4.4	*	2882	*	1880	*	10827	*	5.7	*	##	##	29.66	26.17	1.1
Himachal Pradesh	2783	405	6.8	214	—	—	—	4865	—	—	1288	7146	5.5	—	—	—	—	19.57	20.64	0.9
Jammu & Kashmir	—	647	—	395	—	—	2349	1366	-1.7	—	—	5429	—	—	—	—	—	14.87	NA	—
Karnataka	2426	413	5.9	476	5976	2.4	—	3117	—	1074	1375	10774	7.8	10.0	853	108.0	7.9	29.51	10.63	2.7
Kerala	4747	1288	3.7	1159	25730	5.4	2197	2901	+1.3	933	1152	9149	7.9	9.8	736	85.9	8.5	25.06	28.31	0.8
Madhya Pradesh	1771	309	5.7	360	3659	2.1	2197	3954	+1.8	905	1816	12618	6.9	13.9	982	80.9	12.1	34.56	14.12	2.4
Maharashtra	1934	376	5.1	467	6630	3.4	3421	5018	+1.4	1239	1775	12730	7.2	10.3	1415	101.0	14.0	34.87	16.25	2.1
Orissa	2442	514	4.7	488	6008	2.5	2902	2217	-1.3	1017	1180	12283	10.4	12.1	949	76.5	12.4	33.65	13.14	2.5
Punjab	3642	434	8.4	861	17981	4.9	2537	2390	-1.06	2325	1174	9261	7.9	4.0	991	131.8	7.5	25.37	30.08	0.8
Rajasthan	1097	208	5.3	343	5157	4.7	1861	2931	-1.06	1222	761	11117	14.6	9.1	770	76.6	10.0	30.45	16.41	1.8
Tamil Nadu	3759	837	4.5	530	4549	1.2	2702	2806	+1.03	578	1465	9482	6.5	16.4	950	92.0	10.3	25.97	27.67	0.9
Uttar Pradesh	3276	494	6.6	479	4357	1.3	2323	2029	-1.1	869	1264	6640	5.2	7.6	1014	80.5	12.6	18.19	15.89	1.1
West Bengal	4125	862	4.8	824	10171	2.4	2823	2419	-1.2	1075	1410	12093	8.5	11.2	1082	153.9	7.7	33.13	14.00	2.3
All-India	—	—	—	**477**	—	—	**2756**	**3114**	**+1.1**	—	**1540**	**8882**	**5.7**	—	**1187**	**99.4**	**11.9**	**24.33**	**NA**	—

Sources:
(1) K.N. Prasad, The Economics of a Backward Region in a Backward Economy : A Case Study of Bihar in Relation to Other States, Scientific Book Agency, Calcutta, Vol. I, 1966, & Vol. II, 1967;
(2) Government of Maharashtra, Selected Indicators, August, 1990;
(3) RBI, Occasional Papers, March, 1989;
(4) U.P. State Planning Institute, Inter-State Disparities, April, 1990;
(5) Statistical Abstract of India, 1987;
(6) Figures in Column (20) are estimated from the data furnished by the Joint Director (Mr D. Shankar), Evaluation Division, Bihar State Planning Board and his staff member, Mr. Uday Sinha.
* Average of daily wages of field labourers, plough men and carpenters
\# (*see* Maharashtra) ## (*see* Punjab)

through the years, and new and more value-adding crops might have been introduced. We have to plead ignorance of all this. In regions marked largely by orthodoxies and traditional practices, we have had generally low-order or insignificant increases in output, etc. In fine, we have to examine each item separately before we can conclude in which State which sector — rural or urban — has fared better or worse, and in what degree. Exclusively the rural sector has prospered in the same manner as has the urban sector but *inter se* which sector has prospered more or relatively is a judgment that should be pronounced only after adequate perusal and analysis of the data as well as in full awareness of the qualifications with which the data are essentially hedged.

5

APPROACH OF INDIAN FIVE-YEAR PLANS TO POVERTY AND INEQUALITY

The Government of India Resolution of March 1950 on planning urged that a rapid rise in the standard of living of the people be promoted by efficient exploitation of the resources of the country, production be increased and opportunities to all for employment be offered in the service of the country.

The Directive Principles of State Policy enunciated in Articles 36 to 51 of the Indian Constitution, desire that the ends of the right to work, the right to adequate income, the right to education and the right to a measure of insurance against old age, sickness and other disabilities be attained; ownership and control of the material resources of the country be so distributed as best to serve the common good, and the economic system be so operated that it did not result in the concentration of wealth and economic power in the hands of a few.

The authors of the First Plan said that the urge to economic and social change, to raise living standards and to open out to the people new opportunities for a richer and more varied life came from the fact of poverty and of inequalities in income, wealth and opportunity. They realised that poverty could not be eliminated merely by redistributing the wealth that existed then. One of the chief tasks in the planners' hand was removal of economic inequalities. Attainment of economic equality and social justice was one of the basic objectives of the First Plan. Growth and equity were considered together. A simultaneous advance along both lines was advocated.

The authors of the First Plan realised that only by raising production the inequalities could not be removed. They recognised the need for balancing the advantages of a greater equality of incomes and wealth against the disadvantages of a possible fall in the private savings and capital formation. They emphasised the need for creating in the country an environment conducive to growth, for making the community put forth its best efforts for promoting growth, for creating psychological conditions to provide an incentive to all to give of their best as development called for effort and sacrifice on the part of all citizens.

The formulators of the Second Plan realised that the current levels of living were very low, production was insufficient even for satisfying the minimum essential needs of the population and a large leeway had to be made up before the services and amenities required for healthy living could be brought within the reach of any significant proportion of the population.

The two main objectives of the Second Plan were: first, a sizable increase in the national income so as to raise the level of living in the country, and, second, a reduction in inequalities in income and wealth and a more even distribution of economic power. The Plan wanted a certain minimum national standard of the essentials of civilized life — a kind of a floor to incomes — guaranteed. For this a dynamic force had to be generated in the economy that could lift it continually to higher levels of material well-being.

The sheet-anchor of the Second Plan lay in a socialist pattern of society — a social and economic order based on the values of freedom and democracy, without caste, clan and privilege, in which there was a substantial rise in employment and production and the largest measure of social justice attainable.

According to the makers of the Second Plan, the process of reducing inequalities was a two-fold one: (1) it must raise incomes at the lowest levels and (2) it must simultaneously reduce incomes at the top. Those in receipt of large incomes should make a larger contribution to the public exchequer.

The authors of the Second Plan regarded the ownership of property as the most important single factor responsible for inequalities of income and wealth. For the ownership of property signified taxable capacity. A separate tax on property above the average was, therefore, justified. The authors argued that a ceiling on income had little significance unless it were accompanied by a ceiling on property.

The authors cautioned that in reducing inequalities no damage should occur to the productive system, for that would jeopardise the task of development itself or imperil the very processes of democratic change, which are intended to be strengthened. On the other hand, regard for democratic and orderly change could not be allowed to become a sanction for the existing or new inequalities.

The authors realised that some fiscal measures which lowered inequalities were apt to react adversely on incentives.

The points at which new incomes would be generated and the manner in which they would be distributed would be determined by the policies noted below:

1. The pattern of investment proposed in the Plan.
2. The direction to which economic activity would be canalised as given by state action.
3. Mobilisation of resources.
4. Expansion of social services.
5. Institutional changes in the domain of land ownership and management.
6. Functioning of joint-stock companies and the financial system.
7. Growth of the cooperative sector.

The above policies were to be used in such a manner as to enlarge incomes and opportunities at the lower end and to reduce wealth and privilege at the upper end.

The framers of the Second Plan suggested that positive measures should be adopted to promote a more even distribution of incomes, which were as follows:

1. Promotion of cooperative forms of production.
2. Elimination of functionless rent-receivers.
3. Substitution of private usurious credit by institutional credit.
4. Control of private monopoly.
5. Enlargement of the public sector in strategic lines of production and trade.

Moreover, the conditions that created and perpetuated inequalities had to be altered. The weaker and underprivileged sections of our people should secure opportunities to the greatest extent possible.

The authors of the Second Plan concluded that reduction in income and wealth could follow only from the totality of measures and institutional changes undertaken as part of the Plan.

To the Third Plan drafters, the more immediate problem was to combat the curse of poverty, with all the ills that it produced. The central objective of the Plan should be to provide to the masses of the Indian people the opportunity to lead a good life. The poverty of the underdeveloped countries was an abiding danger to the maintenance of world peace, which required the extermination of poverty, disease and ignorance from every country.

Widespread and appalling Indian poverty was the outcome of a traditional society and a static economy in the past, petrified to some extent by colonial rule, scanty development of resources, low levels of productivity, lack of work, rigidities of the caste system, etc.

Improving the living standards of the masses was a prime objective of the Third Plan. Another was to establish a social order in which justice — social, economic and political — informed all the institutions of national life.

The achieve a rising level of living for all citizens and especially for those in low-income groups or lacking the opportunity to work the essential condition was a high rate of economic growth sustained over a long period. Poverty could be combated only by social and economic advance — by constructing a technologically mature society and a social order which offered equal opportunities to all citizens. Social and economic advance involved basic social and economic changes and the replacing of the old traditional order by a dynamic society and the application of science and technology and far-reaching changes in social customs and institutions.

The authors of the Third Plan attributed inequalities to feudal rights and tenures, privileges and handicaps associated with the social structure. They pointed out that old disparities in the levels of income and opportunity, as reflected in the modes of living, social behaviour and a spurt of acquisitiveness, were disappearing, while new disparities were appearing.

The authors suggested that as a first step in the direction of abolishing poverty the basic necessities, such as food, work, opportunity for education, reasonable conditions of health and sanitation, improvement in conditions of housing and a minimum level of income that ensures tolerable living standards should be provided to the millions that were poor.

The measures suggested in the Third Plan to remedy the problem comprised opportunities for work (in pursuance of which the programme of rural works was to be launched), development of agriculture, development of village and small-scale industries (which would ensure a more equitable distribution of national life), development of a cooperative agro-industrial economy in rural areas, development of organised industry, manipulation of fiscal and monetary devices to provide incentives and to restrict growth of private monopolies, extension of the public sector, development of infrastructure, particularly social overheads, with emphasis on investment in man, institutional reforms like land reforms and the introduction of the village panchayats, promotion of common values and a sense of shared citizenship, and so on.

The three years, 1966–69, which were marked by near stagnation in industry or industrial recession, are called the years of Plan Holiday, covered by the Annual Plans.

The Fourth Plan which commenced in April, 1969, stood for "a fight against poverty and economic equality". Its basic goal was a rapid rise in the standard of living of the people, through measures which also promoted equality and social justice, especially of the less privileged sections of society and to the common man with a view also to unleashing the forces of production. It advocated increased production together with rational distribution of the added wealth. It embodied a burning sense of social justice. This was considered necessary to evoke the people's participation. A fuller life for an increasingly large number of people was the motto before the Fourth Plan. The Plan took cognizance of the deep-seated urges of the people for greater equality, and made reduction of disparities between classes one of the central objectives of developmental planning.

The measures to solve the problem included:

1. More rapid growth of the economy.
2. Special programmes concerning: (a) small farmers, (b) marginal farmers, (c) agricultural labourers, especially those who were landless – turning them into producers, through animal husbandry, small enterprises or land redistribution, (d) forestry for forest labourers and forest dwellers, (e) Scheduled Castes, Scheduled Tribes, and other weaker sections, so that their conditions were ameliorated faster — programmes that spread the benefits of economic growth to them, a task that was necessary in the interests of both equity and growth. Protecting their economic and educational interests with care. Integration of the Scheduled Castes socially within the

community in which they lived. Removal of their relative backwardness. Enabling them to share in the general development process. Integrating the economy of the Scheduled Tribes with that of the rest of the economy. This called for development of the basic infrastructure. Using supplementary resources for other specific programmes of economic development.

3. Increasing the productivity of the weaker sections.
4. Rural industrialisation.
5. Technological progress of the small-scale industrial units.
6. Dispersal of industry.
7. Greater diffusion of enterprise and of the ownership of means of production. Removal or reduction and prevention of the concentration of wealth and economic power. Expansion of the public sector. Nationalisation of banks to pay more attention to the small man's needs as well as to restrict the scope for monopolistic operations of the privileged few. The enforcement of the Monolpolies Act, industrial lincensing and taxation measures.
8. Use of subsidies (commodities such as food and fertilizers were subsidised) – Provision of certain public services free (such as primary education) as also certain goods (free rice/milk to people belonging to the vulnerable groups). Control of supplies of commodities fully or partially.
9. Provision of employment generally wage-employment. Widening opportunities of productive work and employment to the common man, particularly the less privileged sections of society. Continuing rural works programmes but by integrating them with the area development programmes and non-Plan schemes. Running local needs – and local resources – based local plans for generating employment opportunities. Opening service centres in rural areas involving the young entrepreneurs.
10. Reorienting the socio-economic institutions by such methods as the "land to the tiller" legislation.
11. Stabilisation of the prices of essential goods and services. Emphasis on the extension of the public distribution system.
12. Putting the energies of all people to profitable use.

The Fifth Plan was calculated to solve the problems of the poor of all communities, especially Scheduled Tribals, Scheduled Castes, and backward classes. In its opinion, provision of fuller employment was a surest means of providing greater social justice.

At the beginning of the second year of the Fifth Plan the 20-Point Economic Programme was announced on July 1, 1975, with a view to relieving the hardships of various sections of people, particularly the poor and the vulnerable (the latter composed of agricultural labourers and marginal farmers). Some of the points were directed at increasing production, bringing about greater employment and better distribution, removing rural poverty through land reforms, abolishing bonded labour, liquidating rural indebtedness, imposing ceiling on ownership and possession of vacant land and acquiring excess land, restricting the plinth area of new dwelling units, socialising the public distribution of essential commodities, providing drinking water and supplying essential articles at controlled prices to the students coming from poor families.

The Sixth Plan accorded a very high priority to the objective of poverty removal. In the development strategy a progressive reduction in the incidence of poverty received the highest priority. According to its authors, the objective of social justice had two major dimensions:

1. An improvement in the living standards of the poorest groups in society, and
2. A reduction in inequalities in assets distribution. According to them, a trinity of factors worked behind poverty, namely, inadequate rate of growth of the economy, uneven distribution of income and consumption, and a high rate of growth of population.

A meaningful solution to the problem of poverty could, according to the authors of the Sixth Plan, be found only within the rubrics of a rapidly expanding economy. It was only in the conditions of an expanding economy that the attack on the problem of poverty was most effective. A substantial step-up in the over-all rate of growth of the economy created undoubtedly favourable conditions for a dent in poverty.

But having said this, the authors of the Sixth Plan lost no time in qualifying their statement: In the light of past experience, however, it would not be realistic to rely solely on the growth process to work out a solution to the question of poverty. Specific policy measures would be needed not only to influence the composition of output in favour of mass consumption goods but also to ensure a more even class distribution of the output.

That is to say, growth had to be supplemented by more direct and positive means of reducing the incidence of poverty, particularly in rural areas. Determined and positive measures, e. g. restructuring of output, redistribution of income and consumption and redistribution of property, had to be taken, if poverty were to be conquered.

The authors of the Sixth Plan desired that the on-going poverty-eradication programmes aimed at the specified target groups of population were improved and enlarged with regard to their content as well as their coverage, such that the productivity of the poor was upgraded and with it their income was driven up.

Those programmes fell into two major classes – one class concerned with the provision of wage-employment, primarily in the slack seasons and lean months of the year, and their best example was the NREP*, and the other class, preoccupied with provision and transformation of assets as well as skills of those involved and hence generation of self-employment on a permanent footing and their best illustration was the IRDP.*

Close on the heels of the commencement of the Sixth Plan was announced the New 20-Point Programme which made rural employment programme the most important pillar of rural development. Poverty-tagged unemployment-eradication programmes meant that on being employed a person was able to earn enough to sustain himself.

Categorically the Sixth Plan had the following programmes relating to poverty-alleviation:

1. Programmes of direct benefit to the poor through increased public expenditures of social services. The relative share of the poorest groups had to increase in total social consumption. With it the level and distribution of private consumption expenditure had to improve, so also had the per capita consumption to improve. And from this all the degree of social justice had to go up.

---

* On both see our *India's Rural Problems*, Concept Publishing Company, New Delhi-59.

2. A coordinated effort was envisaged that would enable the poor to join the mainstream of economic activity and provide them with an opportunity for advancement.
3. Wage-employment generating programmes like the NREP.
4. Self-employment generating programmes like the IRDP, based on transfer and transformation of assets — milch cattle and provision of credit supplemented by a subsidy scheme.
5. Pursuit with greater vigour and effectiveness of institutional reforms designed to impart an increased redistributive bias to public policies in favour of the poorest sections. Land reforms were an admirable instance of this. Transfer of the land asset was involved in it. It was argued that a redistribution of 5 per cent of the cultivated area from holdings above five acres to small farmers and agricultural labourers would have the effect of increasing income accruing to them by 20 per cent.
6. The Plan had a Special Component Plan for the uplift of the Scheduled Castes, funded by the Centre. Besides, there were special programmes for areas which were drought-prone, tribal and hilly. All these were to strengthen the redistributive bias in public policies.
7. Provision of inputs, credit, services and training, in which the poorer sections were to be treated preferentially.
8. Diversification of occupations in rural areas under 3 and 4 above.
9. Development of the rural infrastructure through such programmes as the MNP so as to improve the quality of life and thereby to help attain social justice.
10. Implementation of the Urban Land Ceiling Act.
11. Further expansion of the public sector. Social control of the financial system. Reorientation of the credit system.
12. Progressive taxation.
13. Suggestion that all the various programmes should be so brought together that they focussed upon the level of the individual households and raised 3,000 of the poorest households above the Poverty Line in each block during the five-year period.
14. In so far as population growth was exacerbating the poverty problem, voluntary adoption of the small family norm should be the thrust of the policy.
15. Careful planning of the organisational framework of the

anti-poverty programmes on the basis of the socio-cultural and socio-economic features of each area.

The Seventh Plan had removal of poverty as its central concern. It declared that socialism stood for economic growth accompanied by social justice and elimination of age-old social barriers that oppressed the weak. It was for expansion and strengthening of the anti-poverty programmes. It proposed to continue at an accelerated pace the special programmes meant for generating wage-employment and self-employment with the end of eradicating poverty in view. Its premise was that the ability of a poorer household to cross the Poverty Level depended on its over-all income from both wage- and non-wage employment.

The anti-poverty programmes became an important element of the strategy of the Seventh Plan. The Plan sought to integrate the anti-poverty programmes and the various sectoral and area development programmes into a comprehensive design for the integrated development of each area. It recognised the mutual inclusiveness of both types of programmes, e.g., the IRDP, the NREP, the RLEGP, the TRYSEM, the MNP, etc. Together these programmes could ensure a more stable flow of income to the poor throughout the year.

In the 1986 version of the 20-Point Programme, poverty-alleviation got the top place. Efforts were redoubled to wipe out poverty, and to expand the employment-oriented anti-poverty programmes at a still faster rate.

The MNP aimed at a further improvement in the living conditions of the poor and their access to education and health. The literacy drive was speeded up. The cooperative endeavour was further promoted. The land reforms measures found a prominent place in the newly carved out 20-Point Programme. Dairy poultry, etc., were emphasised in a bid to diversify agriculture.

The Seventh Plan attached due significance to the following:

1. Social transformation involving structural changes.
2. Growth in awareness.
3. Change in outlook, motivation and attitudes.
4. Provision of opportunities for the poorer sections to display initiative and to stand on their own feet.
5. Minimisation and prevention of leakages which might fritter

away the benefits of the poverty-alleviation programmes.

6. Increased participation of the poor through the elected institutions at the grass-roots level as well as through their own organisations. Studies revealed that the anti-poverty programmes were more successful in those areas where follow-up measures were taken and where people were involved through their representatives.
7. Keeping the cost-effectiveness of the programmes in the forefront.
8. Rendering perception of needs and priorities also a female responsibility and right. That is, taking into account explicitly the special needs and problems of women and children.
9. Every feasible attempt to be made to plug the loop-holes and lacunae in the operation of the anti-poverty programmes.
10. Ensuring that the benefits flowed to those for whom they were really intended.

But the above-mentioned positively anti-poverty approach of the Seventh Plan was partly diluted by an element of ambivalence on the part of its makers, as would be evident from their remarks as under:

– That the resources and capabilities needed for anti-poverty programmes could not be generated in the system unless the economy itself was buoyant and there was a sustained increase in output.
– That the programmes of poverty-alleviation should be regarded as supplementing the basic plan for over-all economic growth in terms of generating productive assets and skills as well as incomes for the poor.
– That it was necessary to ensure that the pattern of over-all economic growth itself was such as to generate an impact on employment-generation and on the development of the less developed regions.
– That the demand for goods and services produced by the poorer household enterprises rose significantly in response to the over-all increase in incomes in the country so that the viability of those household enterprises turned critically on the sustained increase in national income.
– That "while the present strategy of direct attack on poverty through specific poverty-alleviation programmes was justified

> on account of insufficient percolation of benefits to the poor from the over-all economic growth, it should be appreciated that the strategy of direct attack on poverty could not be sustained and would not yield the desired results, if the over-all growth of the economy itself is slow and the benefits of such growth are inequitably distributed".

The Seventh Plan very candidly admitted that the experience of the poverty-alleviation programmes was by no means uniform in the country.*

---

* The terminal year of the Plan witnessed the introduction of the JRY, which replaced the NREP, in the main (see our *India's Rural Problems*, Concept Publishing Company, New Delhi-59).

6

AN AGENDA FOR ACTION AGAINST POVERTY AND INEQUALITY IN INDIA

It is well known to us that nearly three-fourths of our population resides in rural areas and one-fourth of it in urban areas. Per capita consumer expenditure in urban areas is nearly 1.46 times that in rural. The average size of the rural households is 5.21 members and that of the urban 4.85 members, that is a difference of 1.07 times. The percentage of population below the Poverty Line in rural areas is 1.43 times that in urban areas (40.4 per cent versus 28.1 per cent). In 1987 the annual income per rural household capable of lifting it above the Poverty Line was Rs. 6,400. By January 1991 it should have risen to a figure of Rs. 7,750 (approximately) owing to price rise.

In India the projected total population for 1991 is 84.350 crores—63.262 crores in rural and 11.088 crores in urban areas.* This places the number of people below the Poverty Line in rural and urban areas at 25.558 crores and 3.116 crores respectively. In terms of households these come to 4.90 crores in rural and 0.64 crores in urban areas.

Per capita monthly consumer expenditure in urban areas is 1.46 times that in rural areas. Hence, in urban areas we would need Rs. 11,315 instead of Rs. 7,750 per household if it were to be lifted above the Poverty Line.

In rural areas we would need to spend Rs. 37,975 crores and in urban areas Rs. 7,242 crores, or, a sum – total of Rs. 45,217 crores in order to lift the existing households above the Poverty Line. As the action programme is delayed, prices would further rise and the total

---

* According to the 1991 Census, the figures are: Total Population: 843,930,86; Rural Population: 525 million; Urban Population: 160 million, Average Annual Exponential Growth Rate: 2.11 per cent; Density: 267 per km; Sex-Ratio: 929; Literacy Rate: 52.11 per Hundred (63.86 Males & 39.42 Females).

expenditure for the purpose would further increase.

That all households, rural and urban, have equal incomes at Rs. 7,750 per household in rural and Rs. 11,515 in urban areas (when all incomes are equal, social welfare should be maximum in the neo-classical sense), an aggregate outlay of Rs. 2,33,330 crores (1,98,073 crores rural plus 35,257 crores urban) would be needed.

According to the estimate made by us, in 1990-91 NNP at factor cost and at current prices amounted to Rs. 2,47,7564 crores. Of this, 83.5 per cent, i.e., Rs. 2,06,715 crores was on private consumption expenditure. The total outlay for poverty alleviation comes to Rs. 2,33,330 crores, as shown in the preceding paragraph. In other words, what was actually being consumed on private consumption was not enough for the abolition of poverty. The only requirement was that the existing private consumption in the country plus an additional consumption worth Rs. 26,615 crores was redistributed equally among all households. The households consuming above Rs. 7,750 per annum in rural and above Rs. 11,515 per annum in urban areas had to be made to part with their excess consumption, which excess along with Rs. 26,615 crores worth additional consumption* had to be** redistributed among the households that fell below the threshold in rural and urban areas. Thus what was really desired was a process of levelling down combined with another of levelling up at the same time.

To illustrate, in 1983 the top 30 per cent of the rural households were responsible for 50.9 per cent of total consumer expenditure. The middle 40 per cent of them accounted for 33.9 per cent of it. The bottom 30 per cent of them made do with barely 15.2 per cent of it. In urban areas the top 30 per cent of the households claimed 53.3 per cent of it; the middle 40 per cent of them 32.8 per cent of it; and the bottom 30 per cent just 13.9 per cent of it.

In other words, the top 30 per cent households in both rural and urban areas had to share their private consumption with the middle and the bottom 70 per cent. This meant redistribution of existing total private consumption or consumption expenditure among the three classes of society.

The foregoing generalisation needs to be qualified by two factors:

---

* Worth Rs. 18,602 crores, which would have to be siphoned off.

** Giving a sum-total of Rs. 45,217 crores.

One, the nation is not consuming its current income wholly, though not all people are consuming at one and the same level and no one is really starving, malnutrition notwithstanding. Nearly 25 per cent of the assisted households during January-December 1987, belonged to the group of destitutes with per capita per annum consumer expenditure of Re 1 to Rs. 1,225 and 46 per cent to the group of very, very poor with per capita per annum consumer expenditure of Rs. 2,266 to Rs, 3,500. This firms up the evidence that even the most indigent households had a scraping of earning which they spent on keeping their body and soul together. That being so, the total anti-poverty plan expenditure had to be lower to the extent of the sum-total of such expenditures by all groups composing the poor.

The second factor, which is a deduction from the first, is that the nation has a saving whose proportion has grown from the outset of planning and despite a deceleration in the household sector saving is around 20 per cent at present. In 1990-91 it would have been approximately Rs. 49,513 crores. For emancipating the existing rural and urban poor in the country from the bondage of poverty the total public outlay that was needed came to Rs. 45,217 crores (see above), which is less than the quantum of saving done. Were we to reject the consumption redistribution policy in view of the underlying problems and difficulties and opt for an alternative method for bringing immediate relief to the poor who are in teeming millions, then the choice would fall on a policy of redistribution of the current saving. This would obviously be possible by halting the process of capital accumulation, which would have produced its deadly effects before much time passed. This would not be a once-over step; instead it would have to be repeated every year.

In the model we have spelt cut above the estimates made are rough and ready in character but they are adequate for a broad mapping out of the intricacies of the programme. In the second alternative no curtailment occurs in the present standard of living of the non-poor and the poor secure the opportunity of moving from below the Poverty Line to above it. The maldistribution of consumption which the present system involves would remain uncured by such a measure. But society would breathe a new life. The given inequality would have a new lease of life.

Not the whole of the saving identified above is mopped up by the fiscal instruments at present. To net it in toto a Draconian decision would be necessary. Taxation and borrowing would have to be pressed into service at their maximum pitch. This may not be feasible in an order that is subtended on democratic principles and values.

In the configuration of poverty the backwardness of a State sometimes subtly overlaps with it since poverty and backwardness are like mirror twins. Take a State, say, A in a particular year, say, 1986-87. At current prices its per capita income is, say, Rs. 1,802. On the other hand, average per capita income for India is, say, Rs. 2,974. This gives a difference of Rs. 1,172. Take the population of that State at 8 crores. Further take the ICOR of the State at 4.40. Then an aggregate public expenditure of Rs 41,254 crores in that State would have the gap between the all-India per capita income and that State's per capita income bridged. That would be nearly 25 to 27 per cent of the SDP of that State or about 1.6 per cent of NNP of India in that year.

Suppose the richest State which invariably has meant Punjab had a per capita income of Rs. 4,719 in that year. The difference between the per capita income of the State in question and that of the richest State amounted to Rs. 2,917 in that year. With a population of 8 cores and an ICOR of 4.40 that State required a total public outlay of Rs. 1,02,678 crores in order to move up to that level. That amounted to 6.8 times that State's SDP or about 41.5 per cent of India's NNP in that year.

As percentage of its SDP the poorest State's plan outlay was the highest in the Sixth Plan (at 8.6%) and lowest in the First Plan (at 2.12%). Considering this, it would be rash to think that public outlays of the order implied in the above-mentioned figures would ever be planned or incurred.

Parsimonious ways on the part of the capitalist producers (the grave of today who spend little on their personal consumption and save most of their current income in the hope of being gay tomorrow), the thrift on the part of the agriculturists and the workers are the qualities which are wanted even at present. The rate at which the given levels of consumption could be allowed to go up would rise only slowly but the pressure on consumption standards would at least be no worse than before and it might well be possible to permit moderate improvements. Sustained austerity rather than any excessive degree of privation and suffering was called for. As a matter of fact, the First Five-Year Plan had very candidly and unequivocally outlined this approach.

Since planning became an edict of economic policy the country has imposed upon itself a high rate of saving. The rate of capital formation was stepped up through defined stages. Hardships were minimised in the initial period. The country did not go all-out in favour of industrialisation (heavy industrialisation to be precise). The emphasis on labour-intensive techniques ensured that the measure of sacrifice implicit in the matter of consumption was minimum while the economy was being strengthened at the base. The initial levels of consumption were not reduced and excessive privation was not entailed. Additional incomes accrued. Proportionally more was saved and ploughed back into capital formation/investment. Owing to the high rate of population growth shortage of capital rather than shortage of labour proved to be the main limiting factor in development. The total effort put up in each successive Plan had therefore to be larger so as to raise per capita living standards. All in all, the community as a whole, not all fractiles or deciles of it, had a little more to consume of most things than before. But this was not without setting up an inflationary pressure that has never terminated. The period 1950-51 to 1984-85 witnessed a modest, 1.1 per cent per annum rise in per capita consumption, a very small increase indeed.

The exercise incorporating the calculations undertaken so far is illustrative and is intended only broadly to indicate the implications, in terms of effort and return, of alternative courses of action.

The influence of growth rate on consumption level being so very small, not much improvement in the living standards of the people could be recorded. This appeared all the more disappointing when viewed against the base of extremely low per capita consumption. What was worse was the fact that the increase did not seep or trickle down to the poor.

In those regions where per capita SDP has risen and with it per capita food consumption, the chief cause of poverty has been unequal distribution. It is maintained in certain quarters that two-thirds of planning in India has contributed to the deepening process and benefited the haves. Only one-third of it has contributed to the widening process and benefited the have-nots. This is generally attributed to the limited effectiveness of the trickle-down or spread effect. To correct this the Sixth Plan had urged that public policies should acquire a sharper redistributive focus in raising the share of the poorer sections in national income and consumption and in the utilisation of public services. On this view, unless the existing pattern of distribution of incomes is altered, the consumption standards of the poor would remain unduly low.

Opinions veer round the proposition that the given income distribution is not conducive to economic growth. On the other hand, being inequitable in its effect economic growth can and does bring about a little impoverishment. In so far as the rate of growth of the Indian economy has not been related to the distribution of income between different classes, it has not measured up to the welfare of the masses of the people. As growth has gone to the top, more and more families have been pushed to the bottom. In all events the rate of economic growth has more or less affected the proportion of income ensuing to the bottom 30 per cent of the population.

Many, e.g., J.P. Lewis, consider the choice between equity and growth a practical canard. They enjoin on the planners that not only should total income and employment be enhanced but also that the increments in them should be equitably distributed among classes of society. The distributive aim should be particularly relevant to the objective of attaining a national minimum. This redistributive policy may resolve itself, in part, into rationing and, in part, into creation of more income-yielding employment opportunities. Under the former, the public distribution system could be extended to supply the basic goods to the poor at controlled/regulated prices. Side by side, the poor people's entitlement to food ought to be borne in mind, for passive reliance on economic development is not by itself sufficient to realise the goal. From the physically able poor persons the Government would take work and in return give wages, both in cash and in kind. In the latter case a coupon when presented to the fair price shop would serve the purpose. The ration would be subsidised to the degree required. To the physically disabled poor persons the Government would supply free food through the fair price shop on presentation of a coupon. This is the mechanism through which the poverty-alleviation and unemployment-eradication programmes would get dovetailed. This would also integrate more and more meaningfully and effectively the poor into the income-generation process.

As a rule, the pattern of distribution determines the character of growth. It affects the level of employment through its impact on the pattern of consumption via different import and labour contents of the expenditure incurred by the rich and the poor.

India has a strategy of direct assault on poverty and unemployment since the Sixth Plan. The target group orientation of the poverty-alleviation programme was ushered in during the Seventh Plan period. The abortive Janata Government Sixth Plan (Draft) had contemplated abolition of poverty and inequality by expanding employment opportunities, especially for the weaker sections of society. Its philosophy was that poverty could not be attacked sufficiently by depending on raising of the growth rate but instead on launching of direct programmes which would bring forth permanent and gainful employment. The majority of the poor had no other economic asset than their own labour, being in the lowest income-groups. They had to be provided additional opportunities for productive employment so that they earned enough to meet their minimum needs. For the poor were those who could not work to support themselves as well as those with large families.

Provision of more employment to the poor might prove self-multiplying when it pushed up the demand for those goods the production of which required relatively more labour-intensive methods.

It would be more helpful to the remedying of the poverty problem if we were to regard the unemployment problem as plainly and simply a low-end poverty problem. Similarly, the problem of the poor is best regarded as one of their un- or under-employment or low productivity in an important sense. The estimates of the magnitudes of unemployment furnish a striking index of those steeped in poverty, and hence misery and deprivation. In short, the cure of joblessness presumes that first there would be progress towards relieving poverty. In essence, both unemployment and poverty are ramifications of underdevelopment.

Un- and under-employment on a vast scale are both an asset and a liability. They are a liability because they cause poverty. They are an asset because they can be used to remove poverty. Unemployment and low income are closely related. Poverty and un- and under-employment are, by and large, inextricably linked together in India.

It is advisable to calculate the extent by which the volume of employment generated is likely to fall short of that needed to pull the poor up to a level which guarantees at least minimum consumption to them. Providing productive or gainful employment to the poor on as large and wide a scale as practicable would ensure that some income accrues to them. Even in rural areas agricultural income is a far better calculus of the level of living than the rate of employment.

Transfer of surplus labour from agriculture to non-agriculture is a corrective of poverty. To elucidate, in the USA every percentage point fall in the number of farmers has been accompanied by 0.3 percentage point fall in the incidence of poverty.

To put the preceding in a nutshell, income must be redistributed from the top 10 per cent to the lowest 30 per cent. In addition, income distribution should be prevented from becoming more and more uneven as the economy progresses. In other words, any decline in the relative share of the bottom 30 per cent in incremental income must be staved off. When unemployment exists on a broad scale, income redistribution through creation of employment opportunities in favour of the unemployed must take precedence over redistribution among those who enjoy a regular income at or above a level which is just sufficient to maintain a minimum socially acceptable standard of living.

As said above, the contemporary elitist orientation of the production pattern of consumer goods must give way to emphasis on the production of food and other articles of mass consumption. But the production pattern cannot easily be restructured due to the lack of information concerning input-output coefficients for the different sectors of the economy and their likely behaviour subsequent to the restructuring. The repercussion of redistributive policies on the incentives to save and invest would require looking into, besides accrual of income and its taxation, the triad of questions with which they are connected. A drastic redistribution has to be avoided for the reason that it would make resource mobilisation for planned outlay more difficult by worsening the relative economic position of the top 30 per cent, in particular.

The rich and the poor may appear to be living apart but, in fact, they do not. Their employment, income and consumption are interdependent. Harming one involves harming the other. Hence the poverty question has to grapple with the underlying ideological and institutional factors. The poor should be provided with those institutional structures which enable them to exert control over the conditions in which they lead their lives. Their income and living standards cannot rise with economic growth alone; economic growth has to be reinforced with special assistance, say, by means of employment generation. In our example of 49 million households in rural areas, employment to one person per household at the daily wage of Rs. 23.70 assumed as the current wage for 327 days in a year would cost Rs. 37,974 crores, this roughly equals GDS but when adjusted for the average daily income of the household as it exists today, it should amount to a lower public outlay. For eliminating urban poverty through provision of employment an additional budget would be needed. Unless GDS is higher, this may not be practicable. Of course, these models or paradigms are for mere enunciation of the problem. The real resource requirements may differ substantially.

A combination of a strong production base, agricultural or industrial, and an egalitarian income distribution pattern may counteract the growth of poverty. Emphasis on wage goods industries, light industries and capital formation in this order--may reduce disparities of incomes, class-wise and region-wise.

Investment in human capital by developing social services like education, health and housing would be a big step in providing equal opportunities to different sections of the community and hence in bringing about a measure of redistribution of income and providing the basic necessities to one and all.

In India, the ceiling laws apart, the decline in concentration of landownership has been but marginal. Resumption of land by the landlords and eviction of tenants have taken place. While in some parts small and marginal farmers have sold part of their land to the large farmers, in others the latter have also disposed of part of their land to the former and taken to non-agricultural activities or migrated to urban areas. Evidently, the medium farmers have increased their land possessions.

In developing countries the twin levellers of politics are food and land; hence a question posed naturally is: What should be the hue or colour of radicalism pertinent to land reform in India? Experts like Dantwala believe that preventive land reform can be more urgent than positive land reform. Central to the problem is how to redistribute the power and opportunity derived from the system of relations and the consequential apparatus and mechanisms immanent in land ownership and operation as well as the inherited and tradition – and custom-bound institutions among the sections of people bereft of them. In its distillate inequality of incomes is a form of inequality of power and opportunity.

In our country redistributive policies are constrained and distorted by organisational, administrative and entrepreneurial problems. The local bureaucracy is biased in favour of the rural oligarchy. Political, social and religious issues loom large. Economic issues do not surface. They mostly lie low.

A question akin to the above often posed is: Whose pay-off is higher in a country like India: of technological progress or institutional reform? The answer to it is obtrusively difficult and there can be a temptation to be dogmatic in it.

Massive land-hunger has provoked a land-grab movement in some parts of India. The equality-conscious Naxalites have launched a crusade against poverty and exploitation in these areas. The landowners have read the writing on the wall. The rituals and institutions that legitimatised inequalities for ages have been thrown off their moorings and anchorage and have gradually lost their socio-political sanctions. Yet socialism in India has not come to have its conceptual clarity, though its indices of growth have had a wide support and acceptance—reduction of poverty and inequality and unemployment. And the positive advantages of socialism over capitalism have lain in the elimination of these characteristic evils or maladies of the older economic discipline or order. In a truly socialist regime economic activities would meet a double test of growth and equity. *Growth with Equity* is the slogan of today and growth is conterminous with Lower Poverty and Less Unemployment and hence with equity which springs from the two.

We have noted above that investment in human capital with a tilt towards the weaker sections of the community is a powerful instrument of redistribution of real consumption frequently pursued by the Third World countries. Social services like education, health and housing are often identified as a more limited specific functional area within social well-being. Most of them include aspects of both income redistribution and resource allocation between the private and the public sector. Free distribution of these social services is justified on Pareto-optimum grounds if not on any other because they yield externalities in a sufficient measure. A proportionately greater expansion of these social services would be essential to stimulate a shift towards a better balance between social and economic development.

Provision of social services is the hard core of a socialistic state, for it is not founded on democratic pressures as is the case with the Welfare State, and is a necessary pre-condition of democratic stability. Relief is not to be confused with poverty eradication. The gulf that divides the two is analogous to the gulf that divides a

Welfare State from a Socialistic State.

The Fifth Plan was the first articulate attempt at provision, through reasonable time-phasing, of the public or social consumption goods, principally in rural areas, commensurate with the minimum acceptable norms. Being in the nature of transfer payment it was supposed to improve income distribution more than it was supposed to boost economic development.

In India the moderate rise in the general level of individual income achieved so far has failed to reduce the people's dependence on the government for the abolition of poverty; instead it has increased that dependence. While equality of opportunity remains a distant goal in India, to talk of creation of equality of result, which is a stronger and more efficacious goal, is glib and a mere pious wish or a fond hope. Social justice at present connotes not equality at the start of a race but at the finish, equality not of opportunity but of result. If the principle of equality of opportunity was the liberal ethic, that of equality of result is a socialist ethic.

The staunch socialists consider redistribution of consumption a poor substitute of redistribution of property rights, if poverty is really intended to be mastered. To really master poverty the existing assets must be shared with the poor, for that would form an abiding solution to poverty. Assets can be land, livestock, irrigation water, energy, and the like.

The few empirical studies made so far reveal that salaried employment in the private or public sector of one member or more of a family designated as poor has helped it to move up from below the Poverty Line more successfully than has wage-employment or self-employment for only a part of the year.

Authors like Meade have cautioned us against one great danger latent in the provision of more extensive educational opportunities of certain specifications to the weaker sections of society, alone namely, the risk of creating a separate meritocratic elite, given to in-breeding, out of those sections. Were this to materialise, the increase in equality of opportunity may become unequal.

In Table 6.1 we have endeavoured to arrive at the extent of subsidy needed State-wise to lift the poor above the Poverty Line. The relative poverty of the States can be judged on the basis of per capita monthly SDP and per capita monthly consumer/consumption expenditure. The rankings of the States in the two cases are not identical, except in the respect of the two States in the bottom class, namely, Bihar and Madhya Pradesh, two States in the top classes, viz., Punjab and Haryana, and one State in the middle class, that is, Karnataka. Among the richest States, Maharashtra, occupies the third position in terms of per capita SDP but the eighth position in terms of per capita monthly expenditure, while West Bengal's corresponding positions are fifth and fourteenth. That is to say, Maharashtra and West Bengal are poorer if measured by the yardstick of per capita consumer expenditure. On the other hand, among the poorer States, Rajasthan claims the third rank from the standpoint of per capita consumer expenditure but the eighth one from that of per capita SDP, whereas Uttar Pradesh enlists the ninth and the thirteenth ranks respectively from the two stand points.

Obvious from the table is that all other States, except Punjab, would call for subsidy in varying degrees—Bihar the maximum and Haryana the minimum.

The amount of subsidy shown in the table belongs to 1983. Owing to inflation in 1991 the amount would be 65 to 70 per cent higher.

The subsidy would be financed from the general budget which implies recourse either to taxation or to public borrowing or to a combination of both.

Insofar as the people to be subsidised are already spending some money on their consumption needs, the amount of subsidy they need would be less by that amount of expenditure. With the aid of this we can finally derive the total public outlay on subsidy required to wipe out poverty from the face of the country.

For tackling the poverty (or unemployment) problem it is incumbent on our part that we break it up in terms of sectors, classes and regions and do not rely upon any solution to an absolute extent. For fighting existing poverty big effort has to be put in. While the size of poverty is important, its contents are all the more important. Poverty requires measurement because, without this, the magnitude of the task implicit in it cannot be assessed. The acid – test of success of the poverty-alleviation programmes would lie in reaching out to the most needy, the *Daridra-Narayan,* the poorest of the poor or, which is the same things, the rise of the last person, *Antyodaya,* as it is called. Today an individual's acceptability in society is a function of his social as well as economic background. True egalitarianism cannot be attained so long as there prevail in society rigidities of the caste system while class and regional differences act as further barriers to it. It is these factors that make the future of certain regions, bestrewn as they are today with mass poverty and unemployment and low productivity, very dark and uncertain, although there is no need to be unnecessarily alarmed by it.

TABLE 6.1: A tentative model of subsidy-based poverty-alleviation

(Rupees)

State	Per Capita Monthly State-Specific Poverty Line in 1983*	Per Capita Monthly SDP in 1983-84	Amount of Subsidy Per Capita Per Month (2) - (3)	Per Year Subsidy Needed [(4)X5 average no. of members in a Household X 12 months in a year]	Per Capita Monthly Consumer Expenditure in 1983 at 1973-74 Prices
1	2	3	4	5	6
Andhra Pradesh	76	63.2(6)	12.8	768(11)	75.9(4)
Assam	99	48.8(12)	50.2	3012(2)	57.4(11)
Bihar	104	37.8(15)	66.2	3972(1)	45.3(15)
Gujarat	85	76.7(4)	8.3	498(12)	72.6(6)
Haryana	92	90.6(2)	1.4	84(14)	83.0(2)
Himachal Pradesh	—	—	—	—	—
Jammu & Kashmir	—	—	—	—	—
Karnataka	90	60.9(7)	29.1	1746(9)	65.3(7)
Kerala	100	50.7(11)	49.3	2958(3)	73.0(5)
Madhya Pradesh	85	51.2(10)	33.8	2028(8)	59.5(10)
Maharashtra	91	85.5(3)	5.5	330(13)	61.0(8)
Orissa	94	45.7(14)	48.3	2898(4)	52.8(13)
Punjab	92	123.9(1)	29.9 (excess)	1794 (excess)	93.2(1)
Rajasthan	78	59.7(8)	18.3	1098(10)	81.3(3)
Tamil Nadu	99	54.7(9)	44.3	2658(5)	56.7(12)
Uttar Pradesh	87	48.2(13)	38.8	2328(7)	60.1(9)
West Bengal	112	68.5(5)	43.5	2610(6)	46.9(14)
All-India	91	191.0	100.0	6000	61.7

Note: An average household comprises five members.
Figures in brackets indicate the ranks of the States.

* See *Economic and Political Weekly*, March 31, 1990. The Poverty Line has been deflated by the cost-of-living index in the States.

7

MANAGING THE POVERTY-ALLEVIATION PROGRAMMES IN INDIA

Recent studies expose the following drawbacks of management of the existing poverty-alleviation programmes:

1. A dysfunctional diffusion of responsibility.
2. Frequent transfers of the key personnel.
3. Poor communication with current and potential beneficiaries.
4. Weak micro-planning.
5. Absence of computerised information.
6. Absence of follow-up action.
7. Social constraints.
8. Little involvement of the beneficiaries in decision-making.
9. Weaknesses of the other pro-poor programmes.
10. Reluctance of banks to provide financial support on a regular basis.
11. Organisational inadequacies.
12. Lack of clarity in Plan formulation and implementation.
13. Lack of proper monitoring.

Some of the drawbacks are the basic cause of other drawbacks and so if this basic cause is removed the entire effect would disappear. But for this the poverty-alleviation programme will have to be region/area-specific. In other words, to attack poverty, its location, extent and characteristics should be known in detail and in advance. Moreover, the poverty-eradication campaign should have a mass-oriented total approach, for a partial approach would not work. Also, it has to be an admixture of the short-term, medium-term and long-term programmes—a tripartite programme from the standpoint of time.

Of late, there has appeared a growing hiatus between the two objectives—poverty elimination and growth—since no attempt has so far been made to dovetail them adequately and effectively.

A three-pronged policy – increased foodgrains production, increased employment (both of productive and relief types) opportunities, and increased productivity—can surmount the triple problems of poverty, unemployment and inequality. So far as the first problem is concerned, the alternative methods are increasing per capita consumption, reducing the inequality of consumption, or combining the two.

A long-term and viable solution to rural poverty, in particular, would consist in a comprehensive approach to rural development that would be a three-element strategy, namely, (i) Equal or equitable distribution of land and other rural resources, (ii) a gradual process of consolidation and cooperativisation of the cultivated land holdings, and (iii) diversification of the rural economy.

The five basic human needs—food, clothing, shelter, education and medicine—have to guaranteed. And a decent cremation/burial too. These would form the main pillar of development. Food is the first need of man but it is not, and should not be made, everything for the poor. As an "at least norm" it is good but in a developing economy we have to have the **physical index of the quality of life** as the norm, as suggested by economists, such as Khusro. Next to food, salt (the only condiment of the poor), oil (the cooking medium), and fuelwood (i.e. *Nun, Tel* and *Lakarhi*) are the three instrinsic objects of life that keep the poor perpetually looking for employment.

In guaranteeing the right to work, as the first ever remedy of absolute poverty, choice has to be made between wage-employment and self-employment. It is the latter which underscores the importance of land or non-land asset/property as the key to income, and in its advocacy the traditional notion of socialism gets watered down and a new brand of it comes to be paraded as a cure-all of poverty. Those who champion the former take the view that possession of property or its encouragement in whatever degree has been germane to the prevalence of mass poverty in the contemporary society and hence self-employment has to be replaced with wage-employment, preferably in the public sector.

All the same, we have economists like Rath who would like us to blend the two alternatives by providing wage-employment in the Employment Guarantee Scheme type programmes, on the one hand, and self-employment through the IRDP type schemes, on the other.

In either case the employment goal has to be wedded to the development goal, considering their interaction which is very close.

But the poverty-focussed policies and programmes have to go beyond the employment-generation programmes. The Minimum Needs Programmes (MNP) has to be strengthened. The social goods/amenities may be supplied to the poor either in kind or in cash. Reservation of jobs for the weaker sections is another method, and in the past few years it has achieved its goal appreciably, though at the cost of efficiency, the level of which has already been low in our country. The fixation of minimum wages has had a wholesome impact on these programmes, though by escalating rural unrest in the process—a transitional phenomenon, as interpreted by many sympathetic commentators. Welfare measures, especially the social security schemes, adopted have made for a similar impact, though by raising unproductive expenditures, already an enormous charge on the general budget of the Government, Central or State.

Upset by the upsurge of the new approach, those who have preferred an eclectic approach have sought to subordinate the basic human needs goal to the concept of a social minimum that has to be rigidly and stringently enforced by means of avoidance of wasteful conspicuous consumption and control of the production pattern. And in this they seem to have been on a firm ground theoretically because, in the final analysis, production and distribution are interdependent.

Abolition of poverty calls for social transformation as well as economic change. More benefits have to flow evenly among classes. For this is the only mechanism that can narrow down the social distance between different classes. Social exploitation must stop. It is the present inegalitarian social structure that is fanning social tensions, spearheaded by agrarian violence. Humanistic socialism could be a corrective of this. It would be ushered in if the marginalised and excluded sections of our society were brought within the ambit of a comprehensive social policy. Included among these sections are women whose development became an edict of policy first only during the Sixth Plan period.

The social order must be just both in reality and in perception, to borrow the phraseology of the authors of the Eighth Plan Approach Paper. A just social order is not bedevilled by poverty nor plagued by unemployment nor besmirched by gross inequality. Planning should for this purpose become an apparatus also of social transformation.

This brings us to the inequality question. A dent in inequality would be a major factor that could lead to a substantial reduction in poverty. In a general sense a higher rate of growth is itself a solvent of inequality. That is what is implied by *the majesty of the compound rate of growth* providing as it does enduring redress over time, as Patel put it in a recent public discourse. But this advice has to be hedged with a qualification put forth by Dandekar, which is that growth should lift the bottom rather than put up the top. However, this equitable distribution of benefits of growth would require that primacy of place was accorded to the labour factor. With this broad lay-out in the forefront, steps should be taken to prevent rural poverty from being aggravated. Deconcentration of land and of income from land should be encouraged. Property should be redistributed. New technology should be made available to all. Land reforms in its broader sense should be speeded up. Its ceiling part should be unified with its other part pertaining to the supply of inputs, credit and technology so that its full benefit could be reaped. Consequent upon the fiscal and credit incentives extended by the Government to the agriculturists, reinforced by its pro-agriculture price policy, a new rich class has risen from amongst the old and is trying to monopolise opportunities released by the Government for the uplift of the neglected and distressed sections of the rural population. It is, therefore, imperative that the monopolistic and quasi-feudal activities of this new rich class are effectively curbed. In order to arrest further impoverishment of the natural resource-base in the country – side on which a sizable chunk of the rural poor is dependent for its very survival conservatory measures should be enforced. This would necessitate grass-roots management and hence decentralization of planning and administration via refashioned institutions.

Insofar as there is no all-India solution to the poverty problem, the total, tripartite approach to poverty-alleviation would have to embrace a local approach towards the rural problems to which it has to address itself and also involve local people by revamping the Panchayati Raj. The grass-roots level, group-oriented institutions entrusted with the task of Plan formulation and implementation should prove cost-effective and efficient in delivering the goods to the people. Authorities like Hanumantha Rao share the view that decentralisation, if effective operationally or functionally, would also be capable of ensuring the success of land reform policies.

While poverty-alleviation programme is being managed, the rural-urban dichotomy should be paid due attention and its aggravation countered with a strong hand. The reverse resource transfer from rural to urban areas, a latter-day development, should be halted. The criteria and procedures relating to the supply of inputs and finance to the peasantry class should be simplified, with an eye to inequality reduction. At the same time, the pattern of production and commercial activities has to be restructured and streamlined in favour of those belonging to the low-income brackets.

Poverty-alleviation programmes management has to resolve the conflict between number and quality as well as between physical and pecuniary targets, and strive to improve both the quality of the programmes and the quality of the instruments used.

Thanks to the authors of the Eighth Plan Approach Paper who view development as a holistic endeavour of the planner interrelating various dimensions, sectors and disciplines. This make the task of the planner easier.

In our country public measures to alleviate poverty, measures to eradicate unemployment, and measures to mitigate inequality overlap. Public expenditure on social services is calculated to reduce poverty and inequality but to the extent that they include construction works they are designed to combat unemployment as well. In our country Plan expenditure of the Union Government (revenue and capital accounts combined) on social services rose from 10.4 per cent of the total Plan expenditure in 1980-81 to 11.8 per cent in 1988-89. On the other hand, food subsidies, which formed about 32 per cent of total subsidies in 1980-81 fell to nearly 28 per cent in 1988-89. But total subsidies which constituted 9.2 per cent of total government expenditure in 1980-81 increased to 10.3 per cent in 1988-89. This indicated that the proportions of subsidies, benefiting the less poor, such as fertilizer subsidies, and those benefiting the relatively rich like export promotion and market development subsidies had risen. But more objectionable than this was that the relative contribution of indirect taxes to total revenue kept increasing and that of direct taxes kept decreasing. Thus in 1960-61 indirect taxes as percentage of total revenue were 71.2 but in 1980-81 their share had gone up to 82.4 per cent and by 1987-88 it was 85.7 per cent. The corresponding shares of direct taxes were 28.8 per cent in 1960-61, 17.6 per cent in 1980-81 and 14.3 per cent in 1987-88. The relatively poor shouldered the tax burden more than the non-poor. The income redistribution which was sought to be improved by non-conventional means turned adverse to the relatively poor because of the steady flight from direct taxation in this country.

8

CONCLUDING REMARKS ON POVERTY AND INEQUALITY

The poor States face obstacles to delivering goods and services to the marginalised sections of their population sufficient to abolish poverty from their economies.

Inadequate infrastructure for appropriate nutrition, health, sanitation and education programmes contribute considerably to the syndrome of their poverty.

Poverty continues in them because the "poverty of the masses is a necessary cost of the privileges of the rich and because poverty is the carcass that is left behind from the *Trickle-Down* strategy of development aimed at GNP growth, emphasising efficiency and building on the best". This strategy has consisted in limiting consumption, raising savings and investment rates, investing heavily in the protected modern industrial sector of the economy, and thus concentrating of government expenditures on economic rather than social overheads. This strategy has not ensured rapid economic growth and its benefits have not trickled down to the entire population in the form of increased per capita income. Instead relative incomes and standards of living have decreased, sometimes markedly. The absolute incomes of the bottom 10 to 20 per cent have fallen. This strategy has done nothing of a direct nature to improve the development prospect of the rural poor.

In spite of this and because of the direct attack on poverty and execution of rural development programmes living conditions in rural areas have slightly improved for landless labourers and subsistence farmers. But the urban poor have benefited little from this strategy. On the whole, to has abjured any specific policy targeting on the problems of the poorest strata of society.

The overwhelming majority of the constantly remembered 40 per cent of our population living in poverty are rural in origin.

The ending of absolute poverty is one major goal of a new set of development strategies adopted by the States under the aegis of the National Plan. In it poverty is conceptualised as substandard conditions of life. There is in it a recognition of the fact that the definitional problems connected with the term "absolute poverty" are monumental as well as of the fact that the problem of poverty is at once more complex than and normatively distinct from the question of low income. Even then there are reasons for thinking of the problem of poverty in basically income terms. Sheer increases in income per capita would not guarantee higher standards of living for the poor but neither would they inevitably drive their standards of living down.

The fulfilment of basic human needs is gradually being conceptualised by the States as the elimination of absolute poverty and it is to them more a goal than a strategy. The absolute poverty of 40 per cent is a colossal problem which makes the basic human needs strategy appear highly burdensome.

The basic human needs strategy attempts to guarantee a floor to standards of living beneath which no personal income would fall. Inherent in it is the assumption that the fulfilment of basic human needs would automatically produce greater potential earning power among the bottom deciles of the population.

The basic human needs goal of the new development strategy is essentially connected with the reduction of existing inequalities in income and wealth distribution directly and the alleviation of un- and under-employment indirectly. Lately, it has become connected with the elimination of absolute poverty as well.

It is being believed that a new admixture of policies and policy priorities can produce much greater productive employment and thus attack the absolute poverty problem with far greater success than achieved in the earlier periods, and with little sacrifice in the rates of economic growth.

The proponents of the basic human needs strategy do not want to wait for a revolution to occur before adopting it, for they think that there is in the existing circumstances some room for manoeuvre.

One universal demand in the States is that the public services should be so refashioned that they actually benefit those in absolute poverty, i.e., the target groups. Basic education is seen as a critical element in bursting the absolute poverty cycle.

But poverty is so profoundly locked into the structure of the poor

States that only the most profound transformation of economic, political and class relations and culture could enable them to wage a war upon it.

The poor are today integrated with the rich in some functional areas for supply of land, tools and implements, employment, credit, inputs, etc. In the coming years they may need more assured access to the rich. And at some stage or other a cooperative resolution of the pressing problems would become necessary.

The structural or institutional reforms that would become the capstone of the proposed strategy would underwrite the division of gains to the relatively poor, who must be ensured a place and a say in maintaining the services they need by redirecting social change and by redesigning the structure or the institutions.

The structural or institutional reforms may be moderate or drastic. Likewise, the models of such reforms may be many and varied. Seven alternative models come immediately to our mind:

(1) Employment generation.
(2) Redirection of investment.
(3) Meeting the basic human needs.
(4) Human resource development.
(5) Developing agriculture first of all.
(6) Integrated rural development.
(7) A new national economic order.

The policy framework selected should be familiar and tested. Within it a number of capitalist institutions that survive at present may also survive after the structural reforms have taken place.

In managing the poverty-alleviation programmes at the earliest time-point constraints would be many but, as the programmes is intended to be long-term, some of them would be surmounted as the programmes advance. Suspicion would not be unfounded when the confirmed and vehement opponents and critics of the programmes all on a sudden announce their intention to support it to the utmost of their capacity.

The institutions, values and human resources (to organise and administer and monitor) needed for the success of the poverty-alleviation programmes do not exist in many States in the quantities and volume adequate for the purpose in hands.

The programmes have three aspects, namely, the physical, the financial and the socio-political (the last concerns sabotage by the vested interests, leakage of part of public expenditure to the non-target groups, and failure of assets distribution policies).

The resources required for financing the poverty-alleviation programmes must be raised within a State or obtained from the Centre. The financial constraints would ease if aid comes from the Centre.

The poor States work and should work to establish or strengthen their domestic structures in order to ensure economic justice. Self-reliant growth is and should be the real hope in the medium and long term.

Integration of the poor States into the national economy is and would be to the advantage of not only the poor States out also of the nation as a whole. Increased growth performance in them has been associated with their increased participation in the national programmes. It is the fault not of the Centre but of the States themselves that they are its underlings. However, the Centre should respond to both the perceived and real economic needs of the poor States in their war against poverty. The poor States should be on their guard so that the vested interests do not skim off most of the financial assistance meant for the poor to themselves.

The equity issue defined in poverty terms is present in every State to some degree and in a number of poor States it affects the majority of its inhabitants.

The quintessence of equity is either viewed in the struggle against poverty or come across in the degree of inequality obtaining in society and the trends in the reduction or intensification of this inequality. The former is *Equity as Non-Poverty.* The latter concerns itself with the relative shares of resources and opportunities received by different groups and hence with the question of poverty. The latter is *Equity as Distribution.*

By and large, strategies towards poverty-alleviation are not easy to devise so long as the critical links between technology and income distribution, income distribution and decision-makers, and decision-makers and objectives are ignored.

Poverty and inequality persist in the States because *inter alia* the masses in them are immobilized, fatalistic and apathetic.

Relative inequality is constrained by the condition that the poorest receive enough income to survive. Reduction in equality may not mean decline in the average income of the poorest.

In some situations the style of development may be a much more critical determinant of internal equity than the level of income or its rate of change.

Social justice at present signifies equality not of opportunity (*a liberal ethic*) but of result (*a socialist ethic*), not equality at the start of a race but at its finish. In the poor States if the equality of opportunity objective is far from being achieved, it would be rash at this stage to talk of the equality of result objective in their context.

Beyond a certain low level of income, the relationship between equality and income among the poor States is not very systematic, nor is there any indication that inequality is greater in States whose levels of income per capita are similar but whose growth rates are different.

Income is only one of the valued goods at issue when distribution is being examined. Such being the case, at least the increments of capital formation must be redistributed.

It is doubtful if even rapid growth rates could alleviate the absolute poverty problem or significantly alter the present patterns of highly unequal income distribution in the poor States.

The only genre of changes that could make possible serious assaults on the inequity issue would involve socialist forms of economic organisation.

The key challenge for the poor States, whose people are not yet committed to revolutionary methods, is to ensure that the poor get their fair share of whatever growth takes place. The equitable distribution would resolve the poverty issue to an appreciable extent.

Profiles of income distribution, in fact, understate the degree of inequality in the poor States, where market and quasi-market economies make a great deal of sense despite immense empirical variations. When we work with income distribution statistics in market and quasi-market economies, we actually study the statistical outcroppings of a much deeper structure of inequality. More basic stratifications are reflected.

Sometimes the incentives offered to supplement and reinforce the working of these economies have been too weak or too slow-working to produce automatically the right solution. This being so, to an extent, setting of correct prices may eliminate both poverty and inequality, the twin serious maladies often held out against such economies.

We cannot have the new development strategy without structural or institutional reforms of a fundamental nature and we cannot reform institutions if political will is conspicuous by its absence. Such reforms do not imply ejecting some of the constraints from the front door only to readmit them from the back door.

"Mere tokenism" is not structural or institutional reform, for institutional reform is the real restructuring of society.

For a policy to succeed the environment must be congenial to it. Even the best policy would flop if the environment in which it is executed is not congenial.

History bears out that institutions or structures have not so far been transformed through peaceful methods; they have needed mass movements or popular revolutions mounted by new political alliances before this could happen. Thus the revolutionary socialist regimes made a direct assault on privilege and poverty head on and simultaneously. Massive redistributions of power and consumption took place. The market mechanism was interfered with at every turn and even smashed as and when needed. Conventional efficiency criteria in resource allocation gave way to openly political criteria. All available energies were concentrated on achieving certain minimal levels of living and opportunity for all citizens. This necessarily involved "taking from the rich" and "giving to the poor".

Growth and equity may be achieved by the poor States either in the capitalist or socialist manner of things but that would be only at the cost of human rights — freedom as a mockery in a capitalist regime and freedom sacrificed at the altar of regimented central planning in a socialist one.

Were freedom to survive, it is only through structural or institutional reforms that we could achieve growth and equity.

The poor States are after achieving equity and alleviating poverty without having recourse to a social revolution but social revolution cannot in any case be achieved through parliamentary means.

The poor States are in dire need of a profound revolution of their institutions and structures.

Where conditions are not appropriate, even the most efficacious policies prove futile.

If the *raison d'etre*, character or complexion of institutions is apt to change when faced for long with abnormal or adverse conditions, the institutions may feel free to judge their performance by such criteria as are wrong or absurd or their own improvisations in utter disregard of the well-established norms and values with a view to justifying their very existence.* The contemporary conflict of values and attitudes makes us feel as if we are standing today at a watershed of history.

* We all know that universities exist primarily for teaching and research and examinations are secondary, though not inessential. But the performance of universities in certain States has come to be judged in terms of timely conduct of examinations, no matter if teaching is not done even for 50 days in a year as is the situation in several universities at present, and the quality of examinations leaves much to be desired.

PART II

THE UNEMPLOYMENT PROBLEM

9

DIAGNOSING THE INDIAN UNEMPLOYMENT PROBLEM

Growing unemployment is one of the impending problems faced by India, others being poverty and inequality, in rising prices and increasing fiscal and trade deficits.

Unemployment and underemployment are symptoms of far-reaching economic and social disturbances both within the country and in its relationship with the developed countries.

Utilisation of the full potentialities of the human and material resources is today regarded as the first ever leaven of change in the developing countries. It is being increasingly and widely maintained that creation of more jobs would ease tensions and regenerate resources.

The real inequality or gulf between the employed and the unemployed has grown. The unemployed are like the internal colony to the employed. The latter receive more and more at the cost of the former. They are analogous to the privileged classes of the past.

Low productivity in India is manifest from the un- and under-employment of a large part of its labour supply. How to improve the utilisation of labour—to employ more labour, to make it more productive and reward it more handsomely—is the crux of the country's development problem.

Creation of opportunities for productive employment of a growing labour force has assumed top priority in the planning process of India.

The right to an adequate means of livelihood has been provided for in the Constitution. The Directive Principles admit that the right to work and the right to adequate income have to go together. They enjoin on the state to adopt a measure of insurance against old age, sickness and other disabilities. Likewise they recognise the right to education of the people.

There has, of late, been public talk that at least one member of every family must be employed. This may amount to levying a modest duty on wife and husband if both are employed so as to finance an unemployment insurance scheme. The problem that defies solution is the allocation of additional work between the existing underemployed labour force and the new entrants to it. It is being realised that granting the right to work without first creating jobs may be dangerous, as Mohan Dharia is reported to have stated. In its extreme form this may lead to reallocation or even rationing of the existing and potential volume of wage-employment.

The employment goal is still the most important challenge to the Indian planners, who are of the opinion that when unemployment exists on a broad scale, income redistribution through creation of employment opportunities in favour of the unemployed takes precedence over redistribution among those who enjoy a regular income at or above a level which is just sufficient to maintain a minimum socially acceptable standard of living. A policy of work-sharing assumes greater significance than that of income-sharing, notwithstanding the inherent discrepancies between the two.

The above approach is derived from the proposition that mass unemployment in one primary cause of economic inequality. But income redistribution must follow immediately, for poverty being there, solution of unemployment boils down to a re-arranging of the existing distribution of income and wealth. But, more specifically, income redistribution in favour of the unemployed has to precede income distribution in favour of those who are employed, though at lower levels of income.

In short, to provide a minimum of equality of opportunity and establish a socialistic pattern of society provision of full employment would be the first step in a series of steps.

When subjected to the rigorous abstract analysis, Indian unemployment has existed and expanded because the techniques of production chosen so far have not been in accordance with the socio-economic characteristics of the regions concerned and have been influenced in some way or other by the demonstration effect. But there have been also other reasons to this. From time to time there have arisen temporary shortages of labour in particular regions even as there has been a general surplus of unskilled and semi-skilled labour in the country as a whole—a structural maladjustment, as it is called—and such shortages have tended to encourage mechanisation of operations in farming as well as in construction projects. Such a phenomenon could not be remedied because the inter-regional mobility of labour was not enhanced sufficiently. Similarly, the pace of mechanisation could not properly be regulated over the long run of years.

The technology chosen has not been one which could generate maximum employment as well as maximum investible surplus, producing both capacity-creating and income-generating effects to the optimal extent. Moreover, no attempt has been made to weed out the distortions in factor prices that have occurred on account of the state controls and measures affecting them so that appropriate techniques of production could be chosen by the private investors and employers. Use of imported expensive mechanical equipment, whenever and wherever underutilised owing to the presence of a limited market, has resulted in increased average costs of production which have expressed that total factor productivity has fallen, even if labour productivity has increased. To amplify, the corporation tax policy has tended to stimulate frictions in the functioning of the economy and thereby has favoured increased employment of capital, with the result that labour-intensity of output has declined.

Putting the preceding a bit more stringently, we would say that oversize of firms and growth of monopolisation and oligopolisation; rationalisation in older industries like cotton textiles, jute and tea to meet international competition; adoption of the latest and most efficient production techniques, for instance, in iron and steel, chemicals, etc.; mechanisation, for example, in coal-mining; scientific management, etc., in manufacturing; the Green Revolution techniques in agriculture; the progress of R&D; and so forth have had a mixed effect on the capacity of the organised sector to absorb the expected number of workers. A structural blind-alley has been at work in the economy since there has been more demand for specialised and less demand for non-specialised workers, more demand for the educated than the uneducated, and also for the specialised among the educated than the non-specialised among them.

On the other hand, the magnitude of employment in the household manufacturing sector, incorporating the whole gamut of cottage industries, has not risen to the planned size. Responsible for this has been low agricultural growth, as also the low rates of growth of gross value added to important household manufacturing industries. These have not been capable of imparting the expected impetus to the process of employment expansion in the economy.

Rapid population growth has compounded the prevailing unemployment problem. In agriculture, which is a land-based activity, *par excellence*, the amount of labour that could be efficiently employed at any time has been limited by the scarcity of land. The numbers that could be employed by industry have been limited, given the price ratio between the products of agriculture and those of industry. Moreover, there could be only a limited range of feasible price-ratios between the products of agriculture and those of industry because the price of labour could not in any case fall below a certain minimum level in terms of the means of subsistence like food. The conclusion has been explicit – unemployment has resulted from a relatively slow growth of labour demand in both the modern (industrial) sector and the traditional (agricultural) sector combined with a rapidly growing labour supply, especially on account of accelerated population growth and high levels of rural-urban migration.

Those who believed with Mahalanobis that unemployment in India would not be eliminated unless the capital goods sector was expanded sufficiently have been disillusioned.

From a broader, sociological angle of vision, four decades of planned development have meant that while the moorings of the old economic structure have been snapped, no new structure has uptill now become firmly ingrained in its place. The decline of the joint family system is a case in point.

A minor factor has been the march of displaced persons in thousands from neighbouring countries/border States which has aggravated the unemployment problem of the affected States and India as a whole.

An alternative theory accounting for Indian unemployment is couched in terms of the inadequate functioning of the real savings-investment mechanism – the Savings Gap.

Causes of the type of unemployment from which a developing country like India suffers are more complex than those of the involuntary/mass type, i.e., the Keynesian type of unemployment and the Robinsonian type of underemployment. In Keynes's new economics the employment level followed from the income level—a static view. Increasing the latter implied increasing the former well.

Given the ICOR, output and employment could be maximised by maximising the rate of savings and investment.

Expansion of aggregate demand for consumption goods is not the singular remedy of this type of unemployment and has therefore to be supplemented by other policy measures.

But there are yet bigger alternative explanations of Indian unemployment. One such is advanced in terms of the income distribution pattern. According to it, unemployment is rooted in maldistribution of income and consumption. For the pattern of income distribution and consumption and the volume of employment in a country are inter-related. Others relate to a rate of population growth that is fast, an inappropriate composition of sectors and techniques and an inadequent and slower rate of growth of GDP. We have already noted some of these a moment ago.

Unemployment is a major factor in poverty. Idle or unproductive labour is both a curse and a cause of poverty and low levels of living and a potential reserve for development. Unemployment is a manifestation of poverty. It is associated with poverty, as was the experience of a number of developed countries. Alongwith underemployment (which is low-productivity employment) it is concentrated in the poverty-stricken areas. Eighty per cent of the poor and 70 per cent of the unemployed are concentrated in States less benefited by the Green Revolution.

Unemployment is a measure of social distress. The unemployed, the underemployed and the unemployable are caught up in a trap at the bottom of our society and compose its underclass, which has little to withdraw economically but politically it can withdraw its votes, which may decide the destiny of the ruling party. Unfortunately, the fragmented character of this class greatly dilutes its effectiveness.

Both low income accruing to the fully employed and the absence of income to the unemployed are indicators of (a) wasted labour potential and (b) poverty. For any given Poverty Line, the lower the proportion of households and individuals, who are poor, the lower is also the rate of unemployment.

Poverty is a function of technology and productivity, of ownership of means of production, and of exploitation and social arrangements for production and distribution. The incidence of poverty fluctuates with the performance of the economy in its component sectors. The poor have a low asset base. Their educational attainments are low. Similar is the economic lot of the majority of the unemployed. As the small farmers are the real proletariat of today, so are the educated unemployed in urban areas the lumpen proletariat of today.

The largest incidence of rural poverty and unemployment is borne by four types of rural households : (i) rural labour households with land, (ii) rural households operating land below one hectare in area other than the agricultural labour households with land, (iii) agricultural labour households without land, and (iv) non-agricultural rural households. The recent rise in the size of these four types of rural households reflects the correlated increase in their pauperisation, unemployment and underemployment.

The dangers of unemployment and low-end poverty look most inflammable and explosive in the large towns and cities.

Some causes, e.g., population pressure and hence very weak land or capital base per capita, heavy dependency, indebtedness, under-education, small and fragmented holdings resulting in underemployment and the vicious circle of poverty, are common to both unemployment and poverty. The reasons that explain why the non-viable and sub-marginal farmers, the artisans engaged in traditional crafts, the landless agricultural labourers, the share-croppers, oral tenants, etc., are unemployed are the very same reasons as explain why they are so poor.

Apart from the above, the causes and effects of poverty and unemployment are so intertwined and intermingled that they cannot easily be segregated.

In view of **a strong association between poverty and unemployment** a number of economists argue persuasively for the adoption of the poverty norm in order to estimate the desired level of additional employment. In other words, the national norm of a minimum desirable level of per capita consumer expenditure cannot be independent of the national norm of an adequate level of employment in terms of earning.

However, most of the poor are unemployed but not all unemployed are poor. Unemployment is connected more with the question of earning, whereas poverty is connected more with that of spending. But in the final analysis provision of employment is the most effective remedy of poverty. This is tantamount to suggesting that the assault on poverty and unemployment must be simultaneous. Provision of employment opportunities to the unemployed may become the fulcrum that could lift the economy from the depths of poverty and malnutrition and starvation to a state of prosperity and progress. It is cruel to speak to the unemployed without giving them opportunity to work. It is like the dinner in the Aesops' Fables given by the fox to the crane, as someone has put it.

In fine, fuller employment lifts some classes of families and individuals above the Poverty Line more effectively compared to others. Alleviation of low-end poverty calls for rehabilitation more than provision of employment.

States with a higher percentage of agricultural labourers to total working population are, by and large, also the States with lower monthly per capita consumer expenditure in rural areas or (by a twist of the same argument) are the States with larger percentages of rural population living below the minimum consumption level. Thus as Table 9.1 uncovers, the proposition that a higher percentage of agricultural labourers to total working population/rural working population is accompanied by a lower per capita monthly expenditure in rural areas is wholly confirmed in the case of Bihar and more or less confirmed in the case of Gujarat, Himachal Pradesh, Maharashtra, Rajasthan and West Bengal (cols. 4 and 8 of Table 9.1).

More precisely, a comparison of col. 3 with col. 8 brings out that the theory is fully proved in the case of Jammu & Kashmir and more or less is proved in the case of Gujarat, Haryana, Himachal Pradesh, Karnataka, Kerala, Madhya Pradesh, Maharashtra, Orissa, Punjab, Tamil Nadu and Uttar Pradesh.

Oddly, some of the industrially advanced States have higher percentages of agricultural labourers to total working force, betraying the failure of industrialisation to enlarge employment opportunities and skim surplus agricultural labour off the farms.

The incidence of poverty is the highest among the agricultural labour households. Being nearly 30 per cent of total rural households, the agricultural labour households have about 42 per cent of the total rural poor. A little less than half the rural poor are landless labourers and a little more than half are small and marginal farmers. But the two categories overlap since small farmers also work as agricultural labourers. The high incidence of un- and under-employment among agricultural labourers is one paramount cause of the high incidence of poverty among them. The incidence of poverty as well as unemployment is higher among casual than among attached agricultural labourers. The bargaining power of the casual workers is weaker and hence they get lower wages. The minimum

TABLE 9.1: Certain relationships between rural poverty and percentage of agricultural labour to total working population

State	Percentage of Agricultural Labourers to Total Working Population (Rural) 1961	Percentage of Agricultural Labourers to Total Working Population (Rural) 1981	Percentage of Agricultural Labourers to Total Working Force 1981	Percentage of Rural Poor to Total Working Population (Rural) 1961	Percentage of Rural Poor to Total Population (Rural) 1983-84	Daily Status Rural Unemployment(1983) (Percentage) Male	Daily Status Rural Unemployment(1983) Female	Monthly Per Capita Consumption Expenditure in Rural Areas (Rs) 1983
1	2	3	4	5	6	7	8	9
Andhra Pradesh	31.33(1)	36.19(1)	31(2)	69.7(4)	38.7(8)	5.59(5)	4.70(3)	115.4(9)
Assam	3.87(14)	NA	10*(11)	58.3(8)	23.8(13)	1.88(15)	0.50(12)	113.0(11)
Bihar	24.37(3)	35.50(2)	33(1)	73.0(3)	51.4(1)	4.24(8)	1.92(7)	93.8(17)
Gujarat	17.70(10)	22.65(10)	19(8)	45.7(12)	27.6(11)	3.02(13)	1.67(8)	122.7(7)
Haryana	NA	16.11(12)	14(10)	NA	15.2(15)	3.41(12)	0.29(13)	151.8(2)
Himachal Pradesh	NA	2.73(16)	5(13)	NA	14.0(16)	1.17(17)	0.23(14)	150.8(3)
Jammu & Kashmir	1.26(15)	3.49(15)	3(14)	58.5(7)	16.4(14)	8.36(4)	0.21(15)	129.3(5)
Karnataka	18.52(7)	26.78(6)	20(7)	56.3(10)	38.5(9)	4.69(7)	3.15(4)	116.8(8)
Kerala	19.44(6)	28.24(4)	24(4)	69.1(5)	26.1(12)	13.39(1)	6.56(2)	145.2(4)
Madhya Pradesh	18.14(8)	24.24(9)	22(6)	47.0(11)	50.3(2)	1.56(16)	0.67(11)	100.5(15)
Maharashtra	28.94(2)	26.64(7)	24(4)	56.9(9)	41.5(7)	3.99(10)	2.69(5)	110.4(12)
Orissa	17.86(9)	27.76(5)	24(4)	67.8(6)	44.8(4)	5.09(6)	2.68(6)	98.8(16)
Punjab	8.94(12)	22.17(11)	20(7)	33.6(13)	10.9(17)	4.08(9)	1.16(9)	170.5(1)
Rajasthan	4.42(13)	7.32(14)	6(12)	33.1(14)	36.6(10)	3.09(11)	0.92(10)	127.0(6)
Tamil Nadu	21.80(4)	31.73(3)	29(3)	74.9(2)	44.1(5)	12.00(2)	8.55(1)	112.2(10)
Uttar Pradesh	12.45(11)	15.98(13)	15(9)	75.1(1)	46.5(3)	2.16(14)	0.50(12)	104.5(14)
West Bengal	20.47(5)	25.23(8)	23(5)	69.1(5)	43.8(4)	8.80(3)	3.15(4)	104.6(13)
All-India	18.86	24.94	22	61.5	40.4	4.79	2.52	112.4

* For 1971.

Source: (1) K.N. Prasad, *Problems of Indian Economic Development.*
(2) A.N. Agrawal et al, *India.*
(3) R.B.I., *Occasional Papers*, December, 1989.

wages legislation is observed more in breach than in compliance. The incidence of poverty among other labour households is also high, around 38.5 per cent. The marginal farmers constituting nearly 30 to 35 per cent of the total rural poor are mostly self-employed.

As indicated by Table 9.1 (col. 5 versus col. 2), the States having higher percentages of agricultural labourers in their total working population in rural areas have also higher percentages of the rural poor. Bihar and West Bengal furnish the best examples of this, followed by Kerala, Punjab, Rajasthan and Tamil Nadu which confirm the proposition more or less for 1961. A comparison between col. 6 and col. 3 in the Table 9.1 testifies to the proposition for 1981 wholly in respect of Maharashtra and Himachal Pradesh and more or less so in respect of Bihar, Gujarat, Jammu & Kashmir, Orissa, Tamil Nadu and West Bengal.

Some correlation exists between the percentage of agricultural labourers and percentage of the daily status of unemployed. Let us look at col. 7 in relation to col. 3 in Table 9.1. Haryana wholly elucidates the theory. Likewise, the theory is more or less attested to by Himachal Pradesh, Karnataka, Orissa, Punjab, Tamil Nadu and Uttar Pradesh. Somewhat less strictly the correlation is observable in the case of Karnataka in toto and slightly more strictly in that of Haryana, Orissa, Punjab, Rajasthan, Tamil Nadu and Uttar Pradesh, if we set col. 4 and col. 7 side by side.

Table 9.2 seeks to discover the correlation between the extent of poverty and extent of unemployment, both rural and urban in either case, and reaches the conclusion that so far as rural poverty and rural unemployment are concerned, they are wholly correlated in the case of Maharashtra and more or less correlated in the case of Assam, Gujarat, Haryana, Orissa and Rajasthan (compare col. 3 with col. 5). Likewise, urban poverty and urban unemployment are wholly correlated in the case of Maharashtra and more or less correlated in the case of Orissa, Rajasthan and Tamil Nadu (compare col. 4 with col. 6 of Table 9.2).

As far as the intensity of the poverty-cum-unemployment problem is concerned, higher ranks indicate greater intensity (see cols. 7 and 8 of Table 9.2). The problem is equally intense in both rural and urban areas of Karnataka, Kerala and Maharashtra, and more or less equally intense in both rural and urban areas in Bihar, Haryana, Madhya Pradesh , Orissa, Punjab, Rajasthan, Uttar Pradesh and West Bengal. The intensity of the problem in rural areas

TABLE 9.2: Some characteristics of the unemployment problem *vis-a-vis* the poverty problem

State	Percentage of Population to be provided Employment in 1983-84	Percentage of the Unemployed (Rural and Urban) to Total Population of Age 5 years and above (1983)		Percentage of Population below the Poverty Line (1983-84)		Rural Poverty: Rural Unemployment Ratio (1983)	Urban Poverty: Urban Unemployment Ratio (1983)	Per Capita Income (At 1970-71 Prices) in 1983-84 (Rs)
		Rural	Urban	Rural	Urban			
1	2	3	4	5	6	7	8	9
Andhra Pradesh	7.28	10.29(4)	6.49(9)	38.7(8) (33.3)	29.5(6) (25.4)	3.23(11)	3.91(4)	758(7)
Assam	4.70	2.38(14)	7.02(6)	23.8 (22.7)(13)	21.6(11) (18.9)	9.53(3)	2.64(10)	586(12)
Bihar	9.90	6.16(8)	4.76(12)	51.4(1) (44.3)(2)	37.0(2) (31.3)	7.19(5)	6.55(2)	454(15)
Gujarat	4.81	4.69(10)	6.17(8)	27.6(11) (23.8)	17.3(13) (14.9)	5.07(7)	2.41(13)	921(4)
Haryana	3.12	3.70(12)	5.05(11)	15.2(14) (13.1)	16.9(14) (14.6)	3.54(10)	2.89(8)	1087(2)
Karnataka	7.00	7.84(5)	8.75(4)	38.5(19) (33.2)	29.2(8) (25.2)	4.23(9)	2.88(9)	731(7)

Contd.

TABLE 9.2 *Contd.*

1	2	3	4	5	6	7	8	9
Kerala	5.31	19.95(12)	18.05(1)	26.1(2) (22.5)	30.1(5) (25.9)	1.12(15)	1.43(15)	608(11)
Madhya Pradesh	9.24	2.23(15)	4.2(13)	50.3(2) (43.3)	31.1(3) (26.8)	19.41(1)	6.32(3)	614(12)
Maharashtra	6.98	6.68(7)	6.00(10)	41.5(7) (35.7)	23.3(10) (20.1)	5.34(6)	3.35(6)	102(63)
Orissa	8.56	7.77(6)	7.77(5)	44.8(4) (38.6)	29.3(7) (25.2)	4.96(8)	3.24(7)	549(14)
Punjab	2.76	5.24(9)	6.89(7)	10.9(15) (9.4)	21.0(12) (18.1)	1.79(14)	2.62(11)	1487(1)
Rajasthan	6.86	4.01(11)	6.00(10)	36.6(11) (31.5)	26.1(9) (22.5)	7.85(4)	3.75(5)	716(8)
Tamil Nadu	7.92	20.55(1)	12.91(2)	44.1(5) (38.0)	30.9(4) (26.6)	1.84(13)	2.06(14)	657(9)
Uttar Pradesh	9.06	2.66(13)	4.36(12)	46.5(3) (40.0)	40.3(1) (34.7)	15.03(2)	7.95(1)	579(13)
West Bengal	7.84	11.95(3)	10.26(3)	43.8(6) (37.7)	26.1(9) (22.5)	3.15(12)	2.19(12)	822(5)
All-India	7.84	7.31	7.17	40.4 (34.8)	28.1 (24.2)	4.76	3.73	764

Source: (1) Rajya Sabha Proceedings as reported on March 12, 1987.
(2) N.S.S. 38th Round.
(3) National Accounts Statistics.

Note: Figures in brackets under other figures indicate percentages of population below the Poverty Line excluding 14 per cent below 5 years, whereas figures in brackets to the right of other figures indicate the ranks of the States.

appears to be in sharp contrast with the intensity of the problem in urban areas in Andhra Pradesh, Assam, Gujarat, Rajasthan and Tamil Nadu.

In Table 9.2 for estimating the rural poverty-rural unemployment ratio and the urban poverty-urban unemployment ratio in 1983-84/1983 we have used the figures after adjusting them for the child population under 5 years of age amounting to nearly 14 per cent of total population (see those in brackets below other figures in, Table 9.2).

Roughly, the rural poverty : rural unemployment ratio is generally high in the poorer States and low in the richer States. So far as the urban poverty : urban unemployment ratio is concerned, there does not appear to be any perceptible disparity between the richer and the poorer States, though the figures for Bihar, Madhya Pradesh and Uttar Pradesh are quite high.

In Table 9.2 the percentage of population out of the percentage of it below the Poverty Line to be provided with employment in 1983-84 so as to alleviate poverty is given by dividing the percentage of population below the Poverty Line by 5, assuming that one employed person would be supporting five persons, this number representing also the average size of the households. On a daily wage of Rs. 23.70 for 327 days in the year, to employ one person we need an annual outlay of Rs. 7,750. In the country 7.48 per cent of the population would need employment. Supposing the total Indian population in 1991 is 840 million, 62.83 million would have to be employed. This would call for an annual expenditure of Rs. 486,932 million.*

"Full Employment For All" would comprise three types of jobs: (1) Full-time employment for the year round, (2) Full-time employment for part of the year, (3) Part-time employment for the year round. It would require knowledge of what the unemployed and underemployed are spending per head at present, what their percentage is to the total working population, how much money would be needed per month to enable them and their families to maintain themselves, for how many days in the year they have to be employed and for how many hours per day.

---

* At the 1991 Census, India's total population was 843.93 million of them, 63.12 million were to be employed. This called for an annual expenditure of Rs. 489,179 million — an annual *Full Employment Budget*.

For the closing year of the 1960s Dandekar and Rath had estimated that about Rs. 800 crores worth of additional employment had to be created annually to enable the thirty per cent of the rural population, excluding the 10 per cent poorest (who would be given social assistance) to secure a level of living which was 25 per cent below what had been accepted as the nationally desirable minimum.

The V.P. Singh Government had estimated a total expenditure of Rs. 13;000 crores for executing the job guarantee scheme.

10

DEFINING UNEMPLOYMENT AND UNDEREMPLOYMENT IN THE INDIAN CONTEXT

In the developing countries at present the unemployment problem is being discussed in the context of (a) open and partial unemployment, particularly in urban areas, (b) low productivity of labour and seasonal unemployment in agriculture, (c) wide disparities in personal income distribution, and (d) significant disparities between rural and urban incomes.

Underutilisation of labour assumes any of the following five forms:

1. Open unemployment—voluntary and involuntary.
2. Underemployment.
3. Visibly active but underutilised sections of society.
4. Those whose intensity of effort is impaired due to malnutrition or ill-health.
5. The unproductive class(es).

All these forms are interdependent.

Unemployment

Unemployment connotes a state of being without fruitful work. In a sense, it is another name of lack of employment opportunities. It is another aspect of underdevelopment.

The NSS estimates use three concepts : (1) Usual status, (2) Weekly status and (3) Daily status. Usual status refers to relatively long-term, chronic unemployment. It is measured in terms of number of persons. It considers only principal activities. It is more relevant to those in search of regular employment, e.g., educated and skilled persons, who are unwilling to accept casual work. It is concentrated in the 15-29 years age-group. Its rates are high for urban areas and for women. It is available by educational levels and age-groups. The chronically unemployed seek work or are available for work but are unable to find even an hour's work. Weekly status represents seasonal unemployment. Daily status signifies part-time underemployment. It is a most inclusive and significant indicator of the magnitude of unemployment. Data on it are available by household population.

The Janata Government Draft Sixth Five-Year Plan (1978-83) which could last for just two years identified three facts of the unemployment problem, namely, (1) chronic unemployment and underemployment, (2) educated unemployment and (3) female unemployment.

The unemployment problem has a number of facets to it:

(1) Shortage of work opportunities, that is, inadequacy rather than non-existence of jobs.
(2) Underutilisation of manpower.
(3) Low labour productivity.
(4) Growing divergence between inflated attitudes and job expectations of the educated youth and the actual jobs available.
(5) The educated unemployed's aversion to manual work and work in rural areas and preference for white-collar, soft-handed jobs and jobs in urban areas.
(6) Much higher incidence of unemployment among the young.
(7) Very high proportions of the un- and underemployed that are unknown to any advanced country.
(8) Non-comparability of the figures of estimates of un- and underemployment owing principally to differences of reference period and coverage of the labour force.
(9) Dependence of the over-all rates of unemployment on shifts in the employment pattern.
(10) High correlation of the female unemployment rates with the male.

In March 1951, declared unemployment had not amounted to much. However, two conflicting estimates are available. One puts it at 2.5 million and another at 3.3 million. In April 1969, i.e., at the beginning of the Fourth Plan unemployment was estimated at 16 million. But another estimate was as high as 22 million. This is somewhat intriguing. However, the fact that the unemployment situation had assumed a disturbing proportion could not be denied. It was realised that increased investment since the First Plan had been accompanied by more unemployment and underemployment. Development had caused more pains than gains to the community.

In 1971 the Bhagwati Committee put the unemployment figure at 18.7 million. Another estimate for that year was as low as 3.61 million. In 1972-73 the usual "status unemployed" numbered 9.3 million, while all types of unemployment claimed 20.4 million persons. Of them, 10.1 million stood for the "weekly unemployed."

In 1977-78, 12.8 million man-years out of a total of 16.9 million man-years were without daily employment in rural areas. On a typical day 21 million persons were seeking work and were available for work but were unable to find it.

In 1978 the weekly unemployed were 11.2 million. In 1979 their number was much higher, 20.6 million.

The NSS estimates of unemployment in 1977-78 were based on "usual status", "weekly status", and "daily status", though they differed quite significantly. Under the first those who worked less than 14 hours a week were treated on a par with the unemployed. Table 10.1 depicts the State-wise position of chronic unemployment in 1977-78.

But the NSS data are criticised for being inadequate and on the low side.

In 1983 the number of chronically unemployed in India was 4.97 million.

Conceptual difficulties in estimating unemployment stand in the way of a proper appreciation of the problem and hinders the evolution of appropriate remedies.

In March 1985, the number of chronically unemployed was 13.89 million in the age-group five years and above based on the NSS 38th Round. For the age-group 15 years and above the corresponding figures were 13.25 million and 8.77 million. Lastly, for the age-group 15 to 19 years they were 13.10 million and 8.67 million respectively.

To conclude, extremely difficult as it was, measurement of the extent of unemployment was need for assessing the magnitude of the task involved.

TABLE 10.1: Daily status unemployment rates by States in 1977-78 (based on NSS, 32nd round)

State	Unemployment Rates	Share of State in All-India Unemployment	Share of State in All-India Labour Force
Andhra Pradesh	10.67	12.37	9.49
Assam	1.81	0.47	2.15
Bihar	8.01	8.71	8.91
Gujarat	6.24	3.80	4.99
Haryana	6.41	1.22	1.56
Himachal Pradesh	1.92	0.16	0.66
Jammu & Kashmir	5.70	0.52	0.74
Karnataka	9.36	6.61	5.78
Kerala	25.69	11.09	3.54
Madhya Pradesh	3.09	3.21	8.50
Maharashtra	7.99	10.16	10.41
Orissa	8.13	3.81	3.83
Punjab	4.82	1.34	2.27
Rajasthan	2.99	1.92	5.26
Tamil Nadu	15.59	16.48	8.65
Uttar Pradesh	4.12	7.01	13.92
West Bengal	10.15	9.08	7.33
All-India	8.18	100.00	100.00

Source: *Sixth Five-Year Plan.*

Note: (1) The data relate to all ages, five and above.

(2) Totals of figures under cols. 3 and 4 may not each add up to 100 due to incomplete data in respect of Union Territories.

(3) The NSS data for 1972-73 are based on the 27th Round, for 1977-78 on the 32nd Round, for 1983 on the 38th Round and for 1987-88 on the 43rd Round.

Underemployment

Unemployment and underemployment are interconnected phenomena in the Indian economy. Three explanations are offered to account for underemployment prevalent in India in varying degrees, in its different States viz., deficiency of aggregate demand, structural factors and inappropriate factor endowments.

Underemployment discloses three aspects: (1) Time (work for longer hours is wanted), (2) Intensity of work (which turns on the health and nutrition of the workers), and (3) Productivity (which is low because of missing components of production). The underemployed have neither the complementary resources nor the opportunities for increasing their very low incomes to levels comparable to those in modern manufacturing, commerce and services.

Underemployment (which is also called *disguised* or *concealed unemployment*) is pre-eminently a fact or manifestation of low productivity. Part of it is due to the production techniques that are used. Limited employment horizons have tended through the ages to strengthen the hold of underemployment-inducing production techniques on our economy. Given a surplus of labour supply, there has also been less pressure or incentive to maximise labour productivity. The joint family system which until recently looked after the aged, the infirm, the disabled, and the unemployed in the family had concealed the rigours of disguised unemployment in India. The spread of economic individualism and hence the weakening of the joint family system as a social security organisation has brought underemployment more and more into the open.

The incidence of chronic underemployment is widespread. It encompasses the bulk of population. It is not concentrated among a relatively limited number of workers. Long religious holidays, although they often merely underline underemployment conditions, result in a waste of both labour and resources. This is one instance. But instances can be multiplied without any difficulty.

Even most of the gainfully employed in India are underemployed. The rigidity of the Indian social structure has been a deterrent to the ideal utilisation of labour in this country. Over the ages underemployment has become interwoven into the social fabric of India.

Underemployment may be visible or invisible (that is, disguised). Those who work short hours are visibly underemployed. Those who scrape a living somehow or other and those who work below capacity are disguisedly or invisibly underemployed.

Potential underemployment occurs when productivity is abnormally low. To illustrate, labour productivity in Indian agriculture is nearly one-third of that in its non-agriculture.

Underemployment carries with it the possibility of fuller utilisation of the available resources. The purely physical possibility of raising output per unit of labour by using it more intensively is very great indeed.

Given a choice, the underemployed would perhaps prefer more

work in their present occupations rather than seek redressal in fresh opportunities outside. This fact has an important implication for the employment policy.

Such an irrational preference of the labourers for sticking to their existing uneconomic jobs being there, this has to be surmounted by means of economic incentives and disincentives.

Labour enters the production process from the supply side as well as the demand side. The focal point for both sides is higher productivity. Only by raising labour productivity can larger employment be provided at a rising level of real income. This is necessary for boosting the morale of the working population.

The additional work the underemployed would like to do is a more satisfactory and reliable measure of underemployment than the norm of man-years, for the former takes into account factors, such as income levels of the underemployed, the nature of additional work desired by them, the terms on which their labour would be forthcoming, etc., that are pertinent to the issue.

Labour productivity increases when education is improved, training is better and so is management. Part-time training for industrial workers and the apprenticeship training scheme for specified industries are steps in the same direction.

In recent years in our country the quantitative growth in labour force has gone on with qualitative improvement. The literacy level of labour force has grown at an average rate of about one per cent per annum.

In practice it is very difficult to assess the size of underemployment. The determinants of the extent of underemployment are: technology and institutional factors governing supply of farm labour and affecting labour mobility.

Unemployment and Underemployment in Agriculture

Agricultural employment is a fixed coefficient of land. Employment per rupee of agricultural output and per hectare of land turns on variables relating to irrigation, such as the number of pumpsets installed per hectare of land. Such employment rates are seen to be associated with a higher percentage of land operated in farms equal to or less than two hectares.

In India 15.8 per cent of the workforce is engaged in regular wage-employment. Of this 58.1 per cent is self-employed, mostly in agriculture.

The cultivators find full employment for 69 days in the busy season and for 58 days in the slack season. An agriculturist in an eastern State like Bihar finds work, on an average, for about 127 days in the year in the agricultural operations, though he can find some work for a few days in the non-agricultural operations as well. Per acre per day labour amounts to 50 man-days. Agricultural land per agriculturist comes to 2.53 acres. This gives 127 days' work per agriculturist in the year. Intensity of agricultural employment is greater in those States where density of population and pressure on the land are greater. Among those gainfully employed in agriculture the intensity of employment varies as between States from 46 to 91 per cent of the available man-days—with the result that there is a high incidence of un- and underemployment in them. The actual labour input in some other Asian countries is reported to be a multiple of that in Indian agriculture. For example, in Japan it is 3.5 times that in India.

Shifts in the employment pattern are attributable to a variety of factors: changing pattern of land-holding, pressure of population on the soil, and employee-employer relationship. To elaborate, with the spread of the Green Revolution the demand for immigrant agricultural labour in the peak operational seasons has increased. The additional employment created during these seasons has led to an upward pressure on wage rates and has meant a welcome addition to the incomes of landless labourers in the backward areas.

Irrigation tends to increase labour absorption per acre through multiple-cropping and mixed farming. Fertilizer applications per acre have been positively related with employment variables in commercialized agricultural regions.

Above all, however, agricultural employment is affected less by the phases of general economic activity than by seasonal conditions.

Agriculture is overflowing with people. Of the increase in the labour force, 89 to 90 per cent drifts into part-time employment in rural areas or in the informal segment of urban industry and trade or becomes chronically unemployed. Much of the employment in agriculture is at present of the nature of work-sharing, with the same output produced by more hands. The low, poverty-level incomes of the self-employed on the farms and household industries are due to overmanning and lack of know-how.

Rural underemployment is indistinguishable from rural unemployment, which ordinarily assumes the form of rural underemployment both observably and statistically partly owing to sub-division and partly owing to fragmentation of farm-holdings. In agriculture it has two aspects: (1) seasonal idleness of labour and (2) excessively high labour-land ratio. But chronic rural underemployment is twice as large in magnitude as seasonal unemployment in rural areas. This is so because excess labour stays on in agriculture for want of alternative employment.

Although the precise proportion of the rural surplus labour which is likely to migrate to urban areas cannot easily be determined, yet attempts have been made at computing it for the years of planning. A time-worked norm, i.e., 30.41 man-days as the standard labour input required per acre, is stated to yield dependable estimates of rural underemployment. In the NSS exercise the qualitative aspects of rural unemployment are given by the notion of current activity status used and unemployment rates are defined in the light of the disposition of labour time.

In 1951 B.N. Datar estimated that 4.8 million people were underemployed for nearly six years. Around one-third of the labour force occupied in agriculture, that is, about 14 to 18.7 million, was surplus. In 1960-61 rural underemployment was believed to be of the order of 15 to 18 million. Excluding those who worked over 28 hours a week, it amounted to 4.5 per cent of the total labour force in rural areas. After the lapse of almost three decades both unemployment and underemployment in rural areas would now be, on a rough and ready estimate, some 30 to 40 million persons.

The volume of rural underemployment is influenced by the available supply of farm labour and the amount of labour required by the farms. Increasing population adds to rural underemployment. In view of acute shortage of agricultural labour in peak seasons and possibility of agricultural output diminishing on withdrawal of the so-called surplus workforce, economists like Schultz flatly deny the existence of disguised unemployment in Indian agriculture or, alternatively, find it limited broadly to specific areas and specific periods in a year. According to these economists, much of the redundant labour manages to keep itself reasonably employed at the harvesting season. Most people in the villages work for themselves most of the time and exchange labour among themselves. The core of agricultural employment is the "alternative tyranny of rush work and idleness in constant succession".

Seasonal Unemployment in Agriculture

Seasonal unemployment of agriculturists and artisans works out to a figure of nearly 10 per cent of the population dependent on agriculture. Among the rural employed are included many who are part-time or seasonal workers. This inflates the figure and entails an illusion that rural unemployment is low.

The seasons of work and idleness in rural areas are not well marked. They are sporadic. There are seasonal variations in the demand for labour in agriculture. In other words, the load of work in agricultural production fluctuates seasonally and cannot be regularised even with the best of farm management. Idle mandays are often dispersed unevenly over the year.

The foregoing behoves the economists like Schultz who remark that until the production methods alter (for instance, until holdings are consolidated) the marginal product of the rural underemployed is positive, though small.

The above deduction is complicated by the known fact that a sizable proportion of the rural population is economically active in subsidiary occupations.

The proportion of workers (in the age-group 15 to 59 years) engaged in cultivation proper rose from 63 per cent in 1961 to 64.6 per cent in 1971. The 1971 Census revealed that employment on the small and marginal farms was nearly 87 per cent and 52.6 per cent of the total time of adult males and adult females respectively.

The Rural Labour Inquiry demonstrated that between 1964-65 and 1974-75 the number of days for which employment was available to rural workers had declined by 10 per cent for men, 7.5 per cent for women and 5 per cent for children. Similar was the fate of their average earnings.

In 1979-80 agriculture and activities allied to it provided employment equivalent to 80.33 million person years.

Between 1983 and 1987-88 whereas rural population grew by 7.4 per cent, rural employment grew by 4.9 per cent.

The rate of employment in agriculture declined from 2.3 per cent in 1972-73 to 1.2 per cent in 1983 and to 0.65 per cent in 1988.

In 1987-88 there were 51.9 per cent male workers and 24.5 per cent female workers in rural areas.

Differences as between the three concepts of employment (and hence unemployment) are the largest in respect of rural areas, implying that rural areas nurse the highest incidence of chronic unemployment.

A slight deterioration has taken place in the rural female unemployment situation. Self-employed households have both the lowest rates and shares of unemployment. Self-employment has declined in rural areas, notwithstanding the fillip given to it by the IRDP.* In consequence, the demand for casual work of uncertain duration has increased. The self-employed agriculturists and non-agriculturists in rural areas are severely underemployed. Most of the small farms (two hectares or less) are non-viable and their owners are not fully employed on them.

The landless agricultural labourers deserve special mention. Between the 1950s and the 1960s their number rose from 18 to 30 per cent of the rural population. In 1978 there were 53 million landless agricultural labourers in India. At present they number over 64.4 million—35.9 million males, 28.5 million females, being 26.3 per cent of the total workforce and 38.5 per cent of all agricultural workers, 46 per cent of them belonging to the Scheduled Castes and Scheduled Tribes.

Per 100 rural households we have today 60 households with land. Of these, 30 households are marginal farmers, 20 households are small farmers and 10 households have land five acres and above. Among the 40 landless households per 100 households in rural areas we have five artisan households, five small industrial households and 30 landless households.

Over the years the proportion of male workers in agriculture has fallen. On the other hand, the proportion of casual labourers has risen. Today it is 25.9 per cent of the workforce.

Wage-paid employment, which rests on a multiplicity of factors characterising the rural economy in different States, forms an integral part of total gainful employment, agricultural and non-agricultural, though in rural areas themselves, that an agricultural labourer has. Self-employment available to agricultural labourers is small because their own resources are precariously limited. Agricultural labourers and small landholders also undertake

---

* *Via* the Self-Employment Scheme for the Educated Unemployed Youth 1983-84 and the Self-Employment Programme for the Urban Poor launched on September 1, 1986.

secondary occupations to supplement their income.

The landless labourers are at present finding wage employment less and still less as permanent labourers and hence more and still more as casual labourers and are living more and still more as marginal farmers or village artisans. Most of the landless labourers are being driven to the status of casual and intermittent labourers. Shorn of an asset base they are today the most underprivileged and malnutritioned sections of our population. The share-croppers among them are still the victims of social oppression and economic bondage. The unemployment rates are the highest among the households belonging to them. Being one-fifth of the total population, they have 46.7 per cent of the total daily status unemployment concentrated among themselves. Seasonal unemployment hits them hardest. As a result, their incomes are not only low but also uncertain. Superadded to it are the frequent spells of unemployment. The minimum monthly salary was around Rs. 240 per agricultural labourer in 1985. But in the case of family farm labour the relevant price was not the wage rate but instead its real cost.

Table 10.2 belongs to the mid-1950s and the early 1960s, State-wise, for agricultural labourers. It discloses that the earnings of agricultural labourers had fallen between 1950-51 and 1956-57. Compared to the 1985 position, the rise in their earnings was seven times between 1950-51 and 1985 and nine times between 1956-57 and 1985. Between 1950-51 and 1956-57 the number of days of their unemployment had risen in the case of both casual and attached classes, though more than double in the case of the latter.

Percentage of the unemployed persons to total population was the highest in Kerala and the lowest in Rajasthan, according to the 1961 Census.

The tenor of the discussion above is that unemployment in the Western sense affects agriculture and commerce the least in India. Taking the busy and slack seasons jointly, cultivators are unemployed for 30 per cent and agricultural labourers for 35 to 40 per cent of the total number of man-days. Persons who remain unemployed even during the peak seasons in rural areas represent the hard core of the unemployed. The pockets of high incidence of unemployment vary over a period of years because the agricultural employment turns on the extent of rainfall and the extent of rainfall is not constant over the years in any particular region.

TABLE 10.2: Agricultural labour : Its income and unemployment during 1950-51 to 1956-57

State	Income Per Agricultural Worker (Rs.)		Wages Per Day (N.P.)		Unemployment of Male Agricultural Workers (No. of Days in a Year)				Percentage of Unemloyed Persons to Total Population Rural (Census 1961)
	1950-51	1956-57	1950-51	1956-57	1950-51		1956-57		
					Casual	Attached	Casual	Attached	
1	2	3	4	5	6	7	8	9	10
Andhra Pradesh	88.6	104.4	54	57	132	8	126	12	0.07
Assam	164.6	185.9	97	87	71	12	94	67	0.34
Bihar	118.9	88.3	190	154	85	21	120	119	0.10
Gujarat	—	—	—	—	—	—	—	—	0.13
Himachal Pradesh	—	—	—	—	—	—	—	—	0.08
Jammu & Kashmir	—	—	—	—	—	—	—	—	0.13

Contd.

TABLE 10.2 *Contd.*

1	2	3	4	5	6	7	8	9	10
Kerala	105.7	85.9	126	128	125	138	170	145	0.89
Madhya Pradesh	85.0	80.9	79	76	77	12	117	45	0.03
Maharashtra (Bombay)	94.3	101.0	126	91	137	12	113	38	0.13
(Karnataka) Mysore	88.2	108.0	90	84	98	38	118	79	0.05
Orissa	79.1	76.5	72	80	53	7	135	43	0.08
Punjab	140.0	131.8	184	198	155	41	150	32	0.22
Rajasthan	137.5	76.6	123	98	99	19	138	39	0.04
Tamil Nadu	88.3	92.0	97	84	107	24	162	68	0.17
Uttar Pradesh	131.2	80.9	118	92	48	11	124	69	0.06
West Bengal	152.0	153.9	166	143	93	17	113	47	0.58
All-India	104.0	99.4	109	96	90	19	128	68	

Source: (1) Government of India, *Reports* of the Agricultural Labour Enquiry Committees 1950-51 & 1956-57.
(2) K.N. Prasad, *The Economics of a Backward Region in a Backward Economy,* Vols. I & II, Scientific Book Agency, Calcutta-700001 1967-68.

To explain rural unemployment fully we should also look to the local conditions. Were we not to do this, we would not be in a position to appreciate the full potential of the manpower available in the various regions and would not arrive at accurate estimates of the unemployment from which the individual regions suffer. As for the latter, spells of both unemployment and overemployment that are inevitable in agriculture entail problem and difficulties. Very often the urgency of timely operations in agriculture necessitates spells of overemployment when farmers have got to work through day and night or till late at night at the time of sowing, harvesting, threshing, etc. This may be accompanied by spells of prolonged idleness and joblessness and the rural economy would be at a low ebb.

In the absence of other tests, predominance of agricultural workers in the working population and availability of a large number of people for work during the agricultural slack season have been taken as evidence of a high incidence of unemployment, as was done in respect of the Rural Works Programme launched in the earlier days of the current planning era. An important finding is that the larger the unit we take for our study, the more hazardous becomes the estimate of rural unemployment. In spite of this, in 1951 Datar estimated rural unemployment at 1.9 million persons of the working age group for the country as a whole. On the other hand, the First Plan put it at 30 per cent of the total working population (in rural areas). For 1961-62 the NSS 17th Round afforded a figure of 2.6 per cent of the rural labour force as unemployed. Another estimate put it at 5 per cent of it. For 1966-67 it was 2.7 per cent of it, according to the same source. In 1971, 1.73 million people were chronically unemployed in rural areas. For 1972-73 the figure was two million. In 1977-78, according to the NSS data, the percentage of the unemployed to the total rural population in the age-group five years and above was 4.45 for males and 2.45 for females. The extent was 16.9 million man-years without daily employment (in rural areas). In 1979, 16.5 million people, about 8.2 per cent of the total labour force, were unemployed in rural areas. In 1983, according to the same source, the percentage of the unemployed to the total rural population in the age-group five years and above was 4.79 for males and 2.52 for females. Between 1972-73 and 1983 the unemployed rural male force increased from 0.75 to 0.97 per cent and the unemployed rural female force increased from 0.18 to 0.32 per cent. Insofar as the blocks were devoid of the facility of registration the figures of rural unemployment and underemployment were underestimates.

Unemployment and Underemployment in Non-agriculture

The employment problem confronting a typical city of a developing country is, in part, the outcome of "a combination of structural imbalances" or maladjustments, viz., (a) between the growth of the rural economy and that of the urban economy, (b) between the output of the formal educational system and the job market the educated, and (c) between the urban jobs available and the aspirations of the existing labour force.

In a number of developing countries while the rate of growth of the urban labour force has been 4 to 7 per cent, the rate of growth of the urban employment opportunities has been 2.5 per cent. In consequence, there has been surplus labour in urban areas.

The volume of urban employment has remained correlated with the fluctuations in the state of business, transport and industry so much so that any swing in the latter consequent upon any swing in total investment, private and public, has got manifested in a corresponding swing in the former.

The figures on the live registers of employment exchanges were 3.37 lakhs in March, 1951, 5.22 lakhs in December 1953, and 7.05 lakhs in March 1956.

Table 10.3 shows that between 1963-64 and 1964-65 the percentage of the unemployed to total population in urban areas increased in all States, except Madhya Pradesh, Maharashtra, Karnataka, Rajasthan and Uttar Pradesh. The figures of urban unemployment, as given by the 1961 Census, were above those given by the NSS data either for both years or at least one year—1963-64 or 1964-65—in all States, except Kerala, Madhya Pradesh, Punjab, Rajasthan and Himachal Pradesh.

Between 1983 and 1987-88, whereas the urban population grew by 18.7 per cent, urban employment grew by 16.1 per cent. In certain industries, e.g., chemical and engineering, value (gross) added rose at very high rates, which stimulated employment growth.

In 1987-88 there were in urban areas 49.69 per cent male workers and 11.8 per cent female workers in principal occupations and 53.9 per cent male workers and 32.3 per cent female workers in subsidiary occupations. In general, male workers numbered 50.6 per cent and female workers 15.2 per cent in these areas.

TABLE 10.3: Agricultural labour : Its income and unemployment during 1950-51 to 1956-57

State	Percentage of unemployed persons to total population		
	Urban: Census 1961	Urban: NSS 1963-64	Urban: NSS 1964-65
1	2	3	4
Andhra Pradesh	0.60	0.52	0.45
Assam	0.55	0.38	0.42
Bihar	0.77	—	
Gujarat	0.88	—	0.31
Himachal Pradesh	0.50	0.25	—
Jammu & Kashmir	0.67	0.20	0.30
Kerala	1.76	1.67	1.94
Madhya Pradesh	0.37	0.40	0.37
Tamil Nadu	1.13	0.86	1.22
Maharashtra	1.27	0.66	0.53
Mysore(Karnataka)	0.68	0.53	0.44
Orissa	0.54	0.36	0.44
Punjab	0.68	0.21	0.77
Rajasthan	0.34	0.42	0.40
Uttar Pradesh	0.51	0.36	0.26
West Bengal	2.62	0.76	0.92

Source: (1) Directorate of Employment & Training, *Employment Review*.
(2) Census Report for 1961 data.
(3) NSS data for the rest.

Over the years the proportion of regular salaried wage employment for the urban males has come down, whereas that of self-employment has gone up. Earnings of the self-employed have continued to be low and among the urban poor the self-employed have been predominant. The swelling ranks of the lowest strata of urban population, often referred to as the "disinherited proletariat, or the culture of poverty", have been their chief indication.

The urban unemployment problem boils down largely to "an incompatibility between the rapid growth of both urban population and urban labour force and the inadequate growth of productive employment opportunities". The disequilibrium in the urban job supply and demand situation is termed "urban over-employment". Urban unemployment has grown dramatically with growing urbanisation. By and large, the typical urban unemployed is the unmarried dependant.

The current rate of urban unemployment is estimated at 10 to 20 per cent of the urban labour force. Urban unemployment has been fuelled partly by the influx of rural migrants. Agriculture has been spinning off its excess population into large towns and cities. Part of urban unemployment is a spill-over or over-flow from rural areas.

Many consider unemployment in a developing country like India as an urban phenomenon and a phenomenon of the middle class.

As a rule, a big city is caught up in the unemployment trap (or the urban unemployment trap). Creation of additional modern sector jobs at higher wages through increased aggregate demand attracts mass additional migrants from rural areas. Every urban job created induces three or four new job seekers to migrate from the countryside. Urban unemployment instead of falling rises. In consequence, today migration of surplus labour to urban areas is not considered a beneficent process capable of lowering the excessive burden of population on land but rather a process that exacerbates existing urban unemployment.

Urban unemployment is not a viable option of those who have to work irregularly or for very little return in the urban informal sector, the tertiary sector and therefore the rate of urban unemployment cannot accurately be estimated — it is often prone to be an underestimate. The presence of employment opportunities is usually a far greater incentive to migration than wage differentials and there is no law that high wages and new job opportunities would be intimately correlated. The probability of obtaining an urban job is inversely related to the urban unemployment rate, as Todaro concludes.

As a matter of fact, rural and urban unemployment together constitute an organic problem. The higher rates of urban unemployment are the inevitable outcomes of the serious imbalance of economic opportunities between rural and urban areas of most underdeveloped countries. A typical migrant cannot expect to secure a high-paid urban job immediately. It is much more likely that on entering the urban labour market many migrants would either become totally unemployed or would seek casual and part-time employment as vendors, hawkers, repairmen and itinerant day — labourers in the urban traditional or informal sector where ease of entry, small-scale operation and relatively competitive price and wage determination prevails, according to Todaro. Consequently, the migrant must balance the probabilities and risks of being unemployed or underemployed for a considerable period of time against the positive urban-rural real income differential. Though less now that it used to be the case, industrial workers are in some parts of India farmers by choice and factory employees by necessity. Having been pushed rather than pulled, they are no better than fugitives from rural areas.

In 1951 much of Indian unemployment was concentrated in urban areas. Around that time un- and underemployment in non-agricultural occupations accounted for one-fourth of the total agricultural population. According to Datar, 2.5 to 3.0 million persons of the working age were unemployed in urban areas. The ratio of urban unemployment to the urban labour force was 12.0. Bhardwaj's estimate was 2.5 million and his ratio was 11.4. A third estimate was 3.3 million. Prasad's estimate for 1952 was 0.42 million. This was purely industrial unemployment. In 1954 urban unemployment was 2.24 to 2.80 million. Set off against this was frictional unemployment estimated at 0.3 million. The NSS 17th Round for 1960-61 disclosed that 8 per cent of the urban labour force of 15 to 24 years of age and 32 per cent of the urban labour force of age 15 years and above were unemployed. In 1961-62 urban unemployment was 3 per cent of the total urban labour force. In 1966-67 it was 1.6 per cent. In 1971, 1.88 million were chronically unemployed in urban areas. In 1972-73 the number was 2.1 million. In 1977-78 the percentage of the unemployed to the total urban population in the age-group 5 years and above was 5.35 for males and 2.11 for females, according to the NSS data. In 1979, 4.1 million persons, that is, nearly 9 per cent of the total labour force, were unemployed in urban areas. Another estimate for the closing years of the 1970s was 8 to 9 per cent. The NSS findings for 1983 were 5.45 per cent for males and 1.72 per cent for females as proportion to total urban population in the age-group 5 years and above. Between 1972-73 and 1983 the percentage of the unemployed urban labour had increased from 2.87 to 3.11 in the case of males and from 1.00 to 1.05 in the case of females. In 1985, 6.1 million were unemployed, according to the NSS 32nd Round and 4.2 million, according to the NSS 38th Round. In sum, the existing measured rates of urban unemployment are much higher than they were in the past.

Generalising, the incidence of usual status unemployment is

higher in urban, compared to rural, areas and among women than men. Ever since the 1960s recorded unemployment in urban areas has been higher than that in rural areas. This is a situation peculiar to our country. Even during the 1960s the rate of open' urban unemployment was high. But the rate of urban unemployment has been just the visible aspect of the unemployment problem — the tip of an enormous iceberg. This is true of all age-groups owing to differences in the structure of activities, particularly differences in the importance of household and non-household enterprises as between rural and urban areas.

In recent years (say, the 1980s) the percentage of those seeking work on a regular monthly salary has tapered off in urban areas. Also has diminished the proportion of urban females in self-employment in non-agriculture. On the contrary, shares of both sexes in casual labour in non-agriculture in urban areas have risen. The backlog of the unemployed in urban areas has acted as a brake over urban-ward rural migration. To the extent that the additional demand for labour in urban areas has been met by the pool of surplus labour in them, the pace of rural-urban migration has slowed down.

The urban unemployed, comprising the overflow of people from rural areas, lie at the very root of social unrest and individual anomie. The incidence of poverty is increasing in urban areas and decreasing in rural areas.

When urban underemployment is coupled with urban unemployment, the problem becomes all the more alarming. It is in 15 to 24 years age-group that urban underemployment has its maximum concentration.

As for the estimate of urban underemployment, Datar's study gave a figure of 2.1 million for 1951 and the average duration of underemployment was stated to be six months. In 1961-62 urban underemployment was 3.2 to 6.2 per cent of the total urban labour force, depending on whether those who worked over 28 hours per week were excluded or included. In 1972-73 total underemployment, rural as well as urban, was estimated at 7 million. At present the coverage of urban underemployment is said to be nearly 30 per cent of the aggregate urban population.

Perceptibly our towns share with our villages a good measure of the distress entailed by underemployment. The incidence of underemployment and hence underutilization of manpower is highest in the tertiary sector.

11

THE BALANCE-SHEET OF DEMAND AND SUPPLY OF LABOUR-FORCE IN INDIA

The number of people looking for employment turns primarily on the size and age composition of the population of a country. The labour-force estimates take into consideration usual status participation rates. In 1981 the over-all work participation rate of women as a percentage of all women in India was 24 for rural and 11 for urban areas. Those who would enter the labour force over the next 15 years have already been born and the size of the labour force two decades hence would be largely determined by the current fertility rates. The proportion of new labour force entrants unable to find regular jobs is expressed by the marginal unemployment rate.

A triad of explosions — population explosion from 361 million in 1951 to 844 million in 1991, urbanisation explosion from 63 million in urban areas in 1951 to 160 million in 1981 and education explosion from 23.93 million students in 1950-51 to 140.02 million students in 1986-87 — has engineered a situation in which the Indian urban labour force has continued to grow at a very fast rate. One consequence of a high birth rate is that India has a young population of a very high percentage those in age-groups 20-29 were 16.2 per cent of total population in 1981. The age-group 15-19 claimed 9.6 per cent.

In 1951 the labour force was estimated at 145 million. In 1991 it was around 250 million. The current rate of growth of labour force is between 2.2 and 2.5 per cent per annum, while that of population growth is around 2.22 (1971-81)/2.11 (1981-91) per cent per annum. The annual addition to population is about 12 million and to the labour force 4 to 5 million. Two-thirds of the annual addition to total population is in rural areas, and only one-third in urban. During 1990-97, 37 million and during 1995-2000, 41 million are expected to join the labour force.

There is an area of uncertainty in the labour force supply projections in an economy of the Indian type. The complications come from inclusion of children, conceptual differences and area of uncertainty mentioned above. Despite the law to the contrary, child labour prevails in many parts of India, and predominates in certain parts owing to the grinding poverty of the people. But as child education progresses, a decline in the backlog of children counted as unemployed and hence in the net addition to the labour force in age-groups below 15 years occurs. Due to the lack of old age security people continue to work beyond the age of retirement.

Table 11.1 sums up the information on increases in the labour force during the Plan period.

TABLE 11.1: Increase in the labour force

(In million)

Period	Number	Rate (Per cent per annum)
Early 1950s	1.8	—
Mid - 1950s	2.0	—
Early 1960s	3.4	—
1974-79	3.6 to 3.8	—
1980-85	3.9 to 4/6.8	2.5
1960-85	3.2	—
1979-80 to 1994-95	7.2	2.9
1985-90	3.6	—
1985-95	—	2.3
1990-2000	7.3	—

Source: *Seventh Five-Year Plan* (mainly); also other Plans.

Note: On an average, the labour force is assumed to be growing at the rate of 2.4 per cent per annum, which is in excess of the growth rate of population at around 2.35 per cent per annum during 1981-91. The population growth rate was expected at 1.79 per cent per annum during 1981-86 and at 1.63 per cent per annum during 1986-96. The 1991 Census has already demonstrated that these were wrong assumptions.

In 1980, the number of young persons of the age-group 15-29 was nearly 172 million. By 2000 A.D. this was expected to short up to 287 million. Of the 115 million, the difference, nearly half have already entered the labour market.

The Indian plan framers have been expressing growth in terms of both output and employment, although it is quite clear in the context that they have put the emphasis on the former. The output: employment macro-model focuses on the relationship between capital accumulation, industrial output growth and employment generation. Rate of growth of employment equals rate of growth in output minus rate of growth in labour productivity. If in an economy output grows at the rate of 5.5 per cent per annum and employment grows at the rate of three per cent per annum, then the difference of 2.5 per cent per annum is due to the rise in labour productivity.

The ratio of the rate of output growth to the rate of employment growth is the income equivalent of employment growth. Employment in any activity is related as a non-linear function of either gross output or value added but in the case of agriculture it is related as a fixed coefficient of land, the major input.

What effect a structural change in output will have on employment would depend upon the degree and direction of change in each input-coefficient as well as on the corresponding employment potential of each sector. The consumer goods sector is capable of recording an employment growth rate which is higher than its output growth rate.

Increase in employment has taken place in all sectors of the economy since 1951, particularly in recent years. The number of those working on their own has gone up in both the professions and the unorganised sector. The number of those working on daily wages/salaries in the private and public sectors has also gone up substantially.

The maximum rate of growth of employment during the Plan period so far has been five per cent per annum. This was also the position during the Third Plan. The minimum rate of growth of employment at 0.7 per cent per annum prevailed during 1980-88. The rate was 0.8 per cent for 1967-68, 0.9 per cent for 1968-69, 2.82 per cent for 1972-73, 1.51 per cent for 1981 and 0.95 per cent for 1987-88. This gave a rate of 0.7 per cent per annum during 1980-88, 1.55 per cent per annum during the 1980s, 2.2 per cent per annum during the Seventh Plan and three per cent per annum during the Eighth Plan.

Between 1972-73 and 1987-88 the total size of employment grew by around 86 million. The growth rate of employment during 1983 and 1987-88 was 1.55 per cent per year. In 1979-80 total employment amounted to 151.11 million person years. The growth rate of the economy during the Seventh Plan was four per cent per annum and during the Eighth Plan it was five per cent per annum, as against the projected growth rate of 5.6 per cent per annum. During the 1980s the rate was five per cent per annum. In 1989 it was five per cent; and in 1990, 4.5 per cent. Employment elasticity was 0.36 per cent during the Seventh Plan and 0.55 per cent during the Eighth Plan. Growth rate of the economy required during the 1980s to absorb the newcomers to the labour market was 2.2 per cent per annum.

An output growth of one per cent per annum resulted in an employment increase of zero per cent in Punjab, 0.07 per cent in Haryana and 0.19 per cent in Uttar Pradesh. Increases were higher in other States like Andhra Pradesh, Tamil Nadu, West Bengal, Bihar and Orissa.

Four bands compose the employment spectrum: (1) Countable jobs in public services and public enterprises, (2) Countable jobs in large industries in the private sector, (3) Less dependably calculated jobs in cottage and small-scale industries, coming mostly under self-employment and (4) Jobs in commerce, services, etc., that result largely from the employment multiplier effects under (1) to (3)—the employment potential of this band being difficult to calculate.

During the 1980s, as compared to the 1970s, there was a significant drop in the growth of agricultural employment and of both rural and urban employment. The non-agricultural sector employment grew at the rate of 3.23 per cent per annum during the period 1961-82.

Equating the factory or the registered segment of the industrial sector with the organised sector of industry, we find that the organised sector absorbed only a small fraction of the total workforce throughout the Plan period. Factory employment grew at the compound rate of 1.7 per cent per annum during the First Plan; 3.9 per cent per annum during the Second Plan; and 4.7 per cent per annum during the Third Plan. Over the period 1951-51 to 1970-71 employment in the organised sector grew at the rate of five per cent per annum. Total factory employment had amounted to 2.4 million in 1951. In 1970 the figure was 4.7 million. In 1951 the number of workers engaged in mines and factories was 3.46 million. In 1984 the figure was 8.5 million. (In 1979-80 mining alone provided employment equivalent to 0.72 million person years.) Between 1961 and 1976 investment in the modern factory sector rose by 139 per cent and output by 161 per cent, but employment could rise only by 71 per cent. As a result, while employment per unit of gross output decreased by 34 per cent, employment per unit of capital decreased by 28 per cent. The rate of growth of factory employment was 2.50 per cent per annum during 1950-63 and 2.10 per cent per annum during 1963-76. Employment in the organised sector increased from 16.32 million in 1967 to 17.45 million in 1971. At the end of 1981 the total industrial labour force was 6 million. At the end of March, 1976, employment in the organised sector was 20.21 million. At the end of June, 1976, it was 20.14 million.

While over the period 1951-1969 factory production increased at an annual compound rate of 7 per cent, employment increased at a rate less than 3 per cent per annum. Average daily employment in factories was 5.08 million in 1971 and 7.69 million in 1985. The total number of employees in the organised sector was nearly 24.6 million in March, 1985. During the period 1972-73 to 1985-86 the organised sector contributed only nearly 6 million employees per year, on an average. In 1960-61, 12.1 million people and in 1987-88, 25.8 million people found employment in this sector. Between these two years the increase was about twice. During 1980-88 the rate of growth of the organised sector (compound) came to an average of 1.8 per cent per annum. The annual growth rate of organised sector employment was highest at 6 per cent per annum during the Third Plan and lowest at 0.9 per cent per annum (being the average of the three Annual Plans) during 1966-69. During the Fourth Plan the organised sector grew at around 3 per cent per year. At present only about 12 per cent of the increase in the labour force is absorbed in the organised sector. The year-to-year increase in the organised sector employment averaged around 0.8 million (or, say, one million at most). This meant employment wholly for the educated and skilled; still many of them remained without employment.

We now shift our attention to a segment of the organised sector, namely, the manufacturing segment, which also combines segments of the unorganised industrial sector. That is to say, the manufacturing segment covers a much wider field than the organised sector. Unsure about the nature of the data, whether they include the figures relating to the unorganised counterpart of the manufacturing segment or not, we attempt below a chronological picture of the growth of the manufacturing segment.

During 1961-71 the percentage of population employed in manufacturing had fallen from 29 to 25, and in so far as urban employment was influenced by employment in manufacturing, urban employment had also suffered a setback during the period. The annual growth rate of employment in manufacturing was approximately four per cent during the 1970s, and two per cent during the 1980s and of this two per cent, the bulk was in the unorganized segment. The employment: output ratio in the manufacturing industry came down from 1.00 in 1970 to 0.68 in 1982. In 1979-80, 22.01 million people were employed in manufacturing. In a factory employing more than 100 workers, the employment : output ratio was 0.15. The ratio was high in rural and small-scale industries.

During the Plan period village industries producing handloom cloth, ghani oil, flour, rice and *khadi* received an impetus from the increased purchasing power of the rural workers employed in the employment programmes. The handloom industry remained the largest single cottage/village industry in terms of employment. Over 7.5 million people were engaged in it. They had in it full-time work. *Khadi* production provided ordinarily part-time employment. Other village industries, including handicrafts, reduced underemployment in agriculture.

In India the extreme expansion of the services/tertiary sector has occurred long before the accomplishment of either the agricultural or the industrial revoluation in the country. The increase in the percentage of workers employed in trade and commerce has been marginal, no doubt, but in other fields the progress has been impressive, often startling.

In 1951, 26.1 million workers were engaged in the tertiary sector. In 1971 their number was 32.3 million. In 1961, 2.1 million people were occupied in shops, commercial establishments and restaurants. In 1983 the number had shot up to 4.1 million. During the 1980s employment growth in transport, storage and communications slowed down sharply, uncompensated by the spurt in construction employment. The demand for the services of doctors, engineers, lawyers, and other professionals had risen faster than income per head owing to the Bandwagon Effect: income-elasticity of the demand for services is very high and their demand curve rises like a rocket.

A closer analysis would suggest that the urban-based modern sector in India has failed to act as the engine of growth and shorten the transition period. The hope of the planners in the formative period of planning that two-thirds of the increase in the labour force would be absorbed outside the agricultural sector has not been fulfilled. In a period of five years the organised sector has generated, on an average, additional employment for only 4 to 5 million persons. During the years of fastest growth, i.e., the 1960s, manufacturing output growth could exceed employment growth by a factor of one to three or four only.

At its existing level of development, the Indian economy is well poised to provide more employment than before. The first ever exception to the Hindu Rate of Growth (at three to four per cent) appeared during the 1980s when the growth rate worked out at nearly five per cent. It is stipulated now that only if employment in non-agriculture expanded at the rate of six per cent per annum could increasing population in our country be absorbed in employment.

And the economy has to grow at the rate of 10.5 per cent per annum and employment in agriculture and non-agriculture at that of 4.3 per cent per annum if full employment is to be attained in the Eighth Plan. Another calculation predicts creation of 78 million jobs during the Eighth Plan at three per cent per annum growth rate of employment opportunities and hence full employment for all in the economy.

Today the modern industrial sector is sought after not so much for its direct effect on employment as for its indirect effect on it.

The V.P. Singh Government was confident of creating three million additional jobs during the Eighth Plan in the self-employment occupations, micro-enterprises, computer profession, etc. Self-employment for 0.8 million was envisaged to be generated for the educated unemployed in gas agencies, fertilizer agencies, etc.

Tables 11.2 and 11.3 refer to organised registered sector employment—one for 1950-52 and the other for 1980. The former alludes to employment of a varied nature, and contained in it are enterprises and other sources of employment. The latter alludes to employment in enterprises that may fall under the "shops and commercial establishments" column of the former. The two tables do not lend themselves to any comparison. In addition to the difference of coverage of units, the reorganisation of the States in 1956 and the inadequacy of data for 1950-52 render any such attempt infructuous.

Table 11.2 reveals that during 1950-52 the modern sector had a prominent place in Maharashtra, West Bengal and Tamil Nadu from the employment point of view but was least important from the same point of view in Orissa and Punjab. Plantations provided maximum employment in Assam, West Bengal and Tamil Nadu. Maharashtra and Tamil Nadu had good volumes of employment in shops and

TABLE 11.2: Percentage shares of states in employment

State	Factories	Plantations		Shops & Commercial Establishments		Municipalities Number of Persons Employed, September 1952	State Transport Services Number of Employees, 1951	State Public Works Number of Employees, 1952
	Average Daily Number of Workers 1951	Number of all Estates 1950	Average Daily Number of Workers 1950	Number of all Establishments 1951	Workers Employed in All Establishments 1951			
1	2	3	4	5	6	7	8	9
Andhra Pradesh (Hyderabad)	—	—	—	—	—	1.98	13.77	31.22
Assam	2.56	3.78	41.13	0.74	0.78	0.65	4.62	—
Bihar	7.33	Neg.	Neg.	—	—	4.32	2.79 (1952)	—
Himachal Pradesh	—	1.24	0.01	—	—	0.02	4.00 (1952)	1.68
Karnataka (Mysore)	—	16.79	5.79	2.59	3.87	8.26	8.74 (1952)	0.84

Contd.

TABLE 11.2 *(Contd.)*

1	2	3	4	5	6	7	8	9
Kerala (Travancore-Cochin)	—	34.03	8.46	—	—	—	4.40	—
Madhya Pradesh	4.37	—	—	1.22	3.12	37.17	5.56	—
Maharashtra (Bombay)	30.24	—	—	38.77	54.63	16.06	28.19 (1950)	—
Orissa	0.67	Neg.	Neg.	—	—	—	2.4 (1952)	23.20
Punjab	1.89	9.88	0.66	11.29	3.66	3.16	5.07	2.10
Rajasthan	—	—	—	-	—	—	12.05	—
Tamil Nadu (Madras)	16.44	15.82	13.89	38.16	29.40	15.26	12.05	—
Uttar Pradesh	7.96	Neg.	Neg.	—	—	—	32.91	—
West Bengal	25.82	1.21	26.27	—	—	—	8.22	—
All-India	100.0	100.0	100.0	100.0	100.0	100.0	100.0	100.0

Source: *Statistical Abstract of India*, 1952-53.

establishments. Madhya Pradesh, Tamil Nadu and Maharashtra were appreciably represented in employment provided by municipalities. State transport services claimed good percentages in Maharashtra, Uttar Pradesh, Tamil Nadu, Rajasthan and Andhra Pradesh. In respect of employment in state public works in Andhra Pradesh and Orissa had impressive percentages.

Table 11.3 brings out that in 1980 enterprises, agricultural and non-agricultural, gave employment in high proportions in Maharashtra, Uttar Pradesh and West Bengal, whereas Punjab, Haryana and Orissa obtained very low representations from the employment standpoint. So far as agricultural enterprises are concerned, employment generation was on the high side in Gujarat, Karnataka, Rajasthan, Tamil Nadu and Andhra Pradesh and on the low side in Haryana, West Bengal, Bihar and Maharashtra. Finally, in creating employment the non-agricultural enterprises had a lead in Punjab, Haryana and Uttar Pradesh and were backbenchers in no State at all.

In a mixed economy like the Indian economy the volume of employment is a function, in the main, of the volume of public sector plan outlay but, in general, public sector employment accounts for only a small fraction of the aggregate volume of employment in the economy. Another feature of a mixed economy such as the Indian is the predominance of self-employment. At present about 72 per cent of the working force is in self-employment and 11 per cent of it is in wage-employment. The family workers in India have only a nominal attachment to the labour market. Broadly, they neither sell work nor are available for outside work. They work in their household activities without receiving or asking for any wages. Employment opportunities are concentrated in the families which are self-employed. Capitalist farmers, businessmen, manufacturers, traders, operators of the private means of transport, etc., and families relating to them belong to the new class of the rich—they have appropriated a good share of the development gains. Growth of self-employment at the expense of wage-employment has, to an extent, camouflaged the shortcomings and lapses of our planning process.

Tables 11.4 and 11.5 present State-wise figures of employment per lakh of population in March, 1987, in private and public sectors. Table 11.4 illustrates that Himachal Pradesh is the most employed State, while Bihar is the least employed State. In public sector employment Himachal Pradesh is the first and Uttar Pradesh the

TABLE 11.3: Sectoral distribution of registered employment

State	Percentage Share in Total Number of Enterprises (Agricultural and Non-agricultural) in 1980	Number of Agricultural Enterprises as Percentage of Total Number of Enterprises (1980)	Number of Non-agricultural Enterprises as Percentage of Total Number of Enterprises (1980)	Percentage Share in Total employment in All Enterprises (Agricultural and Non-agricultural) in 1980	Employment in Agricultural Enterprises as Percentage of Total Employ- in All Enterprises (1980)	Employment in Non-agricultural Enterprises as Percentage of Total Employment in All Enterprises (1980)
	2	3	4	5	6	7
Andhra Pradesh	9.26	8.75	91.25	8.89	7.57	92.43
Assam	NA	NA	NA	NA	NA	NA
Bihar	5.62	4.88	95.12	5.04	3.37	96.63
Gujarat	6.38	22.84	77.16	6.83	13.21	86.79
Haryana	1.73	3.79	96.21	1.87	2.49	97.51
Himachal Pradesh	0.75	4.98	95.02	0.65	4.18	95.82
Jammu & Kashmir	1.19	6.94	93.06	0.99	5.96	94.04
Karnataka	6.98	11.37	88.63	6.42	11.63	88.37
Kerala	5.04	5.85	94.15	4.90	3.53	96.47
Madhya Pradesh	6.66	6.41	93.59	5.64	5.73	94.27
Maharashtra	10.62	7.64	92.36	13.13	3.76	96.24
Orissa	4.37	6.54	93.46	3.70	4.79	95.21
Punjab	2.26	3.63	96.37	2.48	2.14	97.86
Rajasthan	5.26	11.24	88.76	4.31	7.63	92.37
Tamil Nadu	9.51	6.40	93.60	9.56	7.63	95.88
Uttar Pradesh	11.80	4.13	95.87	10.90	4.12	97.00
West Bengal	9.30	8.38	91.62	10.15	3.00	94.77
All-India	100.00	8.09	91.91	100.00	5.53	94.47

Source: 1. *Statistical Abstract of India* 1985.
2. Bihar State Planning Board, *Selected Plan Statistics*, 1986.

last. In private sector employment Assam tops the list and Himachal Pradesh is at the bottom. Table 11.5 divides the public sector into three classes-Central Government establishments, State Government establishments, and Quasi-Government establishments, both Central and State. It further divides the private sector into local bodies, large units and small units. Thereafter, it gives the percentage shares of the States in number of units as well as total employment in each division. All States have been ranked with regard to each component. In the grand total of units in both private and public sectors Maharashtra comes first and Himachal Pradesh last. The reference year is 1981-82. In the private sector are included only such concerns/establishments as employ 10 or more workers. The larger units are those employing 25 or more workers and the small, 10 to 24 workers.

TABLE 11.4: Employment per lakh of population as on March end 1987

State	Public Sector	(2) as per cent of (6)	Private Sector	(4) as per cent of (6)	Total
1	2	3	4	5	6
Andhra Pradesh	2418.5(11)	78(7)	660.1(10)	22(9)	3078.6(11)
Assam	2270.0(13)	48(15)	2436.5(1)	52(1)	4675.5(3)
Bihar	1909.5(14)	83(4)	369.9(16)	17(12)	2279.4(16)
Gujarat	2585.8(7)	56(13)	1950.9(4)	44(3)	4536.7(5)
Haryana	2958.3(5)	67(10)	1491.1(6)	33(6)	4449.4(7)
Himachal Pradesh	6285.9(1)	92(1)	516.2(12)	8(15)	6802.1(1)
Karnataka	2555.7(8)	7(19)	1009.8(9)	29(1)	3565.5(10)
Kerala	2270.0(13)	52(14)	2023.7(3)	48(2)	4293.7(9)
Madhya Pradesh	2537.4(9)	84(3)	416.3(14)	16(13)	2953.7(13)
Maharashtra	3475.6(2)	61(2)	2146.9(2)	39(4)	5622.5(2)
Orissa	2281.0(12)	86(2)	372.4(15)	14(14)	2653.4(14)
Punjab	3216.4(3)	72(8)	1182.3(8)	28(8)	4398.7(8)
Rajasthan	2461.4(10)	80(5)	572.6(11)	20(11)	3064.0(12)
Tamil Nadu	3046.0(4)	67(10)	1426.0(7)	33(6)	4472.0(6)
Uttar Pradesh	1893.0(15)	79(6)	481.5(13)	21(10)	2374.5(15)
West Bengal	2926.8(6)	63(11)	1689.0(5)	37(5)	4615.8(4)

Source: U.P. State Planning Institute, *Inter-State Disparities*, April, 1990.
Note: Figures in brackets indicate the ranks of the States.

TABLE 11.5: Estimated employment in the private and public sectors (1981-82)

State	Percentage Distribution							
	Public Sector				Private Sector			Grand Total
	Central Government Establishments	State Government Eastablishments	Quasi-Government Establishments (including 14 Nationalized Banks)		Local Bodies	Large Units	Small Units	
			Central	State				
1	2	3	4	5	6	7	8	9
Andhra Pradesh	7.00(5)	5.46(8)	4.99(8)	11.59(2)	11.17(4)	4.40(9)	6.25(7)	6.34(6)
Assam	2.44(11)	3.52(14)	1.46(14)	2.32(14)	0.58(15)	6.91(6)	1.13(15)	3.65(12)
Bihar	5.27(7)	6.11(5)	16.96(2)	3.88(11)	6.88(5)	4.12(10)	4.47(8)	6.53(5)
Gujarat	4.07(9)	3.19(13)	3.69(9)	4.87(8)	11.41(3)	8.70(3)	7.90(5)	5.97(8)
Haryana	0.88(15)	3.55(15)	0.96(15)	3.07(13)	0.71(14)	2.55(12)	2.67(12)	2.26(15)
Himachal Pradesh	0.73(17)	2.57(16)	0.29(16)	1.52(16)	0.20(17)	0.14(16)	0.25(16)	0.97(16)
Jammu & Kashmir	0.81(16)	1.89(17)	0.21(17)	0.30(17)	0.30(16)	0.10(17)	0.14(17)	0.69(17)
Karnataka	3.77(10)	6.03(7)	6.04(5)	6.94(6)	2.08(10)	4.44(8)	6.89(6)	5.02(9)
Kerala	2.28(12)	4.15(12)	2.35(11)	5.83(7)	1.14(12)	6.07(7)	13.84(2)	4.44(10)
Madhya Pradesh	5.91(6)	9.91(2)	9.87(4)	4.52(9)	2.43(9)	2.79(11)	2.77(11)	5.94(7)
Maharashtra	15.07(1)	7.14(4)	11.81(3)	10.23(4)	24.79(1)	19.93(1)	8.62(4)	14.31(1)
Orissa	1.59(14)	5.16(10)	2.84(10)	2.29(15)	0.76(13)	1.08(15)	1.89(14)	2.48(14)
Punjab	1.95(13)	4.52(11)	1.90(12)	3.82(12)	1.43(11)	2.21(14)	3.22(10)	2.79(13)
Rajasthan	5.10(8)	6.04(6)	1.98(12)	4.01(10)	3.85(8)	2.40(13)	2.29(13)	3.88(11)
Tamil Nadu	7.37(4)	8.38(3)	5.25(7)	14.95(1)	4.85(7)	8.40(4)	17.89(1)	8.44(4)
Uttar Pradesh	13.77(2)	12.19(1)	5.59(6)	11.25(3)	15.80(2)	8.16(5)	9.62(3)	10.60(3)
West Bengal	13.45(3)	5.23(9)	17.38(1)	8.58(5)	5.48(6)	14.29(2)	3.65(9)	10.69(2)
All-India	100.00	100.00	100.00	100.00	100.00	100.00	100.00	100.00

Contd.

TABLE 11.5 *(Contd.)*

State	Employment in Central Government Establishments as Percentage of Total Employment in the State	Employment in State Government Establishments as Percentage of Total Employment in the State	Employment in Quasi-Government Establishments as Percentage of Total Employment in the State		Employment in Private Sector as Percentage of Total Employment in the State		
			Central	State	Local Bodies	Large Units	Small Units
1	10	11	12	13	14	15	16
Andhra Pradesh	15.26(5)	21.43(13)	9.58(6)	15.17(1)	15.23(2)	19.90(10)	3.41(8)
Assam	9.24(14)	24.03(11)	4.86(14)	5.27(15)	1.38(16)	54.13(1)	1.07(15)
Bihar	11.16(9)	23.30(12)	3.12(17)	4.30(16)	9.12(5)	18.08(11)	2.37(11)
Gujarat	9.44(13)	13.34(14)	7.52(9)	6.77(11)	16.53(1)	41.78(2)	4.58(5)
Haryana	5.42(17)	39.08(6)	5.15(13)	11.23(6)	2.73(11)	32.27(6)	4.09(6)
Himachal Pradesh	10.48(10)	65.83(2)	3.62(16)	12.97(3)	1.83(15)	4.36(16)	0.91(16)
Jammu & Kashmir	16.15(4)	67.56(1)	3.78(15)	3.65(17)	3.71(9)	4.32(17)	0.73(17)
Karnataka	10.38(11)	29.87(8)	14.64(3)	11.46(4)	3.58(10)	25.30(8)	4.74(4)
Kerala	7.12(16)	23.30(12)	6.46(10)	10.90(7)	2.22(14)	39.19(4)	10.78(2)
Madhya Pradesh	13.76(7)	41.56(4)	24.21(1)	5.76(14)	3.54(11)	13.49(14)	1.61(14)
Maharashtra	14.56(6)	12.44(15)	10.05(5)	5.93(13)	14.99(3)	39.92(3)	2.08(12)
Orissa	8.86(15)	51.70(3)	13.94(4)	7.66(10)	2.66(13)	12.52(15)	2.63(10)
Punjab	9.66(12)	39.51(5)	8.30(7)	11.37(5)	4.43(8)	22.70(9)	3.99(7)
Rajasthan	18.15(1)	38.73(7)	6.21(12)	8.58(9)	8.57(6)	17.70(13)	2.04(13)
Tamil Nadu	12.07(8)	24.75(10)	7.57(8)	14.70(2)	4.98(7)	28.53(7)	7.34(3)
Uttar Pradesh	17.95(2)	28.65(9)	6.43(11)	8.81(8)	12.89(4)	22.08(12)	3.14(9)
West Bengal	17.40(2)	12.19(16)	19.80(2)	6.66(12)	4.43(8)	38.31(5)	11.82(1)

Source: 1. *Statistical Abstract of India*, 1985.
2. Bihar State Planning Board, *Selected Plan Statistics*, 1986.

Note: Figures in brackets indicate the ranks of the States . Since 1966 the rise in the employment of Central Government staff has been of the order of 16 per cent and that in the State Governments', staff has been to the tune of 45 per cent.

Employment in government factories as percentage of total employment in factories was 12.3 per cent (0.43 million/3.48 million) in 1957, 15.6 per cent (0.64 million/4.11 million) in 1962, 19.2 per cent (0.90 million/4.69 million) in 1966, and 22.2 per cent (1.05 million/4.74 million) in 1968. During 1961-86 employment in the public sector grew at an average rate of 3.7 per cent per annum. As against this, employment in the private sector grew barely by 1.5 per cent per annum during the same period. In the private sector employment rose by only 0.3 per cent in 1979-80, as against a growth rate of 2.3 per cent in 1978-79. The number of jobs rose from 7.20 million at the end of March 1979 to 7.23 million at the end of March 1980. Fluctuations in private sector employment were there. To exemplify, in 1966 the private sector gave employment to 6.1 million but in 1971 it employed only six million persons. Over the same period public sector employment increased from 9.4 million to 10.7 million, and half the increase was in the domain of services. Employment in the public sector rose from 15.04 million at the end of March, 1979 to 15.69 million at the end of March, 1980. During 1976-81, while the public sector generated additional employment for a little over two million persons, the private sector did so for about 0.5 million persons. At the end of 1981 the number of employees of the State and Central Governments was between 19 and 20 million.

The organised sector is the hub or pivot of an advanced economy but in India it employs only one-tenth of the total labour force—two-thirds in the public sector and one-third in the private sector. In 1980 the percentage shares of the public and private sectors were 67.6 per cent and 32.4 per cent respectively. In 1988 the public sector provided employment to 18.32 million, which yielded a percentage of 71.3. On the other hand, the private sector gave employment to 7.39 million, which worked out to a percentage of 28.7. Together the two sectors employed 25.71 million people. And this was in the organised sector. More than concern for efficiency, concern for providing more employment explained expansion of the Government sub-sector in the tertiary sector. Some more data on the topic are presented in Tables 11.6 and 11.7.

The Sixth and Seventh Plans embodied certain employment scenarios. Besides, they correlated the annual growth rate of value added and gross output with that of employment within the span of five years. Table 11.8 presents all those data. The increase in standard person years was estimated at about 34 million during the

TABLE 11.6: Some more data on public sector employment by industrial/occupational origins

Year	Central Government	Public Sector ('000)			
		State Goverments	Quasi Goverments	Local Bodies	Total
1961	2,163	3,075	860	1,240	7,320
1987 (Provisional)	3,349	6,668	5,786	2,214	18,028
Railways					
1961	1,163				
1985	1,615				
Posts and Telegraph					
1961	382				
1985	953				
Banking					
1961	133				
1984	731				
Insurance					
1961	56				
1985	117				

Source: *Statistical Abstract of India,* 1985 and 1987.

TABLE 11.7: Some more data on private versus public sector employment by industrial/occupational origins

Industry/Occupation	Public Sector ('000)		Private Sector ('000)	
	1971	1987	1971	1987
Agriculture and Allied Activities	281	557	824	848
Mining and Quarrying	254	942	340	91
Manufacturing	862	1862	394	4409
Electricity, Gas and Water Supply	455	791	46	40
Wholesale and Retail Sale Trade, etc.	367	134	294	277
Transport and Communications	2238	2972	94	52
Services	5746	9587	1032	1588

Source: *Statistical Abstract of India,* 1987.

TABLE 11.8: Projected growth of employment during 1979-80 to 1989-90

Sector	Employment in Million Standards Personal Years (SPYs)				Increase in Employment in (Million SPYs)		Annual Growth Rate of Employment in (per cent)		Annual Growth Rate of (per cent)			
									Value Added during		Gross Output during	
	1979-80	1984-85		1989-90	6th Plan	7th Plan	6th Plan	7th Plan	6th Plan	7th Plan	6th Plan	7th Plan
		6th Plan (Projection)	7th Plan (Estimate)									
1	2	3	4	5	6	7	8	9	10	11	12	13
Agriculture and Allied Activities	80.331	95.25	96.108	114.092	14.920	17.984	3.47	3.49	3.83	2.5	5.20	4.0
Mining	0.724	0.894	1.153 (including quarrying)	1.494 (including quarrying)	0.170	0.341	4.31	5.32 (including quarrying)	11.25	— 6.8 (both and manufacturing)	11.50	— 8.3 (both mining and manufacturing)
Manufacturing	22.012	27.759	26.790	33.466	5.747	6.676	4.75	4.55	6.50	—	7.62	—
Construction	9.286	11.321	10.427	12.624	2.035	2.197	4.04	3.90	5.10	4.8	7.10	4.8
Others (including electricity, railways, other transport, communications and other Services)	38.757	50.164	52.222	65.385	11.407	13.158	5.30	1.80 to 7.76	5.47	6.1 to 7.9	6.36	6.6 to 12.0
Total	151.110	185.339	186.705	227.061	34.279	40.356	4.17	3.99	5.20	5.0	—	6.6

Source: (1) *Sixth Five Year Plan*;
(2) *Seventh Five Year Plan.*

Sixth Plan and nearly 40 million during the Seventh Plan. It is patent from the table that output has to grow faster than employment by 1.25 to 1.50 times in order to cause one per cent increase in employment. With the passage of time the output has to increase at a rate faster still so as to step up employment by the same percentage. The two Plans had expected the actual number of beneficiaries to exceed the estimated figure of jobs since not every member of the labour force might be a full-time worker during the entire year.

TABLE 11.9: Estimates of backlog of unemployment in successive Five Year Plans

(Figures in millions)

	1st Plan	2nd Plan	3rd Plan	Annual Plans 1966-69	6th Plan	7th Plan
1. Backlog of Unemployment at the start of the Plan	3.3	5.3	7.1	9.6	11.3	7.8
2. Net addition to the labour force during the Plan Period	9.0	11.8	17.0	14.0	32.1*	36.3*
3. Total (1-2)	12.3	17.1	24.1	23.6	43.4	44.1
4. Additional employment likely to have been generated	7.0	10.0	14.5	11.0	35.6	40.4**
5. Backlog of unemployment at the end of Plan (3-4)	5.3	7.1	9.6	12.6	7.8	3.7**

* In the age group 15-59 years.
** Estimated in the Seventh Plan document.

Contd.

Source: RBI, *Occasional Papers,* December 1989.

Note: During 1980-85, 35.60 million SPYs of employment and during 1985-90, 40.36 million SPYs of employment were generated. In 1988-89, 850 million man-days of employment were generated through the poverty-alleviation programmes (excluding the IRDP). 100 days' employment was provided to 8.5 million people in lean months. If there were five members per family, then 4205 million people benefited. This amounts to nearly one-sixth of the aggregate numbers of the rural poor.

The estimates of the backlog of unemployment in the successive

Five-Year Plans as made by the RBI team are given in Table 11.9. The message transmitted by the table is unequivocal: growth of employment has not kept pace with growth of labour force. The new projects have failed to absorb the increments in the labour force. Every year the addition to the reservoir of the unemployed has amounted to a figure between 0.5 million and 0.6 million. We have at present a serious and striking imbalance between supply of manpower and demand for opportunities of gainful employment throughout the length and breadth of the country. In a word, unemployment has grown faster than employment. There has been more unemployment at the end of each Plan than at its beginning. Estimates other than those made by the RBI team put the backlog of unemployment at 9 million at the end of the First Plan, 9 million at the end of the Second Plan, 9.5 million at the end of the Third Plan, 22.1 million at the end of the Fifth Plan, 9.2 to 13.8 million at the end of the Sixth Plan and 8.2 million at the end of the Seventh Plan (Table 11.9). The estimated increase in labour force during the Eighth Plan was 37 million.

In 1990 the backlog of unemployment was 28 million, of which 16 million was open unemployment (Table 11.10).

The annual growth rate of employment exceeded the number of new job-seekers during 1973-78 but fell short of the latter thereafter, markedly so during 1983-88, thereby bloating the volume of the unemployed. In 1989 there were 768 employment exchanges. The job-seekers numbered 32.77 million. In 1980 this number had been 16.2 million. Between 1980 and 1989 the increase in the number of job-seekers was at the rate of 8.1 per cent per annum. During the same period the number of placements declined by 5.4 per cent per annum. This came to 0.9 per cent of the total number of job-seekers on the live registers of employment exchanges.

Once more we would like to point out that in India a substantial proportion of labour input in household activities, be it in any sector, is provided by some members of the family, who have but a partial attachment to the labour market. They work in the family unit of activity without receiving any wage. They work on the family farms and similar enterprises as and when required and when there is no such work, they generally hark back to household work. Their inclusion in the labour force and in unemployment estimates becomes highly misleading but their exclusion equally conceals the brute reality of the situation.

TABLE 11.10: Plan-wise backlog of unemployment

(Figures in million)

Plan Period	Backlog of Unemployment at the beginning of the Plan			Net Additional Labour Force Creation	Jobs Created	Backlog at the end of Plan
	Rural	Urban	Total	Total	Total	Total
First Plan	—	—	—	5.5 (non-agricultural)	—	9.0
Second Plan	2.8	2.5	5.3	11.7	8.0	9.0
Third Plan	5.8	1.2	7.0 (revised)	17.0	14.5	9.5
Fourth Plan	7.0	2.5	9.5	—	—	—
Fifth Plan	—	—	—	—	—	—
Sixth Plan	—	—	12.0	37.4	35.6	9.2 (the actual figures works out to 13.8)
Seventh Plan	—	—	9.2 (the actual figure works out to 13.8)	39.4	40.4	8.2

Source: Compiled from the various Five-Year Plans.

12

THE CURRENT UNEMPLOYMENT SITUATION IN INDIA

In our exposition of the poverty and inequality question(s) we have stated a number of facts that are relevant to the unemployment problem as well.* But the unemployment problem calls for a separate treatment because of its topical interest. Table 12.1 gives State-wise percentages of the unemployed to total persons on daily status basis, rural and urban, male and female, for 1978 and 1983 respectively. Usual status unemployment involving irregular unemployment relates to long-term unemployment, while weekly status and daily status unemployment estimates provide knowledge about seasonal and part-time unemployment and underemployment respectively. Bihar with 8.91 per cent share in labour force had 8.71 per cent share in daily status unemployment rate. The estimate of rural unemployment in Bihar at about four per cent was an underestimate.

The regions where economic activity has been expanding at a faster rate have attracted immigration from other regions. Since migration is always selective, at least in regard to the migrant's age, such movement by itself has tended to favour the rapidly growing regions and adversely affected other regions. Capital and credit movements have tended to have an identical impact, that is, of accentuating inequalities. So has trade, with a bias in favour of the more prosperous regions as against the less; also politics and policies.

But in certain cases migration of rural labour (for example, from some districts of Bihar to Punjab) has led to an economic uplift of the concerned households which the public expenditures made in the past had failed to achieve, although the human cost involved in the slaying of a number of migrated workers was not of a mean order.

---

* And *via-versa*, see Ch. 9, for instance.

TABLE 12.1: Percentage of unemployed to total persons of age five years and above on daily status basis (32nd and 38th rounds of NSS)

State	Rural						Urban					
	Male			Female			Male			Female		
	32nd round (July 1977-June 1978)	38th round (Jan.-Dec. 1983)	Increase(+)/ Decrease(-) during the Period	32nd round (July 1977-June 1978)	38th round (Jan.-Dec. 1983)	Increase(+)/ Decrease(-) during the Period	32nd round (July 1977-June 1978)	38th round (Jan.-Dec. 1983)	Increase(+)/ Decrease(-) during the Period	32nd round (July 1977 June 1978)	38th round (Jan.-Dec. 1983)	Increase(+)/ Decrease(-) during the Period
	1	2	3	4	5	6	7	8	9 10	11	12	13
Andhra Pradesh	5.67	5.59	(-) 0.08	6.29	4.70	(-) 1.59	6.77	4.95	(+) 1.82	2.79	1.79	(-) 1.00
Assam	0.76	1.88	(+) 1.12	0.09	0.50	(+) 0.41	1.90	5.34	(+) 3.44	0.25	1.68	(+) 1.43
Bihar	5.73	4.24	(-) 1.49	1.78	1.92	(+) 0.14	4.56	4.24	(-) 0.32	0.96	0.52	(-) 0.44
Gujarat	4.49	3.02	(-) 1.47	1.88	1.67	(-) 0.21	3.49	5.50	(+) 2.01	0.82	0.67	(-) 0.15
Haryana	3.89	3.41	(-) 0.48	0.63	0.29	(-) 0.34	3.67	4.61	(+) 0.74	0.73	0.44	(-) 0.29
Himachal Pradesh	2.03	1.17	(-) 0.86	0.14	0.23	(+) 0.09	3.71	4.27	(+) 0.56	2.83	2.22	(-) 0.61
Jammu & Kashmir	4.94	8.36	(+) 3.42	0.36	0.21	(-) 0.15	4.15	3.29	(-) 0.86	2.07	1.37	(-) 0.70
Karnataka	4.48	4.69	(+) 0.21	4.07	3.15	(-) 0.82	5.73	6.34	(-) 0.61	2.55	2.41	(-) 0.14
Kerala	13.70	13.39	(-) 0.31	8.61	6.56	(-) 2.05	13.76	12.76	(-) 1.00	4.74	5.28	(+) 0.54
Madhya Pradesh	1.84	1.56	(-) 0.28	1.58	0.67	(-) 0.91	3.44	3.61	(+) 0.37	0.63	0.79	(+) 0.16
Maharashtra	3.44	3.99	(+) 0.55	4.09	2.69	(-) 1.40	5.47	4.32	(-) 1.15	2.61	1.68	(-) 0.93
Orissa	4.52	5.09	(+) 0.47	1.55	2.68	(+) 1.13	4.40	6.22	(+) 1.82	1.08	1.55	(+) 0.47
Punjab	2.94	4.08	+) 1.14	0.33	1.16	(+) 0.83	2.45	3.90	(+) 1.45	1.04	2.99	(+) 1.95
Rajasthan	2.65	3.09	(+) 0.34	0.99	0.92	(-) 0.07	2.87	3.18	(+) 0.31	0.52	0.55	(+) 0.03
Tamil Nadu	8.36	12.00	(+) 3.64	5.32	8.55	(+) 3.23	8.04	9.43	(+) 1.39	4.66	3.48	(-) 1.18
Uttar Pradesh	2.48	2.16	(-) 0.32	0.54	0.50	(-) 0.04	3.49	3.95	(+) 0.46	0.38	0.41	(+) 0.03
West Bengal	5.70	8.80	(+) 3.10	0.98	3.15	(+) 2.17	7.05	7.51	(+) 0.46	1.52	2.75	(+) 1.23
All-India	**4.45**	**4.79**	**(+) 0.34**	**2.45**	**2.52**	**(+) 0.07**	**5.35**	**5.45**	**(+) 0.10**	**2.11**	1.72	(-) 0.39

Source: CMIE, *Basic Statistics relating to the Indian Economy*, Vol. 2, *States*, September, 1989.

Migration of rural workers to urban areas in quest of jobs over the years has deprived the villages of their skill and leadership, on the one hand, and caused growing pressure on the existing basic services available in the cities as reflected in the over-increasing social tension in them, on the other.

Technically, a region at a relatively low level of development is said to be possessed of relatively higher employment potential. By the same token, the agriculturally lagging regions can be said to be impregnated with good employment potential absolutely as well as relatively.

The new government at the Centre (which came in towards the end of November 1989) recognised the people's right to work. This was contained in the party's election manifesto. Adequate assistance had to be provided to everyone seeking livelihood such that he earned reasonable income and had access to the minimum amenities of life. According to the framers of the Eighth Plan Approach Paper, the first and foremost goal of a just society was the fulfilment of the basic human needs through maximum possible utilisation of the given power. Gainful employment to all sections of the population (*gainful employment* standing for employment resulting in value addition at least equal to the wage paid and the wage paid has to ensure to the earner his daily bread) was the most challenging task facing the planners. The new plan was expected to look upon growth in terms of provision of meaningful work and a reasonable minimum standard of living and essential amenities to everyone, and that speedily. Growth was considered good only to the extent that it guaranteed employment to all desirous of it, and through it and other supplementary means led to the fulfilment of the basic human needs by all citizens. So far unemployment had proved growth-resistant. Employment was an inextricable and indivisible component of development and the two were catalysts of each other.

Alternatively, employment can be provided for the sake of eradicating poverty (in many cases poverty and unemployment are coexistent and households below the Poverty Line have the concentration of unemployment in them) and/or for the sake of speeding up growth.

Ideally, the right to work should be introduced in a staggered manner. Such right could be meaningful only when the total economy has been remodelled and population growth has been held in check and an appropriate wage and income policy has been evolved. This right has to be processed with caution because the amount involved would be enormous — Rs. 13,000 crores on one estimate. The existing employment programmes involve a cost of Rs. 3,000 crores. The remaining Rs. 10,000 crores has, therefore, to be raised to render the right operational. Further, the right to work should not be construed to mean mere appointment to government jobs. Also, before the right to work is conceded in full, the Employment Guarantee Scheme (EGS) should be executed everywhere in the country to gain experience because the EGS has all the ingredients that would go to constitute a mammoth programme subsequently.

In recent years the employment elasticity with respect to aggregate output has been on the decline in our economy. GDP has grown at the annual rate of nearly five per cent. The labour force has grown at the annual rate of about 2.5 per cent. The population has grown at the annual rate of 2.4 per cent. From 1972-73 to 1977-78 employment grew at the annual rate of 2.82 per cent. From 1977-78 to 1983 it grew at the annual rate of 2.22 per cent. From 1983 to 1987-88 it grew at the rate of 1.55 per cent. During the Sixth Plan the rate of employment generation was 4.32 per cent per annum. During the Seventh Plan it was expected to be 3.99 per cent per annum.

A nagging situation appears to have emerged with acceleration in growth of national income, on the one hand, and with slowing down of employment growth and hence moving up of the pace of unemployment growth, on the other. Employment in the organised sector has grown but sluggishly. The share of this sector in total employment at present is around 10 per cent. During 1966–74 employment growth in the public sector was at the rate of 3.6 per cent per annum, as against the rate of growth of national income at 3.7 per cent per annum. In 1977, 1.81 per 100 persons were employed in general government services and 2.31 persons in the public sector as a whole. During 1975–85 national income increased at the rate of 4.18 per cent per annum, whereas employment in the public sector grew at the rate of three per cent per annum. Employment in construction works has risen at the rate of 11 per cent per annum and has been inextricably linked with the parallel economy. Employment in agriculture grew at the rate of 2.32 per cent per annum during 1972-72 to 1977-78 and at the rate of 1.20 (according to another estimate, 0.65) per cent per annum during 1983 to 1987-88 (the latter being a drought year).

In recent years the tertiary sector that has expanded at the fastest rate has absorbed skilled and trained labour force most of all but the unskilled and unlettered rural labour force in limited numbers only.

Increased mechanisation has been one potent factor to slow down the pace of employment growth in the economy. To elucidate, during 1980-81 to 1984-85 capital intensity grew at the rate of 12 per cent per annum in Central public undertakings, whereas employment grew at the rate of 3 per cent per annum in them. The number of employees per enterprise fell off, in consequence.

Share of manpower cost as percentage of capital employed declined in public enterprises from 15.7 per cent in 1974-75 to 13 per cent in 1985-86. During the same period as percentage of sales revenue it declined from 10.3 per cent to 9 per cent. Manpower cost as percentage of value added fell from 38.7 to 31.8 per cent. While total cost of production increased seven-fold, manpower cost increased five-fold. The wage bill doubled in public administration and public services.

Percentage distribution of employment sector-wise during the Sixth and Seventh Plans in the country is given in Table 12.2.

TABLE 12.2: Sector-wise distribution of employment in India

(Percentage)

	Sector	1984-85	1989-90
1.	Agriculture, Irrigation and other activities allied to agriculture	50.66	50.24
	(a) Crop Sector	31.46	28.94
	(b) Non-crop Sector	19.20	21.30
2.	Mining and Quarrying	0.61	0.65
3.	Manufacturing	14.34	14.73
4.	Construction	5.58	5.56
5.	Electricity	0.55	0.66
6.	Railways	0.82	0.74
7.	Communications	0.51	0.54
8.	Other services	21.02	21.65
	Total	100.00	100.00

Source: The Seventh Five-Year Plan.

Table 12.3 presents gross investment in the private and public sectors in the seven industrial/occupational divisions of the Indian economy during the Seventh Plan at 1984-85 prices as percentage of total investment as well as incremental GDP at factor cost as percentage of total GDP on the same pattern. The investment allocation was computed by using sectoral capital-output ratios estimated on the basis of past data and information on recent trends.

Table 12.4 presents the Incremental Output-Capital Ratio (IOCR) sector-wise for the same industrial/occupational divisions of the economy during the same period as above, capital-labour ratio and output-employment ratio. The employment potential has been calculated in terms of standard person years, each of which was equal to 273 man-days of 8 hours work per day.

Our study shows that increase of employment by one per cent in Bihar in agriculture and allied activities added 1.89 per cent to the SDP, whereas increase of employment by one per cent in non-agriculture added 8.97 per cent to it. On the other hand, one per cent SDP in agriculture and allied activities supported 1.76 persons (0.52 per cent of them doing some work or other, and the rest 1.24 being dependants), while one per cent SDP in non-agriculture supported 0.37 persons (0.11 worker and 0.26 dependant) only.

Persons in self-employment were found to be in highest percentages in agriculture and allied activities, and next came in order trade, restaurants and hotels; community, social and personal services; and manufacturing. Self-employment obtained in lowest percentages in transport, storage, communications, construction, electricity, gas and water supply, mining and quarrying.

The informal sector in urban areas was characteristically self-employed and often beset with both poverty and unemployment. To combat their problem it was suggested by the authors of the Approach Paper on the Eighth Plan that they should be helped to organise themselves with a view to upgrading their techniques and getting better access to working space, credit and marketing channels. Some States (like Bihar) have set up Minorities Financial Corporations to finance self-employment amongst those belonging to the minority communities.

In India 12.4 to 15 per cent of all women are employed in the organised sector. The rest are employed in agriculture and allied activities, community, social and personal services, gas and water supply; transport, storage and communications, in the descending order.

TABLE 12.3: Investment, output and IOCR in the Seventh Plan (1985-90) of India at 1984-85 prices

Sector	Gross Investment as Percentage of Total Investment			Incremental GDP at Factor Cost as Percentage of total GDP		
	Public	Private	Total	Public	Private	Total
1. Agriculture, Irrigation, Allied activities	8.55	10.56	19.11	1.63	15.93	17.56
2. Mining, Quarrying and Manufacturing	13.16	19.29	32.45	12.42	13.22	25.64
3. Electricity	9.97	0.13	10.10	Neg.	3.34	3.34
4. Railways	0.0 (Approx.)	—	0.01	Neg.	Neg.	Neg.
5. Other Transport	3.10	5.24	8.34	2.44	4.50	6.94
6. Communication	0.19	—	0.19	3.00	Neg.	3.00
7. Other Services	Neg.	Neg.	24.18	1.88	2.48	4.36
Total	47.83	52.17	100.00	41.38	58.62	100.00

Source: *The Seventh Five-Year Plan.*
Note: The investment allocation was computed by using sectoral capital: output ratios estimated on the basis of past data and information on recent trends.

The questions facing the planners are: At what rate should the different sectors – agriculture, industry and infrastructure – grow so as to enable employment in the total economy to grow at the rate stipulated by the plan? How could these various sectors be made to grow at that rate? How would growth of employment at the stipulated rate affect the growth rate of the various sectors? What should be done so that employment grows at the stipulated rate? In trying to answer these questions changes occurring in demand and supply and their interrelations have to be carefully examined.

At the given level of its development and being the poorest State of all Bihar would need relatively less investment per man to be employed in the primary sector, slightly more of it for the same purpose in the services sector, and definitely far higher investment in the secondary sector than in the services sector for that very purpose in view of the inadequacies of the infrastructural facilities in the secondary sector.

TABLE 12.4: Sector-wise capital: output, capital: labour and labour: output ratios in the Seventh Plan (1985-90) of India at 1984-85 prices

Sector	Gross Investment Required for Re 1 worth more of Additional Output (Rs.)			Gross Investment for One more standard person year of Employment (Rs.)			So much Rs. Worth of Increase in Output required for one more standard person day of Employment
	Public	Private	Total	Public	Private	Total	
1	2	3	4	5	6	7	8
1. Agriculture, Irrigation, and Activities Allied to Agriculture	2.93	3.63	6.56	15332	18933	34265	19.11
2. Mining, Quarrying and Manufacturing	3.09	4.54	7.63	60503	88602	149105	71.54
3. Electricity	17.99	0.23	18.22	2522	Neg.	2522	140.16
4. Railways	16.99	Neg.	16.99	3137	Neg.	3137	184.67
5. Other Transport	2.59	4.85	7.24	137	278	415	57.35
6. Communication	7.71	—	7.71	853	—	853	110.56
7. Other Services	1.05	2.29	3.34	37.18	49.06	86.24	86.24
Total	2.88	3.15	6.03	140	153	293	48.25

Source: *The Seventh Five-Year Plan*.

Note: The employment generated by the targeted levels of economic activity was calculated in terms of Standard person years, each of which was equal to 273 mandays of work at the rate of 8 hours a day.

During the Fifth Plan period the rural labour force was provided employment in local construction works (mainly earth works). The IRDP, the NREP, the RLEGP, the Special Area Programme, and so on, were embarked upon to provide rural people with employment in creation of infrastructure, social forestry, afforestation, etc., during both the Sixth and the Seventh Plan period. Minimum wages paid to each worker amounted to Rs. 8.50 per day (part in the form of subsidised foodgrains). But an equal amount had to be spent on every employed worker per day to meet the non-cost requirements of the NREP. The RLEGP cost more per man-day – Rs. 22 during the Sixth Plan and Rs. 33 during the Seventh Plan in Bihar. The assets built benefited the weaker sections most.

The NREP and the RLEGP did not create sufficiently useful, labour-intensive jobs at times and in places most needed. They met only about nine per cent of the demand for work from the poor in rural areas. The NREP provided nearly 40 per cent of the total incremental employment in the rural areas. The wages actually paid under it and the RLEGP were lower than stipulated owing to leakages and corruption implicit in the process.

The IRDP promoted self-employment but the emphasis on the livestock asset was excessive, which meant that the beneficiaries only for a short period enjoyed improvement in the scale of production and productivity.

The employment provided under the 20-Point Programme cost less than Rs. 12 per man day during the Seventh Plan period.

The much-advertised JRY (introduced in April 1989) was a compound of the NREP and the RLEGP. A sum of Rs. 2,100 crores was made available to the States and Union Territories by the Centre for it during 1989-90. The funds were remitted directly to the district collectors for disbursement to village panchayats. Handling of funds directly by village panchayats rendered the bureaucratic machinery that had sprung up over the years since the Community Development Project days, particularly to serve the Panchayati Raj, redundant. Direct remittance of funds to districts deprived the State Governments of the use of those funds for bolstering their ways and means position in times of need, besides of assuming additional power in allocating funds between localities, between sectors, and even between eligible beneficiaries, and thereby deriving political mileage from it.

The JRY failed to attain the target during 1989-90. Of the target 27 million people could not be provided employment. Consequently, the number of the jobless shot up sharply.

In the coming five years what type of employment would be provided by a sector shall depend on what the present employment and what the present output-structure in it are.

It appears that the time-worn suggestions, that is, suggestions made in the last four decades, have not been acted upon or have been acted upon only in part so that they are being suggested again for the

Eighth Plan, namely, all undeveloped wasteland should be developed, all land that can be reclaimed should be reclaimed, contour-building unexecuted so far should be executed, field channels, not so far constructed, should be constructed, unimproved rural roads should be improved, and social services unprovided uptil now should now be provided. Such works would last as avenues of fresh employment for some decades to come, no doubt, but these are more time-consuming than providing employment by developing labour- intensive industries.

Sectors in descending order of rate of growth of potential employment are: electricity, mining and quarrying, non-crop sectors in agriculture, communications, services, roads, manufacturing, construction, agriculture, crop-sector in agriculture, and railways. (Under construction housing has backward and forward linkages in employment generation.)

Capital assets-formation is eminently suited to providing seasonal employment to agricultural labourers. The watershed development programme has a special appeal from the point of view of employment potential insofar as it focuses on the integrated development of catchment areas, waste and pasture lands and areas under crops.

Another merit of this programme is that the landless agriculturists can be provided participatory opportunities. As would be evident from the employment potentials of different economic activities compiled above, not much hope could be pinned on agriculture for providing employment continuously and in substantial numbers. Agricultural operations have grown in their capital intensity in the last two decades or so. More foreign exchange is now needed to supply one unit of fertiliser and pesticide to the farmer than was the case before. Agricultural employment has not expanded in the same proportion to output expansion also in agriculture in recent years as happened formerly. Therefore, the planners' attention has to shift increasingly more to alternative avenues of employment, avenues that have propinquity to agriculture or even to horticulture and cattle-raising. Dandekar's calculation brings out that only one-fourth of the additional demand generated by additional employment in the coming plans would be for agricultural output and the remaining part would be for non-agricultural output. Agriculture has begun throwing cultivator out of crop production. The dwindling of the average size of operational holdings and the proliferation of marginal holdings have together, perhaps, imparted a fillip to this trend. Agriculture now employs relatively more workers than cultivators, compared to the position before. The NSS 38th Round has revealed that a shift is taking place from agriculture to non-agriculture. Thus there is no alternative to providing additional employment to the rural labour force which is non-agricultural or of moving people from main agricultural operations to subsidiary and auxiliary agricultural operations that are and would be more remunerative, and, of course, trying to absorb them in a *bridge* or transitional sort of employment say, in construction works, off-farm as well as off-factory jobs, until such time as the surplus population mopped up from agriculture is re-employed in industry. In the meantime, the requisite resource back-up would be organised, and another spark added further to the inflationary process during the gestation period of construction works extinguished only by increasing the stock of wage-goods. Within agriculture employment multiplication would be governed by natural resources including soil and water which are available, the land tenure system that exists, efficiency of and commitment to the goal on the part of administration, marketing and other supporting facilities, and so forth.

The new employment policy ought to be predicated upon a stock-taking of the old. It is essential to evaluate the impact of the past employment programmes on the macro-level of employment and its sectoral and sub-sectoral levels as well as types of labour, besides their impact on those benefited or not benefited, or partly benefited and partly harmed. Mere multiplication of such programmes without an eye to the returns on investment made in them is, to quote Patel, a recipe for perpetuating poverty, not for removing it. This would necessitate that while evaluating growth of employment opportunities we juxtapose it with gains in economic and technical efficiency in order that the process could be sustained for a longer period. Only assets that are productive and durable and turn out goods that are cost-effective and viable from the angle of the market without requiring subsidy should be created. During the Eighth Plan even those who obtain intermittent employment in agriculture or non-agriculture are to be treated as productive workers and have to be brought into the mainstream of development by giving them the needed assistance. The employment projects that are selected should concur with the development thrust, be it in agriculture or in industry or in the whole economy, i.e., tend to become assimilated in it.

To be precise, in fixing up the employment programme four aspects have to be borne in mind : (1) *Time* – number of hours or days spent on doing gainful work, (2) *Income* – whether the earning is sufficient or insufficient to bring the worker above the Poverty Line, (3) *Willingness/Recognition* – whether the worker has anyhow been employed, and so is looking for a better opening benefiting his education and training and, (4) *Productivity* – net value added, actual and potential.

Economic and technical efficiency to be improved through modernisation should be so devised as to avert adverse repercussions on rural employment and income distribution.

It is necessary that agricultural labourers are guaranteed minimum wages (consistent with the Supreme Court's judgment) instead of subsistence wages, as in the past, and good working conditions but ordinarily these should not be in excess of their marginal productivity and should conform to the maximum "what the traffic would bear", otherwise they would have a negative effect on production, which in turn would mar employment prospects in agriculture and non-agriculture. It is in this context that the rural employment policy, if over-stretched, would clash with the agricultural labour policy.

In conclusion, there can be no single solution to any one problem but only a series of solutions, and no solution can be used to the full extent, for it is in the nature of, problems to hang together like a spider's web.

Table 12.5 contains figures of job-seekers on the live registers of employment exchanges in 1970 and during 1980-88 in different States. From them a rough idea of the growth of unemployment among the educated can be formed – rough because not all those who are educated and unemployed get themselves registered with the employment exchanges. Among those who get themselves registered are many who have some employment, intermittent or part-time, but are not content with it because it does not befit their education and training and carries less wages than they deserve; also because not all States have so far developed this mechanism in the number and localities as desired for want of resources; further because the same persons get themselves registered with more than one employment exchange; and, lastly, because there are those people who are

TABLE 12.5: Number of job-seekers on the live registers of employment exchanges : 1970 & 1980-1988

(In '000s)

State	December end 1970	March-end								Percentage Change in 1988 over 1980
		1980	1981	1982	1983	1984	1985	1986	1988	
1	2	3	4	5	6	7	8	9	10	11
Andhra Pradesh	279	1,288	1,472	1,568	1,843	2,058	2,203	2,360	2,679	108.0
Assam	465	324	322	374	394	474	510	643	841	159.6
Bihar	319	2,112	2,149	2,469	2,587	2,661	2,662	2,538	2,649	25.4
Gujarat	154	431	481	521	582	627	642	788	777	80.3
Haryana	83	334	367	383	467	458	473	488	580	73.6
Himachal Pradesh	14	125	149	161	171	200	312	334	348	374.4
Jammu & Kashmir	14	54	52	59	68	68	69	79	126	133.3
Karnataka	241	557	609	634	697	747	788	958	996	78.8
Kerala	294	1,243	1,354	1,848	2,051	2,343	2,457	2,532	2,914	134.4
Madhya Pradesh	247	765	838	876	909	1,069	1,159	1,497	1,697	121.8
Maharashtra	328	1,117	1,283	1,426	1,583	1,965	2,163	2,546	2,598	132.6
Orissa	150	431	455	495	490	540	574	762	753	74.7
Punjab	94	408	463	493	523	530	540	654	608	49.0
Rajasthan	128	331	365	394	411	482	534	714	826	119.8
Tamil Nadu	400	1,002	1,129	1,260	1,354	1,620	1,755	2,146	2,478	117.3
Uttar Pradesh	426	1,382	1,418	1,510	1,676	1,886	1,959	2,752	2,975	108.0
West Bengal	585	2,179	2,645	2,849	3,542	3,974	4,114	4,005	4,341	99.2
All-India	**4,069**	**14,690**	**16,198**	**18,029**	**20,120**	**22,603**	**23,915**	**27,034**	**29,568**	**101.3**

Source: CMIE, *Basic Statistics Relating to the Indian Economy*, Vol. 2, *States*, September 1989.

satisfied with their present positions just for the sake of the real advantages they enjoy in spite of the low nominal rewards received by them. For some of these reasons a poorest State like Bihar shows a low percentage of growth of educated unemployment and a low absolute number of the educated unemployed vis-a-vis its population, as compared respectively to Maharashtra and West Bengal.

Table 12.6 gives the break-down of the registered unemployed in June 1988 according to the level of their education State-wise. It is clear from the table that the matriculates are unemployed in overwhelming numbers and that the incidence of educated unemployment declines as we move from the lower to the higher level of education.

TABLE 12.6: Educated job-seekers on the live registers of employment exchanges: 30 June, 1988

(in '000s)

State	Total No. of Jobseekers on the Live Registers	Matriculates	Graduates	Post-Graduates	Total (2 to 4)	Col. (3) as percentage of Col. (1)	Col. (2) as percentage of All-India Total (Percentage Share of the State)
1	2	3	4	5	6	7	8
Andhra Pradesh	2,587	783	190	20	993	38.4	8.8(3)
Assam	862	301	50	3	354	41.1	2.7(8)
Bihar	2,645	972	248	6	1,226	46.4	8.8(3)
Gujarat	798	357	48	5	410	51.4	2.7(7)
Haryana	576	233	42	6	281	48.8	1.7(10)
Himachal Pradesh	352	176	21	7	302	57.7	1.0(11)
Jammu & Kashmir	128	20	12	4	36	28.1	0.3(12)
Karnataka	1,020	458	92	9	559	54.8	3.4(6)
Kerala	2,826	1,392	99	14	1,505	53.3	9.5(2)
Madhya Pradesh	1,676	91	147	38	276	16.5	5.4(5)
Maharashtra	2,612	1,158	165	21	1,344	51.5	8.8(3)
Orissa	737	258	90	8	356	48.3	2.4(8)
Punjab	601	184	61	11	256	42.6	2.0(9)
Rajasthan	831	159	102	14	275	33.1	2.7(7)
Tamil Nadu	2,503	791	189	48	1,028	41.1	8.5(4)
Uttar Pradesh	2,852	651	354	70	1,075	37.7	9.5(2)
West Bengal	4,318	1,210	417	24	1,651	38.2	14.6(1)
All-India	**29,412**	**9,676**	**2,484**	**328**	**12,488**	**42.5**	**100.0**

Source: CMIE, *Basic Statistics Relating to the Indian Economy*, Vol. 2, *States*, September, 1989.

Note: Figures in brackets indicate the ranks of the States.

A peculiarity of educated unemployment is its structuralness. That is to say, a surplus of the highly educated coexists with a shortage of desired technical manpower, more so in the rural areas. Another peculiarity, though economically inconsistent, is that the educated unemployed in our country have a reserve price, arising out of their lack of a true sense of dignity of labour, which prevents them from accepting jobs taken up usually by semi-educated persons.

The Eighth Plan Approach Paper regarded over-emphasis on higher education as being responsible for educated unemployment.

About 45 per cent of the total educated unemployed are located in the rural areas but not all of them figure in the registers of employment exchanges. It is largely the educated in the urban areas who face unemployment and poverty and constitute what is called the *lumpen proletariat*. Surveys disclose that urban unemployment is much smaller in volume than rural unemployment but the percentage of the urban educated unemployed to total urban population is higher. Bulk of unskilled casual labour in urban areas, by and large in the informal sector, is unemployed and poor. The social and political tensions touched off by urban unemployment are far more acute than those triggered off by rural unemployment. Poverty in rural areas and unemployment in urban areas have relative dominance over total unemployment and total poverty respectively.

Educated unemployment is a socially volatile phenomenon. The riff-raff we notice in our society today is not in the least ascribable to this phenomenon. Only the absence of organisation among the educated unemployed (they have not resources enough for the purpose and are also dispersed in space) acts as a brake over the agitation and prevents it from spreading and assuming the form of a mass movement. It makes the agitation localised in space as well as in time.

Educational reform is the first antidote to the existing malady but it would take time before such reform could be devised and implemented. Meanwhile, the educated unemployed could be absorbed in extension works required in the delivery of credit and inputs to agriculturists and small producers, in the anti-illiteracy drive, in the health awareness programme, in tackling environmental degradation, and so forth. There is also room for increased brain drain. Apart from this, those who possess technological and managerial skills can be provided with jobs that technological upgradation would throw up in the coming years. Soft-ware business services are another avenue of employment for these persons.

A paradoxical situation obtains in our society. With unemployment growing at different levels more and more households are being thrown out of employment. Not even one member (after the retirement from service of the members erstwhile employed in some cases) in a household is employed. On the other hand, employment is getting, concentrated in the fewer number of families – wives working along with their husbands; a large number of the employed doing more than one paid work; those already employed managing to get their wards employed in their own organisations or elsewhere, even if they have inferior merits; employment going to the nearest kin of the employees dying prior to the age of superannuation, on grounds of compassion, or an any other ground, thanks to the power wielded by the employees association.

Before we conclude this, we would like to add that employment programme management is a new area. The decentralised organisational agencies must possess management competence to manage the programme effectively and successfully. Compartmentalisation of administration short of proper coordination, can have a disastrous effect. Integration of the regular plan programme with the employment programme, coordination between and among area levels, integration of the district credit plan with the district development plan, rural-urban integration, public participation in district planning through its own bodies as well as the Panchayati Raj bodies, and so on, are the different facets of this management through the techniques that have to be duly considered and abided by if achievement of success is the goal of the planners in the realm of employment.

Management and monitoring of either the anti-poverty or employment-generation programme or a cross of both should focus on fulfilment of the physical targets, and attach only the minimum necessary significance to fulfilment of the monetary targets because the emphasis on the latter has resulted in a number of abuses which render the scenario most depressing. Judging performance by the amount of money allotted to different projects/programmes/schemes utilised within the time-span, whether utilised properly or otherwise, has played havoc with planning in this country and virtually made a mockery of it. Everybody is aware of this but everybody tends to pass over it because he knows that those above him are the real patrons of this corrupt practice.

Leakages, misuse and wastage of funds, outright corruption, frauds, embezzlement, false receipts, and what not, are met with everywhere but are disregarded, condoned and easily forgotten. While this is the common landscape, we have also a good many cases where large funds remain unutilised and have therefore to be surrendered. This is generally due to the non-existence of eligible projects in anticipation of fresh grants or an inordinate delay in the preparation and approval of a project by the competent authority or simply because the expected amount of work was not put in. A third class of cases enshrines projects that are left incomplete or simply put aside in the mid-stream on account of an acute shortage of funds or quietly deferred until such time that further instalments are released. Misallocation, mismanagement of funds and their badly phased release intensely vitiate and inhibit planning. Examples abound of the district planners not knowing how and where to spend the plan funds sanctioned to their districts. In consequence, funds — large in size and dimension — are wasted on irrelevant or non-existent heads. Projects (new or on-going) figuring in the annual plans are indicated as completed and the funds earmarked for them shown as disbursed much ahead of the schedule in order to enable the district officials and their henchmen to grab the funds and take out of them their illegal booties, even when, in truth, there is no trace of any such project having been started or at most only of its foundation-stone having been laid by some VIP (who dedicated it to the people of the district, as if it were funded by his own hard-earned money or of his forefathers), or the work related with it has progressed only to a very limited extent and is far from being completed – all these various forms and stages of project execution are assumed to be on a par for the purpose of withdrawing the funds tagged to a project. All these *paper horses* are being created and made to run unchecked and incessantly because there is no system of physical audit and verification, for one thing, and, for another, because funds have also been placed at the disposal of the people's representatives to the legislature for allotment, persons having no legal accountability or responsibility within the corpus of the existing rules of public administration. What is worse, bulk of the funds sanctioned for an administrative unit are released and shown as disbursed around the last month of the financial year. Where the projects have been successfully executed, they are being used for parties other than those for which they were originally meant. To give some examples, low-cost houses are used to tend the cattle and to store fodder and other articles. Functional houses that are constructed are rented by the concerned functionaries, who reside in their own posh houses (or vice-versa). Villages shown as wholly electrified on paper have to make do with the kerosene lamps. We have *ghost* schools and colleges. Lakhs of handpumps lie unused for want of washers (the price of a washer being Rs. 10). Roads that are constructed are such that they do not last more than one year and hence justify reconstruction every year and when reconstructed are shown as new roads every time. More objectionable than this is that the same roads are constructed or reconstructed and repaired by more than one government department every year or in every new Plan. In certain cases the same persons were declared as poor by more than one government department and buoyed with funds, one after another while a large number of equally poor people were not approached by a single department. Sheer discrimination or mere distance might have been the reason for this, though nothing can be said definitely or emphatically or positively.

The non-poor fool the bureaucrats in the garb of the poor because the bureaucrats are impatient to have the beneficiaries among whom they could distribute the funds with both hands within the little time available. The "*melas*", presided over by people who have distinguished themselves politically, rehearse and react the same play in a more grandiose manner. The non-weaker sections have little difficulty in obtaining the authorised official's certificates on payment of an absurdly low price to prove that they belong to the weaker sections. They thus swindle and intercept the privileges meant for the latter. The poor and the members of the weaker sections do not figure in the voters' lists in large numbers. Besides, they do not have any chance of getting the ration card.

Bunker Roy, one of the senior-most bureaucrats (retired), whose writings have stimulated us to produce a digest of the drawbacks and snags of the poverty-alleviation and unemployment-eradication programmes in the foregoing paragraphs, comments aptly as follows:

> "If this is the scenario and the government has decided to be a party to these abuses, then the solution only lies with the rural community and the amount of pressure they can bring to bear on the system. Awareness programmes, a proper and effective feedback system designed to embarrass the administration, an information system on government facilities that have collapsed, an organised community fully made aware of their rights and the subsidies they are entitled to, a campaign of legitimacy that informs the comity of the laws in the country for their own protection and welfare – these are strategies that will take time to yield results but in many parts of the country pressure from below has changed government thinking and lessened corruption. But in

some States pressure from above – the Chief Ministers' level – has put great checks on the corrupt practices in the administration at its top, dubbed publicly as a *jehad* or crusade. But in truth the efforts are diffuse and sporadic and have not been accompanied by public appreciation and enthusiasm because neither all the crusaders are above fault in their own private lives, nor have they proved their competence to run the government, as evidenced by the total collapse of civic life and facilities. The appeal of this measure is rapidly diminishing. Just as in the field of environment, community groups have to be mobilised, so also have they to be mobilised to change decisions in the field of drinking water, education, health and energy. The important thing is to hasten slowly *(Times of India*, March 30, 1991).

The kernel of the long discussion so far is that misutilisation of the given funds is a more convincing reason for the present economic malaise than the lack of funds. The public authority at all levels of administration has behaved like the proverbial prodigal in matters of public expenditure, be it revenue or capital. We are living in a land where the penny has become wise and the pound foolish. Self-help and self-reliance being theologies for mere preaching by the public agencies, in practice the public agencies have almost gone crazy with funds flowing from outside in incredibly large amounts and trying to parade them without weighing the pros and cons of incurring marginal expenditures in the light of the twin laws of diminishing marginal utility and equi-marginal marginal utility. Extravagance has become their creed as well as cult. The public at large has been so indifferent to this that the public agencies have found themselves absolutely unshackled and unbridled as actors as well as a betters in this process of an unending loot and wastage of public money.

13

INTER-REGIONAL VARIATIONS IN THE EMPLOYMENT AND UNEMPLOYMENT PATTERNS IN INDIA

Employment opportunities are not equally distributed in the country. Their availability reflects the history and ecology of economic growth, particularly industrialisation. An inverse relationship between the percentage of literate population and the participation rate of the workforce is noticeable in States, such as Bihar, Madhya Pradesh, Orissa, Rajasthan and Uttar Pradesh, which are all backward States — this is a coincidence. The number and timing of the peak seasons in agriculture probably varies from region to region, depending on the cropping pattern and the intensity of cropping in them. Wage employment is more prevalent in States with higher per capita incomes and higher levels of commercialisation. The employment pattern of adult male agricultural labourers exhibits considerable variations among different States.

The RBI's (i.e., A.K. Nag's) study demonstrates vast and sharp divergencies in employment growth as between States during 1983-1988 *per se* and in employment growth, as compared with population growth. These are portrayed by Tables 13.1 and 13.2. Some States, e.g., Gujarat and Haryana, that have experienced low rural employment growth have made good the loss in better urban employment growth. Other States like Bihar have gained from neither rural nor urban employment growth. Still others like Rajasthan and Punjab have benefited from relatively high employment growth in both rural and urban areas. On the whole, States like West Bengal and Gujarat have done best, while States like Bihar and Himachal Pradesh have done worst.

The regional rates of un- and underemployment in India are not apparently at some critical level well above the national average such that action could be precipitated as often demanded under conditions of cyclical slumps and are somehow or other level with the general half-dead – or quasi-equilibrium economic situation. Some striking traits can be noted: Off-season agricultural unemployment is concentrated in the eastern and southern regions. At the existing levels of technique, surplus agricultural labour tends to vary pronouncedly from region to region and appears to be concentrated in Bihar, Orissa and in some States of the central and southern regions. Agricultural wages are influenced seasonally on account of this. A vital factor in the employment of the surplus labour is the regional distribution of new non-agricultural activities. Rural underemployment varies markedly from locality to locality with variations in the intensity of production, fertility of the soil, type of farming practised, density of population, and other cognate factors. Rural underemployment is less articulate in Punjab and Gujarat and more articulate in Bihar, Kerala and Karnataka.

TABLE 13.1: Statewise data on change in population (5+) and in employment by principal status for rural areas between 1983 and 1987-88

State	Absolute growth in Population (million)	Growth in Population (per cent)	Absolute Growth in Employment (million)	Growth in Employment (per cent)	Difference between (3) & (5)
Andhra Pradesh	2.2	5.9	0.6	2.7	(-) 3.2(7)
Assam	1.7	10.7	0.3	6.1	(-) 4.6(10)
Bihar	3.8	8.9	0.1	0.5	(-) 8.4(16)
Gujarat	1.5	7.2	0.2	1.5	(-) 5.7(12)
Haryana	1.0	10.7	0.1	3.9	(-) 6.8(15)
Himachal Pradesh	0.3	8.7	0.4	2.1	(-) 6.6(14)
Jammu & Kashmir	0.4	8.9	0.2	15.5	(+)6.6(2)
Karnataka	1.7	7.2	0.4	3.4	(-) 3.8(8)
Kerala	1.4	7.2	0.6	8.8	(+)0.4(5)
Madhya Pradesh	2.6	7.0	0.2	1.2	(-) 5.8(13)
Maharashtra	2.1	5.8	0.3	1.3	(-) 4.5(9)
Orissa	1.3	6.2	0.2	1.7	(-) 4.5(9)
Punjab	0.6	6.0	0.3	8.2	(+)1.2(3)
Rajasthan	2.5	10.1	1.3	10.1	0.0(6)
Tamil Nadu	1.8	6.1	1.1	7.0	(+)0.9(4)
Tripura	0.2	12.6	0.4	7.5	(-) 5.1(11)
Uttar Pradesh	6.0	7.4	2.6	8.3	(+)0.9(4)
West Bengal	2.5	6.8	1.7	13.7	(+)6.9(1)
All-India	**35.04**	**7.4**	**10.4**	**4.9**	**(-) 2.5**

Source: RBI, *Occasional Papers*, December, 1989.

Note: Population refers to persons in the age-group 5 and above. Employment refers to usually employed by principal status. Figures in brackets indicate the ranks of the States.

TABLE 13.2: State-wise data on change in population (5+) and in employment by principal status for urban areas between 1983 and 1987-88

State	Absolute Growth in Population (million)	Growth in population (per cent)	Absolute Growth in Employment (million)	Growth in Employment (per cent)	Difference between (3) & (5)
(1)	(2)	(3)	(4)	(5)	(6)
Andhra Pradesh	2.3	19.2	0.8	17.3	(-) 1.9(9)
Assam	0.3	16.4	0.1	17.8	(+)0.6(6)
Bihar	1.8	21.9	0.3	11.6	(-)10.3(16)
Gujarat	1.5	15.4	0.9	29.7	(+)14.3(1)
Haryana	0.7	26.1	0.2	17.2	(-) 8.9(15)
Himachal Pradesh	0.4	12.5	(-) 0.2	(-)19.9	(-)32.4(17)
Jammu & Kashmir	0.2	16.3	0.1	19.0	(+)2.7(4)
Karnataka	2.1	20.2	0.6	15.8	(-) 4.4(13)
Kerala	0.7	15.8	0.25	16.3	(+)0.5(7)
Madhya Pradesh	2.4	23.5	1.0	28.5	(+)5.0(3)
Maharashtra	3.2	15.5	0.9	11.7	(-) 3.8(12)
Orissa	0.8	27.5	0.2	19.4	(-) 8.1(14)
Punjab	0.8	18.2	0.3	18.4	(+)0.2(8)
Rajasthan	1.6	23.5	0.6	25.1	(+)1.6(5)
Tamil Nadu	1.8	12.2	1.1	18.0	(+)5.8(2)
Uttar Pradesh	4.4	23.1	1.4	21.1	(-) 2.0(10)
West Bengal	1.7	12.5	0.5	9.0	(-) 3.5(11)
All-India	**28.5**	**18.7**	**9.05**	**16.1**	**(-) 2.6**

Source: RBI, *Occasional Papers*, December, 1989.
Note: Figures in brackets indicate the ranks of the States.

There are considerable and wide variations in the incidence of unemployment between regions/States. At the same time what comes out in sharp focus is the regional unevenness in the character of the unemployment problem. The inadequately developed States are substantially replete with chronic un- and under-employment. In some States the unemployment situation may assume alarming proportions before the turn of the century. In some States at present the level of unemployment is above the national average; in others it is below it. Relatively high unemployment and net outmigration are aspects of a relative paucity of economic opportunity in a region where the immigrant labour forms a considerable proportion of the total population; it is instrumental in depressing the wage level there.

Rural unemployment is much less prominent in those States

whose rural economy is more diversified and which encounter less population pressure. Open unemployment, that is, registered unemployment, affects the educated labour force of the States in a wide range of 0.3 to 14.6 per cent in share terms – West Bengal has the highest percentage share and Jammu & Kashmir has the lowest. Educated/registered unemployment is more or less co-terminus with urban unemployment, which is higher in those States which have either a higher density of population, or which have a higher percentage of working force, or which have a higher literacy rate or which have a higher urban-rural ratio of population. Urban male unemployment is very high in Kerala, Tamil Nadu and West Bengal.

Unemployment among skilled hands in tertiary activities, e.g., transport and communication, predominates in States which lack surfaced roads.

More explicitly, there are wide variations in educated unemployment as between States. It is much more critical in the eastern region. The incidence of professional and technical unemployment is higher in the comparatively less industrialised States, such as Punjab, Haryana, Rajasthan and Kerala. The southern region is more fraught with uneducated unemployment. Unskilled workers tend to move from the less to the more prosperous States. They form an appreciable proportion of the registered unemployed.

The foregoing estimate is based partly on the NSS data and partly on the Employment Exchanges data, and their underlying flaws have been overemphasised. Furthermore, the different NSS studies have preferred not to adhere to one and the same set of definitions and concepts. These account for the limitations of the conclusions reached by us in this and other sections.

14

APPROACH OF THE FIVE-YEAR PLANS TO THE PROBLEMS OF EMPLOYMENT AND UNEMPLOYMENT

The problems of employment or unemployment have been a matter of vital concern to the Indian planners and policy-makers from the right beginning. The First Plan considered the level of employment a welfare index. Attainment of full employment was one of its three main objectives. Opportunities for the fuller utilisation of the idle man-power had to be created, according to it. Elimination of unemployment was, in the opinion of the framers of the First Plan, the most important challenge of their time.

The Second Plan aimed at achieving larger increases in production, investment and employment. It realised that full employment was a far more difficult goal than expansion of employment opportunities, which became one of its four chief objectives. But larger employment opportunities were to be generated at higher levels of income. This was necessary for boosting the morale of the working population. The authors of the Second Plan saw no conflict, in the long run, between a policy directed at maximum growth of output and income and a policy directed at full employment. They thought that the unemployment problem was resolvable only by a series of intensive and planned efforts lasting over a pretty long period. To them, development stood for removal of unemployment and opening up of employment opportunities for all at rising levels of real income.

The Third Plan advocated utilisation to the fullest extent possible of the inadequately utilised manpower resources of the country, and ensuring of a substantial spurt in the employment opportunities was one of its five central objectives. It contained a suggestion that attempts at the generation of more employment opportunities should be concentrated in areas of high incidence of chronic underemployment.

In between the completion of the Third Plan and the commencement of the Fourth Plan three years lapsed, for which the country had three annual plans, which continued the policies of the past.

The formulators of the Fourth Plan realised ruefully that the tempo of economic development achieved during the previous three plans had been insufficient to provide productive employment to all and, therefore, wanted that tempo to be accelerated with a view to providing productive employment to all. They proposed specific measures for widening opportunities for productive work and employment at a sufficiently higher level of income for the common man and particularly the less privileged sections of society. They suggested avenues for fuller and more employment in agriculture. They favoured employment at a sufficiently high level of efficiency. They felt that employment opportunities would expand as the economy became more self-reliant. Expansion of employment remained an objective with them.

The framers of the Fifth Plan were the first to clearly perceive compatibility between growth and elimination of poverty and unemployment. They retained expansion of employment as one of the objectives. They regretted that much remained to be done in respect of creation of diversified and dispersed employment activities. They were strongly of the view that the Indian economy had reached a stage where larger availability of resources made it possible to launch a frontal attack on unemployment, underemployment and poverty and also to assure adequate growth. This made them desire maximisation of all possible openings for productive and meaningful employment, which, they thought was the major solvent or cure of poverty. They stressed the need for creating employment opportunities for the poorer sections of the population, including the marginally employed, so that their relative economic condition improved.

It appears from the preceding that the first five Five-Year Plans had an investment-cum-growth-oriented plan strategy. This can be interpreted to mean that the creation of employment opportunities for a quarter of a century since Independence was viewed more or less as an adjunct to or a by-product of the development strategy. Aside from this, the employment programmes were formulated and implemented in isolation of the on-going development projects.

However, in all honesty it cannot be denied that the Fifth Plan, in contradistinction to the Second Plan, had an element of pessimism in it in that it doubted the capability of the investment-oriented strategy or capital accumulation process to take care of the unemployment problem by itself.

The aborted Janata Draft Sixth Plan admitted that growth and employment were in conflict. It was the first plan to give employment the pride of place. It was the first plan to have an employment-oriented plan strategy consequent upon the realisation that the process of growth was no alchemy for the provision of employment to everybody as also observation of the concrete reality that those at the "wolf points" of poverty, i.e. on the verge of starvation, had been least benefited by whatever economic development the country had been able to achieve. For the removal of poverty and unemployment a high growth rate was not considered a necessary condition by the Sixth Plan, though the trend growth rate of 4.7 per cent per annum was recognised by it as one of a number of conditions conducive to it (that is, removal of poverty and unemployment), viz., redistribution of income, increasing demand for labour-intensive goods, accelerated investment in rural infrastructure and social services. The growth rate could at best be a secondary, not a primary, condition, according to the authors of the Sixth Plan.

The Sixth Plan had progressive reduction of unemployment as one of its key objectives. Very high priority was accorded to it, as was to removal of poverty. The Plan was seized of the imperative need of maximising employment. With employment as the norm of the Plan policy, development was, according to its proponents, to be channelled in those directions which could help all citizens to earn their daily bread. The architects of the Sixth Plan ascribed perpetuation of poverty and unemployment to the undervaluation of human resources and the overvaluation of material resources. But this assertion is not free of a certain amount of ambiguity. In one strain it is stated that meaningful solutions to problems of unemployment and underemployment (as also to poverty) could be found only within the ambit of a rapidly expanding economy, that a carefully balanced growth scenario and an adequate growth rate of GDP would result in a net increase in employment, measured in Standard Person Years, i.e., 3.4 per cent per annum, which was significantly higher than the growth rate of the labour force, i.e. 2.4

per cent per annum. But in another strain it is pointed out that the feasible growth rate of GDP, between 5 and 5.5 per cent per annum, would not allay these maladies unless supplemented by other direct methods, such as a less uneven distribution of income and consumption and a less rapid rate of growth of population (the two other causes of the persistence of these economic ills) as well as choice of an appropriate composition of sectors and techniques that generated employment without affecting adversely the growth in productivity in conjunction with specific employment schemes. Without a determined effort in these directions a substantial reduction in unemployment and poverty would not be possible. Concludingly, not only was reduction of unemployment made secondary to alleviation of poverty by those who drafted the Sixth Plan but also made ambivalently dependent on growth by them. This is why the Sixth Plan cannot be said to be employment-oriented in the same sense that the Seventh Plan can be said to be so.

The Seventh Plan set four cardinal objectives, namely, growth, modernisation, self-reliance and social justice before itself. But "the central element" in its development strategy was "the generation of productive employment", that is, expansion of employment opportunities consistent with increase in productivity. On this ground the Seventh Plan may be said to have become employment-oriented. It emphasised policies and programmes appertaining to increased employment opportunities. It espoused a direct attack on unemployment (as also on poverty and regional imbalances). But its aim at a significant reduction in the incidence of poverty (let alone that in regional imbalances) was a concomitant of its emphasis on the generation of productive employment. The Seventh Plan predicted a four per cent per annum growth of employment potential that would be competent to meet the exigencies of a 2.6 per cent growth rate of labour force in general that of rural labour force being slightly lower, at 2.0 per cent per annum). Employment had to grow in agriculture at the rate of 3.5 per cent per annum, and in non-agriculture at the rate of 4.5 per cent per annum. The creators of the Seventh Plan hoped that the employment-oriented strategy would bring about a qualitative, structural change in the economy in the sense of a new production pattern, and the two would interact uninterruptedly within the time span of the Plan and thereafter.

So far as the approach of the Eighth Plan, as drafted by the Planning Commission during the period of V.P. Singh was Prime

Minister, is concerned, we have summarised it in another section in an earlier chapter.

The reconstituted Planning Commission by Chandra Shekhar expressed an opinion that a time-bound decentralised phased programme of not less than ten years was essential to fulfil the commitment of "right to work" which, as a fundamental right, may be laudable but perhaps had, in fact, the making of a most serious and complex commitment. Such unemployed youths as were prepared to work in rural areas that had nearly 70 per cent of our population had to be given priority in selection. However, the majority of our poor could be given the right only in a phased manner, spanning at least a decade or even longer.

The national consensus has always favoured eradication of unemployment at the earliest and conceding to all those who are unemployed equal rights to feasible opportunities for future employment. We have had in this country a body of opinion advocating this, even if it involved loss of scale economies as well as social surplus, and hence a slower rise in the incomes of the rest of the community in the long run. Employment ought to be provided in the short run to those at the bottom rung of our society. On the other side, we have had the insistence of those who were convinced that the country had not yet reached the stage where people, one and all, could enjoy the right to an adequate means of livelihood.

15

THE SPECIAL PROBLEM OF EDUCATED UNEMPLOYMENT IN INDIA

We would start off in this section with an inventory of the data for the Plan period based on the live registers of the employment exchanges, assuming that they furnish an approximate idea of the trend in the growth of the number of the educated unemployed, if not of their absolute number in any year on account of the fact that only a fraction of the unemployed educated registered themselves with the employment exchanges in the earlier years — the figure for 1954 is around 25 per cent, but with the passage of time the percentage has definitely gone up.

The number of registered job-seekers was 0.28 million in December, 1951:

Technical	:	41469
Clerical	:	85057
Unskilled	:	162445
Total	:	288971

In 1960 the number of persons on the live registers of employment exchanges was 1.6 million. In 1961 it was 1.83 million.

Table 15.1 presents State-wise data on the unemployment situation during 1961-66 and in 1970. In 1970 the number of registered unemployment was 3.7 million. Unemployment, specially of the technically trained persons, was acute during 1966-69. The States with larger populations and higher literacy rates had higher percentages of registered unemployment. Those which were better off were in a position to create more employment opportunities.

TABLE 15.1: The unemployment situation in 1970

State	Year : 1970 Total No. of Application for jobs	Year : 1970 Percentage Share of the State	Percentage Rise in Employment and Unemployment during 1961-66	
			Employment	Unemployment
1	2	3	4	5
Andhra Pradesh	2,16,254	6.9(7)	25.4(7)	31.4(12)
Assam	55,358	1.7(15)	0.0(13)	145.0(2)
Bihar	2,87,742	9.2(5)	12.4(12)	126.5(3)
Gujarat	1,28,658	4.0(110)	16.7(10)	39.0(11)
Haryana	59,040	1.8(14)	—	—
Jammu & Kashmir	8,022	0.2(16)	—	—
Kerala	2,41,331	7.6(6)	35.9(4)	3.0(13)
Madhya Pradesh	1,98,492	6.2(9)	19.0(9)	169.0(1)
Maharashtra	3,02,030	9.5(4)	40.1(3)	64.8(6)
Mysore(Karnataka)	2,10,799	6.6(8)	43.2(2)	98.5(4)
Orissa	1,22,560	3.7(11)	14.7(11)	82.2(5)
Punjab	83,811	2.6(12)	47.7(1)	54.1(8)
Rajasthan	82,677	2.5(13)	—	—
Tamil Nadu	3,52,371	11.2(2)	19.6(8)	51.5(9)
Uttar Pradesh	3,19,666	10.2(3)	25.9(6)	39.7(10)
West Bengal	4,96,475	16.1(1)	32.9(5)	61.4(7)

Source: Directorate of Employment & Training, *Employment Review*, Government of India.

Note: Figures in brackets indicate the ranks of the States.

In 1978 the number of the registered unemployed was 12.7 million.

The number of job-seekers on the live registers of the employment exchanges showed a rise of 13 per cent from 14.33 million in December, 1979, to 16.29 million in December, 1980. The number of registered job-seekers was 23.5 million in 1984.

Between 1961 and 1984 the number of registered job-seekers had risen at the rate of 11.7 per cent per annum.

The number of registered job-seekers was 30.2 million in 1987-88.

Between 1950-51 and 1987-88 the number of registered job-seekers had multiplied by 100 times.

Table 15.2 has a wider time-scale as one of its co-ordinates, that is, from 1952 to 1988. It also contains data on the literacy rates in 1951 and 1981. With risen literacy rates the number of persons registering themselves with the employment exchanges naturally shot up, though it is extremely difficult for us to postulate any correlation between the extent of registered unemployment and the rate of literacy in the States. Similarly, it would not be plausible or convincing, were we to insinuate that the percentages of the populations below the Poverty Line in different States have had any correlation with the States' percentages in total registered unemployment.

The supply of the educated labour force has increased rapidly because its private cost has been low and because a higher educational degree has meant better employment.

The employment exchanges do not appear to have made much of a dent on the unemployment situation in the country.

As Table 15.3 shows, in 1989 vacancies notified through employment exchanges and university information and guidance bureaux were nearly 9 per cent of total registrations. Only 0.01 per cent of job-seekers on the live registers of employment exchanges had notices of vacancies. Placements were just half the total number of notified vacancies, which, in turn, were only 2 per cent of all vacancies.

The employment exchange figures do not and cannot furnish a reliable idea of the total volume of unemployment for obvious reasons,* though they are more prone to be underestimates rather than overestimates.

The employment exchange data suffer from urban, male and educational biases.

Educated unemployment is one part of total or general unemployment. It is the spearhead of urban unemployment.

A change in the number in the live registers of employment exchanges can be taken as a broad indicator of the trends of unemployment in the economy.

Educated unemployment is pre-eminently coordinate with open unemployment. Open unemployment encompasses non-educated rural and urban unemployment as well, but only secondarily.

The educated unemployed are those who have obtained at least a matriculation or a higher secondary education certificate. Many of

---

* For details see K.N. Prasad, *Problems of Economic Development in the Third World,* 1980, pp. 176-78.

TABLE 15.2: The unemployment situation

State	Number * 1952 End	As Percentage of All-India Total	Literacy Rate 1951	Number* March 1988 ('000s)	As Percentage of All-India Total	Literacy Rate 1981	Percentage of Population below the Poverty Line 1983-84
1	2	3	4	5	6	7	8
Andhra Pradesh (Hyderabad)	27852	6.3(4)	13.2(9)	2679	9.1(5)	29.9(9)	36.4(7)
Assam	8214	1.8(9)	18.3(6)	841	2.8(11)	NA	23.5(13)
Bihar	27162	6.2(5)	12.2(10)	2649	8.9(6)	26.2(13)	49.5(1)
Himachal Pradesh	—	—	7.7(14)	348	1.1(13)	42.5(5)	13.5(17)
Jammu & Kashmir	—	—	—	126	0.4(14)	26.7(12)	16.3(14)
Karnataka(Mysore)	—	—	19.3(5)	996	3.3(10)	38.5(7)	35.0(8)
Kerala	—	—	40.7(1)	2914	9.8(4)	70.4(1)	26.8(11)
Orissa	4954	1.1(10)	15.3(7)	753	2.5(12)	34.2(8)	42.8(4)
Punjab	22693	5.0(7)	15.2(8)	1234 (Punjab:654) (Haryana:580)	4.2(9) (2.2+2.0)	40.9(6) (Haryana:43.7)	13.8(16)
Madhya Pradesh	20821	4.5(8)	9.8(12)	1497	5.1(8)	27.9(10)	46.2(2)
Maharashtra (Bombay including Gujarat)	62351	14.2(3)	20.9(3)	3375 (Maharashtra: 2598 (Gujarat:777	11.4(2) (8.8+2.6)	47.2(2) (Gujarat 43.7(4)	34.9(9)
Tamil Nadu(Madras)	89053	20.3(1)	20.8(4)	2478	8.4(7)	46.8(14)	39.6(5)
Uttar Pradesh	88471	20.1(2)	10.8(11)	2975	10.1(3)	27.2(11)	45.3(3)
West Bengal	62321	14.2(3)	24.0(2)	4341	16.7(1)	40.9(6)	39.2(6)
All-India	437571	100.0	16.6	29568	100.0	36.2	37.4

* On the live-registers of employment exchanges.

Source: (1) *Statistical Abstract of India,* 1952-53. (2) *Census of India*

Note: Figures in brackets indicate the ranks of the States.

TABLE 15.3: The unemployment situation in 1989 *('000)*

State	Registrations	(2) as Percentage of All-India Total	Vacancies Notified	(4) as Percentage of All-India Total	Placements	(6) as Percentage of All-India Total	Live Register (Cumulative Figures)	(8) as Percentage of All-India Total
1	2	3	4	5	6	7	8	9
Andhra Pradesh	459.4	6.9(2)	62.2	10.3	27.4	9.3	2818.9	8.6(2)
Assam	179.2	2.7(5)	11.1	1.8	6.3	2.2	973.7	2.9(4)
Bihar	804.3	12.2(1)	28.1	4.6	15.4	5.3	3048.7	9.3(1)
Gujarat	173.0	2.6(6)	35.4	5.9	14.2	4.9	939.0	2.8(5)
Haryana	204.5	3.1(4)	28.6	4.7	6.9	2.4	574.0	1.7(6)
Himachal Pradesh	102.7	1.5(7)	10.5	1.7	6.9	2.4	418.5	1.3(7)
Jammu & Kashmir	23.3	0.3(8)	2.0	0.3	0.4	0.1	125.5	0.4(8)
Karnataka	300.0	4.5(3)	22.3	3.7	8.3	2.8	1242.7	3.8(3)
All-India	6575.8	10.0	600.2	100.0	289.2	100.0	32776.2	100.0

Source: Directorate of Employment & Training, Government of India, *Employment Review*. Data were furnished by employment exchanges and University Information and Guidance Bureaus.

Note: Figures in brackets indicate the ranks of the States.

the nominally educated are probably in the category of persons who leave school before matriculation or obtain a bare pass class in higher examinations.

Higher percentages of unemployment among the educated rather than among the illiterate working class constitute the crux of the people.

Even though the educated manpower currently accounts for only 10 per cent of the total labour force (of age-group 15 to 59 years), the problem of educated unemployment looms large because of the investment by society of enormous sums of money in education and training. Per student public expenditure increases steeply with the level of education and training. Therefore, the society is intensely seized of the necessity of properly utilising the educated manpower.

The dimension and gravity of educated unemployment varies from State to State.

In 1953-54, 8.6 per cent of the total number of the educated were unemployed. They numbered 0.24 million.

The unemployed graduates and post-graduates numbered 26,800 in 1955 and 1,21,500 in 1957.

In 1957, 33.4 per cent of the total employment exchange registrations were those made by the educated unemployed .

In 1961 the percentage of the educated unemployed to the total unemployed was 32.3, as given by the employment exchange data, and 25.7, as given by the census data.

In 1968-69, 20.5 per cent of the total number of the educated were unemployed.

In 1971, 13.2 per cent of the total number of 2,88,460 educated persons were unemployed. The number of educated job-seekers increased from 1,02,600 in 1967 to 20,53,300 in 1971. In 1971 the percentage of educated unemployment to total unemployment was 45.1, as based on the employment exchange data, and 29.6, as based on the census data. The percentage of unemployment was highest (17.7%) among the matriculates and non-matriculates and lowest (3.5%) among those who possessed the doctorate degree. The incidence of unemployment was heaviest (20%) among those who had some technical or vocational training. It was next heaviest among those who had been science students.

In 1972, 48 per cent of the total employment exchange registrations were those more by the educated unemployed. Their total number was between 6.9 million and 8 million, inclusive of 10 to

12 per cent of the unemployed who were not registered.

The unemployed graduates and post-graduates numbered 3.5 million in 1977.

The number of educated job-seekers increased from 6.93 million in June, 1979, to 7.66 million in June 1980.

In 1981 the percentage of educated unemployment to total employment was 50.6, as based on the employment exchange data, and 46.8, as based on the census data.

In 1983 the percentage of educated unemployment to total unemployment was 50.8, as based on the employment exchange data.

The number of the educated unemployed was 24 million* in 1985 and 33.2 million in 1990. Of these, 26 per cent were graduates and professionally qualified persons and the rest, 74 per cent, were matriculates and higher secondary passes.

Employment among the educated grew at the rate of over seven per cent per annum during 1983-88, whereas general employment grew at the rate of 1.55 per cent per annum during the same period. But the supply of the educated unemployed grew at a faster rate during that period. Unbridled supply, nay, oversupply culminated in the devaluation of the graduates' worth in the market. The number of persons seeking clerical posts went up spectacularly.

The educated comprise 40 per cent of the openly unemployed in India. The percentage for Punjab is 59 and for Haryana 47. The rates of open unemployment are high in Kerala (17.07%), West Bengal (6.06%), Punjab (5.86%) and Haryana (4.04%). The high rates of open unemployment in the better-off States are generally accompanied by a high proportion of the educated among the unemployed.

Among the job-seekers, the proportion of the educated unemployed is very high.

The category of the young educated with education up to the secondary level and above form nearly 11.5 per cent of the total young labour-force but account for about one-third of total unemployment.

About 23.8 per cent of the educated unemployed are secondary-level, and 9.4 per cent graduate and above level.

But not all matriculates and graduates seek employment.

---

* Another estimate is 4.8 million.

Those in the 15 to 29 years age-group subsume about 11.5 per cent of the total educated unemployed but comprise approximately 33.2 per cent of total unemployment.

The incidence of unemployment is much higher among the more educated in the 15-24 years age-brackets.

Three-fourths of the educated unemployed are men and 45 per cent of them are in rural areas.

The educated unemployed have generally to wait for long before they are employed.

A special study in 1958-59 of the Delhi University graduates disclosed that 3.3 per cent of those who had graduated in 1950 and 7.2 per cent of those who had graduated in 1954 were still unemployed. Of those employed, one-fourth of the 1950 batch graduates and two-fifths of the 1954 batch graduates worked as clerks. The picture in other universities was probably far less favourable.

The period of waiting by an educated unemployed had increased from 62.4 weeks in 1953-54 to 95 weeks in 1968-69. But when employment was obtained, the costs of such a long waiting were offset.

The capacity of any economy to absorb the educated is a function of its structure as well as its rate of growth. Educated unemployment exists in India because the expectations of the educated have not conformed to the structure of the economy or its rate of growth.

The real culprit for the prevalent malaise is the failure of the market of educated labour.

The out-turn of graduates is on a mass scale. Their market is glutted/saturated with their supply.

Blaug refers to two notable conundrums : (1) The short-run conundrum relates to why the wages of the educated people do not fall sufficiently either far or fast until all the unemployed are employed and (2) the long-run conundrum concerns the fact that when the wages of the educated people fall, their supply keeps on rising as fast as before.

Education today is positively correlated with unemployment. More education implies more open, more urban unemployment. An inverted U-shaped educated unemployment curve is typical of developing countries — the rate of educated unemployment is lower for primary school-leavers but higher for secondary school-leavers. For University graduates it is lower than that for secondary school-leavers.

Educated unemployment takes after a pyramid. The unemployment rates fall off at the higher educational levels. Of the total educated unemployed, 71 per cent are matriculates.

A higher level of education is generally associated with better employment, a higher level of income and a better status in society.

Life spent in an academic institution is socially acceptable and is at huge public cost. Outside it life fails to get a start — and if it gets a start at all, it is hard and uninteresting.

The disenchantment of many educated employed with their present positions is in utter discord with their self-image. For their jobs do not match or correspond with their qualifications and expectations.

It is unquestionable that education improves the vertical mobility of labour.

Income becomes embodied in education which cannot be redistributed, though society can benefit from an individual's education on account of its external economy effect.

Students go in for higher education in spite of their knowledge that it is no good on account of what Myint terms the "fallacy of misplaced concreteness".

In the face of the prevalent rates of educated unemployment in the country students persist in demanding higher education more and more not only because it provides status and prestige but also because it still pays off handsomely to them in terms of future earnings, even after allowing for the private costs of education and the possibility of being unemployed for a considerable period of time and because it is, besides being a producer good, also a consumer good and hence a conventional need for a sizable chunk of the population.

The graduates are being shoddily turned out. Devoid of chiselling and polishing and proper motivation and orientation, they betray absolute lack of self-discpline and work culture. Both students and their teachers pursue their non-academic economic interests more vigorously and energetically, more devotedly and committedly than their academic interests.

Considering the fact that the least educated are often the most marginalised among the educated employed, as far as possible, the more educated unemployed should not be employed at the cost of the less educated unemployed.

The mismatch or imbalance in demand and supply of the educated has arisen because the creation of graduates and post-graduates is not poised, not geared, not attuned to the manpower needs of the different sectors, regions and classes of the economy. Alongside has stemmed a maladjustment between the educational system and the socio-economic needs of the country.

There are idle men but there are no jobs for them. There are vacant jobs but there are no suitable candidates to fill them. There are vacant jobs and also suitable candidates to fill them but they are not being filled. The given administrative machinery is so much preoccupied with day-to-day law and order problems that it has no time left for taking stock of vacancies and getting them filled in the regular way. Ad hoc and arbitrary appointments are the only remedy in such circumstances.

On the one hand, many trained persons have failed to find jobs. On the other, people with the desired kind of skill and training have not been available. Evidently, this has been due to a communication gap between institutions producing trained persons and establishments and departments demanding them.

There has been a misbalance between literary or general education, on the one hand, and vocational, technical or specialised education, on the other. By comparison, technical education has been better planned than general education in the teeth of unending pressures for admission.

In 1951 the intake in degree as well as diploma courses had exceeded the output of technical hands in engineering and technology, as Table 15.4 shows.

TABLE 15.4: Technical education (1951)

	Output		Intake	
	Degree Courses	Diploma Courses	Degree Courses	Diploma Courses
Engineering	2152	1923	3755	1935
Technology	675	1338	885	1523

Source: *First Five-Year Plan.*

Whereas the number of the educated unemployed in technical professions, as registered with employment exchanges, was 41,469 in

December 1951, that in clerical positions was 85,057 — a difference of over 200 times.

The average level of education of the unemployed appears to have risen sharply in recent years.

Disparities in the level of education are larger in urban than in rural areas.

The educated unemployed from rural middle class families swell the ranks of the unemployed in urban areas.

The educated unemployed would not accept jobs below their education and skill level and they would not starve either because they are maintained by their parents and guardians and other relations and hence they would even prefer to remain voluntarily unemployed.

The educated unemployed are after white-collar, soft-handed jobs. They have a distaste for agricultural and manual work. They despise it.

Stereotyped schemes for rural or urban employment cannot provide a reasonable answer to the problem of educated unemployment.

Openings for the educated unemployed are : In the primary sector as village-level workers, agricultural research officers and assistants; in development of scientific agriculture, as agricultural census officers and farm managers; in co-operatives; in the Minimum Needs Programmes, the rural works programme, inland fishery, block-level planning, dairy, processing, marketing and trade operations, rural small industrial centres, other industries between cottage and large industries, rural banking, establishments of democratic institutions at the district, block and village levels, tourism — both in wage-employment and self-employment. Expansion of these openings will help rural areas to retain the services and leadership of their educated youth. However, the primary remedy of the educated unemployment consists in expanding avenues of self-employment.

Education, public health and other social services have been the biggest absorbers of the educated unemployed. All the same, the public sector's capacity to absorb the educated unemployed in these spheres is not limitless.

The secondary remedy of educated unemployment lies in expanding the organised sector substantially.

The above concerns demand-side management. On the supply

side, an overhaul of the educational system is long overdue. This means combining vocational teaching with school education before the students become helplessly spoilt and begin to detest vocational education. Secondly, educational facilities should not be developed in those directions in which they are likely to aggravate the existing unemployment problem. Thirdly, so that the educated do not become unemployable refresher courses should be run at short intervals. At present a sizable number of the unemployed graduates are literally unemployable. Along with this, the current unemployed should be made more employable through short-term training/vocational programmes. Fourthly, the educated unemployed ought to be motivated towards manual work through means like the orientation camps. They should be taught the dignity of labour and encouraged to take up manual work until they could secure white-collar and soft-handed office jobs. They (especially the technical/professional graduates) should be motivated to shake off their disinclination for and prejudice against working in rural and undeveloped areas and to become barefoot professionals and technicians but at the same time some of the unattractive service conditions of such posts should be improved. Fifthly, the educated should be motivated to discard their locational preferences. They seem to suffer from regional immobility, except at fairly high levels. Sixthly, supply should be adjusted with demand by means of suitable incentives and opportunities. There exist surpluses of supply of educated persons with regard to certain occupations and professions and shortages in others. It is still difficult to get persons of one's choice to man the productive processes in certain departments and industries. These are the index of structural maladjustments : apprenticeship training ought to be imparted. This would enable the employers to have experienced hands. The employers should also try to expand facilities for practical in-plant training to meet the requirements of the apprenticeship legislation. Even now technically qualified persons are likely to secure employment sooner than generally educated persons. Simultaneously, the educational system should be streamlined to meet the rapidly changing pattern of personnel requirements. Seventhly, vocational counselling and guidance services should be further developed. Finally, the upper-caste and upper-class bias of higher education should be weeded out of the present order.

The resource back-up for the purpose of fully tapping the existing reservoir of the educated unemployed is far from adequate in the country.

The problem of educated unemployment has assumed such a form and such a proportion by now that the country may ere long be compelled to ration employment among the educated persons.

The manpower situation of today is the outcome of what has happened before. Likewise, the present developments in the demographic, educational and economic fields would determine what the manpower situation would be in the future. But the demographic, educational and economic factors act and react on one another, with the result that significant changes in one or more of them are bound to be reflected in the manpower situation in due course of time. Hence, education, employment and development should become catalysts of each other. The three have to be linked in a virtually supportive manner. That is to say, it is necessary to evolve an integrated employment, education and development strategy.

A determined effort will have to be made to promote self-employment by providing training, credit, marketing and guidance facilities – the wherewithal to achieve greater productivity from the assets they work upon. All appointments should be made through local employment exchanges.

Public undertakings and state-aided agencies should prefer local candidates, qualifications being equal.

Manpower planning, which is a sort of advance planning, is needed for assessing demand and making provision for supply of manpower in a progressing country. Manpower planning is manpower budgeting. It is necessitated by the fact that although educated manpower is about 10 per cent of the total labour force in developing countries, the public expenditure on provision of educational facilities to this section of society is a substantial figure.

Under manpower planning manpower needed for the fulfilment of the targets of growth of different sectors of the economy is developed. Manpower planning purports to ensure the proper linkage of economic planning with manpower and educational planning so that no plan programme later suffers from a lack of the trained manpower which is needed.

Under manpower planning skills are developed consistent with the level of technology, the local environment and the development process in line with the felt social needs.

The twin objectives of manpower planning are : (1) Planning supply to match forecasts of manpower requirements and (2) planning economic development with the sole aim of the full employment of the existing labour force. But these do not necessarily coincide because the manpower requirements might be met and yet the excess supply of the educated people might be left unemployed.

One precondition of the success of manpower planning is that information should be widely disseminated through vocational counselling and guidance services. Another is the arranging of crash training programmes with a view to reorienting the educated unemployed/employed.

But such programmes in technical education, in particular, tend to centre on quantity and totally ignore quality. This should deliberately be avoided. Similarly, regional or inter-speciality imbalances in the demand and supply of the broad categories of the trained personnel must thoughtfully be eliminated.

In India the District Manpower Planning and Employment Generation Council pursues a disaggregated approach to the unemployment problem. It prepares a manpower budget for the district. It identifies avenues of self-employment, sound from the point of view of cost, return and risk. It also conducts training programmes. It comes under the decentralised approach adopted in the Plan, which supposes that the district employment plan is competent to tackle the educated unemployment problem.

The long-term objective of manpower planning should be to reach an equilibrium between growth of educated labour force and employment opportunities.

Lastly, the country should judiciously examine the worthwhileness of encouraging the highly qualified to go abroad to work there. In 1966, 20,000 educated Indians were employed abroad. In 1989 the number of Indians who had gone abroad for employment was 1.2 lakhs.

International migration or *Brain Drain* is often out of the fear on the part of the more qualified persons that if they stayed behind in their own country, they would in all probability get locked up in inferior and poorly paid posts for the whole of their life (and their brain would be in the drain, as some one put it jocularly).

To the extent international migration has occurred, it has eased the task of the Indian Government but has cost the nation dear.

The solution of the problem of the educated unemployed should be viewed in its two component parts, viz., the backlog and the new entrants, and the short-term and the long-term time-phasing of the programme should be hammered out.

The former Deputy Chairman of the Planning Commission, Mohan Dharia, had suggested that such unemployed persons from rural areas as could not be accommodated in the IRDP of the respective villages as well as the unemployed from urban areas willing to join and work in rural areas should be allowed to join the *Land Army* which would attend to the work of huge wasteland development, afforestation, minor and major irrigation, road projects, etc.

16

SOME GENERAL REFLECTIONS ON THE UNEMPLOYMENT PROBLEM IN INDIA

The unemployment question in India has the following aspects:

1. An over-all, aggregative aspect.
2. Rural and urban dimensions.
3. Appearance in different forms, such as involuntary/chronic unemployment, disguised unemployment/underemployment and seasonal unemployment (ignoring frictional and technological unemployment).
4. Educated unemployment versus general/non-educated unemployment.
5. The backlog of the unemployed and the new entrants.
6. Sectoral, regional/spatial and class distribution of unemployment.

As a rule, a fresh demand for labour is created from increased national output consequent upon increased investment expenditure.

The employment potential of a Plan is based on data showing how employment responds to the different kinds of investment stimuli, indicating additional employment per unit of investment and/or increase in output in different sectors, population available for gainful employment, manpower requirements of all branches of economic activity, etc.

It is difficult to assess accurately the effects of a plan on the employment situation prevalent in an economy. The estimates of employment effects are subject to a considerable degree of uncertainty. The estimate of increased employment may be so much of a guess that one and the same estimate can be produced for widely varying totals of the Plan outlay.

All estimates of employment assume absence of any major,

significant change in any direction. They assume that production and employment would not be allowed to fall below their existing levels. They assume that development programmes would be carried out with efficiency and economy and in a continuous, on-going manner.

The estimates made would be more meaningful and reliable for public policy if distinctions were made in the demand and supply of labour in terms of their location, rural-urban residence, self- and wage-employment, etc., and the demand likely to be generated in different regions for different categories of labour were identified.

In estimating the employment potential of the proposed increased output, allowance must be made for productivity changes, the known phenomenon of proportionally more work and less pay and less leisure and fewer holidays in the private sector, as compared to the situation in the public sector, creation of full-time and part-time jobs, and so on.

The private sector employees' estimates of employment should be tested in the light of objective standards. For they estimate their future labour requirements by assuming that additional production would lead to a proportionate rise in employment. This assumption is dependent on the volume of idle labour engaged, the revised man-machine ratio consequent upon the installation of new machinery, the rationalisation schemes under contemplation, etc.

In evaluating the employment impact of the Plan projects and programmes, the imperfections of the labour market cannot be ignored. They include, besides the usual text-book imperfections, the tendency of employment to beget employment, that is, the concentration of employment in the already employed families, because of personal influences or on compassionate grounds, caste considerations, reservation of posts, vacancies reserved for demobilised war personnel, preferences shown to displaced persons, appointments of the nearest kith and kin of persons dying in harness or killed in battles or wars, caste or communal riots and accidents while travelling by the public modes of transport (which amounts to denial of employment opportunities to others), higher castes taking up menial jobs in government or semi-government departments and then sub-letting them to members of lower castes, persons employed on full-time basis in government departments doing other jobs or businesses privately on a part-time basis in *benami* (fake) names, and the like.

Plan outlays on employment programmes are supposed to create more than proportionate employment *directly* as well as *indirectly* by activising those resources which could not be fully utilised through other developmental programmes, some of them providing built-in correctives. The aim is to create continuing employment. Such *employment multiplier effects* are visualised in two phases—construction phase and post-construction phase, which would be the *continuing phase.* The latter is regarded as attainable only through the cumulative effects of a variety of schemes in different sectors.

To put it differently, an economic activity provides direct employment in the sector concerned but it also provides indirect employment by creating demand for intermediate output by other sectors.

The immediate effect of direct employment in the primary and secondary sectors lies in stepping up the degree of utilisation of persons currently underemployed in these sectors. In agriculture underemployment gets reduced nearly thrice the amount of new employment provided in it by the development programmes. The rise of employment at the farm level is the primary employment effect, while the rise of employment at the level of marketing and distribution of the additional output is the secondary effect. A larger proportion of the generated employment opportunities ordinarily escapes to the non-agricultural sectors.

Increase of direct employment in the primary and secondary sectors enhance indirect employment in the tertiary/services sector. Indirect employment is automatic responses in employment. It is 52 to 56 per cent of direct employment generated in the development projects. In agriculture it is 30 per cent. This is how the earlier plans calculated them.

The secondary or multiplier effects of investment on employment take more time to mature and manifest themselves but they are more impressive. They rest on a complex of factors, viz., the amount of increased output, the elasticity of demand for the products comprising the increased output and the extent to which it induces the growth of technically related activities. The mechanism comprising them is inversely related to the leaks like savings, payment of taxes and purchase of goods produced in other areas. It is stronger in those areas where external economies are present in sufficient quantity.

In socio-economic overheads indirect employment is 1.52 times the direct employment. In construction works indirect employment is

1.60 times the direct employment. In minor irrigation indirect employment is nearly half the direct employment. In major irrigation it is thrice the direct employment.

In some other countries the multiplier effect of a two-year programme of basic works for every unit of employment tended to be as low as only 0.3 unit because investment was scattered in a large number of areas, mostly retarded; on low-yield projects of the relief-type, involving short-term operations and in the nature of transfer payments meant to improve income distribution; and because the leaks of investment and operating expenditures to outside areas were high.

Investigations point out that in our big cities one formal job created three informal jobs. Where subsistence farming obtains, no employment mutiplier effect is realised. The employment stimuli are transmitted only to the extent that subsistence farming can produce a remarkable surplus of foodgrains and industrial raw materials.

Areas specialising in rapid-growth activities (i.e. *tough* activities) like energy, communications, construction, heavy electricals, metal, chemical, etc., have displayed net upward proportionality shifts in total employment. Their multiplier effects are far-reaching in impact.

Areas specialising in slow-growth activities (i.e., *smooth* activities) like mining, forestry, agriculture, food processing, etc., have exhibited net downward proportionality shifts in total employment. Their multiplier effects are limited in impact.

Each State has its *meat* (more prosperous) areas as well as its *bone* (less prosperous) areas also from the point of view of agricultural production, just as the different crops have different elasticities of labour absorption with regard to output. According to a study[1] in recent years (1980-81 to 1986-87), wheat, paddy, and sugarcane have tended to employ relatively less labour, whereas groundnut, cotton, jute, *jowar* and *bajra* have tended to employ relatively more labour. But in this there are inter-State variations. The range of labour absorption in as much as 25 man-days per hectare for gram in Haryana and 376 man-days for sugarcane in Maharashtra. For paddy Madhya Pradesh generates an employment of 72 mandays per hectare, compared with 159 mandays in Tamil Nadu. In sugarcane Bihar's figure is 122 man-days, as against 377 man-days per hectare in Maharashtra. In the case of wheat, Madhya Pradesh generates 46 man-days a hectare, while Bihar employs 92 man-days. Mustard has a range of 34 man-days in the case of

Haryana and 72 man-days in the case of Assam. In groundnut the range is from 61 man-days in the case of Gujarat to 136 man-days in the case of Orissa. Broadly speaking, States which have made major strides in recent years in particular crops employ more labour, compared to States which have already reached a certain level of development. Wheat in Bihar, groundnut in Orissa, soyabean in Madhya Pradesh, mustard in Assam (followed by Rajasthan) and tur in Uttar Pradesh are some instances. This confirms the hypothesis that in the process of agricultural development farmers do employ more labour in the initial stages. However, when growth in production and yields reach a high level, the employment intensity diminishes.

The moral of the above is this: Given the fact that over-all employment intensity of agriculture is on the decline and a spread of technology in new areas would be less labour-intensive that it was in the traditional Green Revolution areas, it becomes imperative that crops with high second-round employment effects are identified. Crops with high direct labour absorption are sugarcane, paddy, cotton, and jute in the same order.

It is generally held that in the realm of agriculture more than elsewhere it is possible to identify those alternatives that generate employment immediately as well as enhance agricultural productivity so that the community can enjoy the fruits of both increased output and increased employment.

The improved agricultural practices (which normally require more labour) and increased yields (which should normally require more labour to harvest) should be accelerating rural employment.

In India for one per cent increase in yield per acre, labour input increases between 0.50 and 0.75 per cent. Were the yield per acre doubled, employment could conceivably rise by 50 per cent.

It is estimated that in east India an investment of Rs. 1,150 crores on minor irrigation covering 1.5 million hectares would generate 412.5 million man-days of direct employment alone, leave aside indirect employment generated and an increase in agricultural production worth Rs. 5400 crores in five years. Tube-wells create demand for both types of agricultural workers, permanent and casual.

The immediate employment ėffect of higher income in rural areas is not articulate but as the trend of rising income becomes firm, employment opportunities proliferate. Villagers need many services and in many areas they are capable of paying for them. These needs have only to be identified and educated people organized and assisted to take up the jobs on self-employment basis. The Seventh Plan particularly realised the need to generate employment opportunities for the educated youth in rural areas.

It is felt that increased market orientation of agricultural production in the eastern States would provide more effective employment opportunities.

It would be expedient to state here that the over-all, nation-wide, estimates of unemployment, underemployment and employment potential of a Plan are not enough. Their regional distribution is equally essential for planning. For the purpose of evolving an appropriate public policy it is necessary to identify factors influencing the levels of rural employment on a regional basis. The additional employment generated in rural areas must fit in with the location, skills and idle time of the unemployed. Agricultural planning executed on the basis of a comprehensive area approach is likely to prove effective in generating additional employment through ancillary activities involving animal husbandry, better utilisation of conventional waste materials, and so on. But area-specific employment planning through agriculture calls for a multi-level approach. So far we have been preoccupied with agriculture.

Let us now take up industry. Since Independence the Big Push for rapid industrialisation has been the catch or code word for development in India. Among other hopes, one hope pinned on it was that it would generate a significant number of employment opportunities. Among other policies, one policy has been to encourage development of industrial activity in identified backward districts. A package of measures was put into effect for bringing about an all-round advance of industry in the country. Industry expanded. Expansion of industry created a large volume of downstream employment through forward linkages. Food processing industries provided large employment per unit of final demand. Construction, metal products, electrical equipment, chemicals, animal husbandry and gur and khandsari had the largest employment potential. Cement, sugar and plastics produced the largest employment linkage effects.

But we have noticed elsewhere in this chapter that the above hope was not realised. Mining and organised industry employed 10.7 per cent of the working population in 1951; in 1981 this figure had risen to 12.9 only. This is one of the most glaring failures of the development process in India. The opportunistic predictions regarding the ability of modern industries to absorb the rural migrants did not materialise. The limited change that has occurred in the occupational pattern is largely the consequence of development. At its present rate of contribution, mining and organised industry would have to raise their employment by 17 per cent per annum simply to absorb the increase in a total working force growing at the rate of 2.2 per cent per annum but it would not be possible to achieve such a high rate of employment growth in these sectors. Perhaps no other country can do this.

A sad experience of four decades of industrialisation in this country is that creation of more urban, modern sector jobs without simultaneous attempts to improve rural incomes and employment opportunities results in the paradoxical situation where more urban employment has led to at once to higher levels of urban unemployment and lower levels of agricultural output in some parts of the country on account of labour shortage in them.

On the eve of our independence rural labour was universally alleged to be less than perfectly mobile but with the development of transport facilities rural labour has now become over-mobile in many parts of the country. Urbanisation progressed by 2.55 times between 1951 and 1981, while industrialisation by 6.08 times. The percentage of population in towns and cities greatly exceeded the proportion engaged in manufacturing. In 1981 urban population was 23.3 per cent of total population. Towns with 100,000 and above population claimed 60.4 per cent of aggregate urban population; towns with 50,000 and above but below 100,000, 11.6 per cent and towns with 20,000 and above but less than 50,000, 14.4 per cent. Urbanisation has progressed due in part to the natural growth of urban population and due in part to the exodus of rural population to towns and cities.

Search for wage-employment has brought unemployment more and more into the open. Urban unemployment is largely open unemployment and a sizable chunk of open unemployment is the staple input of the employment exchanges' live registers. It is for this reason that the employment exchanges data are taken as satisfactory indices of the trend of urban unemployment in the economy.

Economists advise that rural migration to urban areas must be moderated by minimising the imbalances between economic opportunities in rural and urban sectors, which presumes improved tone and quality of rural life. Manipulation of urban-bound migration must be founded on a proper understanding of the factors behind it. The factors are demand and supply side determinants, originating primarily from economic causes—push, pull and push-back factors, as they have been classified in the existing literature.

While the rural economy is being revitalised, the urban industrial base should be further extended and expanded and the anatomy of the towns and cities revamped. The informal segment in the urban economy should be strengthened and linked with the modern, formal segment in it. As the employment situation improves in rural areas, the drift of rural population into towns and cities would slacken, and to that extent the problems of urban unemployment would also become manageable and the strain on civic amenities would be relieved. Urban job creation is generally more difficult and costly to accomplish than rural job creation owing to the high costs of providing these amenities. But there is another reason as well: Since transportation of food into urban areas involves some wastage, a shift of workers to urban areas from rural areas would lead to a decrease in the total quantity of food available for consumption, and hence to a decrease in the total number of work units. The upshot of this analysis is therefore this that the main venue of production for maximising employment has to be for some years yet to come the country-side. Dispersal of industrial activity would antidote labour absenteeism which has been one of the complaints of urban mill-owners against rural workers employed in their concerns (that they go back to their villages during harvest and sowing seasons, etc. causing much inconvenience to the urban factories). Lately, implementation of several rural works programme and projects, on the one hand and increasing difficulty of finding employment in urban areas, on the other, have stemmed the tide of rural efflux to towns and cities.

Realisation that organised industry cannot be relied upon for meeting the ever-worsening unemployment situation in the country has forced the Indian planners to turn more and more towards the unorganized industry, comprising cottage, *khadi*, village, handicraft and small-scale industries for throwing up avenues of employment for the rural and urban unemployed. Next to agriculture, it is these avocations that employ a great number of people in directly productive activities falling into the class of secondary activities. Rural industrialisation has gained immensely from rural electrification. Projectised programmes have been executed to regenerate the decadent cottage industries and to further uplift household industries like handloom-weaving, sericulture and carpet-weaving, brass utensil works, etc. Besides introducing technical improvements, fiscal, credit and production support has been extended. In order that the unorganised industries exploit their employment potential to the full fiscal instruments employed have included policy of reservation, policy of excise protection and policy of tax incentives. The unorganised sector has now increased access to risk capital and scarce raw materials.

It is rightly believed that promotion of the unorganised industries would take off the claimant problems of un- and under-employment. Appropriate and timely use of these various policy measures should reinforce the unorganised sector's capability for further generation of employment.

We know that employment in agriculture is seasonal. The slack period is inevitable. Underemployment is widespread. But it is concealed by the joint family system. It is how we define it that determines what its extent is. The numbers engaged in agriculture and activities allied to it are large in relation to the work, which connotes that they are infested with underemployment. The underemployed have some work to do but are willing to take up additional work, if provided. Increased work opportunities in household industries and in rural works can remedy under-employment and seasonal unemployment. The rural works projects should be such as can be switched on and off as and when needed. But this presupposes the intensification and diversification of the rural economy and conduct of agriculture on a scientific basis. Manoeuvre of factor proportions in rural production is conceivable if productivity of the already employed labour in it increases so that surplus labour is shifted to other lines of production in rural areas. Lowering of the given high labour : land ratio would be in the interests of both the rural and urban sectors. Policies should be directed at reducing labour demand in purely agricultural operations and raising labour demand in activities derived from and related to and dependent upon agriculture. A pyramid of rural industries based broadly on the cooperation and collective effort of a group of villages may modernise the rural economy in a decentralised manner. Cooperative and constructive effort is possible where a felt need is in existence.

The employment generation programmes must go on till the rural economy is reorganised and built up on a more permanent basis through rural and decentralised industrialisation and agricultural and cooperative development gathers sufficient motive power to develop and forge ahead on its own steam and momentum and out of its own volition.

Rural reconstruction would involve a compound to wage- and self-employment. Opportunities for gainful self-employment will have to be assessed and those composing the unemployment reservoir induced to accept self-employment as far as practicable. But promotion of self-employment is connected with the contraction of the public sector, which is an ideological issue. In an economy in which self-employment preponderates, it is not possible to judge how a given increase in the employment potential is likely to get diffused among the labour force, even if such an increase could somehow or other be estimated. Notwithstanding this, the details of both types of employment have to be thrashed out, properly delineated and matched.

Given the low elasticity of response of employment to output increase in the organized sector, it is evident that if employment has to grow as far possible at the same rate as output, both mixes—product-mix and technology-mix—must, of necessity, be labour-intensive. Adoption of an appropriate technology and an appropriate mix of techniques, assuming a suitable structure of production that investment and organizational support, would make the process of change in the technology field smooth. In any case the rigidity of capital-output ratios has to be overcome and factor endowments should govern technological choice, and productivity remaining more or less the same, labour-intensive techniques and processes should be preferred. This is the first step. The second step lies in regulating technical change so that it is gradual and smooth rather than abrupt and unsetting with a view to protecting and enhancing employment. Reliance on labour-intensive techniques is not basically antithetical to a higher growth rate, as the experiences of Japan, Taiwan and Korea have shown. In the conditions of our people and in the context of what planning has yielded in the past 40 years it would be erroneous to look upon the question of efficiency of the economic system in isolation of the question of employment but simultaneously nothing should be done to give the impression that inefficiency is regarded as a positive virtue, for that would be no less absurd. Low productivity limits the over-all size of income, thwarts the use of labour on works which do not add immediately to the supply of currently needed consumer goods and keeps down the size of the market. The trade-off between productivity and employment would desire India to increase labour productivity by improving technical efficiency. For the problem of employment in a developing country such as India has got twin aspects in relation to development: in the first place, making the maximum use of idle labour for the purpose of economic development, and, in the second place, increasing the productivity of labour so that larger employment can be provided at rising levels of real income. The employment creation policy should assure at least the current level of wages to the newly employed as well as to the already employed. And with improved productivity wages should move up. Full employment has meaning and content only when it is able to provide higher money as well as real incomes all-round.

The rural-urban dichotomy should end and yield place to the rural-urban continuum if agriculture and industry have to become more and more interrelated activities and the norm of policy becomes "walking on two legs". The real need of the hour is an agricultural base with an industrial superstructure. The pattern and priorities of public investment would hinge on the type of agro-industrial complex visualised. In the larger framework of economic integration between urban and rural sectors trade diversion from outside and trade creation from within could be a source of gain, besides the achievement of a compromise between growth and equity.

It is needless to state here that generally growth creates employment via capital formation as an independent entity and as implicit in embodiment of technological knowledge, and construction is a major part of capital formation. This is examined in a separate chapter. Growth-derived employment is the product of real investment but also determines its pattern significantly. As capital formation gathers speed, employment creation is at a faster rate. To the extent employment is a consequence of growth and capital formation is the king-pin of growth or provides its main thrust, increases in real saving must suitably match the planned increases in capital formation. But it is out of the frustration engendered by the failure of rising GDP to evoke a corresponding rise in employment, presumably because of the faulty factor proportions for which a developing economy like India has opted that further dependence on growth is considered unworthwhile and reliance on specific, direct employment-oriented policies and measures has increased emphasis in the reallocation of emphasis. That the problem of unemployment nagged the planners as did that of poverty right from the beginning of the First Plan should disabuse the minds of the critics of their oft-quoted criticism that the Indian planners were enamoured of the growth-oriented cure of unemployment, although the temptation on their part to delude themselves into such a line of thought at intervals cannot totally be denied. It was way back in the Fourth Plan that a comprehensive programme of action had been proposed for increasing employment immediately as well as increasing its future potential.

Any number of illustrations of the planners' concern for employment and policies formulated for the elimination of unemployment can be given Plan-wise. The central object of the community development programme in the First Plan was to mobilise local manpower for a concerted and co-ordinated effort at elevating the whole level of rural life. The emphasis was inevitably on improving the level of agricultural productivity. Included in the plan was an extensive programme for village industries prepared primarily with the object of increasing rural employment. The construction activities were to provide employment immediately and the capital assets built up were to provide employment in the production processes at the next stage. Perennial irrigation by making double cropping possible was expected to reduce seasonal unemployment. The First Plan hoped that with progress in capital formation and with establishment of the trend of rising incomes, growth of effective demand would be triggered off and with this would the process of employment generation spurred further, first in agriculture and industry and then in activities contingent upon the two sectors. For example, construction of brick kilns and saw-mills would provide supplementary employment. A statement of total production, additional production, expenditures involved, and employment to be created, village industry-wise, was prepared. The problem of educated unemployment received a separate treatment.

The Second Plan tried to spell out the distinction between an employment-oriented plan and an optimum-scale investment-oriented plan — the former implied a lot more than did the latter. The employment problem had three sides to it—the sectors, the regions, and the classes. For creating new employment the Second Plan reposed great hope in the diversification of the industrial pattern, a suitable policy on location of industries, special measures to assist small-scale and cottage industries, maintenance of economic activity continuously at high levels, provision of adequate training facilities and measures to promote geographical and occupational mobility of labour. It realised that the extent of employment to be provided turned on the supply of tools and equipment as well as on that of wage goods. It was the expectation of the Plan that irrigation and land reclamation would absorb new persons and reduce underemployment, that increased agricultural production and increased employment opportunities outside agriculture would have very much the same effect and that promotion and reorganisation of the unorganised industries would lower underemployment in them. One full chapter was devoted to the employment aspects of the plan. Additional employment to be generated during the Plan was estimated sector-wise, allowing for both primary and secondary effects of investment outlays in the private and public sectors. The problem of the educated unemployed received due attention in one section of the chapter on employment. A number of orientation and training sectors were set up to orient the educated to the requirements of the developing economy.

The Third Plan computed the additional employment opportunities that were to result from the plan expenditures. Apart from this, it was the first to contemplate organizing of *special works projects* in rural areas on a mass scale at a total cost of Rs. 150 crores. It devoted one chapter to the exposition of employment and manpower, which contained estimates of additional employment in the non-agricultural sectors. It believed that in agriculture additional employment would spring from soil conservation, afforestation, land reclamation, flood control, settlement on land and the utilisation of irrigation facilities.

The rural works programme envisaged by the Third Plan comprised five categories of works so as to tackle the problems concerning unemployment (seasonal and chronic), underemployment and wage- and self-employment for semi- and un-skilled persons.

The Third Plan made a thread-bare analysis of the problem of the educated unemployed with special reference to personnel requirements and training programmes.

In the Fourth Plan more employment opportunities were expected to stem from extension of irrigation, especially minor irrigation, multiple cropping, soil conservation, ayacut and special area development and private house-building in rural areas and from public sector investments in mining and industry, transport and communication and power in urban areas. Manpower planning received a separate treatment in the Plan.

The employment programmes embodied in the Fourth Plan were in consonance with the guidelines indicated in the World Employment Programme of the International Labour Organisation. They were: development of agriculture, rural infrastructure, rural electrification, water management, rural industries, decentralisation and dispersal of industrial investments, rural and urban housing, etc. Considerable emphasis was laid on labour-intensive schemes and productive employment on a sufficiently high level of efficiency. Policies restricting and inhibiting growth of employment were to be removed during the plan. All programmes were given an employment-orientation to the extent they admitted of it.

Special programmes for sub-marginal and dry farmers, rural works in drought-prone districts (by way of unemployment relief), dairy and milk supply schemes, development of the land and marine fisheries, the Employment Guarantee Scheme of the Maharashtra Government and the "Right to Work" Guarantee Scheme of the Gujarat Government, promotion of self-employment among engineer entrepreneurs, etc., were the highlights of the Fourth Plan.

The Fifth Plan emphasised the three interrelated aspects of an employment policy — the first concerning the need for implementing a programme using the strategic foci employed in the Plan, such as irrigation, agricultural extension involving the use of HYVs, etc.; the second relating to the need that all the aspects of the rural employment generation programme should be interwoven with the local development strategy; and the third pertaining to the creation of a secure rural tenantry and a productive small farmer base by means of tenancy reform. In respect of employment generation in non-agricultural sectors the Fifth Plan did not have anything new or original to say, except emphasising that the fulfilment of the production targets might prove to be a long step towards the attainment of the goal of full employment.

The Sixth Plan employment policy consisted of two major goals: reducing underemployment by increasing the rate of growth of the number of the gainfully employed and reducing unemployment estimated on the basis of usual status, commonly known as open unemployment. Employment meant employment for 273 days in a year with 8 hours' work a day . It became the *Standard Person Year Index*. The Sixth Plan was unique in pin-pointing productive or gainful employment and in organising employment as part of development, which was a positive approach, as contrasted with providing relief employment to the unemployed, which was a negative approach.

The Sixth Plan derived the employment generation capacity of a sector by studying its past employment performance against its growth performance. Employment in an activity was related as a non-linear function of either gross output or value added. In agriculture it was a fixed coefficient of land, the major input.

The Sixth Plan was the first to interlink the rural development and the rural employment programmes. It was also the first to synchronise the study of unemployment with that of poverty. The employment potential of irrigation, command area development and flood control obtained special attention in the Plan.

The Integrated Rural Development Programme (IRDP) first proposed in the Union Budget of 1976-77, and commenced from April 1976, was partly modified in 1978-79, and made to subsume the SFDA, the MFAL, the DPAP and the CAD programmes. The DD Programme was introduced in 1977-78. The "food for work" programme was launched in the same year. The TRYSEM came in 1979. The NREP was introduced in 1980. The RLEGP was ushered in 1983.

The Sixth Plan contained a separate chapter on manpower and employment. It decided to continue some old programmes such as the Operation Flood II Dairy Development Project, the Fish Farmers' Development Agencies, the MNP, etc., for expanding employment opportunities. It contained also a new deal for the self-employed. Its *Women and Child Development Programme* had an employment focus.

The composite – poverty-cum-unemployment alleviation — approach continued to be a characteristic feature of the Seventh Plan as well. The NREP, the RLEGP, the MNP, the IRDP, the TRYSEM, the DWCRA, the DPAP, the DRDA, etc. – all were so conceived and mapped out that they closely interacted in accelerating development and employment during the Seventh Plan period. In

April 1989 the JRY for the rural poor was announced. It replaced the NREP. By November 1989 the NRY had been inducted as an analogous anti-poverty (for the urban poor) programme.

Before we conclude this section, we would like to enumerate the landmarks or turning-points or epochs in the area of employment planning so far:

1. *First Plan:* It stressed programmes and schemes with significant employment potentials (plus some relief-type rural works).
2. *Second Plan:* It sough to provide employment opportunities to 10 to 12 million persons.
3. *Third Plan:* It opted for productivity-based programmes to surmount underemployment and seasonal unemployment. Instances are the IADP (1962), the IAAP (1963), the HYVs Programmes (1965). If combined relief-type rural works programmes on pilot basis.
4. *Fourth Plan:* It embarked upon a three-year crash Rural Employment Programmes (1971) and the Pilot Intensive Rural Employment Projects (1972-73 to 1974-75). Under the Rural Works Programmes, the Employment Guarantee Scheme as launched by Maharashtra in 1972-73, the SFDA and MFAL in 1971 (MFAL merged with SFDA in 1975) and the twin DPAP and DDP (the impact of the Bhagwati Committees Report 1973 could be seen writ large on the first of the twins).
5. *Fifth Plan:* It was instrumental in initiating the FWP (1977-78), the MNP (1977), the CAD (1975), the TRYSEM (1979)—programmes which were both productivity – and employment-based.
6. *Sixth Plan:* It pioneered the IRDP (1978-79)—which became a plank of the new 20-Point Programme in 1982 replacing the SFDA, the Operations Flood II Dairy Project, the Fish Farmers' Development Agencies (these three were to provide work opportunities to the poor families in their present occupations), the NREP (1980) for those uncovered by the first three, the EGS by Tamil Nadu, Madhya Pradesh and Karnataka, programmes for the Scheduled Castes and Scheduled Tribes, the RLEGP (1983), area development schemes, agro-service centres, integrated dry land agricultural

development, special programmes for the Scheduled Castes and Scheduled Tribes, etc. The Self-Employment Scheme for the Educated Unemployed was introduced in 1983-84. Composite loans were granted by banks for the purpose.

7. *Seventh Plan:* The JRY (April 1989) and the NRY (November 1989) and the Self-Employment Programme for the urban poor were launched (September 1, 1986). Per 100 persons, who were poor in urban areas, one beneficiary with a monthly income under Rs. 600 was selected. Bank loans and capital subsidy were granted.

From the list given above, the rural focus of the employment programmes is unmistakably clear. These programmes have been of a wide and varied nature—most of them have catered for unskilled workers but some have trained and skilled workers also in mind (for example, the FWP and the MNP); others have had those with general or technical education and some others have had those with training in mind (for instance, the TRYSEM). Some programmes have been designed with particular classes of society in mind (for example, the RLEGP for landless labourers, the TRYSEM for the rural youth, the DWCRA for women). Employment has been provided mostly through execution of construction works. By and large, the employment programmes had a double purpose–to alleviate poverty at the same time that they eliminated unemployment. Such direct methods of assault on poverty and unemployment have been more effective than indirect ones. Creation of income has gone hand in hand with creation of assets just as development of production and improvement of productivity (as under the IRDP) have gone side by side with generation of employment and removal of poverty (as under the NREP). Some programmes (e.g., the FWP, the NREP, the JRY) have provided wage-employment; others (e.g., the TRYSEM, the IRDP, the NRY) have provided self-employment in primary and secondary sectors. Employment has been given on a discriminatory basis in some programmes (preference for the weaker sections and the weaker sex or, for those without assets or with grossly inadequate assets, as under the JRY and the NRY). In some programmes accent has rested on payment of wages in kind (as under the FWP). While some programmes have gone on throughout the year, others have offered employment during the slack and lean seasons (as under the JRY).

That the special employment programmes have benefited the rural people cannot be denied, even if the contention that some households have benefited more than others cannot be refuted or it cannot be gainsaid that some bogus and undeserving households gained, while a number of genuine and deserving ones were left out. The IRDP has given impetus to activities with lower capital : output ratios. The FWP engendered an awareness among the wage-earners about the amount of wages paid. It took into consideration the level of development and the dimension of un- and underemployment. It served as a good medium for using the surplus foodgrains in the bufferstock where they were adding to the storage costs. By embarking upon short-term projects the FWP, the NREP, the JRY, etc., have created works of durable utility that have added materially to production.

Despite the announcement of the NJR not much attention has been called to the urban poor who have generally got temporary employment in the unorganised sector. They are now to be provided employment in various works, for example, tree plantation, slum improvement environmental sanitation, construction of houses for the economically handicapped, and so forth.

The employment programmes have aimed at providing not only employment but also employment at reasonable wages. They have kept the technical skill requirement of the programmes at such levels that even those with lower levels of technical skill are benefited. They have also tried to rehabilitate the technologically unemployed by giving them positive assistance and assuring appropriate location. In rural areas they have been affianced to some component or other of the new agrarian technology—irrigation, HYVs, fertilizers and agricultural extension. They have attempted to remedy seasonal unemployment by promoting outlets, such as mixed farming, and rural crafts and by employing agricultural labourers on rural capital works, such as road-building, minor irrigation works, bund-making, embankment-making, rural electrification, repair of old wells and tanks, construction of storage buildings, reclamation of marshy lands, soil replenishment, flood control, social forestry, water harvesting, and so on. These works have been suffused with large direct and indirect employment and income effects. An external economy effect is, as noted above, mass rural consciousness aroused against underpayment of wages and in favour of stabilisation of wages in rural areas and arresting of the unruly rise in the price of foodgrains in rural areas.

But the conducting of the employment programmes has encountered a host of difficulties. Workers have been dispersed over wide areas. Their availability has been irregular and uncertain. In many cases the workers had difficulty in working as a disciplined work-force. They have not been quite amenable to sustained team-work. Low procurement, low grain reserves, lack of bank credit, inadequate rural infrastructure, etc., have compounded the difficulty of the employment programmes. The programmes have been liable to degenerate into income-augmenting relief or dole type make-work/work-sharing schemes, that is, pseudo-employment. Besides, each programme, in addition to being a source of funds, jobs and influences, has been attractive as a political and economic power-base, as also a vehicle of certain felt needs and social urges. Control of a programme has symbolised not only some control over funds and jobs but also symptomatised some power or authority to influence, to dominate and to exploit the groups relying on the programme.

That in many fields the already employed have been doing un- or under or counter-productive work because of the relief or dole character of the projects is an ideal of which the Indian planners have been consistently seized and as such they have been continuously suggesting that the employment programmes should be linked with the development programmes organically but in this their success has been only qualified. All the same, interknitting of the employment generation and resource utilisation strategies and programmes at the local level in the rural sector is important from the point of view of food management, which has been a prime adjunct of the employment policy. In its final analysis, employment generation rests on the food situation and the position of food stocks with the public sector agencies. We know that those whose incomes increases with development of the economy command larger quantities of essential commodities like foodgrains and create difficulties for those whose incomes remain more or less fixed in spite of development or, alternatively, rise after a lag. In so far as only 10.5 per cent of our total population is dependent on the public distribution system and a little more than half the urban market (nearly 55 per cent) is dependent on the open market, bulk of the onus for crisis management so far has devolved on the buffer stocks rather than on the public distribution system *per se*. Such being the situation every kilo of grain saved from wastage is akin to an additional kilo of it raised from the soil, as it were. Thus employment provided to the workers *in situ* would prevent the loss and wastage of grain inherent in its transportation from the village to the town, besides the cost of transportation and storage there. Food production and consumption could be made to coincide in locus by this method. The growers with surplus grain would be more willing to part with it were they in a position to see with their own naked eyes that it was being deployed for projects that would ultimately benefit them as well, no matter if they benefited others too. The task of mobilisation of marketable surplus would become easier and simpler to handle to that extent.

Roughly, the average productivity of labour employed in the public sector has been lower than that of labour employed in the private sector. Productivity of labour employed on a temporary basis in the public sector has been higher than that of labour employed on a permanent basis in it. Unionisation has severely eroded the work ethic or culture in the public sector. The contractors make the workers do more work than the salaried managers in the public projects. Even the public spirit is down now-a-days. Self-employment, therefore, scores heavily against wage-employment in the public sector in respect of productivity. The IRDP-type of policy programme seems to be the most appropriate one, according to this criterion, subject to the proviso that it could get rid of its present defects. The sum-total of subsidy and loans should be such that it serves as a capital base sufficient to generate a permanent income which enables the family to repay its debt in some years and at the same time to rise above the Poverty Line[2] Since assets are provided through beneficiary-oriented and target-oriented projects, an assessment of the employment and unemployment situation by the household type is helpful in according priorities to the selected target groups.

In a broader perspective, an institutional restructuring aimed at by means of land reforms should ordinarily have facilitated by now a better utilisation of the labour force. Land reforms have been attempted ever since Independence as a tool for achieving a more equitable distribution of the grains of development. The step taken to reduce larger farms to smaller farms under the land ceiling legislation was expected to result in a more intensive utilisation of labour (increased use of labour per unit of land) and hence more rural employment. The erstwhile landless labourers were expected to employ themselves and the members of their families more usefully in cultivating the land given to them as part of the surplus land redistribution policy.

But the above-mentioned expectations have been realised only piece-meal, not wholly. An array of reasons is advanced to account for this. However, the most palpable reason has been the ideal-real gap typical of a soft state like India. Performance at the implementation level has given a cruel lie to the intentions expressed at the policy formulation level. Policies have lacked the needed political will and the inner motive-force and hence tended to be simply exhortations and appeals to the charity and goodwill of the landlords.

This brings us to the pertinence and relevance of the *regional approach to the problem of unemployment-eradication*. For each separate regional unemployment situation calls for a different method of solution. It is necessary to identify the factors which influence the levels of rural employment on a regional basis. It is generally supposed that the employment potential of the development strategy is higher at the regional or local level, that the inflation-unemployment dichotomy is less severe when a regional approach is assumed. By the same token, it is believed that agricultural planning carried out on the basis of a comprehensive area approach is likely to prove effective in generating additional employment through ancillary activities involving animal husbandry, better utilisation of conventional waste materials, etc. Area-specific employment generation in agriculture requires a multi-level, aggregative or holistic approach. Spatially and structurally more balanced public investments are essential for remedying the unemployment problem.

There is no doubt that translating the general prescriptions for increasing employment into precise policy measures tailored to the needs and possibilities of the country and the individual States is a formidable task. However, the State-wise details of employment in the private and public sectors as well as of unemployment presented in this study should help the planners in deciding the directions in which efforts for enlarging opportunities would be appropriate. The critical zones marked by chronic unemployment have to be salavaged first. The employment policy at the State level must reflect awareness of both the level and the problem of structure of unemployment.

Each State should strive hard to realise the employment potential of the programmes and projects under its Plan and take into account the extent to which these could be supplemented with other measures. Finally, additional employment created should closelv assort with and correspond to the location, skills and idle time of the unemployed (speaking of idle time, we are led to the necessity of dovetailing seasonal fluctuations in project employment with those in agricultural employment).

The Third Plan had suggested that the problem of unemployment should be broken up by districts, if a greater impact on it were to be made and as much of it as possible should be tackled directly with the help of a three-tier — district, block and village – plan.

One advantage of the regional or local orientation of the employment programmes is that at that plane resource constraint is felt with less severity. Moreover, at it resources can be augmented and utilised more efficiently. Its another merit is that local leadership can, assuming that it is not tainted by casteism or communalism, supply the catalytic agency and the vital ingredient of organisation. As a result, local knowledge can be tapped and popular participation can be enlisted. Its third advantage is derived from the avoidance of transport and housing costs which are commonly latent in projects which have their site away from a cluster of villages.

But field surveys have brought to light certain drawbacks of the area-specific programmes. Firstly, sufficient attention has not been paid to the possibilities of making a larger impact on the employment problem at the district and block levels by carefully adapting them to local needs and by mobilising and harnessing local resources, such as unemployed artisans and agricultural labourers, the educated unemployed, and so on. Secondly, the employment approach at the area level (district, block or village) has not been worked out with that amount of flexibility which suits local conditions and resources, the problems in different areas being essentially different. Thirdly, projects that have become an integral part of district planning have not satisfied the tests of financial viability and technical feasibility. Fourthly, in some regions where employment planning has assumed a regional or local complexion it has tended to be at odds with the basic tenets of national planning owing to the sharply antagonistic political affiliations of the local leadership. Local planning has failed to adjust and harmonise with national planning. Fifthly, in several areas wage conditions have not been satisfactory, with the results that the workers have had grumbles and have therefore, felt disgruntled. The quantum of employment provided has been measured in terms of jobs, not in terms of the income accruing from them. As a matter of fact, an excellent indicator of progress on the employment front is the movement of real wages over time. The unemployed persons on being employed need and claim more food to eat than they did when they were idle. Moreover, wages should rise also when productivity rises, when work given is productive, when skills improve, etc. The Government may motivate the workers to voluntarily opt for saving out of their risen real income. Sixthly, more often than not, the success of an employment programme has been judged by the amount of the some sanctioned money spent on it within the prescribed time period. Lastly, whatever the employment targets, high or low, they have been let down by the actual performance that has often failed to live up to the expectations. This failure has been attributed in most cases to the lack of requisite organisational and input support, on the one hand, and absence of enthusiasm and fervour on the part of the people involved, on the other. Planning has become routinised impersonalised and institutionalised. Instead of being organic it has become mechanical. The administration has not proved itself equal to the task. The patterns of organisation and incentives have been orthodox. The failure of the administration to translate the promise held out by the Government into achial performance has left the people cold, inert and listless. But these problems are not insuperable. It would not be difficult for the people to recaputre some of the idealism and the sense of adventure and euphoria that had inspired our freedom struggle for our planning process, if they are really determined.

The entire planning strategy became employment conscious perceptibly with the inauguration of the Sixth Plan, as we have noted earlier. Precedent to the Sixth Plan, employment-creation was more or less peripheral rather than central to the plans – on their border rather than within their territory. While choosing between alternative paths to growth, their relative effects on the employment situation were to be considered carefully. The employment potential of the various Plan programmes was to be optimised in keeping with the long-term needs of the economy. Programmes and projects with a higher employment potential were to be given preference. In order that this happened, the following were to be kept in the forefront: (1) The existing level of employment was to be maintained, (2) The programmes and projects were to be undertaken with the requisite degree of efficiency and economy, (3) Their continuity was to be maintained with a view to stabilising employment. (In other words, the employment generation process was to be made cumulative like the growth process. In so far as certain inelasticities were inevitable care was to be taken to ensure that inconsistencies did not develop in demand and supply of inputs and outputs.) (4) Such employment patterns were to be favoured as minimised the total time needed for attaining full employment by the nation as a whole. With this end in view the employment programme had to be time-phased with independent goals—during the short-term of five years the goal was to at least absorb in productive/gainful employment the equivalent of new entrants to the labour force so that the distress caused by the non-availability of jobs could be mitigated and during the short-term the focus of policy was to lie on agriculture and the unorganised segment of the secondary sector, while during the long-term the goal of policy was to remove the backlog of unemployment, for which the organised segment of the secondary sector and the tertiary sector was to be the focus. The planners were alive to the fact that elimination of unemployment in a developing economy was by its very nature a somewhat long-term problem which occasioned steady and persistent efforts. (5) In balancing demand and supply of unskilled and semi-skilled labour in terms of areas, occupations and time, which posed the need for improved outward mobility of labour, the land army, the labour-cum-development banks, the construction corporations and the border roads organisations had to play their respective parts. Implicit in this was the necessity of keeping the employed useful by organising short in-plant or in-service training programmes. Attached with it more generally was the question of harnessing the abundant human resources that India had got, as also improving their capabilities for further development.

So far we have been concerned with the application of theories relating to employment and unemployment. It is advisable at this point in the discussion to set one significant theoretical prediction in bold relief: In the ultimate, the success of the employment-oriented plan strategy has to ensue from the manipulation of the production pattern, which presupposes the emergence of a desirable structure of social wants, that is, an appropriate distribution pattern. To put it in an unvarnished language, the problem of employment generation is an intrinsic part of the problem of distribution of the gains from the development process. The unemployed cannot find employment unless the employed are prepared to accept some erosion of or inroads into their present standard of living. A social responsibility devolves on that section of the population which has hitherto benefited disproportionately from planned development as well as on those who have been fortunate enough to enjoy superior access to educational and professional skills. The objective of full employment would not be realised without a stricter economic discipline and greater readiness on the part of the relatively well-to-do classes to accept restraints on their rising consumption in order to release resources for the faster development of the economy and for implementing specific employment programmes. As a matter of fact, the cost of maintaining the growing numbers of the openly unemployed is higher consumption now at the expense of a slower rate of growth of output in the future.

The day is not very far off when the country would be polarised hard and sharp into two broad compartments, one consisting of the employed and the other of the unemployed, and the latter acting as an internal colony to the former. To stave off that situation it would be incumbent on the part of the planners to provide for fuller employment and to distribute the increment in employment in an appropriate manner so as to assure everybody a national minimum. Full employment would be the best form of social security for this country. It would also be the surest means of promoting greater social justice.

To substantiate, the annual rate of growth of employment with redistribution of consumption expenditures in favour of the poor classes would be higher by at least 15 per cent than that without redistribution. More explicitly, in the short run, the newly mobilised labour is a charge on the available supplies of essential commodities, which betoken its redistribution, and this makes probably for a rise in the real incomes of those newly employed and a fall in the real incomes of those who are previously employed. To an extent, such redistribution is at once obligatory and desirable. But certainly not beyond that because food prices would hike, entailing mass suffering and discontent.

The existing situation is far from this ideal. The bottom 20 per cent of the population secures only 11 per cent of the public spending. The top 20 per cent of the population share 35 per cent of it. Public expenditure in India contributes by way of provision of social and merit goods which is free 20 per cent to the household real income (this is a rough estimate) of the poor with a monthly income of less than Rs. 100. For the income bracket (i.e., over Rs. 1,000 per month) it is five to seven per cent. The upper middle quintile has a share of 24 per cent. The middle quintile has a share of 17 per cent. The lower middle quintile has a share of 13 per cent. The bottom 40 per cent has a total share of 24 per cent in aggregate public expenditure.

Inasmuch as population growth at a rapid rate acts as a hindrance to per capita income, family planning has been considered a useful instrument in the nation's encounter with poverty and unemployment. In the final analysis, the success of our efforts in wiping out unemployment and poverty from the land would turn on the extent to which we succeed in bringing down the rate of population growth. Therefore, the voluntary adoption of the norm of the small family is to become an item on the agenda of action against poverty and unemployment.

The unemployment problem is a manifestation of the economic development problem. Unemployment has been at the centre of the stage in the drama of economic development. Jobs have been milled out by growth but not in that number needed to absorb the entire increase in the labour-force. The percolation effects of growth have been limited because the income levels have been low and have bristled with some leakage. The rate of growth of the GDP during the Plan period (1950-51 onwards) has not been adequate for the purpose—a far greater rate has been needed. The rates of growth of agriculture and organised manufacturing too have been lower than the desired rates. Something has been fundamentally amiss or out of accord with the specific employment programmes. To offer one example: In the poorer States the population stock is far younger and hence requires far more new jobs at an ever-increasing rate, compared to the situation and its remedy in the richer states.

In the country as a whole whereas employment growth decelerated during the 1980s, national income growth accelerated. This was ample proof of some contradiction or other bedevilling our Plan strategy. A plan for economic development exists for the utilisation of available human resources in a manner that would maximise the rate of growth. Over a period of five years there may arise a degree of conflict between a policy of full employment and a policy of stepping up the rate of development. But over a sufficiently long period the two policies should not necessarily conflict and would find a resolution.

Prior to the Sixth Plan a larger proportion of the employment opportunities generated went to the non-agricultural sectors. But since the Sixth Plan the agricultural sector has had the larger. All in all, the growth process, as induced by the Plans, and the specific employment creation programmes launched in the economy unleashed a large number of employment opportunities, though not fast enough to absorb both the unemployed from the previous years and the new entrants to the labour-force during the Plan period. This was because the output targets were not attained, which was because the policies and programmes were not implemented efficiently and successfully and because their employment effects came to be spread out more widely and evenly from the Third Plan onwards. Limits on employment growth were set first by the amount of investment to be made in a Plan and then by the difficulty of varying the pattern of investment, for another thing. Only a marginal variation in the investment pattern was possible and the readjustment of priorities that was feasible could yield only small results in terms of employment. The last limit was set by the international environment appertaining to trade, aid and technology transfer. From all evidences it appears that the scale of the unemployment problem would increase dramatically in the years that lie ahead.

Before we conclude this section, we would like to stress the necessity of continuously testing the assumptions which are made while estimating the volume of employment that would flow from the given development programmes, of compiling information on the manner in which employment responds to different kinds of investment stimuli, of conducting technical studies regarding the employment component of various types of investment and of the relationship between direct employment resulting from an act of investment and further increases to employment to which the former leads over a period of time, of estimating additional employment per unit of investment and/or increase in output in different sectors and the relationship of employment per rupee of output with output per hectare (the last two depend on variables relating to the use of fertilizer per hectare, tractorisation, irrigation, number of pump-sets per hectare of land, levels of investments, level of inequality of operational land holdings, and so on). However, the fact that the statistics are flawsome and faulty should not and cannot delay action against unemployment.

NOTES

1. *Economic and Political Weekly*, September 29, 1990.
2. The IRDP, as a government in instrument to alleviate rural poverty, assists selected poor househods in rural areas to cross the Poverty Line by providing productive assets and inputs to the target group in all blocks. Per capita subsidy was Rs. 1837 and per capita credit was Rs. 5494 in the 1989-90 Annual Plan. The rate of subsidy is 25 per cent for small farmers, 33-1/3 per cent for marginal farmers, agricultural labourers and rural artisans, and 50 per cent for the tribals.

17

CONSTRUCTION AND EMPLOYMENT GENERATION DURING THE PLAN PERIOD

Construction has a significant role to play in any economic planning geared to the elimination of unemployment. Engineering is the backbone of capital formation. In many fields of development construction accounts for a substantial proportion of the expenditure. During the first two Plans in India construction claimed almost one-half of the aggregate investment. In 1965-66 the percentage of investment in construction to total investment was 54.6. In 1955-56 it had been much higher, 70.3 per cent. But the proportion of employment in construction to total employment was more or less unchanged. It was in the Fifth Plan that construction was treated as a separate sector and an exclusive provision was made for it. Table 17.1 furnishes statistical information on construction for the period spanning the past four plans.

Building industry generally claims almost half of total constructional employment. In fact, housing is a highly employment-intensive activity. Irrigation provides nearly one-third; transport one-seventh; and the rest is provided by communications and other heads.

Construction is a function of the gross fixed capital formation. We can roughly estimate the rates of national income, savings and investment from the rate of employment in construction.

As net investment declines relatively to gross investment with the level of development moving up, so does construction expenditure relatively to equipment expenditure.

Construction investment is largely for extension of the given infrastructure but, next to it, it is on its improvement. The construction projects admit of phasing and time-profile adjustment.

There has been in rural areas massive capital formation by way of construction. The rural areas are today not as isolated as they were before.

TABLE 17.1: Construction in the Indian economy

Employment Provided:	*1971*	*1979-80*	*1987*	*1989-90*
(Percentage of total)	5.83	6.2	4.89	5.6
In Public Sector	5.03		4.66	
In Private Sector	0.80		0.23	
Additional Employment Generated:				
Sixth Plan . . . 3.2 per cent of total				
Seventh Plan . . . 5.4 per cent of total				
Total Main Workers (1981):				
As Percentage of total	. . . 1.6			
Males -do-	. . . 1.8			
Females -do-	. . . 0.8			
Rural -do-	. . . 1.0			
Urban -do-	. . . 4.0			
As Percentage of Fixed Capital Formation				
1980-81 . . . 51.9				
1986-87 . . . 46.8				
Percentage Share in NDP	*At Current Prices*		*At 1970-71 Prices*	
1960-61	4.7		4.6	
1970-71	5.4		5.4	
1980-81	5.2		4.9	
1985-86	—		4.4	
1987-88	6.2		—	
Percentage Share in Gross Value added at Factor Cost				
1970-71	5.3			
1980-81	4.7			
1985-86	5.4			
1989-90	2.3			

Source: National Accounts Statistics, 1991.

Construction can be a category of investment as well as an output and in both cases concrete and hence explicit. It can provide employment over a dispersed space.

Private demand for construction is limited in the developing countries. Besides, it is generally sporadic and unstable. This places an increased responsibility on the government for the maintenance and expansion of the level of construction employment.

Incremental capital-output ratio for construction was 3.39 during the First Plan, 1.97 during the Second Plan, 2.24 during the Third Plan, 1.63 during the Annual Plans, 1.50 during the Fifth Plan and

1.27 during the Sixth Plan. During the Fourth and Seventh Plans the ratio was very high. Increased emphasis on labour-intensive methods lowered the ratio in some of the other plans. The fact that, while the gross value added through construction is fully shown under it, the investment under this item is partly diffused over and incorporated in other sectors, makes the ratio a ratio of dubious value.

Certain types of construction lend themselves easily to labour-intensive methods and labour becomes the primary factor in them. Construction facilitates adherence to the comparative advantage maxim in exploitation of the existing factor endowments. It is on this ground that construction was held by the authors of the Fifth Plan to be the leading sector for creating additional employment. Apart from this, construction offers a high employment potential, about seven per cent, against the over-all employment growth rate of less than two per cent per annum.

On an expert view, mechanised methods of construction appear to have only a narrow economic advantage over manual methods when the low utilisation of equipment is taken into consideration.

The labour-output ratio in construction hinges on (i) design and raw materials, (ii) quality of labour and (iii) techniques of production. The capital equipment needed in construction is relatively small and is available from indigenous sources. In addition, there is a large volume of surplus labour and a good supply of most materials. The multiplier effect of construction is usually regarded as satisfactory. Investigations reveal that in India in order to augment employment by one per cent investment in fixed capital requires to be raised by 2.64 per cent. That is to say, if investment in fixed capital increases by one per cent, employment would increase by 0.38 per cent. If wages rose by one per cent, then labour supply would rise by 0.50 per cent. Were the employment of wage-workers to be increased by one million, their total wage bill would have to be raised by 0.08 per cent. If the cost of living of the working class rises by one per cent, its wage bill would rise by 0.02 per cent.

The amount of constructional activity which can desirably be undertaken in India is unlimited. However, the employment effect of constructional activity is bound to vary with the proportion of construction in total fixed capital formation.

Accent on the labour-intensive methods of construction need not always denote slower production, for there can be several cases where by putting more workers on the job, the production time under the labour-intensive methods can be made to synchronise with the capital-intensive methods.

All the same, there are also types of construction for which the time, cost, quality or other technical considerations assuredly favour the use of machines instead of men.

Employment in construction is characterised by casualness, irregularity and instability. On an average, a skilled worker is employed for 9.3 months and an unskilled worker for 7.5 months in a year in it. Some salient factors responsible for this are: excessive supply of unskilled labour, existing recruitment methods and lack of a close correlation between investment planning and manpower planning.

Construction cannot go very far without an adequate supply of steel and cement. Where heavy equipment is needed, foreign exchange requirement can be of substantial value.

The limits to the expansion of fixed capital formation are also the limits to the expansion of construction activity, namely, expansion of overheads is limited by the market or by the amount of capital available for construction investment, which means supply of savings and/or foreign capital, or supply of plant which forms part of the construction project (land acquisition is obstructed for years on end and works cannot therefore commence), or for want of organising ability (needed for compensating the losers and charging the beneficiaries), or by shortage of skill.

Construction activity in India betrays three short-comings: lack of economy and speed (cost-overrun and time-overrun), lack of efficient construction organisation and bottlenecks in the supply and movement of construction material and equipment. In certain cases, more than the rise in prices of materials and wages increased cost owing to delay for some reason or the other was the pre-eminent factor. Improved project preparation, sponsorship and spawning of efficient construction organisation, and liquidation of bottlenecks are the suggested remedies of these problems.

Some other suggestions may be made here. In the first instance, the various projects have to be planned carefully in relation to one another. Secondly, for every stage of development planning a spectrum of projects should be chosen and kept on the shelf so that continuity is not disturbed in both the plans and the gains that flow from the projects. The projects ought to form a continuous and integrated operation. Thirdly, the short-period and long-period gestation projects should be properly balanced and dovetailed. Fourthly, priority should be accorded to the growth-potential-generating projects in time-scheduling of the band of projects. Lastly, new construction programmes should be taken in hand as soon as those already in progress are complete and workers (particularly the skilled ones) should be transplanted/redeployed smoothly from one project to the other without causing too many frictions and keeping the resulting hardship to the minimum.

Time is of crucial significance in construction for, on it turn a great number of events, such as the pace of rotation of fixed resources, obsolescence of investment, immobilisation of social resources, economic efficiency of a given dose of investment, and so on. The scale should be adequate to sustain growth and at the same time to obviate any likely waste of resources. Anticipated gaps or lacunae should be component parts of the perspective plan so that they are surmounted prior to the launching of the future plans. Perspective planning has the merit of ensuring timely decisions.

The demand for all products of all constructional trades rests directly on the total volume of investment and is peculiarly fluctuating since the rhythm of this fluctuation is derived in an exaggerated form from the rhythm of activity of industry as a whole. A 10 per cent spurt in the industry's need for mechanical construction may engender an 80 or 100 per cent increase in the actual mechanical construction.

In a mixed economy the best course of action consists in organising the investment programme in such a manner that the progress of construction and technical innovation follows a smooth path of ordered development into the future until the ideal goal of capital saturation is attained. Furthermore, the distribution of construction work between projects of different categories in relation to the future is integral to the distribution of labour in production in a balanced manner.

Construction had been accorded to the highest priority during the Sixth and Seventh Plans. The 1980s, therefore, witnessed a spurt in construction. To substantiate, in 1971 employment provided in the construction sector was 0.9 million in the public sector and 0.16 million in the private sector. In 1979-80 employment in construction amounted to 9.29 million person years. In 1987 construction gave employment to 1.2 million workers in the public sector and to 0.6 million in the private sector. Between 1971 and 1987 the increase in total employment was 0.18 million, that is, nearly 20 per cent.

18

A CLOSE-UP VIEW OF THE INDIAN UNEMPLOYMENT PROBLEM

Let us begin with an interpretation of the statistics contained in Table 18.1 which demonstrate that between 1951 and 1981 in India a two to four per cent fall occurred in the percentage of the population occupied in the primary sector. In 30 years this gave an infinitesimal rate of change per year. If the decline in the percentage of population engaged in the primary sector is taken as a measuring-rod of structural transformation and hence the progress of an economy, then India is still many miles away from its final destination. Structural change in the Indian economy appears to be an improbability for many years to come.

Occupational Distribution of Working Population

In 1987-88, 65.5 per cent of the workforce was engaged in agriculture, which should not be confused with the primary sector as is the common tendency. This was even less than the percentage India had in 1981 (68.7 or 70.6).

The percentage of population, engaged in plantations, declined between 1951 and 1981, probably due, in part, to the foreign interests which had invested their capital in them left the country after Independence and due, in part, to the setback these export-oriented activities had to suffer subsequently in the international market (Table 18.2).

Employment in the agricultural sector grew at the rate of 2.32 per cent per annum during 1972-78 and 0.65 per cent per annum during 1983-88.

During 1951-81 the secondary sector provided employment to a larger percentage of the population – 1.5 to 3 per cent more over three decades. Included in it was mining, which accommodated a slightly higher percentage of the working force during the period (Table 18.3).

TABLE 18.1: Percentage distribution of workers by industrial/occupational categories in India (census data)

Industry/Occupation	1951	1981
Primary Sector	*72.1*	*68.7/70.6*
1. Cultivators	50.0	41.6/42.1
2. Agricultural labours	19.7	24.9/26.3
3. Livestock, Forestry, Fishing, etc.	2.4	2.2/2.2
Secondary Sector	*10.6*	*13.5/12.9*
4. Mining and Quarrying	0.6	0.6/0.5
5. Households and other than Household Industry	9.0	11.3/10.9
6. Construction	1.0	1.6/1.5
Tertiary Sector	*17.3*	*17.8/16.5*
7. Trade and Commerce	5.3	6.3/5.9
8. Transport, Storage and Communications	1.5	2.7/2.5
9. Other Services	10.5	8.8/8.1
Total	100.0	100.0/100.0

Source: Tata Services Ltd., *Statistical Outline of India*, 1989-90.
Note: Both sets of figures as available are given.

TABLE 18.2: Employment in plantations

('000s)

Year	Tea	Coffee	Rubber	Total
1951	1018	151	43	1212
1985	839	29	24	892
				(1.35 times decline)

Source: 1. *Indian Labour Statistics*, 1979;
2. *Packet Book of Labour Statistics*, 1988.

TABLE 18.3: Employment in mines by types of minerals

('000s)

Year	Coal	Mica	Manga-nese	Iron	Lime stone	Others	Total
1951	352	52	56	20	16	53	549
1985	551	4	18	44	49	123	789
							(1.43 times increase)

Source: 1. *Indian Labour Statistics*, 1979;
2. *Pocket Book of Labour Statistics*, 1988.
Note: Average daily number of workers employed.

In 1987-88, 10.8 per cent of the labour-force was occupied in manufacturing itself and 3.7 per cent in construction. Employment in manufacturing grew at the rate of 5.10 per cent per annum during 1972–78, and 2.1 per cent per annum during 1983–88. Employment in its organised segment grew at the rate of 1.44 per cent per annum and that in its unorganised segment at the rate of 4.57 per cent per annum during 1972-88. The latter sector provided about 76 per cent of total employment in the manufacturing sector in 1987-88. Employment growth in construction and mining has never been depressed.

Table 18.4 brings to light the expansion of employment in the organised segment of industry during 1951-81, according to the type of factories. In certain industries the pace was high but not as high as was desired. On the whole, the organised sector had provided employment to the growing labour force at a rate lower than that at which it had itself grown.

The share of the modern industrial sector in total urban employment remains small. This has been so despite its enjoying protection in all ways possible. It has become all the more capital-intensive in the past few decades. Within it has developed a labour aristocracy. It has been financed partly by its own savings from the newly generated income and partly by the net flows from the agricultural sector. The traditional industries have consistently lost their old grandeur to the modern industries which have exploited the available technological opportunities as far as possible largely under support from the State.

In 30 years (1951 to 1981) the tertiary/services sector could absorb the increasing work force only by 0.5 to 1.1 per cent. Employment in this sector expanded at the rate of 3.17 per cent per annum during 1972–78, 4.69 per cent per annum during 1978–82 and 2.50 per cent per annum during 1983–88. In 1987-88, 8.2 per cent of the working force was engaged in the community, social and personal services.

Although the figures of censuses of two different years or more are not comparable because of a variety of reasons, such as changes in the definitions of terms used or in their coverage, reorganisation of the States, inclusion or exclusion of this or that economic activity, say, mining and quarrying, etc., yet Table 18.5 which presents State-wise data on occupational distribution of the population and gives figures of those engaged in agriculture according to their class would prove very useful in marking off the central trends in the occupational pattern in our country. As time has rolled on, the primary sector, particularly, agriculture, has absorbed more and still more of the population in the country, invariably in all States, in some States at a rate faster than the all-India average, and in others at a rate slower than that. Both the redistributive and protective land reform policies have contributed their respective mites to this, and the States which have marched more successfully and with greater speeds have had more, and not less, people pressing on the land, as the theory would tell us.

TABLE 18.4: Employment in factories

('000s)

Estimated Average Daily Number of Workers Employed			
Types of Factories	1951	1981	Increase (Times)
I. Government and Local Fund Factories	237	1818	7.6
Textiles	3	273	91.0
Printing, Publishing and Allied Industries*	20	127	6.3
Manufacture of Machinery (other than electrical)	22	152	6.9
Manufacture of Electrical Machinery	10	106	10.6
Transport Equipment	127	228	1.8
Electricity, Gas & Steam	8	86	10.7
Others	49	845	17.2
II. Other Factories	2299	5476	2.4
Textiles	1131	1530	1.3
Food except Beverages	335	943	2.8
Tobacco+	122	165	1.3
Chemicals & Chemical Products	74	370	5.0
Non-metallic Mineral Products	110	358	3.2
Basic Metal Industries	95	357	3.7
Manufacture of Machinery (except Electrical Machinery)	76	359	4.7
Transport Equipment	68	213	3.1
Others	293	1180	4.0

Source: Statistical Abstract of India, 1986.

* From 1971 onwards includes paper and paper products.

\+ From 1971 onwards includes beverages.

TABLE 18.5: Statewise and sector-wise classification of the working population

(Percentage)

State	In Primary Sector		Percentage Fall/Rise during	Cultivators		Percentage Rise/Fall during	Agriculture Labourers		Percentage Rise/Fall during	Others	
	1951	1981*	1951-81	1961	1981	1961-61	1961	1981	1961-81	1961	1981
1	2	3	4	5	6	7	8	9	10	11	12
Andhra Pradesh	67.3	87.1	(+) 19.6	40.2	32.6	(-) 7.6	28.6	56.7	(+) 28.1	31.2	30.7
Assam	73.2	NA	NA	NA	NA	NA	NA	NA	NA	NA	NA
Bihar	81.0	87.1	(+) 6.1	53.8	43.7	(-) 10.1	22.9	35.4	(+) 12.5	23.3	20.9
Gujarat	61.6	91.0	(+) 29.4	53.3	37.7	(-) 15.6	14.7	22.8	(+) 8.1	32.0	39.5
Haryana	66.6	70.7	(+) 4.1	63.8	44.9	(-) 18.9	6.9	16.4	(-) 9.5	29.3	38.7
Himachal Pradesh	NA	76.8	—	NA	—	—	—	—	—	—	—
Jammu & Kashmir	NA	82.5	—	NA	—	—	—	—	—	—	—
Karnataka	NA	88.1	NA	54.1	38.4	(-) 15.7	16.4	26.6	(+) 10.2	29.5	35.0
Kerala	54.9	88.0	(+) 33.1	20.9	17.2	(-) 3.7	17.4	28.2	(+) 10.8	61.7	58.6
Madhya Pradesh	81.2	84.5	(+) 3.3	62.7	51.1	(-) 11.6	16.6	24.1	(+) 7.5	20.7	24.8
Maharashtra	61.6	88.2	(+) 26.6	46.1	34.8	(-) 11.3	23.8	26.8	(+) 3.0	30.9	38.4
Orissa	72.4	88.9	(+) 16.5	56.8	47.0	(-) 9.8	17.0	27.6	(+) 10.6	26.2	52.3
Punjab	66.6	68.4	(+) 1.8	46.2	36.3	(-) 9.9	9.6	22.8	(+) 13.2	44.2	40.9
Rajasthan	NA	83.8	NA	73.6	62.2	(-) 9.4	4.1	7.3	(+) 3.2	28.3	30.5
Tamil Nadu	63.0	91.3	(+) 28.3	42.1	29.4	(-) 12.7	18.4	31.4	(+) 13.0	39.6	39.2
Uttar Pradesh	74.2	81.7	(+) 7.5	63.8	58.0	(-) 5.8	19.9	16.3	(-) 3.6	24.3	25.7
West Bengal	53.4	88.1	(+) 34.7	38.5	30.6	(-) 7.9	15.3	24.8	(+) 9.5	46.2	44.6
All-India	69.8	86.9	(+) 17.1	52.3	41.5	(-) 10.8	17.2	25.1	(+) 7.9	30.5	33.1

Contd.

TABLE 18.5 *Contd.*

State	Percentage Rise/Fall during 1960-61	Total 1961/1981 (5+8+11)/(6+9+12)	Secondary Sector 1951**	Secondary Sector 1981	Percentage Rise/Fall during 1951-81	Tertiary Sector 1951	Tertiary Sector 1981	Percentage Rise/Fall during 1951-81	Total 1951-1981 (2+15+18)/(3+16+19)
1	13	14	15	16	17	18	19	20	21
Andhra Pradesh	(+) 5.5	100.0	12.7	6.9	(-) 5.8	20.0	6.0	(-) 14.0	100.0
Assam	NA	NA	14.8	NA	NA	12.0	NA	N.A.	—
Bihar	(-) 2.4	100.0	8.0	7.5	(-) 0.5	11.0	5.4	(-) 5.6	100.0
Gujarat	(+) 7.5	100.0	13.8	4.6	(-) 9.2	24.6	3.8	(-) 20.8	100.0
Haryana	(+) 9.4	100.0	8.5	15.2	(+) 6.7	24.9	14.1	(-) 10.8	100.0
Himachal Pradesh	—	—	NA	17.9	—	NA	5.2	—	100.0
Jammu & Kashmir	—	—	NA	11.5	—	NA	5.0	—	100.0
Karnataka	(+) 5.5	100.0	NA	6.5	NA	NA	5.4	NA	100.0
Kerala	(+) 3.1	100.0	19.3	5.8	(-) 13.5	25.8	6.2	(-) 19.6	100.0
Madhya Pradesh	(+) 4.1	100.0	7.4	10.7	(+) 3.3	11.4	4.8	(-) 6.6	100.0
Maharashtra	(+) 7.5	100.0	13.8	7.6	(-) 6.2	24.6	4.2	(-) 20.4	100.0
Orissa	(+) 26.1	100.0	10.6	6.0	(-) 4.6	17.0	5.1	(-) 11.9	100.0
Punjab	(-) 3.3	100.0	8.5	14.4	(+) 5.9	24.9	17.2	(-) 7.7	100.0
Rajasthan	(-) 2.2	100.0	NA	10.3	NA	NA	5.8	NA	100.0
Tamil Nadu	(-) 0.4	100.0	13.2	4.5	(-) 8.7	24.8	4.2	(-) 20.6	100.0
Uttar Pradesh	(+) 1.4	100.0	8.5	11.3	(+) 2.8	17.3	7.0	(-) 10.3	100.0
West Bengal	(-) 1.6	100.0	15.3	6.3	(-) 9.0	31.3	5.6	(-) 25.7	100.0
All-India	(+) 2.6	100.0	10.5	7.8	(-) 2.7	19.7	5.3	(-) 14.4	100.0

* Including Mining and Quarrying.
** Including Mining.

Source: (1) K.N. Prasad, *Economics of a Backward Region in a Backward Economy*, Vol. I, 1966.
(2) *Census of India, 1981*.

The percentage of cultivators has fallen in every State (the figures include their dependants). Quite a bit of land has passed out of cultivation into construction works. In several areas cultivation has become a less attractive pre-occupation of the people. As a result of sale and purchase, there are now fewer persons or families owning the same area of land, and as they are designated as cultivators, naturally the outcome is a fall in their total number.

The percentage of agricultural labourers (their figures are inclusive of their dependants) has risen more or less evenly in all States, except Uttar Pradesh, where it has recorded a marginal decline (this finding is questionable). Ejected from their lands the small and marginal farmers, largely tenants, have swelled the ranks of agricultural labour. The rate of population growth has been higher for the agricultural labourers' households. In rural areas the artisans and craftsmen do not hesitate to take up agricultural work when faced with a choice between survival and starvation. Sweeping as it would sound, the rise in the number of agricultural labourers has been not a little in proportion to the unsuccess on the front of land reforms in a number of States, although the hand of other reasons cannot be denied.

For those who have been neither cultivators nor agricultural labourers the problem of finding employment has been most acute and vexatious. In States where non-agricultural employment opportunities have not expanded *pari passu* with constantly increasing labour supply, migration has been the only alternative coming to their succour. In States where people in the primary sector have found engagements other than those of cultivators and agricultural labourers the extent of migration has been moderate.

Turning to the secondary sector we find that the all-India trend has been negative. If such has been the case, then the little rise in the percentage of working force employed in the secondary sector must be attributable to the remaining 8 to 10 States which might have done better to alter the all-India picture disclosed by Table 18.1. Some States have experienced de-industrialisation where the secondary sector has not expanded, be it in its organised or its unorganised segment, in case either mining or construction in them has not declined or if the rates of growth of mining and construction have been insufficient to outweigh the fall in the rate of growth of manufacturing, organised and unorganised.

Some States, such as Haryana, Punjab, Madhya Pradesh and

Uttar Pradesh, have fared better so far as the growth of the secondary sector is concerned.

Our reference to the State-wise occupational distribution of the working population had disintered such inter-State disparities as were masked by the all-India figures. Still more light can be shed on this aspect of the problem.

In our endeavour to cast further light on this aspect of the problem under investigation we would be helped a great deal by Tables 18.6, 18.7 and 18.8. Take up first Table 18.6. Between 1971 and 1987 in the organised sector the position industry-wise disclosed a rise of 9.5 per cent in the public sector and a fall of the same percentage in the private sector in the aggregate volume of employment provided. Employment in agriculture, mining and quarrying, manufacturing, electricity, gas and water supply and services increased in the public sector, while employment in other industrial divisions decreased. In the private sector, employment increased in electricity, gas and water supply, construction, transport, storage and communications, and services, while it decreased in the remaining industrial divisions. It can be deduced from this that electricity, gas and water supply and services are the two industrial divisions which do not show any clash between the private and public sectors. In other words, the public sector in these occupations does not crowd out the private sector. As the economy expands, so does the public sector in its firm commitment to occupy more and more of the commanding heights of the economy and to cutout the dead-wood by ushering in technological innovations in some of these areas. Trade, wholesale and retail, etc., is the industrial division which has shown a declining trend in the public as well as the private sector, which may be the outcome of increasing scale of operation of the units in both sectors in these lines.

Table 18.7 has a purpose – to establish that with the rise in the percentage of the area of land in the possession of the marginal and small farmers, which are the main sources of supply of agricultural labour, next in importance to the landless agricultural labourers, from 20.9 to 28.6 per cent and the simultaneous rise in the percentage of all holdings owned from 69.9 to 76.2 per cent, the intensity of labour employed on them had increased, with agricultural production increasing in result, during 1970-71 to 1985-86.

TABLE 18.6: Employment in the organised sector by industry division

Industry	(As Percentage Distribution of Total Employment)			
	1971		1987	
	Public Sector	Private Sector	Public Sector	Private Sector
Agriculture, etc.	1.5	4.5	2.2	3.3
Mining and Quarrying	1.0	2.3	3.7	0.3
Manufacturing	4.6	22.5	7.3	17.3
Electricity, gas, water , etc.	2.5	0.2	3.1	3.2
Construction	5.0	0.8	4.6	4.9
Wholesale trade, Retail trade etc.	1.8	1.7	0.5	1.6
Transport, Storage and Communications	12.7	0.5	11.7	11.9
Services	32.1	5.7	37.7	44.0
Total	61.4	38.6	70.9	29.1

Source: Tata Services Ltd., *Statistical Outline of India*, 1989-90.

TABLE 18.7: Size-wise classification of operational holdings

Size of Holdings (Hectares)	Percentage Distribution					
	Number of Holdings			Area of Holdings		
	1970-71	1980-81	1985-86	1970-71	1980-81	1985-86
Marginal (Below one ha)	51.0	56.5	58.0	9.0	12.2	13.1
Small (1 ha to 2 ha)	18.9	18.0	18.2	11.9	14.1	15.5
Semi-Medium (2 ha to 4 ha)	15.0	14.0	13.6	18.5	21.2	22.2
Medium (4 ha to 10 ha)	11.2	9.1	8.2	29.7	29.7	28.7
Large (10 ha and above)	3.9	2.4	3.9	30.9	22.8	20.5
Total	100.0	100.0	100.0	100.0	100.0	100.0
Average Size of Holdings	—	—	—	2.28	1.84	1.68

Source: Tata Services Ltd., *Statistical Outline of India*, 1989-90.

Table 18.8 presents data on distribution of employment in the two broad types of enterprises, agricultural and non-agricultural, spread in rural and urban areas, as indicated by the 1980 Economic Census. The average size of enterprises in agriculture was small in rural as well as urban areas – in rural areas 10.2 per cent of all employees were employed in 11.6 per cent of all enterprises, while in urban areas 1.4 per cent of all employees were engaged in 2.4 per cent of all enterprises. The average size of the non-agricultural enterprises was smaller than the average size of the agricultural enterprises, as would be evident from the data contained in the table – in rural areas 89.8 per cent of all persons were employed in 88.4 per cent of all enterprises, while in urban areas the corresponding figures were 98.6 per cent and 97.6 per cent respectively. Finally, the percentage of hired workers was higher in urban areas than in rural – 66.9 per cent, as against 41.0 per cent.

A careful analysis of the same data State-wise in Table 18.9 suggests that the growth rate of enterprises has been quite high in certain States and quite low in other States. In terms of the number of workers the rate of growth has been higher in a few States. The number of female workers has been high in a fewer States. Some States which did well from the standpoint of enterprises with premises have also a large number of poverty-stricken enterprises without premises. Identical was the case when the problem was approached from the standpoint of enterprises using or not using power.

Digressing, for a while, to the abstract side of our present question, the labour-force may be defined as the number of persons willing to work, n, which number is composed of those actually working, l, and those willing to work but unable to find jobs, i.e., unemployed, u. Thus $n=l+u$. We define the percentage of the labour-force unemployed as $U=u/(l+u) \times 100$ and the percentage of the labour-force employed as $\mathbf{L} = l+(l+u) \times 100 = 100\text{-}\mathbf{U}$.

Among the economic factors that determine the volume of employment are: (a) rate of economic growth, (b) productive structure, (c) industrialisation and incorporation of new technology, and (d) various institutional factors which influence the relative prices of capital and labour.

TABLE 18.8: Employment in agricultural and non-agricultural enterprises

(in million)

	Rural				Urban				Total			
	Number of Enterprises	Percentage Share	Number of Persons Employed	Percentage Share	Number of Enterprises	Percentage Share	Number of Persons Employed	Percentage Share	Number of Enterprises	Percentage Share	Number of Persons Employed	Percentage Share
1	2	3	4	5	6	7	8	9	10	11	12	13
Agricultural Enterprises	1.30	11.6	2.48	10.2	0.18	2.4	0.40	1.4	1.48	8.0	2.88	5.4
Non-agricultural Enterprises	9.89	88.4	21.95	89.8	7.05	97.6	28.75	98.6	16.94	92.0	50.70	94.6
All Enterprises	11.19	100.0	24.43	100.0	7.22	100.0	29.16	100.0	18.41	100.0	53.58	100.0
Of which Hired Workers	—	—	10.02	41.0	—	—	19.53	66.9	—	—	29.55	55.1

* According to the 1980 Economic Census.

Source: Tata Services Ltd., *Statistical Outline of India*, 1989-90.

Note: Agricultural enterprises exclude crop production and plantation.

Women labour-force participation rate generally fluctuated during 1951-81. It was 23.4 (per 100 women) in 1951, 28 in 1961, 14.2 in 1971 and 20.8 in 1981. In the organised sector it was 11 per cent in 1971 and 12.4 per cent in 1979. Female employment was concentrated in low-scale, low-wage, and drudgery-involving jobs. Over 90 per cent of the aggregate female employment was in the unorganised sector. This was a product of their low training.

The unpaid economic activities of women and their contribution through work in the domestic sector remain unreported in the census. This would amount to around 25 to 39 per cent of the GNP.

Women are employed in agriculture, animal husbandry, activities allied to agriculture such as storage, marketing, food processing, in plantations, in marginal occupations supplementing the family income, and so forth.

Some of the new technologies have displaced women from many of the traditional activities. In families from which the men migrate to other places their women have to deputise for them in numerous ways, which denotes their increased responsibility and work.

Peculiar social conditions permit women of certain castes and communities to leave their homes and work outside but do not permit women of other castes to do this. Economic compulsions are the chief explanation why we have working women and why their number is growing.

Generally, female participation rates tend to fall off in the early stages of development with the contraction of opportunities for self-employment and unpaid family work in agriculture. But with development gathering momentum women pour out of their households in rising numbers for taking up paid employment, and the total number of female job-seekers is persistently on the rise because of this.

According to Datta and Sundaram, the north-eastern States display very high female work participation rates. Next in order come the southern States. Oddly, Kerala which tops in female literacy rate employs only 13 per cent of its female population of the working age-group on paid work. Some of the economically better-off States exhibit low female work participation rates.

The rate of growth of employment was 2.82 per cent per annum during 1972-78, 2.22 per cent per annum during 1977–83 and 1.55 per cent per annum during 1983-88. It has been estimated that only 3 per cent per annum growth rate of employment can provide work to all in this country by 2000 A.D.

TABLE 18.9: State-wise employment in enterprises (rural & urban)

State	Number of Enterprises (1990) (in lakhs)	Growth Rate during 1980-89 (per cent)	Number of Workers (1990) (in lakhs)	Percentage Increase (1989-90)	Number of Female Workers in All Enterprises (Rural & Urban) (1990) (in thousands)	Number of Hired Female Workers in Own Account Enterprises (Rural & Urban) (1990) (in thousands)
1	2	3	4	5	6	7
Andhra Pradesh	24.60 (4)	52.4 (2)	65.30 (4)	38.6 (2)	1711 (1)	692 (3)
Assam	4.81 (12)	NA	13.26 (12)	NA	160 (12)	125 (12)
Bihar	—	—	—	—	—	—
Gujarat	14.93 (7)	25.6 (10)	44.67 (7)	22.3 (11)	748 (7)	290 (8)
Haryana	4.53 (13)	41.8 (4)	13.08 (13)	34.3 (4)	137 (13)	106 (13)
Himachal Pradesh	1.80 (14)	29.5 (9)	4.58 (14)	32.9 (6)		
Karnataka	17.04 (6)	23.9 (11)	50.04 (5)	29.4 (8)	1175 (3)	701 (2)
Kerala	12.22 (8)	40.2 (5)	31.39 (8)	28.0 (10)	791 (6)	626 (4)
Madhya Pradesh	18.65 (5)	39.1 (6)	48.11 (6)	46.2 (1)	892 (5)	299 (7)
Maharasthra	26.25 (3)	42.7 (3)	87.03 (1)	28.9 (9)	1242 (2)	766 (1)
Orissa	10.99 (10)	36.8 (7)	25.91 (10)	33.0 (5)	464 (9)	151 (9)
Punjab	6.33 (11)	36.6 (8)	17.51 (11)	31.1 (7)	167 (11)	132 (11)
Rajasthan	11.75 (9)	21.9 (12)	27.99 (9)	20.8 (12)	317 10)	149 (10)
Tamil Nadu	—	—	—	—	—	—
Uttar Pradesh	26.41 (2)	21.9 (12)	67.97 (3)	18.3 (13)	657 (8)	300 (6)
West Bengal	27.95 (1)	64.0 (1)	72.84 (2)	36.3 (3)	995 (4)	413 (5)

Source: *Financial Express*, March 22, 1991.
Note: Figures in brackets indicate the ranks of the States.
Dissatisfied with the quality of enumeration the Census Commissioner rejected the data collected from Bihar and Tamil Nadu.

As a result of employment growing at a rate slower than the rate at which the labour force has grown, unemployment has accumulated and poverty has responded less in proportion to the public outlay expended on it for at least 16 years.

We have noticed before that one peculiarity of the Indian mentality consists in this that self-employment in agriculture is craved most of all, whereas, among other occupations, services, be they in the private sector or the public sector, are sought after most fervidly by those willing to be wage-employed. Not all communities are temperamentally suited for self-employment, nor are all occupations suited for it. Self-employment is more demanding than wage-employment in terms of investment — material and human, skill and experience, and propensities like innovation, risk-taking and uncertainty-bearing. Those who prefer a quiet and smooth, steady and soft (as contrasted with venturesome and hard) life, an income that is fixed stable, and some power and influence which attends particular jobs, naturally opt for paid work more in the public and less in the private sector. These are the principal factors that account for the growing relative importance of services in late years.

Table 18.10 depicts growth of employment in the organised sector between 1961 and 1988. Employment increased absolutely in both private and public sectors during this period, 2.6 times in the public sector and 1.4 times in the private sector. But in percentage terms employment increased by 12.9 per cent in the public sector and so decreased by the same percentage in the private sector. As far as the rate of growth of employment is concerned, it was 2.4 times more rapid in the public sector in 1971 but only 1.4 times more rapid only in 1988. The public sector surpassed the private sector in providing employment in the organised sector, no doubt, but over time its pace of so doing suffered an eclipse, partly because it contracted relatively to the private sector, as measured by the amount of public sector plan outlay, partly because it had to adopt relatively more capital-intensive modes of production, and partly for other reasons enumerated in these pages before.

The Unemployment Scenario/Vista

Table 18.11 attempts to summarise the information on growth of employment and unemployment in India in the course of 15 years, from 1972-73 to 1987-88, giving their rural and urban breakdowns side by side and following the triple concepts of unemployment, as used by the NSS studies. In 1990-91 the backlog of unemployment measured by the usual status criterion was 13 million, which amounted to 3.77 per cent of the total workforce. But on the basis of the weekly status concept the backlog of unemployment in the beginning of 1990 was 16 million. Twelve million people were underemployed, according to the NSS data. So altogether un- and under-employment worked out of 28 million in the country. Private estimates had gone up to 120 million for December 1989, on the other hand.

TABLE 18.10: Growth of employment in the organised sector

Year	Public Sector		Private Sector		Total Number of Employees (million)
	Number of Employees (million)	As Percentage of Total	Number of Employees (million)	As Percentage of Total	
1961	7.05	58.3	5.04	41.7	12.09
1988	18.33	71.2	7.42	28.8	25.75
Increase :					
Times	2.6	1.2	1.4	−1.4	2.13

	Rate of Growth of Employment		Times
	Public Sector	Private Sector	
	(per cent per year)		
1971	3.4	0.9	2.4
1988	1.7	0.8	1.4

Source: Tata Services Ltd., *Statistical Outline of India*, 1989-90.

Considering that the number of people living in rural areas is about thrice that living in urban areas, the proportion of employment, on daily status basis, has been higher and increasing in rural areas (3.3 times, 3.5 times, 4.5 times and 4.7 times), as compared to urban areas. As for unemployment, its burden, on daily status basis was, again, was shared by rural areas less in the earlier years than in the later, in proportion to the distribution of population (1.8 times, 2.9 times, 3.3 times and 4.3 times). At present rural areas are bearing the relative burden of unemployment more, as calculated on this criterion.

TABLE 18.11: Aggregate employment and unemployment by current weekly and daily status

(Figures in million persons/person days)

	Employment			Unemployment		
	Rural	Urban	Total	Rural	Urban	Total
			Current Weekly Status			
Round and Year						
43 - 1987-88	212.7	64.9	277.6	9.5	4.5	14.4
38 - 1983	203.0	55.1	258.1	8.2	4.0	12.2
32 - 1977-78	189.0	39.7	228.7	7.3	3.4	10.7
27 - 1972-73	185.0	37.2	222.2	7.4	2.6	10.0
			Daily Status			
Round and Year						
43 - 1987-88	208.1	62.4	270.5	11.4	6.4	17.8
38 - 1983	187.2	52.3	239.5	16.1	5.5	21.6
32 - 1977-78	171.8	37.6	209.3	14.3	4.3	18.6
27 - 1972-73	168.6	35.6	204.2	15.0	3.5	18.5
			Usual Status Chronic			
Round and Year						
1971	—	—	—	1.77	1.88	3.65
1973	—	—	—	1.83	2.04	3.87
1978	—	—	—	2.00	2.37	4.37
1983	—	—	—	2.20	2.77	4.97

Source: National Sample Survey Organisation (NSSO) — Key Result of Employment and Unemployment Survey — All-India (Part I), NSS 43rd Round (July 1987—June 1988).

Note: A person who did not work even for one hour during a reference period of one week preceding the date of inquiry (weekly status) on any day of the preceding week (daily status) or any day during the preceding 365 days (usual status) but was seeking or available for work during that period was deemed to be unemployed.

On the basis of the chronic unemployment criterion, the relative burden has been borne more by urban areas, and that decreasingly too 1.25, 1.18, 1.11 and 1.06 times respectively, when considered against the backdrop of their relative population shares.

Some striking inter-State features of the unemployment problem were highlighted by Visaria. The data for Gujarat and Maharashtra showed that according to both the conventional definition and a more comprehensive measure (designed to capture involuntary idleness within the reference week), the incidence of unemployment was markedly higher among those whose usual activity was casual labour. The self-employed (including the employers) and family helpers reported a much less-than-average level of unemployment or underemployment. The casual labourers were over-represented among the bottom deciles in terms of their per capita expenditure. They reported a lower-than-average level of literacy and education and were generally younger than other workers. Those in rural areas were predominantly agricultural labourers with no land or very small land holdings. Two distinct groups among urban casual labourers were agricultural labourers and miscellaneous workers in the "net elsewhere classified" category.

The incidence of unemployment (in terms of person days) in 17 major States of India showed a statistically significant, positive association with the male labour-force. That is, the importance of casual labourers in the labour-force seemed to explain a good part of the inter-State variance in unemployment rates. Visaria suggested that such differences in the structure or composition of the labour-force might account for some of the differences in unemployment rates reported for different as well. Also, with an increase in the share of casual labour in the labour-force, unemployment rates estimated through surveys could be expected to rise in India.

Table 18.12 can be stated to be an epitome of the educated unemployment situation in India. Since planning was inaugurated, the extent of educated unemployment has soared nearly a hundred times. Educated unemployment is the outcome of misdirected investment. The output of educated persons has exceeded what the economy could take at their current prices. Employment opportunities have not expanded at the same rate at which education has expanded. This has brought educated unemployment in its train. The capacity to absorb educated persons is a function of the structure of the economy and of the rate of its growth. If more educated people are produced than the economy can absorb, the consequence is not more growth but more unemployment of the educated. This is so because the expectations of the educated are not reflected structure by the of the economy. If the educated would take whatever jobs were going, they would always find work, to cite Lewis.

TABLE 18.12: Employment exchange statistics

Year	Number of Employment Exchanges at the end of the period	Monthly Average Number of Employers using Exchanges ('000)	Number of Vacancies Notified ('000)	Number of Registrations During the Period ('000)	Number of Placements Effected ('000)	Number of Applicants on the Live Register at the end of the Period ('000)
1951	126	6	486	1,375	417	329
1987	755	9	600	5,976	343	30,539
Increase (Times)	6.0	1.5	1.2	4.3	–1.21	92.8

Source: 1. *Indian Labour Statistics*, 1979.
2. *Indian Labour Journal*, March, 1989.

Among the unemployed we have secondary school leavers, university graduates and professionals having received university training. A majority of these have rich parents or guardians or government or university or UGC stipends, scholarships or fellowships to support them for the period they refuse work other than the specific modern sector jobs for which they have been trained. We have in India an overproduction of the educated or high-talent manpower.

A remarkable characteristic of educated unemployment is the tendency of unemployment rates to increase with the level of education in each age-group.

The steady upgrading of the educational requirements for jobs and the corresponding devaluation of the existing educational qualifications leads to a further increase in the demand for education, as people seek more education to increase their chances of employment. Dore terms this the "diploma disease".

The decision to seek a higher level of education is based on the expected earnings, not on the earnings actually received when employed. So long as the private costs of education are low, and so long as earning differentials among people having different levels of education are high, the expected earnings at higher levels of education are sufficiently large to make the investment in education appear profitable. This is one reason why the private demand for education has remained high in spite of the presence of ever-growing educated unemployment. Growing unemployment among the educated may make the parents think several times before they agree to spend money on the education of their children beyond a certain level, had education been not so heavily subsidised by the state as it is at present; at times the subsidy: private investment ratio is two to five, depending on the level of higher education. Financial support for an indefinite period from their parents lowers the incentive of the educated unemployed to quicken the search for employment, which is in most cases for a clerical job, which has, of course, the advantage that in it they would not have to soil their hands. This is their notion of a remunerative job whose return would compensate for the investment made in their education and, if they failed to get better jobs, clerkship was surely in the line and also suited the particular type of education they had gone in for.

A suggestion made with regard to the educated unemployed who prefer to return to their village homes and are prepared to continue to live there, provided they secure some job or other there is that they should be retrained and hence refurbished and retooled by running special adult educational or vocational programmes so as to take up the work of teachers, extension workers, minor administrators, and so on. Alternatively, they should be assisted in various ways to shift to the self-employment sector. This is a task fraught with problems and difficulties. For one thing, formal education does not countenance self-employment. In India government jobs carry a particularly high prestige value and provide maximum security with minimum amount of work and hence have immense fascination for the educated young people. The private sector jobs come next which sometimes captivate enterprising young people still more but they extract maximum work from the salaried staff and in many areas lack security. Higher salaries with better perks become the off-setting attractions.

Recognition much earlier in the day of the inability of the growth process to release an adequate number of jobs for those looking for them made the Indian planners regard self-employment as a unique solution to the problem of underdevelopment, being in value equivalent to self-government, and hence one that assured full development of the personality of the persons involved. But the recent experiences in this realm have not been in unison with their stipulations. During 1972-88 a progressive shift occurred from self-employment to casual wage employment.

Unemployment, general or educated, is concentrated in certain regions. In the eastern region Calcutta has the maximum concentration. In the southern region Tamil Nadu with 7.52 per cent of total population accounts for 14.6 per cent of the total unemployed. Tamil Nadu, Andhra Pradesh, Kerala, West Bengal and Uttar Pradesh which constitute 48.2 per cent of the total population account for 56 per cent of aggregate unemployment. Maharashtra, Bihar, Rajasthan, Karnataka and Gujarat comprise 34.4 per cent of the total population but account for 28 per cent of aggregate unemployment. Orissa, Madhya Pradesh, Haryana, Punjab and Assam claim 18.5 per cent of the total population but 14 per cent of aggregate unemployment. Open and disguised unemployment rates range from 25 per cent to 30 per cent, according to different studies. Conceptual differences, nature of the State economy–predominantly agricultural or pre-eminently non-agricultural — rate of growth, rates of literacy and education, etc., are the various factors that lie at the root of the inter-State disparities in employment and unemployment.

With abundant labour supply but with less than requisite amounts of complementary factors the States have to be very selective in emphasising the areas in which fresh employment opportunities are to be generated. The old reliance on the trickle-down strategy has to yield place to direct programmes directed at alleviating poverty and eradicating unemployment. In the current decade agriculture would by all appearances obtain the primacy of place in the allotment of direct programmes. Care should, however, be exercised to prevent agriculture from becoming more capital-intensive and more large-scale. The more employment-intensive agricultural operations become, the larger the number of people that would find employment in them directly or indirectly. Extension of means of irrigation to the small order farms, keeping in mind the need to protect the environment against any likely hazard, would make rich contributions to this goal. Agriculture should try to diversify itself and embrace animal husbandry and pisciculture and horticulture so that the gains and losses inflicted by the natural factors and the market forces are interbalanced and the principle of comparative costs is put to an effective use in the arena of agriculture and allied activities.

Direct programmes are needed not only by rural areas but also by urban areas. An integration of the formal and informal sectors in urban areas brought about by a number of instruments and devices would improve the capacity of non-agriculture to absorb the growing labour force, more and more in the current decade and in the decades to follow.

The lesson of this exposition is that there is no gain-saying that the objective of **work for all** was highly desirable and its achievement would be the true touch-stone of the success of the final strategy for any five-year Plan that would be in the coming years on the anvil.

PART III

A CRITIQUE OF THE RECENT DEBATES

19

RECENT THOUGHTS ON POVERTY, INEQUALITY AND UNEMPLOYMENT IN INDIA

Employing per capita SDPs as the basis for relatively ordering the States as more or less rich/poor is open to serious objections as we have seen at length earlier and as we would see, though briefly, presently. That this measure is oblivious of the distribution of income among the people, particularly among their lowest strata, is its Achilles' heels, its most deplorable loophole.

Let us set aside for a moment this drawback and rank the (fifteen non-special category) States according to their respective SDPs during 1950-51 to 1988-89, as done in Table 19.1. From this table it appears that over the entire period 10 States suffered a setback in their relative positions. Of them, seven had their ranks lowered by one point only, two by two points and one by three points. All the four States in the eastern region had their ranks reduced—West Bengal by three points. The remaining five States had maintained their ranks intact. Three of them were in the southern region. They enjoyed relative stability.

Within this span of 38 years there occurred in different years variations in the relative positions of the States. This is presented in Table 19.2. Two States stand out as being unique—Punjab and Bihar—in maintaining their positions consistently—Punjab the first rank and Bihar the second over the whole period.

The total ranks, as contained in column 8 of Table 19.1, when allocated region-wise, lead us to a situation in which the western region (with Gujarat and Maharasthra) comes out as the best in performance with 37 total ranks; the northern region (with Haryana, Punjab and Rajasthan—Rajasthan is a drag) second with 74; the central region (with Madhya Pradesh and Uttar Pradesh) third with

TABLE 19.1: Changes in per capita SDP as measure of changes in relative poverty of States during 1950-51 to 1988-89

State	(At 1960-61 Prices)		(At 1970-71 Prices)		(At Current Prices : New Series)		
	1950-51	1960-61	1970-71	1980-81	1984-85	1988-89 (Quick Estimates)	Total Ranks [(2) to (6)]
1	2	3	4	5	6	7	8
Andhra Pradesh	258(7)	275(3)	585(10)	647(7)	2086(10)	3211(8)	44(8)
Assam	335(10)	251(12)	535(12)	558(10)	2182(8)	2786(11)	62(10)
Bihar	181(14)	215(14)	402(15)	425(14)	1479(15)	2266(15)	87(13)
Gujarat (with Maharashtra)	381(3)	362(4)	829(4)	904(4)	3131(4)	4742(4)	22(4)
Haryana (with Punjab)	(1)	(3)	877(3)	1058(2)	3325(3)	5274(2)	13(2)
Karnataka (Mysore)	287(5)	296(6)	641(8)	687(6)	2508(5)	3612(5)	34(6)
Kerala	304(9)	259(10)	594(9)	620(8)	2178(9)	3054(9)	53(9)
Madhya Pradesh	236(12)	260(9)	454(13)	518(14)	1675(14)	2739(12)	74(11)
Maharashtra (Bombay)	373(2)	409(1)	783(5)	964(3)	3384(2)	5155(3)	15(3)
Orissa	252(13)	216(13)	478(14)	529(12)	1707(13)	2625(14)	79(12)
Punjab	404(1)	366(3)	1070(1)	1378(1)	4110(1)	6227(1)	8(1)
Rajasthan	256(8)	284(7)	651(7)	535(11)	1818(11)	2923(10)	53(9)
Tamil Nadu (Madras)	245(6)	334(5)	581(11)	584(9)	2341(7)	3593(6)	43(7)
Uttar Pradesh	271(11)	252(11)	486(2)	519(13)	1768(12)	2698(13)	62(10)
West Bengal	471(4)	390(2)	722(6)	797(5)	2473(6)	3423(7)	29(5)
All-India	—	—	—	—	—	—	—

TABLE 19.1 *Contd.*

State	1955-56 (Per capita final product)	1957-58 (Per capita Income)	1960-61 (Per capita Income)	Total Ranks [(9) to (11)]	Total Ranks [(5) to (7)]
1	9	10	11	12	13
Andhra Pradesh	(9)	(8)	(9)	26(9)	25(7)
Assam	(6)	(2)	(6)	14(4)	29(9)
Bihar	(13)	(12)	(13)	38(12)	44(14)
Gujarat	(5)	(5)	(4)	14(4)	12(4)
Haryana	(3)	(1)	(3)	7(2)	7(2)
Karnataka	(6)*	(6)	(6)*	18(5)	16(5)
Kerala	(10)	(11)	(7)	28(10)	26(8)
Madhya Pradesh	(11)	(7)	(10)	28(10)	40(13)
Maharashtra	(2)	(5)	(1)	8(3)	8(3)
Orissa	(12)	(13)	(12)	37(11)	39(12)
Punjab	(3)	(1)	(3)	7(2)	3(1)
Rajasthan	(7)	(4)	(11)	22(7)	32(10)
Tamil Nadu	(8)	(10)	(5)	23(8)	22(6)
Uttar Pradesh	(4)	(9)	(8)	21(6)	38(11)
West Bengal	(1)	(3)	(2)	6(1)	16(5)
All-India	—	—	—	—	

Source: (1) A. Mazoomdar, *Bihar : A Case in Development*, Delhi, 1990, for cols. (2) to (5).
(2) *Economic Survey*, 1990-91, for cols. (6) and (7).
(3) K.N. Prasad, *Economics of a Backward Region in a Backward Economy*, Vol. 2, for cols. (8)-(10). Figures of per capita income have not been reproduced.

Note: Figure in brackets indicate the ranks of the states.
* Improvised.

136; the southern region (with Andhra Pradesh, Karnataka, Kerala and Tamil Nadu) fourth with 174; and the eastern region (with Assam, Bihar, Orissa and West Bengal—with its declining economic fortune West Bengal has not been a prop) fifth and last with 257 rank points.

Allocated among the States according to their grouping[1] as Top Five, Middle Five and Bottom Five, the total ranks bring out that Top Five have the best position with 92 points, Middle Five the second position with 222 points and Bottom Five the third position with 364 points. This is proof of concentration of poverty in the eastern region, which has three of the Bottom Five States.

Were we to confine our vision to the earlier years, namely, 1955-56, 1957-58 and 1960-61 (see column 12 of Table 19.1) and compare them with the later years, namely, 1980-81, 1984-85 and 1988-89, we would discover that the inter-State disparities or imbalances, as indicated by per capita SDPs, were narrower in the earlier years than they were in the later years. That is to say, they had widened with the passage of time.

The year 1970-71 stands almost at the centre of the 38-year period. Making it the point of reference, we find that the inter-State disparities, as measured by per capita SDPs, were slightly wider in 1970-71 but were slightly narrower in 1988-89. In other words, in the first 20 years of planning they had slightly increased and in the last 18 years of it they had slightly decreased.

Poverty: Recent Exercises

The P.V. Narasimha Rao Government has adopted the old figure of 40 per cent of the total population as the population below the Poverty Line in India in 1987-88. In 1990 out of the total population of 830 million, 340 million people were reported to be below the Poverty Line. In 1984-85 the number of the poor in our country had been put at 273 million. Thus in about six years another 67 million people have joined the army of the poor in our country.

The Rajiv Government had claimed that between 1977-78 and 1983-84 nearly 36 million people had crossed the Poverty Line. This was partly due to the impact of growth and partly due to the impact of the anti-poverty programmes. But in any case this could not have been achieved on a permanent, self-sustainable basis. Also, this assertion was a bit suspect because the achievement was claimed for a period which witnessed a sudden spurt in the volume of unemployment: unemployment rising, poverty falling, a paradoxical situation which purported to refute the received theory.

TABLE 19.2: **Variations in ranking of the States in terms of per capita SDP**

	1950-51	1970-71	1980-81	1988-89
Top Five				
Punjab	1st	1st	1st	1st
Haryana	—	3rd	2nd	2nd
Maharashtra	2nd	5th	3rd	3rd
Gujarat	—	4th	4th	4th
Karnataka	4th	8th	6th	5th
Middle Five				
Tamil Nadu	5th	11th	9th	6th
West Bengal	3rd	6th	5th	7th
Andhra Pradesh	6th	10th	7th	8th
Kerala	8th	9th	8th	9th
Rajasthan	7th	7th	11th	10th
Bottom Five				
Assam	11th	12th	10th	15th
Madhya Pradesh	13th	13th	14th	12th
Uttar Pradesh	12th	2nd*	13th	13th
Orissa	14th	14th	12th	14th
Bihar	15th	15th	15th	15th

* This seems absurd; if true, this may be by fluke.

Source: Derived from Table 19.1.

More recently, according to the Planning Commission, the incidence of poverty declined steadily from 51.5 per cent (equals 291.5 million) in 1972-73 to 29.9 per cent (equals 237.4 million) in 1987-88. The Planning Commission has used an over-all price deflator to estimate real consumption. It considers the CSO data a better measure of real aggregate consumption than the NSS data. In its opinion, the NSS organisation underestimates household consumption, whereas the CSO data has a less erratic pattern. However, it considers the NSS data on size distribution of per capita consumer expenditure satisfactory. But the Planning Commission fails to take into account differences in prices in different States as well as differences in prices between the rural and urban areas. It should also be noted here that both years, 1972-73 and 1987-88, were years of severe drought. The Planning Commission has uniformly scaled upwards the NSS consumption data by 27.5 per cent for 1987-88. The Planning Commission estimates err on the low side. Furthermore, the Planning Commission's Poverty Line remains fixed. In consequence, a large number of persons are pulled above the Poverty Line rather artificially.

For 1987-88 the percentage of rural poverty is put at 32 and that of urban poverty at 19.

Minhas and Visaria questioned the Planning Commission data and came out with their own estimate: That in 1972-73, 54.9 per cent of the total population (equals 311 million) was below the Poverty Line. By 1987-88 the percentage had fallen to 42.2 (equals 361.2 million). In the Planning Commission's estimate there was a fall of 22 per cent and of 54 million people. In Minhas-Visaria's estimate there was a fall of 12 per cent but a rise of 24 million people. Minhas and his associates denied that the NSS organisation underestimated household consumption. They treated the NSS data as satisfactory. They called the CSO data as inflated. The CSO data are subject to a large margin of error. Minhas and associates used consumer price indices that were more specific to the rural and urban areas as well as the middle range of the population whose per capita consumption was closer to the Poverty Line.

For 1987-88 Minhas estimated the percentage of rural poverty at 48 (equals 283 million) and that of urban poverty at 37(equals 77 million)—the sumtotal being 360 million people.

The NSS had calculated the percentage of poverty for the year 1977-78 at 14 to 15 per cent. Between 1972-73 and 1977-78 there was a dramatic improvement. But this finding is open to grave doubts.

In its 1990 report the World Bank considered poverty the most pressing problem of the developing countries. According to the Bank, the 1980s were for many of the world's poor a "lost decade", a disaster indeed, and economic growth in the Third World was virtually growth without development. The Bank defined poverty in terms of the inability of a person to attain a minimal standard of living. Evidently, this concept had a close affinity with the PQLI index. The Bank took Rs. 370 per head per year as the threshold of poverty. It measured the extent of poverty with the aid of (1) the head count index (percentage of population below the Poverty Line) and

(2) the poverty gap (aggregate income shortfall of the poor as a percentage of aggregate consumption).

According to the World Bank, between 1973 and 1983 the extent of poverty in India fell by 11 percentage points, of which seven percentage points were between 1977 and 1983. The decline in the extent of poverty in India was very much dependent on the increase in the total purchasing power commanded by the agricultural sector of the country. During 1973-83 purchasing power commanded by the agricultural sector in India had risen by less than 1 per cent per annum, although during 1977-83 it rose by 1.5 per cent a year. Obviously, the 1977-83 sub-period saw a better performance than the 1973-77 sub-period.

For 1985 the World Bank put the number of the people below the Poverty Line at 420 million.

According to the 1991 report of the World Bank, absolute poverty in India declined from about 55 per cent in the early 1960s to only 45 per cent in the mid-1980s.

Estimates show that aggregate rural poverty declined substantially between 1973-74 and 1986-87 from 60.6 to 41.5 per cent. In 1987-88, 32 per cent people in rural areas were reported to be below the Poverty Line.

In percentage terms rural poverty did not increase between 1984-85 and 1991.

According to other estimates, 52 per cent of the total rural population lives in conditions of primary poverty and 75 per cent in conditions of destitution.

The percentage of population grinding out a meagre and inadequate, even pecarious, existence is the highest in the primary sector. For the many impoverished rural dwellers bare subsistence and survival is the only goal of their life. These sections of society have remained largely untouched by the development that has taken place so far. Ordinarily, subsistence and survival levels of living assort logically well with subsistence farm production lacking specialisation and diversification.

Inadequate access to land and capital for the majority of farmers and technological backwardness or stagnation keeping agricultural productivity at a low level are the two prime reasons for rural poverty. By comparison, the rural poor have been poorer than the urban poor. But the recent fall in rural poverty has been by a greater percentage than that in urban poverty. Minhas' estimate of urban poverty at 36.5 per cent in 1987-88 is stated to be on the high side considering that a lot of collateral evidence based on the surveys of urban consumption supports a lower percentage. Urban poverty is analogous to urban unemployment in that like the latter it is an out-growth of rural poverty and unemployment. Just as rural unemployment dissolves itself into urban unemployment, so does rural poverty dissolve itself into urban poverty. But this parallelism smacks of an old aroma which has since become less attractive.

In the Marxian analysis, poverty and distress are firmly linked to the forces of history and the intrinsic nature of capital. Access to income-earning assets/opportunities and capacity to respond to them arc the two principal determinants of the degree of poverty. Hunger is primarily a function of poverty. The poor suffer most when the times are hard. Rural poverty has invariably been affected significantly by the nature of harvests, whether good or bad. An inverse relationship has been posited between rural poverty and per capita output for the rural population. In addition, rural poverty has been positively related with prices.

Severity of poverty is measured by the gap between an average poor person's income and the Poverty Line. In 1973-74 the severity of rural poverty in India was estimated at 18.8 per cent, which had come down to 10.5 per cent by 1986-87.

Rise in per capita income has been rejected as an indicator of fall in the poverty ratio, for it might be that most of the rise is among the top 25 per cent of society and very little of it trickles down to the bottom levels, i.e., 40 per cent of society whose living conditions therefore do not change.

The percentage of population below the Poverty Line is influenced by the nature of agricultural harvest, good or bad, in a given year as well as the price series used for comparison and adjustment to relate the NSS estimates of consumer expenditure to the CSO figures of aggregate national consumption.

The percentage of the poor people in India has diminished steadily. Growth has had an impact. Its fruits have trickled down to the lower strata of society. The consumption equalisation measures have also contributed towards poverty alleviation. The wage employment schemes too had a favourable dent on poverty, even in the years of drought. The development strategy and the growth pattern that emerged from it made an impression on the issue of poverty and want. These are facts which cannot be denied.

That wealth has increased and poverty has decreased is confirmed by certain indicators. A NCAER survey (spanning the period 1986-1990) has revealed that Indians own as many as 120 million wrist watches, 60 million bicycles and 54 million radio sets. Families with an annual income of Rs. 25,000 or less account for one-third of all purchases of refrigerators, washing machines, VCRs and motor-cycles. This spending spree is ascribed to the strong demonstration effect produced by TV advertising. The low-income households (those spending less than Rs. 1,250 a year) comprise 420 million people. The middle class is constituted by about 290 million or, say, 300 million people living in 58 million households. Of these, 20 million households, that is, 100 million people compose the middle, upper middle and higher income groups. Thirty-eight million households or 190 million people form the lower-middle income households. The middle class in India is thus very much in the market economy. It is the backbone of the market, which draws the bulk of its sustenance from this very class.

The market of manufacturing goods is not only widening but it is also deepening. A sizable proportion of different kinds of durable consumer goods is absorbed by the bottom 60 per cent of the income earners and that proportion is constantly rising.

To put it differently, the spending spree goes well beyond the middle class in enveloping the consumers. Thus the share of rural markets in packaged consumer goods rose from 28 per cent in 1984 to 37 per cent in 1989.

To summarise, it would be unwise to read too much meaning into the absolute magnitudes of the different estimates related above. The margin of probable error is large in every estimate. The estimators themselves would not like to swear by the precision of the statistics they have used. Therefore, we cannot be very sure of the exact level of poverty but we can certainly say whether it is on the decline or not—not the magnitude but the direction of the change, i.e., its sign – rise or fall. To quote Mohan (N.C.) and Anklesaria Aiyar (S.S.), "In sum, while the Planning Commission's estimates of poverty look too low, Minhas' estimates look too high. The truth may lie somewhere in the middle. The incidence of poverty has probably fallen less sharply than suggested by the Commission but by more than (that) indicated by Minhas" (*Times of India*, 13.9.91).

Let us now turn to the familiar proposition that economic growth is necessary to reduce poverty but experience so far shows that it has proved insufficient. Social expenditures expand opportunities for the poor but, again, they may not be enough. When interpreted, this should imply that without rapid growth neither income inequality nor poverty can be alleviated. All the same, economic, growth is not a precondition for satisfying basic human needs but a consequence of it. Satisfying the people's basic needs would create economic growth through its trickle-up effect. In India economic expansion, in general, and agricultural development, in particular, and, to crown it all, anti-poverty programmes—a triad of measures—would be essential to get rid of the trinity of our problems, namely poverty, inequality and unemployment. The trickle-down effect is an indirect route and is not infrequently insubstantial in its impact. Even then it has to be relied upon as a complementary measure and not to be discarded on account of its extremely tardy nature.

In our country the development strategy has so far encompassed the anti-poverty programmes. It has been the planners' supposition that the agricultural sector would interact dynamically with these programmes. Three kinds of poverty-alleviation programmes have been in operation: (1) As set creation under the IRDP; (2) Self-employment generation; and (3) Wage-employment provision through rural works. Through public employment, rural infrastructure which benefits the poor has been built and maintained. Such an infrastructure has also cushioned their incomes during spells of unemployment. It has also been built and maintained otherwise. A comprehensive design of the work to be done either at the district level or at the block level embracing the various beneficiary-oriented programmes, sectoral programmes and area schemes was hit upon quite late in the day to combat poverty in conformity with the exigencies of a holistic approach towards the reconstruction of the rural economy in its entirety.

But the anti-poverty programmes have been replete with several pitfalls and lacunae. Leakages of funds meant for them, to the extent of 85 per cent (recall what Rajiv Gandhi had publicly confessed as Prime Minister), have been alleged. Secondly, only limited growth of entrepreneurship has so far resulted from the self-employment schemes. Manual work guaranteed in the rural works has been of a restrictive nature. In the Seventh Plan Rs 25,000 crores was expended on these programmes. Despite this enormous expenditure the situation on the ground level remains even today much the same. At the implementation level not all the poor have been treated equally.

On the contrary, the target groups such as the weaker sections, such as the Scheduled Castes and Scheduled Tribes, have received a preferential treatment. Not only was employment provided to them but also their economic and educational interests were promoted. Past experience, however, bears out that the benefits of most of the programmes intended for the poor have either not reached them at all or if they have reached particular groups of them, they have not reached them in full measure.

Lack of awareness on the part of the potential beneficiaries of these opportunities is a great hurdle in their proper sharing.

Apart from this, some of the effort made by the planners to speed up growth in order to enable the economy to break out of the poverty trap has been dissipated by the appearance of new problems in their bid to remedy some of the old problems.

Last but not least, the programmes still smack of being a mere extension of relief works executed in the earlier days, thus reminding us more of the persistent poverty than of the progress made though slow and limited. Old habits die hard.

On balance, the resources stretched and spent so far have, however, kept the poor off the wolf points. The poverty-orientation of the development strategy has definitely benefited the poor. However, a great deal yet remains to be done if the basic human needs of the poor are to be satisfied.

Inequality: Recent Approaches

Equality has two aspects, according to the 1991 report of the World Bank: one, income distribution; two, incidence of poverty. There is no clear link between growth and changes in income distribution, in either direction. But economic growth is strongly associated with a reduction in the incidence of poverty. Growth reduces poverty.

An unbalanced growth of agricultural production and increased inequality in the regional distribution of income have often been attributed to the Green Revolution in India. The new technology has aggravated inequalities among regions because its introduction has not been uniform in them. Regions with better irrigation facility (the chief input behind the preponderance of wheat in northern and north-western States and rice, especially rabi rice, in the IADP districts and the eastern region) or assured rainfall and assured supply of modern inputs, a congenial socio-economic set-up and the necessary will on the part of the people and their leaders and the administrative and organisational machinery have derived maximum benefit.

Although average consumption grew slowly during 1977-83, inter-State consumption inequality declined during the period.

In recent writings it has been suggested repeatedly that inequality can be lessened by paying special attention to the stimulating of growth in the more backward regions of the country. At the same time, the distribution of output, region-wise, class-wise, crop-wise and sector-wise, should become more even than before, as also maintain the pace in that direction.

The 1991-92 Budget: A New Twist to the Old Policy

In his speech on the occasion (July 22, 1991) of presenting the 1991-92 budget the present Finance Minister of India, Dr. Manmohan Singh, a distinguished Indian economist with global acclaim, observed, "The basic challenge of our times is to ensure that wealth creation is not only tempered by equity and justice but is harnessed to the goals of removal of poverty and development for all." Dr. Singh pointed out very candidly that in so far as the poor were not essentially part of the market they were not served by it properly. For markets could serve only those who were part of the market system.

In his budget the poor are not required to tighten their belts, instead the increased food subsidy is supposed to guarantee to them their customary food packet and increased outlays on anti-poverty schemes are supposed to absorb a larger number of job-seekers.

Suggestions on Poverty-Alleviation Programmes

In its 1990 report the World Bank emphasised a dual approach to reduce poverty: (1) Efficient labour-intensive growth, based on appropriate market incentives, physical infrastructure, institutions and technological innovations, and (2) Adequate provision of social services, including primary education, basic health care and family planning services. But the Bank suggested that this approach should be supplemented by (i) transfer of assistance in cash or kind to those who did not have other benefits, and (ii) provision of safety nets to those who were most vulnerable to income-reducing shocks. Safety nets included guarantee of food security through food-price subsidies, food rations or food supplementation schemes.

A three-pronged attack on poverty was prescribed by the World Bank, namely, (a) Economy-wise and sector-wise policies to shore up and revamp rural development and urban development, (b) Specific policies to improve the participation of the poor in the growth process, e.g., increasing their access to land, credit and public infrastructure and services, (c) Tackling the resource-poor regions in a fashion different from tackling other regions. The Bank thought that, aside from this, the poor could be made wealthier by redistributing the existing assets such as land and by stepping up public investment in augmenting the quality of life of the poor in the country side (the Minimum Needs Programme comes to our mind as a leading example).

In the words of the World Bank, "The evidence . . . suggests that rapid and politically sustainable progress on poverty has been achieved by pursuing a strategy that has two equally important elements. The first element is to promote the productive use of the poor's most abundant asset, labour. . . . The second is to provide basic social services for the poor."

Any feasible policy of immediately improving the living conditions of the poor should be three-pronged:

(1) Creating conditions for a viable subsistence economy in poor rural areas. Measures include expanding the amount of land under cultivation, introducing higher-yield types of indigenous cereals, instruction in and paving the way for ecological forms of landuse, and promoting rural cottage and small industries. Making productive land available to the landless masses is a necessary, and possibly sufficient, condition for improving living conditions in rural areas. In other words, all experience points to the fact that rural poverty cannot be eradicated without comprehensive land reforms.

(2) Creating jobs and income in the mega-city slums. The failure of attempts to expand employment in the formal sector (due primarily to capital-intensive methods of production and labour aristocracies) is generally accepted. The alternative is to support the informal sector, the shadow economy of the urban poor, through small credits on easy terms and on-the-job training, without smothering productive potential

by "formalising the informal". This is so because the small informal businesses use labour-intensive technology to produce for the pocket and tastes of a local market, the "marginalised masses".

(3) Providing basic social services for the poor: health (bare-foot doctors being one means), housing (through building cooperatives) and rural education (learning for the ideal utilisation of land). Experience suggests that authoritarian regimes are less inclined to take this seriously than democratic governments.[2]

The key remedy consists in the empowerment of the poor, that is, establishing a people's economy. Basic needs development is less concerned with things and more with people, by themselves, for themselves. In concrete terms, grassroots initiatives and small development projects, tailored to meet the needs of the people concerned and tap the resources of collective experience and knowledge, self-initiative and self-help would subserve the end best of all.

Policies calculated to alleviate poverty would have to cover both urban and rural areas. Development policy must become the political expression of the fight against poverty. The basic needs of the poor people should move centre-piece. All decisions should be taken via democratic procedures. Leadership must uphold and consolidate them because it cannot replace them.

The Unemployment Scenario and Spectrum

The Seventh Plan had expected the employment potential to grow at the rate of four per cent annum (thus adding 40 million jobs) and the labour force at the rate of 2.6 per cent per annum (thereby adding 39 million persons to the labour market). But average employment growth during 1983 to 1987-88 was at the rate of 1.5 per cent per annum only, although GDP grew at the rate of over 5 per cent per annum during the period. The labour force grew at the rate of about 2.5 per cent per annum. That is to say, employment opportunities did not grow *pari passu* with increase in the labour force. The backlog of unemployment further accumulated. The VPS vintage Planning Commission pronounced this growth of employment more slow than the growth of labour force, a confirmation of the distortions dilutions, compromises and adhocism inherent in the planning process.

As Table 19.3 brings out, some shift of the rural manpower has taken place from the agricultural to the non-agricultural sectors, specially to the tertiary/services sector. But the shift has not been of an order capable of causing structural changes of any special import in the economy.

TABLE 19.3: Occupational distribution of working population during 1951-81

Sector/Industrial Categories	1951	1961	1971	1981*
1. *Primary:*	72.1	71.8	72.1	70.6
Cultivators	50.0	52.8	43.4	42.1
Agricultural labourers	19.7	16.7	26.3	26.3
Livestock, forestry and others	2.4	2.3	2.4	2.2
2. *Secondary Sector:*	10.7	12.2	11.2	12.9
Mining and quarrying	0.6	0.5	0.5	0.5
Large and Small Industries	9.0	10.6	9.5	10.9
Construction	1.1	1.1	1.2	1.5
3. *Tertiary Services Sector:*	17.2	16.0	16.7	16.5
Trade and Commerce	5.2	4.0	5.6	5.9
Transport, Storage and Communication	1.5	1.6	2.4	2.5
Other Services	10.5	10.4	8.7	8.1
Total	100.0	100.0	100.0	100.0

* Based on five per cent sample data. The figures include marginal workers also.
Source: Registrar General, India.

After breaking the non-agricultural sector down into its constituent parts as organised and non-organised, we find from Table 19.4 that during 1974-89, that is, a span of 15 years, organised sector mining and quarrying could create fresh jobs at the maximum rate, followed by "other services". The next area in which people could find employment with comparative ease was trade and transport. Manufacturing employment grew at the rate of 1.44 per cent per year. The construction works created further employment at the minimum rate of 0.37 per cent a year.

TABLE 19.4: Growth in employment during 1974-89

Sector	Annual Growth (per cent)	
	Organised	Unorganised
Mining and Quarrying	2.78	14.81
Manufacturing	1.44	4.57
Construction	0.37	9.73
Trade and Transport	1.70	10.24
Other Services	2.77	4.13

Source: Illustrated Weekly, April 27-28, 1991.

On the other hand, in the unorganised sector construction employment expanded at the rate of 9.73 per cent per annum. Mining and quarrying released additional employment at the fastest pace. Trade and commerce were only next to them from this standpoint. Manufacturing outpaced "other services" in the provision of more employment in the unorganised sector. People looked for employment in the organised sector but secured it in the unorganised sector in most cases. The organised sector subsumed medium and large enterprises, infrastructure, public administration and organised services. Between them these absorbed in the concluding years of the 1980s, 0.5 million persons every year, on an average.

Manufacturing is one of the divisions of the organised sector. From 1972-73 to 1987-88 employment in it grew at the rate of 3.6 per cent per annum. Over two-thirds of the total reported employment was in it. In 1977 it employed 69.5 million persons. By 1989 the number had sagged to 68.6 million — a marginal fall.

For a different point of view we are required to go to Papola's paper. He argues in his paper that in recent years employment growth in manufacturing has, in fact, been higher than the over-all growth in the economywide employment — 3.6 per cent versus two per cent (approx.). In the organised segment of manufacturing the rate of growth of employment was less than 1.5 per cent per annum. Bulk of the manufacturing sector employment being in the unorganised segment, its share in production increased from 67 to 76 per cent and it registered a growth rate of 4.6 per cent per year in employment during the same period.

What could be the reasons for the slow growth of employment in the manufacturing sector? First of all the common argument is that the rise in capital intensity per factory and per employee that has been occurring is the chief reason. Table 19.5 is illustrative of this contention/theory/explanation. Between 1970-71 and 1985-86 per factory fixed capital shot up over four-fold, from Rs. 13 to 59 lakhs; per employee the rise was still bigger, around five times, from Rs. 20 to 120 lakhs. Mechanization in non-agriculture commenced in an intense form in the mid-1970s. This was followed by the age of computerisation. Enquiries into the affairs of small firms disclose that they are more or less capital-intensive like big ones in one and the same line of business. In factories, with capital investment above Rs. 20 lakhs per factory, fixed capital per employee was Rs. 1,27,035; in factories employing less than 50 workers fixed capital per employee was Rs. 22,686. These figures belonged to 1984-85. Credit subsidies induced many small firms to adopt relatively capital-intensive techniques. The number of employees per factory fell from 66 in 1970-71 to 57 in 1985-86. The net outcome was that the shift towards improved, high technology in manufacturing, organised or semi-organised or unorganised (defined in terms of total capital investment) made rapid inroads into the relative share of the labour-intensive units. The gain in productive efficiency which resulted from this was to the detriment of employment creation.

The second explanation is carried out in terms of the decline of competition and the increased recourse to protectionism or tariff. The 1990 World Bank report revealed that the effect of effective industrial protection had been a fall in the level and growth of labour use in the formal sector. Let us substantiate this with an example: During the 1980s the lowly protected industries by using only 43.1 per cent of total fixed capital provided 77.7 per cent of total industrial employment. On the contrary, the highly protected industries, which used 53.2 per cent of fixed capital, provided employment to 18.5 per cent of total industrial employment. As economists like Parikh assert, had half the capital in the highly protected industries used the same capital: labour ratio as the lowly protected industries, industrial employment would have been 40 per cent higher. It should further be indicated here that the cost of labour was no less high in the highly protected industries. By the same token, the policy of reservation for the small sector—a case of internal tariff—has not led to any appreciable gain in employment, as discovered by the World Bank.

TABLE 19.5: Capital employed per factory and per worker

	1970-71	1980-81	1984-85	1985-86
Per Factory (Rs. crores)				
Fixed Capital	0.13	0.31	0.54	0.59
Productive Capital	—	—	0.77	0.83
Inputs	0.15	0.49	0.80	0.91
Wages and Salaries	0.01	0.04	0.06	0.07
Number of Workers	66	63	61	57
Number of Employees	—	—	78	73
Net Value Added (Rs. Lakhs)	4.9	12.4	20.8	23.0
Fixed Capita to Net Value Added Ratio	2.78	2.51	2.58	2.63
Per Worker				
Fixed Capital Per worker (Rs. Lakhs)	0.20	0.49	0.90	1.03
Fixed Capital Per Employer	—	—	0.69	0.80
Inputs (Rs. lakhs)	0.23	0.78	1.32	1.59
Wages Per Worker (Rs. thousand)	2.55	6.52	11.09	12.18
Productive Capital Per Employee (Rs. thousands)	23	55	98	112
Gross Output Per Employee (Rs. thousands)	26	75	134	161
Net Value Added Per Employee (Rs. thousands)	6	15	27	31
Employment Per Employee (Rs. thousand)	—	—	13	14
Employment to Net Value Added Ratio	0.53	0.51	0.51	0.48
Fixed Capital to Net Value Added Ratio	—	—	2.63	2.58
Fixed Capital to Gross Output Ratio	—	—	0.52	0.50
Net Value Added to Gross Output Ratio		—	0.20	0.19

Source: Annual Survey of Industries, issues of various years.

A third reason advanced, though only at times and rather erroneously, is concerned with the structural changes that have taken place in the shape of shifts of industrial groups in employment and output. But this view-point is countered by Papola because such changes have not had any perceptibly adverse effect on employment generation in the organised manufacturing sector as a whole.

A fourth reason assigned is the recent labour legislation, which reportedly has tended to incite labour unrest, to create a labour aristocracy (100 days' leave in a year, 10 times more wages than causal labourers' wages, etc.) to entail problems associated with the management of a larger work force and to pose difficulty in retrenching unwanted workers. But this theory is overruled by Papola, who notices little point in it and finds little evidence in support of the highly protective labour legislation argument.

A fairly good percentage of employment in manufacturing has been concentrated in a few towns. To illustrate, in 1971 nearly 27.5 per cent of it was concentrated in nine towns. But in late years growth of urban employment has decelerated from 4.31 per cent per annum to 3.89 per cent per annum consequent upon sluggish growth of the organised sector.

The 1980s witnessed the introduction of three schemes: (1) Self-employment programmes for the urban poor launched in 1986, (2) The Nehru Rozgar Yojana (NRY) started in October 1989, (3) The Scheme for Self-employment for the Educated Unemployed Youth ushered in 1983-84. The National Front (V. P. Singh) Government decided in April, 1990 that funds for the NRY would be channelled through the State Governments, which would decide on the manner of distribution of those funds to the urban bodies. District-level urban development authorities may be set up for the purpose of this particular programme.

Employment in small-scale industries increased from 5.6 million in 1976-77 to 10.7 million in 1987-88 at the rate of 7 to 9 per cent per annum. In *khadi* and village industries employment increased from 1.92 million in 1970-71 to 4.07 million in 1986-87, at a slightly faster rate.

The tertiary or services sector, a heterogeneous sector, expanded dynamically, responding to the emergency needs of the unemployed and like a sponge soaked up part of the unemployment among the semi-literates and the illiterates, and became overgrown in the process—the informal sector first, in urban and, then, in rural areas, well connected by means of transport and communications. The tertiary sector is, by and large, a self-employed sector, as are the *khadi* and village industries and small-scale industries. The share of the self-employed in the sector rose from 41 per cent in 1972-73 to 43 per cent in 1987-88. In Maharashtra, for each job in a registered factory there were seven jobs in the unemployed or self-employed type of enterprises. The proportion of the self-employed was higher in the less industrialised States.

We have in India a mixed economy. Employment is provided by both private and public sectors. As Table 19.6 depicts, between 1977 and 1989, that is, 12 years, employment increased from 20.5, million in the aggregate to 26 million and in the aggregate of the 5.5 million increase, the private sector's share was just 0.6 million, i.e., 11 per cent, the rest going to the private sector. In the primary sector, while the private sector reduced employment by 0.6 million, the public sector raised it by 0.4 million. In the secondary sector, the private sector's employment fell to the extent of 2.9 million, whereas the public sector's employment rose by a measley 0.1 million; and in the tertiary sector, while employment in the private sector went up by 3.5 million, that in the public sector went down by 2.5 million. Included in the 26 million-strong units were registered shops and establishments and other concerns, engaged in the creation of utility in its varied forms in the economy as a whole, whether in the private or in the public sector. In absolute numbers, there was an increase in the share of the public sector from 13.7 to 18.5 million. In the private sector the increase was from 6.8 to 7.4 million. Both sectors were complementary, not competitive. They interacted.

In the 12 years, as mentioned above, the Centre's share in the public sector employment declined from around 22.4 per cent to around 18.3 per cent. The Central Government's jobs formed merely one per cent of total employment in the country.

Much of the growth in the public sector employment took place during the 1960s and the early 1970s–in the wake of nationalisation of the banks and development of rural banking. The subsequent years saw retrenchment of employees in the nationalised textile mills. Since the 1970s the pace of employment generation in the public sector has slowed down. No large-scale public sector undertaking of the size of Bokaro or Durgapur has appeared on the industrial map of the country in recent years. Between 1981 and 1989, 33.36 lakh more persons were employed in the public sector—Central and State–all departments, directly administered and all public undertakings responsible to the legislature included.

The Centre's relative share diminished from 22.4 per cent in 1977 to 18.3 per cent in 1989; that of the State Governments' moved up from 36.4 to 37.2 per cent during the same period; also that of the quasi-governments and local bodies from 42.2 to 44.5 per cent.

TABLE 19.6: Percentage distribution of employment in the private and public sectors as on March 31

Occupation/Industry	1977		1980		1984		1989(P)	
	Private	Public	Private	Public	Private	Public	Private	Public
Agriculture, Hunting, etc.	12.2	2.6	12.8	2.8	11.1	2.9	11.6	3.0
Mining and Quarrying	1.9	5.5	1.7	5.2	1.5	5.5	1.3	5.1
Manufacturing	60.6	8.9	61.1	9.6	60.9	10.1	58.7	9.9
Electricity, Gas and Water, etc.	0.5	4.1	0.4	4.3	0.5	4.3	0.5	4.6
Construction	1.2	7.3	1.0	7.0	0.9	6.6	0.8	6.3
Wholesale and Retail Trade, etc.	4.0	0.5	3.8	0.7	3.7	0.7	3.8	0.7
Transport, Storage and Communications	1.0	17.9	0.9	17.5	0.7	16.9	0.6	16.3
Financing, Insurance, Real Estate, etc.	2.7	2.4	2.8	4.5	2.9	5.4	3.2	6.2
Community, Social and Personal Services	16.9	52.8	15.5	48.4	17.8	47.6	20.5	49.1
Total	33.3	66.7	32.4	67.6	30.3	69.7	28.7	71.3
	(-6.8m)	(-13.7m)	(-7.2m)	(-15.0m)	(-7.3m)	(-16.8m)	(-7.4m)	(-18.5m)

Note: The Centre's Share in Public Sector Employment:

1977	1980	1984	1989(P)
22.4	21.0	19.6	18.3

The State Government's Share:

1977	1980	1984	1989(P)
36.4	36.3	36.4	37.2

The Quasi-Governments and Local Bodies' Share:

1977	1980	1984	1989(P)
42.2	42.7	44.0	44.5

Source: Economic Survey, 1990-91.

The organised sector includes all establishments employing 10 or more workers. But it employs only one-tenth of the total workforce. The public sector stands to the private sector in the ratio of approximately 2 : 1 in the provision of employment. Half of the public sector employment is engaged in government administration. The poverty-alleviation and employment-generation programmes have created considerable employment for the rural folk for varying spells in a year. Employment made in the public sector is through various means, open competition, promotion, appointment on compassionate grounds in very large numbers, through the back-door, through reservation, through fiat, and what not. As Table 19.7 shows, during 1961-80 public sector employment grew at an average rate of 3.7 per cent per annum, whereas private sector employment grew at 1.5 per cent per annum. Barely 80 lakh people are employed in the organised private sector. The rate of growth of employment in this sector has been just a fraction of a percentage point.

TABLE 19.7: Growth of employment in organised sector in India

(in Lakhs)

Year/ Period	Numbers of Persons Employed			Annual (Compound) Growth Rate of Employment		
	Public	Private	Total	Public	Private	Total
1	2	3	4	5	6	7
1961	70.50	50.40	120.90	—	—	—
1966	93.78	68.10	161.88	—	—	—
1961-66	—	—	—	5.9	6.2	6.0
1969	100.95	65.30	166.25	—	—	—
1966-69	—	—	—	2.6	1.3	1.0
1974	124.86	67.94	192.80	—	—	—
1969-74	—	—	—	4.4	0.8	3.0
1979	150.45	72.08	222.53	—	—	—
1974-79	—	—	—	3.8	1.2	2.8
1980	150.78	72.27	223.05	—	—	—
1981	154.84	73.95	228.79	—	—	—
1986	176.78	73.57	250.35	—	—	—
1979-86	—	—	—	2.3	0.3	1.7
1961-86	—	—	—	3.7	1.5	3.0

Source: R.Datta and K. P. M. Sundharam, *Indian Economy.*

During 1961-86 the non-agricultural sector employment grew at the rate of 3.23 per cent per annum. Employment grew at the fastest rate in mining and quarrying, consequent upon take-over of the private coal-mines in March 1952, and there occurred a large-scale transfer of employees from the private segment to the public segment. Nearly 56 per cent employment in manufacturing was provided by the private sector. This sector grew at a very slow pace during the period. The tertiary/services sector grew more rapidly in the private sector than in the public sector—the rates being 3.4 and 6.1 per annum respectively.

After 1974-75 percentage increase in emoluments of the public sector employees has exceeded the percentage increase in average all-India consumer price index (see Table 19.8). Read alongwith Table 19.5, this is not disquieting, for net value added per worker has also kept pace with this rise in wages per worker. It is only through accelerated growth that more employment at higher wages could be created. Were growth to slow down, increased employment could be provided only at falling wages. Immediately the problem was not one of giving more employment at rising wags but rather one of giving more employment even at wages less than the going so that all seeking employment could be provided employment. Higher wages can wait for some time to come.

TABLE 19.8: Changes in public sector employees' emoluments

Year	Per Capita Emoluments of Public Sector Employees (Rs.)	Percentage Increase in Per Capita Emol-uments of Public Sector Employees	Percentage Increase in Average All-India Consumer Price Index (1960-100)
1	2	3	4
1971-72	5920	—	—
1974-75	7402	25.03	65.10
1977-78	10048	69.73	58.75
1980-81	14239	140.52	108.85
1983-84	21549	264.00	184.90
1986-87	28820	386.82	251.04
1989-90	43665	637.58	345.31

Source: Economic Survey, 1990-91.

The rate of net addition to employment in the Central and State

Governments and other public-sector departments during the 1980s is given in Table 19.9. It is clear from this table that the rate was highest in 1983. By 1989 it had slackened to the minimum. In most government departments appointments had not been made against vacancies, some of a long-standing nature, with the result that the age-structure/profile of the employees had become somewhat skewed and lopsided. This had affected productivity and efficiency adversely.

TABLE 19.9: Net addition to employment Central and State Governments and public sector

(in lakhs)

Year	Addition	Cumulative Total
1981	4.06	—
1982	4.62	8.68
1983	5.10	13.78
1984	4.13	17.91
1985	4.00	21.00
1986	4.14	25.14
1987	3.04	28.18
1988	3.33	31.51
1989	1.85	33.36

Source: Illustrated Weekly, April 27-28, 1991.

Note: To go back to the past, share of the Government Sector in total factory employment during 1957-68 was as under:

Year	Total Factory Employment (In millions)	Employment in government factories (In millions)	(3) as percentage of (2)
(1)	(2)	(3)	(4)
1957	3.48	0.43	12.3
1962	4.11	0.64	15.6
1966	4.69	0.90	19.2
1968	4.74	1.05	22.2

Source: K.N. Prasad, *Economic Development in the Third World (India's Economic Problems)*, Sterling, 1980.

The Five-Year Plans have invested huge sums of money in

projects and programmes from the First Plan onwards and have employed large numbers of people on them. The private sector has also played its part in this task but we do not have figures of private sector investment Plan-wise. Therefore, when we say that a certain number of people were employed in the economy at the end or in the course of a particular Plan, wc have in our mind the combined investment of the two sectors which resulted in the creation of that additional employment in a particular sector or a part of it or in the economy as a whole. A look at Tables 19.10 and 19.11 would disclose that an additionally appointed person added to the national product during the First Plan only six of the total outlay on him. This might have been so because of the glaring lack of the infrastructure at the outset of planning in this country, when an enormous amount of money had to be spent on the furnishing of the needed infrastructure in order to employ one more person. In the Second Plan the marginal product of the additionally employed persons rose to 55 per cent of the total Plan outlay on him. The infrastructural base of the economy had expanded and this was why the marginal product was driven up from six per cent to 55 per cent. In the Third Plan a further improvement had occurred—the marginal product was 77 per cent of the Plan outlay on the newly employed persons. During the Plan Holiday it fell to 71 per cent of the Plan outlay on the average newly employed person. (We do not have with us figures for the Fourth and Fifth Plans.) In the Sixth Plan period the marginal product remained unchanged (at 71 per cent of per person Plan outlay.) But during the Seventh Plan there was a crash in the marginal product of the additionally employed persons. It stood at a very low figure of 25 per cent. Perhaps a fetish of employment generation as a long step, a stride, towards poverty-alleviation might have led to this sordid situation.

During the Second Plan per employee product was valued at Rs. 2,567, according to Table 19.11, and at Rs. 2,068 to 7,947, according to Table 19.12, depending upon the sector in question. On the other hand, the same panel of tables bears out that in the same Plan per employee Plan outlay was Rs. 4,672 in the first case and Rs. 5,398 to 24,732 in the second case, resting upon what sector was taken into account. The ratio of per employee product to per employee Plan outlay ranges between 1 : 1.82 in one case and 1 : 2.16 to 1:3.11 in the other. Low labour productivity is writ large on these figures and the picture turns more depressing when we hedge our remark with the necessary qualification that the per employee investment made during the period in the private sector has been excluded but had it been included labour productivity would have been still lower. Growth on its own and direct action by design have together generated the given volume of additional employment but the cost involved has been extremely high and has continuously risen because the economy has for the most part of the planning era been caught up in the throes of inflation.

TABLE 19.10: Plan-wise public sector outlay on creation of employment per person

Plan	Public Sector Plan Outlay (Rs. crores)	Additional Employment likely to have been generated (Millions)	Public Sector Plan Outlay per Employee (Rs.)
1	2	3	4
First Plan	1960	7.0	2800
Second Plan	4672	10.0	4672
Third Plan	8577	14.5	5915
Annual Plans	6625	11.0	6022
Fourth Plan	15779	—	—
Fifth Plan	39426	—	—
Sixth Plan	97500	35.6	27387
Seventh Plan	180000	40.4	44554

Source: (1) *Five-Year Plans*;
(2) RBI, *Occasional Papers*, December, 1989.

TABLE 19.11: Plan-wise productivity of the labour employed

Plan	Increase in NNP at 1970-71 Prices at the end of the Plan (Rs. crores)	Increase in NNP at Current Prices at the end of the Plan (Rs. crores)	Per Employee Product at Current Prices (Rs.)
First Plan	2867	121	173
Second Plan	3204	2567	2567
Third Plan	2064	6650	4586
Annual Plans	3215	4759	4326
Fourth Plan	3627	11710	—
Fifth Plan	9943	25238	—
Sixth Plan	11164	69452	19509
Seventh Plan	35517	127827	31407

Source: Five-Year Plans.

TABLE 19.12: Certain sector-wise ratios during the second plan

Sector	Public Sector Plan Outlay (Rs. crores)	Additional Direct Employment Generated (lakhs)	Per Employee Public Sector Plan Outlay (Rs.)	Additional Output Generated (Rs. crores)	Public Sector Plan Outlay : Output Ratio	Per Employee Product (Rs.)
1	2	3	4	5	6	7
Agriculture, Community Development, Irrigation, and Flood Control	1054	9.06	7947	720	0.68	7947
Power	427	1.96	21785	—	—	—
Industry (including Cottage and Small-scale Industries) and Mining	890	16.03	5552	785	0.38	4897
Transport and Communications and Commerce	1385	5.60	24732	425	0.30	7589
Professions and Services including Government Administration	1044	19.34	5398	400	0.38	2086

Source: Second Five-Year Plan.

Table 19.10 embodies the average capital-output ratio for the different sectors during the Second Plan period. It varies from 0.30 to 0.88—the figures are on the low side for the simple reason that the investment made by the private sector does not form part of it and implicit in it is the assumption that the entire Plan outlay is capital formation, that is, real capital or real investment.

We take a big leap forward from the Second Plan to the Seventh Plan in Table 19.13. As the two tables (Table 19.10 and Table 19.13) are juxtaposed, per employed person investment through public sector Plan outlay is Rs. 44,554 in the Second Plan period and Rs. 15,332 to Rs. 8,56,527 in the Seventh Plan period, relying upon which sector is involved. Average of the last two figures works out to Rs. 4,35,929, which is over nine times the first figure. In other words, the public sector has now to spend almost nine times more to have one person employed. But this conclusion is upset when total capital investment per person, as visualized in the Seventh Plan, is considered. That ranges from Rs. 34,265 to Rs. 1,49,105, giving an average of Rs. 91,685, which is twice the figure during the Second Plan. Entry of the private sector in investment from 0 to 69 per cent in certain sectors relieves the burden on the public sector to the extent of seven times.

TABLE 19.13: Sector-wise labour-investment ratio in the Seventh Plan.

Sector	Total Capital Investment Per Person* (in Rs.)	Share of Public Sector Investment (in Rs.)
1	2	3
Agriculture and Allied Activities**	34265	15332(45)
Mining, Quarrying and Manufacturing	149105	60503(40)
Electricity	697387	688415(99)
Railways	856527	856527(100)
Other Transport	113443	37430(33)
Communications	232784	232784(100)
Other Services	78730	24717(31)

* To provide employment to him for 273 days in a year at the rate of 8 hours a day.

** the crop sub-sector would provide around 40 per cent and the non-crop sub-sector 60 per cent of the total employment in this sector.

Source: Seventh Five-Year Plan.

Note: Figures in brackets are (3) as percentage of (2).

At the operational level we have to disaggregate the aggregative figure into its component parts. Assuming that a certain amount of money is spent under a Plan (we take the cue from the Second Plan) and as a result, 1000 persons find employment, it would be of immense interest to try to know how this volume of additional employment, which is in the nature of *direct employment,* would be apportioned among the different economic activities, sector-wise. Table 19.14 is an attempt in that direction. It brings out that 520 more persons would be employed *indirectly,* the employment multiplier being 1.52. The present position is not very far different from the 1956 position insofar as the structural change that has taken place in the economy is limited. The technological advance made in the different sectors has led to that situation but it has not only been very slow, it has also been confined to particular areas, sectors and lines of production. In a nutshell, the pattern of occupational distribution of the working population as it obtains today is only slightly different from what it was in 1956, notwithstanding the engineering with it by the Plan authorities, which has been piecemeal and has taken the form of mere tinkering with a larger number of segments, the only mighty step having been in the sphere of public undertakings, where employment grew by leaps and bounds from 59 lakhs in 1961 to 176.8 lakhs in 1987, from 59 per cent of the economy-wide employment to 70.6 per cent of it, but only in those very economic activities, and that too in the organised sector only. Employment in the organised private sector was 73.95 lakhs in 1981 and 73.64 lakhs in 1987; in the private sector, all organised, the corresponding figures were 154.84 lakhs and 180.25 lakhs.

Through consumption expenditure, through savings and through capital formation, the public sector, or better, the government sector can control and does control the pattern of demand and hence the pattern of production and through the pattern of production, the pattern of employment and the choice of techniques of production in various directions. In 1950-51 tax-GDP ratio was 6.56; in 1986-87 it had risen to 16.92. In 1986 the Government's (all) current revenues as percentage of GNP were 13.3 and its expenditures were 16.4 per cent. Plan outlays as percentage of the Central Government's total expenditure were 40.7 in 1980-81 and 33.8 in 1988-89. The Government sector commanded 7.5 per cent of NDP (4.5 on public administration and defence and 3.0 on public enterprises) in 1950-51; in 1984-85, the corresponding figure was 24.5 per cent (9.0 plus 15.5).

TABLE 19.14: **Total employment effect of public sector plan outlays***

Sector with Activities			Number of Persons Employed: Directly	Indirectly
I. *Primary Sector*			79	41
Of which				
(i) Forestry, Fishery, National Extension Service and Allied Schemes		79		
II. *Secondary Sector*			230	119
Of which				
(i) Large and Medium-scale Industries and Mining		144		
(ii) Cottage and Small-scale Industries		86		
III. *Tertiary Sector*			691	360
Of which				
(i) Construction		403		
Of which				
(a) Agriculture and Community Development	50			
(b) Irrigation and Power	70			
(c) Industry and Mining (including cottage and small-scale industries	76			
(d) Transport and Communications (including railways)	24			
(e) Social Services	133			
(f) Miscellaneous (including government services)	50			
(ii) Irrigation and Power		9		
(iii) Railways		48		
(iv) Other Transport and Communications		34		
v) Education		59		
(vi) Health		22		
(vii) Other Services		27		
(viii) Government Services		98		
Total			1000	520

Grand Total: Direct Employment : 1000 + Indirect Employment : 520** = 1520.
(Value of the Employment Multiplier (*K*) : 1520/1000 = 1.52).

* Assuming that 1,000 persons get employed directly in the economy as a result of a given outlay in the public sector in the Plan.

** Indirect employment would be in trade and commerce and other activities.

Source: Based on the figures contained in the *Second Five Year Plan.*

Note: By multiplying direct employment by 0.52 we can arrive at indirect employment.

The public sector saved 1.7 per cent of GNP and invested 3.5 per cent of it in capital formation in the First Plan, in the Sixth Plan the two figures were 4.0 per cent and 11.8 per cent respectively. For the private sector the corresponding figures were 8.7 per cent and 18.6 per cent for the First Plan and 7.2 per cent and 12.3 per cent for the Sixth Plan. The public sector's share in total capital stock was 26 per cent in 1960-61 and 37 per cent in 1979-80, the figures for the private sector being 74 per cent and 63 per cent respectively. In the mixed economy the private sector was the dominant partner from this angle of the vision, though over one-fourth to one-third share of the government sector was not insignificant from the point of view of imparting a thrust, setting the pace at which and the direction in which the economy as a whole had to move.

Table 19.15 throws a flood of light on the question how even as the national income growth rate has accelerated, the employment growth rate has decelerated. The old economists regarded the national product as a determinate of the quantity and quality of labour. The planning economists regard the level of employment as a determinate of the level of output/income. If the level of output/income is less than the optimum at which full employment prevails, a dose of public investment could drive up the level through the multiplier. The NSS data analysis displayed that during 1972-73 to 1987-88 annual compound growth rate of aggregate employment worked out to 2.1 per cent—1.6 per cent for rural and 4.0 per cent for urban areas—which was close to the population growth rate. Continuously from 1970 to 1982, the elasticity of employment growth to output growth levelled off—1.00 in 1970, 0.98 in 1971, 0.90 in 1976, 0.81 in 1980 and 0.68 in 1982. Between the second year of the Fourth Plan (1970-71) and the second year of the Seventh Plan in the factories the number of workers declined from 58,19,000 to 42,31,000, that is, by 4.5 per cent per annum, while the value of output rose from Rs. 13,768 crores to Rs. 1,20,155, crores, i.e., by 13.8 per cent.

In all the Plans bulk of the increase in employment was in the unorganised sector. Between 1972-73 and 1987-88, a 15-year span, the total size of employment in India grew by around 86 million, according to the NSS data. Out of these, the organised sector contributed about six million till 1985-86. In the 15-year span the share of the organised employment to aggregate estimated employment remained constant at a low level of about 8 per cent.

TABLE 19.15: National income growth versus employment growth during the plans

Plan	Increase in NNP (at (1980-81 prices) (Rs. crores)	Average Annual Growth Rate (Per cent)	Increase in: Labour Force (in million)	Increase in: Employment Generated (in million)	Increase in: Backlog of Unemployment (in million)	Increase in Employment (all sectors): Number (in thousand)	Increase in Employment (all sectors): Annual Compound Rate of Increase (Per cent)
1	2	3	4	5	6	7	8
First Plan	48288 - 40454 = 7834	3.6	9.0	7.0	5.3-3.3 = 2.0		
Second Plan	58602 - 48288 = 10314	4.0	11.8	10.0	7.1-5.3 = 1.8		
						16192-12090 = 4120	6.0
Third Plan	65734 - 58602 = 7132	2.4	17.0	14.5	9.6-7.1 = 2.5		
						17491-16192 = 1299	1.6
Annual Plan	73285 - 65734 = 7551	3.7	14.0	11.0	12.6-9.6 = 3.0		
Fourth Plan	86010 - 73285 = 12725	3.3	—	—	—		
						20207-17491 = 2716	2.9
Fifth Plan	102937 - 86010 = 16927	5.0	—	—			
						22879-20207 = 2672	2.5
Sixth Plan	133972 - 102937 = 31035	5.4	32.1	35.6	—	4.8 (minus the figure for Annual Plans)	
						25056-22879 = 2177	1.8
Seventh Plan	168892 - 133972 = 34920	5.6	32.1	35.6	−(-)1.1		

Source: RBI, Occasional Papers, December 1989.

Calculations show that 5.5 per cent per annum growth rate of GDP in India might yield a three per cent per annum growth rate of employment. It would be worth our while to note here that the correlation between the rate of growth of output and rate of growth of employment in the short term is neither simple nor unique. Further, from the standpoint of operation or implementation to suggest that growth of output in such and such sectors would throw up so many jobs has one implication absolutely distinct from the suggestion that so many persons have to be provided employment in such and such sectors, as a result of which output produced in those sectors would be such and such.

It has been customary to consider output as a function of a given input or a given combination of inputs—interchangeable among themselves. Only when an input has become permanently fixed or a derivative of some other factor of an original, exogenously determined factor, or useless in the sense of adding nought to the total product or even causing a dent in the total product, has that factor been dismissed as a factor capable of genuinely contribution to the total product. Growth is a progenitor of employment but growth connotes a multiple of things. To illustrate, it denotes labour-displacing technological change. To avert such technological changes in an economy that attaches greater weightage to welfare maximisation by methods such as employment generation than to efficiency maximisation, employment takes the place of a determinant and output that of a determinate. On the contrary, in an economy that attaches greater weightage to productivity/efficiency maximisation output assumes that role of the conductor of the orchestra and employment plays to its tune, to speak figuratively, if this be permitted.

The Unemployment Measures

Of the three NSS data-based measures (usual status : measure of long-term unemployment of maximum duration of a year; weekly status : measure of those unemployed in the preceding week; and daily status : measure of those unemployed on the day of the survey), the third is the best, the most comprehensive of all. In respect of rural areas differences as between the three measures are the largest. The magnitude of the usually unemployed persons was estimated at around 12 million during July 1987-June 1988. Of this, two million were in secondary work. So 10 million were chronically unemployed in India—5.3 million in rural areas and 4.7 million in urban areas.

In 1980, according to the Planning Commission's estimate the backlog of unemployment was 113 million. The 1981 Census put the number of persons seeking or available for work at 19.42 million. Of these, 10.92 million were males; 62 per cent of them were in rural areas. In the 1961 Census the number of unemployed persons had been put at 1.4 million, of whom 0.8 million were in urban areas. Between 1961 and 1981 there had taken place a stupendous rise in the volume of unemployment. Planning had failed to remedy this endemic human problem. The Planning Commission put the backlog of unemployment at the end of the Seventh Plan, that is, 1989-90 at around 3.75 million only. This was surely on the lower side.

According to S. Mundle, open unemployment in India might escalate by anything from one million to ten million in the next few years depending on how fast the economy grows.

Critics appear to be converging to the view that reliance on the proposed 5.6 per cent per year rate of growth would not put an end to unemployment and poverty and inequality, problems which are to be faced at the same time with the supplementary method of direct assault by means of specific programmes.

While we have, on the one side, economists such as Mundle who see unemployment rising in its dimension, on the other, we have economists like P. Visaria and B. S. Minhas, who declare that unemployment has fallen substantially between 1983 and 1987-88. The impression created by them has gained ground. Measured by person-years the unemployment rate is undoubtedly falling. In addition, underemployment is yielding place to fuller employment.

The Rural Landscape

Two diametrically opposed views are afloat currently in relation to rural employment: One, that it is rising; the other, that it is falling. Let us examine them, in turn.

Rural employment may be viewed as a compound of agricultural and non-agricultural (rural) employment. Its level is a function of: (1) the level of rural demand for non-agricultural goods and services produced locally, (2) the level of extra-local demand for rural products/services, and (3) the location, scale and technology of activities catering to these demands.

Up to the end of the 1970s additional areas were brought under cultivation. Double-cropping spread in areas which were supplied with irrigation facilities. Farm output rose and with it rose farm employment. In areas where multiple cropping became possible more demand was created for labour. In such areas even off-season became an unheard-of thing. The HYVs accompanied by increased use of fertilizers and irrigation water and increased need for weeding and application of pesticides and insecticides contributed towards the expansion of employment.

During the 1980s a gradual shift occurred in favour of manufacturing and services, particularly in rural areas. Agriculture became diversified and wedded to subsidiary and auxiliary activities. More in the advanced States and less in the backward States pockets emerged where economic development emanated from getting people out of agriculture by introducing subsidiary and auxiliary activities and providing employment during the slack and lean seasons. Horticulture, animal husbandry and dairy, goat/pig/poultry farming, fishery, social forestry, sericulture, etc., were embarked upon. These were both land- and labour-intensive. Rural incomes increased. Besides, their instability was controlled to a fair extent, particularly in areas which were drought-prone and remote (in the eastern and north-eastern regions) and which were exposed to fluctuations in employment and hence in income. Also, in degraded areas unemployment and underemployment were the highest in intensity and incidence.

In several other pockets dispersal of agro-industries has provided the necessary impetus to rural development.

Estimates made bring out that rural non-farm employment has grown at the rate of five per cent per annum, seven times as fast as farm jobs. Building of infrastructure in its broader sense in rural areas in recent years has transformed their very character and shortened the hiatus between a village and a small town. At the same time it has stemmed the tide of urban-bound rural migration. This is an event which has been eulogised by economists like Anklesaria Aiyar, who read a still more glorious future into it. With the debut of the infrastructure, avocations complementary to it have also sprung up in the countryside, e.g., trade, transport, agro-processing, construction (which employs 70 per cent of the female labourers), hotels, restaurants, tea-stalls, country and snack bars, stalls selling *pan* and *bidi* and *pan masala,* mechanical repair shops, etc. A veritable boom in rural non-farm employment is the outcome (the supply of domestic servants to towns has steeply fallen because of this factor also). A network of service centres in rural areas has opened out opportunities for the young entrepreneurs. Rural employment in rural electrical machinery and parts has had the maximum rate of growth — 21.5 per cent per annum. The traditional rural industries, handicrafts, and occupations have expanded under the IRDP and other rural development programmes. Under the same programmes modern avocations too have got a fillip—servicing and maintenance of electric pumps and engines, cow-dung gas plants, repairs of tractors, tempos, scooters, bicycles, etc. Construction works have expanded at the rate of 11.2 per cent per year, rural chemical production employment at the rate of nine per cent per annum, rural transport employment at the rate of six per cent per year. Oddly, rural industry has not fully reflected this trend. Rural manufacturing has risen at a meagerly rate of 2.85 per cent a year. Rural handloom weaving has grown at the rate of less than one per cent per annum. The concessions extended to rural industries have not produced the expected results.

Total employment in small-scale industrial units (registered and unregistered—of the latter some are located in semi-urban and even rural areas of the prosperous States), which was 3.9 million in 1974 rose to 6.7 million in 1979 and to 10.7 million in 1987, giving 14.2 per cent and 7.4 per cent rate of growth per annum respectively. Total employment (part-time and full-time) in *khadi* and village industries was 19.21 lakhs in 1970-71, which increased to 46.26 lakhs in 1989-90. This gives 7.4 per cent rate of growth per year. In 1981, of 14.9 million employment in manufacturing 7.7 million (51.7%) was provided by household units, 1.1 million (7.4%) by small-scale units 3.0 million (20.1%) by medium-scale and 3.1 million (20.8%) by large-scale units. Fixed capital employed per employee in a small-scale interprise was Rs. 2,018 in 1965, Rs. 3,706 in 1974-75, Rs. 16,582 in 1978-79. In 1981-82 in units employing less than 50 employees fixed capital invested per employee was on an average Rs. 13,077.

According to a survey conducted by the BITCO, on March 31, 1981, average capital investment per person in all types of registered small-scale industrial units in Bihar was Rs. 28,600 (the highest amount being Rs. 2,99,000). On an average, nine persons were employed in a small-scale unit (the maximum number being 36). Per employee fixed capital investment in medium-scale units was Rs. 4,044 in 1965, Rs. 7,935 in 1974-75 and Rs. 27,610 in 1978-79; that in large-scale units was in these years Rs. 17,753, Rs. 30,536 and Rs. 68166 respectively.

Insofar as the rural industrial and non-industrial units come within the ambit of the IRDP, during 1980-85, per capita investment was, on an average, of the order of Rs. 2,876, of, which Rs. 1,873 was credit and Rs. 1,003 subsidy, the subsidy-credit ratio being 1 : 1.87. During the period (which is the period of Sixth Plan) the total number of beneficiaries was 165.6 lakhs, of which 64.6 lakhs (39%) belonged to the Scheduled Castes and Scheduled Tribes.

Semi-urbanisation, or preferably, rurbanisation, i.e. urbanisation of rural areas is one momentous latter-day development which seems critical to additional employment creation in the rural hinterland of the cities in India in the foreseeable future. Within a few years a cluster of growing villages has finally dissolved itself into a small town and become the cradle of output and income creation. Punjab is a notable case. Its urbanisation has taken the path of small town development. Ludhiana district, the nerve-knot of the Green Revolution in Punjab, is the most urbanised district in the State. In the country as a whole, during 1971-81 the highest growth of employment was achieved in towns with populations between 29,000 and 50,000.

From the preceding we may conclude, as have others, that expanding agriculture is the only way to mitigate unemployment. For organised industry has so far failed to release the requisite number of jobs, and the resource constraint/crunch in the Government is so very stringent and formidable at present that Government jobs cannot be created to the extent desired. Papola has estimated that in 1984-85 the agricultural sector created employment potential at the rate of 3.5 per cent, whereas the rural labour force grew at the rate of about two per cent in that year. This was a happy augury. Given the present rate of growth in our population and hence in our work-force, one feels inclined to concur with Papola and others who think alike that even a relatively high growth rate in industrial employment is not likely to produce a major structural change in employment either in the short run or even in the long run.

The authors of the Seventh Plan had premised similarly: with a high rate of industrial growth, the excess rural population could not fully be absorbed in the organised industrial sector and hence additional employment had to be generated in rural areas through intensification of activities in agriculture and cottage and village industries, diversification of rural economic activity and a massive programme of construction and capital accumulation. There is a pressing need for ensuring more balanced investment for agricultural growth on a more dispersed and decentralised basis, with the focus resting on areas with-huge incidence of poverty and unemployment. The problem of creating additional employment opportunities is, in essence, inseparable from that of their diversification.

Rural employment has expanded particularly since 1980, first under the aegis of the NREP and the RLEGP and, then, under the Jawahar Rozgar Yojana (JRY). During the Sixth Plan period by spending Rs. 1,874 crores on the NREP 17,750 lakh man-days worth employment were created (at the rate of Rs. 10.55 per man-day) and during the same period by spending Rs. 394 crores on the RLEGP 2,630 lakh man-days worth employment was created (at the rate of 14.98 per man-day). During the Seventh Plan the expenditure on the NREP was Rs. 3,092 crores and employment generation was 14,780 lakh man-days (at the rate of Rs. 20.92 per man-day). During the same period an expenditure of Rs. 2,640 crores on the RLEGP created employment equivalent to 11,500.1 lakhs man-days (Rs. 22.95 per man-day). From April 1, 1989, the NREP and the RLEGP were merged into the JRY. In 1989-90 by utilising Rs. 2,272.60 crores employment equal to 8,283.25 lakh man-days was created (which works out to Rs. 27.42 per man-day). Funds for the JRY are allocated by the States to their districts on the basis of index of backwardness. This index is formulated on the bias of : (1) Percentage of agricultural labourers to main workers in rural areas, (2) Percentage of the Scheduled Castes and Scheduled Tribes population to total rural population and (3) Inverse of agricultural productivity per hectare. The weights assigned to the three criteria are 20, 60 and 20 respectively. Some of the States have pleaded that the weight assigned to the first criterion should be revised to sixty.

We now pass on to the second line of thinking or belief: in so far as in many areas absorption of labour in agriculture is falling off, agriculture cannot be relied upon for creating additional employment in the coming years. Conventional wisdom has it that as production rises, employment also rises *pro tanto* with it. This held good till the end of the 1970s: as agricultural output rose, so did agricultural employment with it. But in the period subsequent to the 1970s this proposition has been disproved, negated. Studies by S. Bhalla, A.K. Singh and D.S. Tyagi cast sufficient light on this aspect of the problem. S. Bhalla found in the case of five States, namely, Uttar Pradesh, Rajasthan, Madhya Pradesh, Tamil Nadu and Bihar, that farm employment in them fell while farm output rose. These States accounted for nearly half of the total population of India. In some States (Haryana and Punjab included) during 1977-78 to 1987-88 the amount of labour used per hectare of land declined (though this decline was neutralised in part by multiple cropping and in part by the shift of farmers to the use of labour-intensive alternatives, such as cultivation of vegetables, horticulture, dairying, etc.).

Of late, growth of rural employment has decelerated from 2.5 per cent per annum to (another estimate is 2.32)—during 1972-73 to 1977-78 – to nearly 1.0 per cent (another estimate is 0.74, a third is 0.65and a fourth is 1.4 per cent) per annum during 1982-83 to 1987-88. This came to one-third of the rate of growth of population.

In 1983-84 only 11.7 per cent of the male workers and 0.3 per cent of the female workers found farm jobs.

What has led to falling agricultural employment? One explanation is conducted in terms of the phenomenal rise in agricultural wages in recent years. As agricultural wages have risen, farmers have curtailed their use of labour and increased their use of other inputs. This is what is called the Substitution Effect of a price change. More agricultural wages have signified lesser numbers of agricultural workers employed by individual farmers, with the result that total agricultural employment has sagged.

Agricultural wages have risen because the cost-of-living of the agricultural workers has risen. Prices of wage-goods have risen and, in consequence, wages have risen.

Agricultural wages are fixed statutorily. The Governments have prescribed the minimum agricultural wages below which the workers cannot be paid lawfully, though through mutual agreement or because of their weaker bargaining power the workers may and do accept wages lower than the minimum. In some States the statutorily fixed agricultural wages are on the high side in the existing circumstances and no farmer can agree to pay those wages. Most States had fixed statutory minimum agricultural wages during 1975-76. By the end of 1978 such wages had been fixed in 22 States and Union Territories. Minimum agricultural wages and their fixation, their revision and their implementation are parts of the

20-Point Programme.

In certain States the landed interests have been opposed to the payment of minimum agricultural wages. The agricultural workers in the States have organised themselves into armies or *senas* with a view to coercing their employers into paying these wages. On the other hand, their employers also have similarly organised themselves into armies or *senas* so as to give a short shrift to the agricultural workers, particularly those who are landless and hence poorer. These are living examples of bilateral monopoly.

Employment-generation programmes have been executed lately quite vigorously by the Government and the statutorily fixed wages have been paid in rural areas. "More jobs at higher wages" has been the motto, the slogan of the Government. The result of this move has been that casual wages in non-farm rural activities have been generally 40 per cent higher than casual wages in farming.

Another explanation is executed in terms of the decayed work ethic of today. This has not spared even the lower order of the workforce in our society. Discipline is loose and it is a herculean task to take work from the field workers. Restriction of hours of work is insisted upon by the workers with an aggressiveness, with a vengeance nowadays which was unknown only some years ago. Work on the crop-fields, is strictly speaking, of a nature that is oftener than not at the mercy of Nature and hence hours of work cannot strictly be restricted as can they be in respect of a factory or workshop. Apart from this, an average field worker of today gives less and less of his labour per hour in return for the wages he receives than his counterpart only some years ago. He works less hard and wants to while away the time somehow or other. If the real contribution of an average worker is falling, the farmer would be in quest of another input which would give him a return that is at least equal in value of the price he has paid for it. This is, therefore, another reason for the substitution of agricultural labour by other inputs. Farmers have started economising on labour no sooner than real wags paid to it have risen. But the legal minimum agricultural wages have not been adhered to in payment by farmers in a good many States. The Government machinery has also not enforced them enthusiastically and conscientiously as expected of it. For instance, we have Gujarat where minimum agricultural wages have been enforced lukewarmly. Rajasthan furnishes another instance where labour has been offered under the JRY at less than half the statutorily fixed minimum wages for a full day's work. But this does not warrant us to suggest that agricultural wages paid to any worker in any part of the country should be lower than the living wage capable of guaranteeing to him his own consumption as well as that of the members of his family. It is the duty of the state to see to it that this happens. Higher agricultural wages can be paid only if they correctly mirror the labourers' marginal productivity. Where their marginal productivity is low, their wages cannot and should not be high.

At this point in our analysis we would like to stress a point not appreciated in the normal course. It is this that if wages paid under the employment-generation programmes are higher in keeping with the statutory minimum wages than those paid for other types of work in one and the same locality, workers from those types of work would flock to those programmes, with the result that instead of job creation there would be job diversion. To tide over this eventuality, economists like Anklesaria Aiyar recommend that employment could be offered for half a day only at half the higher wage rate. By this method more people could be employed for a larger number of days in a year.

Another outstanding factor which has made rapid inroads into the customary level of employment secured by agricultural labourers in agriculture is the increased mechanization of the agricultural operations. With the onset of the Green Revolution cultivation has tended to become more capital-intensive in recent years. In every one rupee worth of agricultural output land at present contributes Rs. 0.27, labour Re. 0.30 and capital Re. 0.43. Increased use of capital has tended to retard the growth rate of employment of labour in several parts of India.

Agricultural mechanisation has displaced labour in many regions and to that extent proved labour-saving. Credit subsidisation has encouraged mechanisation and thereby lowered the demand for farm labour. Subsidies for mechanisation have had more or less an identical effect. In regions where labour-saving devices have been adopted, the number of days of employment of agricultural labourers in a year has exhibited a declining tendency. What has transpired has been typical of a system plagued by distortions and dilutions. Tractors have been hired instead of bullocks, combine harvesters instead of manual harvesting, mechanical threshers instead of manual ones. Transfer of paddy seedlings has been abandoned inasmuch as farmers have reverted to broadcast sowing. Weeding has been reduced. All this has occurred because agricultural wages have risen sharply.

But the foregoing calls for some qualification. In the first instance, provided prices of other inputs remain unchanged, investment in agricultural mechanisation does not displace labour. This was a finding by S. Bhalla in five States, namely, Uttar Pradesh, Rajasthan, Madhya Pradesh, Tamil Nadu and Bihar. In the second instance; on large farms in developed regions the labour-displacing effect of tractorisation has been watered down to an extent by its labour-absorbing effect. Farm mechanisation has thrown up avenues for self-employment of the rural youth in repair and fabrication of implements. Moreover, it has helped to augment agricultural production. As a result, the farmers' income has risen. The favourable impact of the Green Revolution on indirect employment has exceeded its favourable impact on direct employment (this is a finding which is in sharp contrast to the model we have constructed on the basis of the statistics supplied in the Second Plan where 1,000 persons' direct employment caused indirect employment of 520 persons only, with the result that the value of the Multiplier was 1.52 — in this case the value would be much higher). The Green Revolution has enabled the richer States, such as Punjab, Haryana and Rajasthan to attract low-paid labour from the poorer States like Uttar Pradesh (its eastern part) and Bihar and Orissa. In the peak season nearly one-third of the total labour force employed in a agriculture in Punjab had come from other States.

To cut the long story short, mechanisation or no mechanisation, rising agricultural wages largely explain why rising farm output denoted falling farm employment. This should please development economists, for this heralds a movement of the economy to a higher plane of advancement, that is structural transformation.

Coming now to the other side of the picture, the unemployment side, the NSS data grossly underestimated rural unemployment by putting it at only a little over one per cent of the rural population. The truth is that rural areas harbour the highest incidence of chronic unemployment.

The notion of disguised unemployment or underemployment remains in the Indian context, particularly its rural counterpart, very imprecise and vague, woolly and hazy, a misnomer, so to say. There is a dearth of convincing evidence supporting its existence in Indian agriculture as an empirically valid concept. For the insufficient supply of field workers for the coming at the peak times is a great disclaimer of this concept. Casualisation of the rural male worker which was a distinct phenomenon of the 1980s has further complicated the estimate of its dimension, although it has suggested a step-up in its dimension. Otherwise, on the basis of the NSS measure—the gap between daily status and weekly status unemployment—of underemployment, in 1987-88 its estimate comes to 0.4 per cent from rural males—a trivial figure.

The Urban Situation

The share of casual labour in urban unemployment rose from 12.6 per cent in 1972-73 to 17 per cent in 1987-88. Urban unemployment, as registered by the Employment Exchanges, was 30 million in 1990. Those in the 15 to 59 age brackets were 80 per cent. The rural migrants in the cities accounted for the expansion of the informal sector of the urban economy at a terrific rate. This sector is "an odd amalgam of all those heterogeneous segments which are not encompassed by the formal sector" but it is, in the main, a self-employment sector.

Migration is not only the offspring but also the creator of rural inequality. The economic distance between rural families becomes longer owing to migration and the remittances that flow perennially from it. Immigrants in urban areas usually settle in localities where their relations and castemen live, for love of security and fraternity, by clinging to old roots and seeking familiar faces in an alien and hostile environment, as Bhagwati puts it. Interregional differences in languages, food habits, ways of industrial recruitment, and the like discourage rural-urban movements. The public sector Plan outlays in rural areas on a vast scale and on a running basis, the various measures to shore up the countryside, the development of small towns adjoining the bigger ones and cities as satellite towns, and, last but not least, the sea change in the availability of infrastructural facilities in the rural side, conjoined with the futility of search for better living in urban areas, have all combined and conspired to entail a push-back of the rural migrant to his original habitat. As efforts are intensified in these directions and as avenues of employment are released in an increasing number in the villages themselves, not only that rural exodus to towns would taper off but also some people resident in urban areas would change their mind and finally decide to settle permanently in the villages, with the result that we would have migration in its reverse gear in a couple of decades. People would work in towns and live in villages (subject to assurance of security of life and property which is becoming increasingly rare in a growing number of villages). Criminalisation of social life in all its ramifications and facets constitutes one explanation of downward migration of the rural folk.

Registered educated unemployment amounted to nine million in 1990. The employment exchange data are not quite reliable, excluding as they do huge numbers of those unemployed in rural areas and including as they do a large number of already employed people not content with their present jobs and wanting to have better ones. An acute shortage of washermen, roadside barbers, iron-smiths, carpenters, domestic servants, and so on, felt more intensely in urban areas, is a manifestation of the people's dislike and distaste for their caste-determined avocations and their innate desire to inundate and invade the rank and file of the office clerks with their own services — public employees, a fair percentage of whom enjoy great security of employment and earn total emoluments disproportionate to their positions and their productivities (which latter are continuously diminishing, thanks to the eclipse of work ethic and absence of fear of loss of employment in view of very strong unionisation) and, the lack of correct perception of what dignity of labour is, which is at the head of all other motives.

Of the nine million educated unemployed in 1990 almost half came from West Bengal, Andhra Pradesh, Tamil Nadu and Maharashtra. The educated unemployed crowded the cities having been brought up on a false, mistaken conception of the impending situation in which these cities were supposed to unfailingly provide them with some kind or other of employment that would enable them to make their both ends meet, a thing which was beyond the capacity of smaller cities in the existing circumstance to ensure.

Such is the depraved and prevert mentality of the educated children of the farmers that they do not want to stick to farming. The graduates who are without employment are averse to selling fruits and similar goods which would surely earn for them their daily bread. Instead they avidly long for clerical jobs, which are far less productive. It is for the attendant status and glamour of the posts that they misplace their choice. Not even blue-collar jobs have any appeal for them — only white-collar ones, a dependable passport to an easy life, without hard work, without toil and trouble, without irk and worry, without much wear and tear. They are prepared to part with their few assets in order to grab such jobs. In this bid they become the underlings of the politicians and middle men who exploit them right and left. They have degrees but they have not the knowledge to enable them to successfully compete at the tests held for the purpose. The administrative wagon of the Government crawls so painfully that several thousand vacancies pile up for years and also take years to fill, so much so that the young reach their middle age by the time they are appointed. Political pressures end in relaxation of the age bar. A relatively older person when employed would naturally add less to the national product than he would have done had he got the same post some years earlier when his faculties were at their highest peak. If the revenue expenditure on the administrative services is nomenclatured as unproductive, there certainly is some modicum of warrant for so doing, for the general trend today fully testifies to it.

The unemployment rates for the female graduates were 30.4 per cent in rural areas and 18.7 per cent in urban.

The FWP, NREP, RLEGP, and their several precursors did a kind turn for the uneducated unemployed in rural areas (one form in which this happened was a rise in the prevalent wage rate) but not for the educated unemployed in those areas. The unemployment rates are lowest for the illiterates, since they are willing to take up any job.

The Future Horizons

At least five million more young and able-bodied persons would be looking for employment every year. The targeted levels of economic activity should, therefore, by generating employment from year to year in an uninterrupted sequence. The 1991-92 budget proposes to create a new national fund to provide compensation and retraining to industrial workers who lose their jobs as a result of the new commercial and industrial policies of the Narasimha Rao Government. The Rao Government desires to create 10 million new jobs per annum on an average during the next decade, and the Planning Commission has been advised to so chalk out the Eighth Plan that it reflects this goal set by the Government.

The Rajiv Government vintage Planning Commission had stated in its Eighth Plan Approach Paper that the backlog of unemployment would become unmanageable in the years to come unless the rate of productive employment generation got accelerated substantially to around 10 million new work opportunities per year.

The 1990-91 budget under the V.P. Singh Government introduced an Employment Guarantee Scheme (EGS) for the drought-prone areas and areas with acute problems of rural unemployment. Were this scheme to be run for the country as a whole after the pattern of the Maharashtra State Employment Guarantee Scheme, it would cost the nation Rs. 13,000 crores a year (about 3.25 per cent of GDP in 1989-90). Were this amount to be set apart from the Plan outlay, that would seriously jeopardise the Plan itself or, alternatively, would give rise to rampant inflation, as argued out cogently by A. Ghosh, a former member of the V.P. Singh vintage Planning Commission. Another calculation within the caveat of the JRY gives a figure of Rs. 1,35,000 crores a year at the existing minimum wages. Still another estimate (by Joshi) comes to Rs. 39,600 crores, almost one-tenth of GNP. This omits the huge army of the village-level workers which would be required to set the scheme going. Be it the EGS or the JRY, its effective and successful implementation turns, in the ultimate analysis, on the food situation in the country and, more particularly, on the position of food stocks with the public sector agencies. This is so because more expenditures on employment generation would impinge on food prices via increased food demand, if all the variables involved in the process are not in harmony with one another.

But, aside from the logic of this argument, the guarantee of employment to an unemployed person even for a short period is bound to act as a substitute for unemployment insurance. Employment is followed by receipt of income by the unemployed, the majority of whom are and would be, as a rule, the landless labourers wholly bereft of a resource base.

Assuming wages to remain inflexible, an expanded public works programme, according to Mundle, would cost Rs. 3,500 crores to 4,320 crores to employ 6 to 8 million people for 182 days in a year.

Limitations of the Data

The estimates of employment to be generated during a Plan period are founded on certain norms about employment potentials of selected investment.

The same norms are again used to calculate the likely size of employment actually generated during the Plan period.

The difference in these two estimates arise due to differences between planned investment and actual investment.

In view of the difficulties experienced in estimating the volume of investment in the non-corporate segment of the private sector, more specially in agriculture and small-scale industries, estimates of employment generation are, of necessity, subject to an unknown margin of error.

The norms adopted for a large part of the unorganised sectors are quite arbitrary "almost a shot in the dark", as the Dantwala Committee had observed.

Basic sources of data on employment and unemployment have inherent weaknesses due to the peculiarities of the employment situation.

Some Guide to the Programmes

With the object of scaling down the proportion of the workforce engaged in agriculture to 60 per cent or so in the fore, it has been stipulated that a four-fold increase in the numbers engaged in mining and factory establishments would have to be brought about and the investment priorities would have to be reordered according to these requirements.

Resources should be reallocated by subsidising more and taxing less those sectors which give more employment and by subsidising less and taxing more those sectors which give less employment. To stimulate the widest possible adoption of multiple shifts in as many lines of production which would tackle, to a degree, the problem of industrial (including mining, gas, power and water supply) employment, fiscal and credit measures would have to be taken.

Lastly, due attention must be paid to the quality of the public works, the choice of projects and the dovetailing of the projects with the regional eco-system so that the employment provided is viable and as such the resources spent on it are, as a matter of fact, put to productive uses. The Government employment schemes at higher wages often culminate in construction works of inferior quality and of shorter duration --- to that extent they are unproductive, remembrances of the relief works of the earlier days built by workers living on doles.

The poverty-alleviation and employment-creation programmes

would succeed if they have an appropriate supportive environment, for one thing, and if the technical change brought about is employment-friendly or intensive, for another.

The strategy for employment growth so far pursued needs to be reformulated in order that increase in employment is on all fours — all of a piece — with technical and economic efficiency; otherwise growth itself would not be sustainable over a long period. This is what the World Bank opined and predicted in its report of 1990.

Papola avers that what is seen as a technological change at a relatively aggregated level may, in fact, represent a structural change at a more disaggregated/decomposed level of commodity classification. Of course, from the standpoint of employment the question of pattern of production is more pertinent than that of choice of technique.

Treating rural electrification as a harbinger of technological progress, and predicating on the experiences reaped in the last 15 years or so in this realm, we would suggest that more resources should be directed to such areas as have evident industrial potential.

We suggest further that in view of the communications bottleneck much of the produce of rural industries should be meant for local consumption.

The Public Distribution System (PDS) should ensure increased supply of grain in the fair price shops as well as in the market with a view to facilitating as smooth, unstifled progress of the programmes and for arresting price hike. It is commendable that in late years the PDS has injected huge stocks of grain in the economy, which has smoothened the advance of the programmes and tamed grain price.

What we have endeavoured to suggest above is a corollary of our economic appraisal but we would agree with our critics that the implications of poverty, inequality and unemployment far transcend purely economic parameters — against the vast empire of social science of which economics is just a territory, and it is the political decision which finally draws the curtain over issues, if evaluated chiefly in the light of economic criteria or tests or considerations.

NOTES

1. In terms of their respective per capita SDPs.
2. G. Braun's article in *Economics,* Vol. 42.

20

THE EPILOGUE

In order to surmount poverty, inequality and unemployment a number of conditions must be satisfied. Development should be all-round and orderly. Ownership and control of material resources should be so distributed as to serve the common good. The managers of the economy should see that the operation of economic system does not result in the concentration of wealth and economic power in the hands of a few. Rural-urban disparities should be narrowed. The programmes addressed to poverty-alleviation and unemployment-eradication should not be fragmented and be immune to contradictions and overlap. All programmes should be devoid of the pervasive leakages alleged in the past. The entrenched elites should not be in a position to pre-empt the programmes. These programmes should not be misused as instruments of political patronage.

The needs of ordinary people and the quality of their life should become the focal point of planning. Adequate employment should be generated. The basic standard of living should be ensured to everyone, specially the poor. Integrated area planning should be emphasised through democratic decentralisation.

The right to work should constitute the keynote of the reoriented plan strategy. More attention should be given to rural development.

The programmes for rapid economic development have to be carried out in many directions. The advance would be rapid if the process of interaction is preferred and relied upon, and if a new sense of direction and purpose is given to the community. The interrelation between technical and social aspects of the process of development must be close. The planning process should be viewed as part of a wider process, that is, the social process.

An economy to continuously expand must fulfil certain basic conditions. For one thing, the community should have the will to progress. For another, it should show readiness to develop and adopt new and more efficient methods and processes of production. Thirdly, it should improve its general productivity through technical progress. Fourthly, the economic structure must be diversified. Industry should expand rapidly, and the state should implement a positive policy with regard to industrialisation. The terms of trade between agriculture and industry should stand in balance, neither favouring one nor disfavouring the other. Conditions in the agricultural sector should be poised towards an over-all economic improvement. Productivity per person engaged in either agriculture or industry should maintain the desired level, and the pressure of population on land should progressively decrease. However, for some more time to come the joint family system should be prevented from disintegrating further because it possesses a stupendous shock-absorbing capacity. Foreign trade should react favourably on the pattern of economic life by generating the impulse for development along new lines.

The whole environment should be suited to economic progress. The prevalent pattern of production and employment should be suitably altered by introducing appropriate changes in the new investment priorities. Both economic priorities and the pattern of spending should be restructured so that much more could be got out of what is actually spent.

The public programmes should try to plug leakages and waste so far insinuated against them.

One class of the basic conditions of economic development comprise the institutional conditions, including economic and social and political organisation. These have to function as powerful levers of growth and development. In shaping the pace and pattern of development the psychological and social setting has an important part to play. Such psychological conditions have to be created as provide an incentive and impetus to give of their best.

The responsibility for promoting economic development should not become concentrated in the hands of certain classes; it should instead be decentralised among all classes.

Needed is a re-adaptation of social institutions and social relationships adequate to meet the needs and aspirations of the people. Each stage of economic development is influenced by and influences the given economic and social stratification and hence is one condition fundamental to development. As such, the existing socio-economic framework has to be remoulded so as to enable it to accommodate progressively those basic urges which manifest themselves in the demands for the right to work, the right to adequate income, the right to education and to a measure of insurance against old age, sickness and other disabilities. In its ultimate analysis and in its quintessence economic development is not merely rechannelling economic activity within the existing socio-economic framework but rather refashioning it so as to accommodate increasingly the seminal human propensities. The inner forces must be strengthened. New institutions should be installed. The hump of cramped or abortive development, characteristic of underdeveloped countries, should be overcome. More progressive ideas should be accepted, for this is germane to development, and the prevalent institutions should undergo the necessary transformation with a view to being in a position to assimilate them. Safeguards should be devised beforehand against special problems thrown up by the divergences in the economic and social interests of different sections of society. Measures should be adopted to ensure that in the process of development the forces of growth from within are not stifled by attempts abruptly to superimpose preconceived patterns of life and activity on particular sections of the community.

The final desideratum of planning ought to be to restore man to a new sense of dignity, to remake him.

Needed is a relatively new phase in policy-making and administration. The 1990 Approach Paper gave a call for restructuring governmental institutions so that they could serve the selected Plan objectives with political determination and will. That call must be attended to.

Last but not the least, policies and programmes chalked out in the areas of poverty, inequality and unemployment should reconcile themselves with the fact that there are so many intractable and indeterminate, or partially known factors at work in the life of a community that the responses of individuals or of groups of individuals and of classes cannot always be predicted in advance, and that policies can at best be recommended on the basis of the best judgement — generally of the fiduciaries — forthcoming at the time of formulating them.

The New Approach of the Planning Commission[1]

The state is to concentrate on protecting the interests of the poor, and the under-privileged.

The Planning Commission will play an integrative role and help in the development of a holistic approach to policy formulation in critical areas such as backward areas development.

The Planning Commission would create a social security net through employment generation.

It would generate adequate employment to achieve a near full employment level by the turn of the century.

Employment generation is listed as one of the priorities towards human development which would be the main focus of the Eighth Plan.

The phenomenon of growing unemployment has, of late, emerged as a major problem and therefore expansion of employment opportunities has to be a central objective of the planning effort. An accelerated expansion of employment opportunities is necessary both for poverty-alleviation and effective utilisation of human resources for economic and social development of the country. During the past two decades, employment has grown at a rate of about 2.2 per cent per annum, but due to a faster increase of labour force at about 2.5 per cent, the backlog of unemployment has been rising. A declining trend in the employment elasticity with respect to GDP growth in recent years has made the task of accelerating the growth of employment more difficult. A deliberate and conscious effort in the direction of employment orientation of the growth process is therefore essential.

It is considered necessary and reasonable to set the goal of employment for all in a time-span of the next ten years. An assessment of the present backlog of unemployment and the likely additions to the labour force suggest that this goal would require generation of additional 10 million employment opportunities per year on an average, which means about a three per cent average annual growth of employment. A relatively high rate of economic growth combined with a pattern of sectoral growth yielding a higher aggregate employment elasticity would be necessary for achieving the rate of employment growth envisaged. Raising employment elasticity in the aggregate would require faster growth of the sectors, sub-sectors and areas which have relatively high employment potential. A geographically and crop-wise diversified agriculture, wasteland development for crop cultivation and forestry, rural non-farm sector, small-scale manufacturing, urban informal sector, rural infrastructure, and housing and services, have been identified as sectors and areas as constituting the basic elements of an employment-oriented growth strategy.

It also needs to be recognised that in addition to the generation of new stable employment opportunities of the order of 10 million per year, which will take care of the open unemployment, it would need to be ensured that those underemployed and employed at very low levels of earnings are able to raise their productivity and income levels. Upgradation of technologies of the self-employed in the traditional and unorganised sectors and their improved access to credit and markets would need to be ensured. Also, it would be necessary, in the meantime, to continue programmes for providing supplementary work to the underemployed poor in infrastructure building and other activities.

Employment generation and poverty-alleviation objectives are ultimately related to growth. However, that growth has to be accompanied with a sharper regional focus of reduced disparity and more dispersed benefits. The lagging regions and the weaker sections of the society, if not protected fully, are more likely to be left behind in the natural process of growth. Adequate protection will have to be continued to be provided to the poor and the weaker sections of the society. Adequate food supply, control on inflation, effective working of the public distribution system and developmental programmes which generate adequate employment are among the main components of the strategy which will take care of the poor.

Though the progress of agriculture in the recent period has been satisfactory, there are striking regional and crop imbalances. Productivity varies considerably from one region to another. The benefits of the Green Revolution, which remain confined at present to the north and north-west, must spread to other parts, more particularly to the eastern region, which has adequate rainfall, fertile soil and unlimited scope for stepping up agricultural production. Since two-thirds of the cultivated area is still unirrigated and largely rainfed, a more balanced regional development would call for a greater emphasis on dry-land farming. Agriculture and allied activities on which two-thirds of the workforce are still dependent must continue to receive a major emphasis in our planning effort.

The state would address specifically to the needs of the houseless, poorer households, SCs and STs, women and other vulnerable groups. The long-term objective is provision of "Shelter for All".

Given the competing demands on available resources, however, the achievement on this score will inevitably need to be spread over a reasonable span of time.

Agricultural growth in the eastern region would be accelerated. The reproductivity of agricultural land would be greatly improved by tapping underground water by construction of large number of tube-wells. Flood control measures in the eastern region are equally important.

An integrated programme of local area development of selected villages would be promoted for poverty-alleviation through increase in employment, appropriate land reforms and meeting housing needs.

An amount of about Rs. 6,500 to Rs. 7,000 crores per year is being spent on different employment generation/poverty-alleviation and similar other programmes. It is felt that a better impact on the problem of poverty could be made by decentralising the planning and implementation components of these programmes at the local area level. Funds under the various heads can be pooled together and allotted to the villages on the basis of certain criteria which can be evolved at the Centre. Every block will be required to prepare a detailed and integrated development plan with emphasis on infrastructural development. This will lead to a better utilisation of existing resources with creation of assets locally required. Adequate funds and co-ordination role should be retained at district levels for the inter-block level programmes and schemes. It is also possible to dovetail basic social services of education, family planning, health, sanitation, water supply and epidemic disease control for the poor, in this framework of local development plan.

The Rural Development Ministry would be advised by Planning Commission to change their plan provisions as provisions for an integrated local area development programme. Planning Commission will identify programmes of other Ministries and State Plans which can go into this integrated programme which, while continuing with the emphasis on employment will ensure creation of rural infrastructure of a minimum standard quality. The programme will be designed in a manner that gives optimum operational flexibility to the district and block levels.

The pattern of growth by broad sectoral divisions of the economy as consistent with the overall growth scenarios in GDP is described in Table 20.1. The growth rate in value added in agriculture is three per cent in the lower growth scenario and 3.3 per cent in the higher growth scenario. The pattern is consistent with the growth in consumption brought about by income growth and its distribution.

TABLE 20.1: Sectoral growth rates and shares of gross value added at factor cost

Sector	Gross Value Added (Per Cent Per Annum)			Sectoral Share (Per Cent)		
	1980-81 to 1989-90 (trend Growth)	1992-93 to 1996-97 (Projected) Scenario		1991-92	1996-97 Scenario	
		I	II		I	II
1. Agriculture	2.9	3.0	3.3	27.66	24.42	24.31
2. Mining and Quarrying	6.8	7.5	8.0	2.04	2.23	2.24
3. Manufacturing	7.0	7.3	7.7	21.50	23.29	23.28
4. Electricity, etc.	9.1	8.2	8.8	2.40	2.71	2.71
5. Construction	3.6	4.3	4.6	5.13	4.82	4.80
6. Transport	7.6	7.2	7.7	5.94	6.40	6.43
7. Communication	6.1	6.3	6.6	1.17	1.21	1.20
8. Other services	6.4	6.1	6.5	34.16	34.92	35.00
Overall Growth Rate	5.5	5.6	6.0	100.00	100.00	100.00

Source: Planning Commission, *Objectives, Thrusts and Macro-Economic Dimensions of the Eighth Plan*, December, 1991.

Employment implications of growth are presented in Table 20.2. The labour force is expected to grow at the rate of 2.2 per cent per annum during the Eighth Plan. With the planned pattern of investment and production, the employment potential will grow at 2.8 per cent per annum in the higher growth scenario and at the rate of 2.6 per cent per annum in the lower growth scenario. In absolute terms, a growth rate of 2.8 per cent per annum implies generation of nine million jobs per annum during the first half of the Eighth Plan and about 10 million jobs per annum towards the latter half of the plan. Thus, it may just about meet the target of 100 million jobs in a decade. Growth at the rate of 2.6 per cent per annum as implicit in the lower growth scenario will mean about eight million jobs per annum during the first half of the Eighth Plan and nine million jobs

TABLE 20.2: Sectoral value added and employment growth during Eighth Plan (1992-97)

Sector	Sectoral Growth (Value Added) (Per Cent Per Annum)		Employment Elasticity			Employment Growth (Per Cent Per Annum)	
	Scenario-I	Scenario-II	(a) Achieved 1977-78 to 1983	(b) Achieved 1983 to 1987-88	(c) Possible Targets for 8th Plan	Scenario-I Using Elasticity as in (c)	Scenario-II Using Elasticity as in (c)
1. Agriculture	3.0	3.3	0.49	0.36	0.50	1.50	1.65
2. Mining and Quarrying	7.5	8.0	0.67	0.85	0.85	6.38	6.80
3. Manufacturing	7.3	7.7	0.68	0.26	0.50	3.65	3.85
4. Construction	4.3	4.6	1.00	1.00	1.00	4.30	4.60
5. Electricity, etc	8.2	8.8	0.74	0.48	0.50	4.10	4.40
6. Transport & Communication	7.0	7.5	0.92	0.35	0.60	4.20	4.50
7. Other services	6.1	6.5	0.99	0.42	0.70	4.27	4.55
Total	5.60	6.00	0.54	0.30	0.46	2.59	2.79

Source: Planning Commission, *Objectives, Thrusts and Macro-Economic Dimensions of the Eighth Plan*, December, 1991.

per year during the latter half of the plan, approaching a rate of 10 million jobs a year towards the end of the decade. It may be pointed out here that even these employment projections are based on a set of assumptions, which, though feasible, would require an effort to realise and, therefore, the projections are optimistic. The employment elasticity in agriculture, for example, will have to rise to the same level as observed during the period 1977-83. This is possible only if a major effort is made to bring about very significant increases in agricultural intensity and agricultural productivity in the eastern region and in dry agricultural belt. These regions have lagged behind in agricultural growth and hence, a new spurt in growth will bring about additional labour absorption of a similar nature as was experienced in Punjab, Haryana and Western Uttar Pradesh during the 1970s. Export-oriented intensive cropping (vegetables, flowers, plantation crops, fruits, spices, etc.) offers further scope for employment.

Similarly, the pattern of industrialisation and choice of technique, where possible without sacrificing productivity, have to be such as to increase the possibility of labour absorption in manufacturing and other sectors. Increasing employment in unproductive jobs will ultimately limit the possibility of expansion of employment and will curtail the growth potential of the economy. Services have to play a major role in generating employment. Expansion of productive services raises the production efficiency of the economy as a whole. The thrust of the next round of liberalisation has to be on the services sector. Entry into the services and the "informal" sectors has to be made free of innumerable rules, regulations and bureaucratic hurdles. The road transport sector needs to be particularly liberated from such strangleholds. With sustained efforts in a number of directions only it would be possible to achieve the employment targets.

The savings of the Government at the Centre and in the States taken together, which was positive in the Sixth Plan, turned negative during the Seventh Plan. Government dissavings amounted to 1.48 per cent of GDP in 1988-89, rose to 2.05 per cent of GDP in 1989-90 and is estimated to have reached 2.2 per cent in 1990-91. The situation is not likely to be any better in 1991-92. For example, in the case of the States, the assessment of financial resources made jointly with them as also the budgets presented so far show that the balances from current revenues in 1991-92 would be about (–) Rs. 2500 crores.

This assessment also shows that the State Electricity Boards would show a deficit of Rs. 1600 crores. Looking at the trends in additional resource mobilisation by the States in recent years, these deficits are likely to turn out to be higher. The savings of the public sector which include both Government and public sector enterprises are such that the bulk of the public sector investment is being financed by borrowing. Even in the changed context, there is a certain minimum investment which needs to be made in the public sector and unless government savings show a distinct improvement, this task will become almost impossible. However, the challenge must be met and the fiscal management both at the Centre and in the States must move in the desired direction of generating more savings so that the minimal level of investment envisaged in the public sector can be realised.

Improved fiscal management by the States and the Centre must aim both at increasing revenue and restricting expenditures. With regard to revenue some of the areas which may need increased attention are: increasing the direct taxes as a proportion of GDP, minimising exemptions and concessions in the computation of taxable income and widening the tax net through such measures as presumptive taxes and bringing agricultural income under the tax net. Besides the disinvestment of shares of public sector enterprises to an extent larger than contemplated in the recent budget, the sale of public sector enterprises which are not in the essential core sector may form part of an overall strategy to raise receipts. Rationalisation of subsidies and a more appropriate pricing of certain products and services, such as electricity, water and transport are also relevant. As for expenditures, besides the containment of growth in some areas, the duplication of functions by the Centre and the States can be avoided leading to a more rational distribution of the staff. Pruning of defence expenditures is also needed, if the effort to contain the overall expenditures is to succeed.

A General Summing Up

We have noted above that absolute poverty is defined by income levels below which even minimum standards of nutrition, shelter and personal amenities cannot be maintained. Only by adopting an arbitrary standard could it be illustrated that a person is in a state of absolute poverty, say, when he or she has an annual income equivalent to rupees so much (at a certain base year's prices). Absolute poverty is explained more by the lowness of per capita income than by the unequal distribution pattern of incomes.

We have also noted above that relative poverty is defined in terms of per capita income of the country to which one belongs. It reflects extreme differences in levels of living between the top and the bottom strata of society. To provide a quantitative illustration, total number of people with per capita income below one-third of the average per capita income of their own country is estimated, which often comes to 40 per cent of the population. This concept has an advantage over the absolute concept because it is not quite possible to quantify the reasonable minimum or high standard of living — a notion basically impregnated with value premises or judgements disliked by many. Thus Okun asks what the minimum income would be on which a family of four could subsist in a community, and his answer falls in a range of 40 to 60 per cent of the medium, not the mean, family income of the community.

We have seen above Sen's Poverty Index which is an ensemble of three elements, namely, (1) the relative number of the poor, indicating the incidence of poverty, (2) average income shortfall of the poor, indicating their average deprivation, and (3) the distribution of income among the poor, indicating their relative deprivation.

For measuring the intensity of poverty we have to employ the Gini Concentration Ratio/Coefficient.

Among the percentage of population below the Poverty Line we have those who are unemployed and poor, those who are fully employed but have very little earning because of low productivity or low wages, those partly employed who earn very little because of low productivity or low wages, and so on.

It is general perception that increasing poverty with increasing GNP tends to become a permanent feature of developing countries. Their low level of development results in a huge backlog of poverty. The supposed automatic trickle-down mechanism is not effective because a major section of society has not equal access to the opportunities of producing or obtaining income from incremental GNP and because intersectoral trade-off imbalances prevail.

A small section of the Indian rural society dominates a number of factors and product markets simultaneously, markets having price and non-price links. The market participants occupy differential positions which defy a uniform model or framework of behaviour and its prognostication. The rural rich are barely 10 to 12 per cent of the total number of the rural households. About six per cent of the big farmers out of nearly 81 million farm households account for around 40 per cent of the total land — this is gross concentration of ownership of holdings.

The propensity to consume of the higher income groups is high, not low, in developing countries. The state policies have favoured their increased expenditures on durable consumer goods: cars, houses, foreign trips, foreign education for their children, and so forth. Those among the rich who commit the sin of saving do so in forms that are not conducive to investment. Between the two stools they are unimportant actors in the play that development presumes.

Rural inequality is associated with the rents received and acquired by the landowners, not with their profits, which have slow growth and that too at the expense of rents. The Ricardian situation prevails in patches where agricultural prosperity is an established fact. In other places where the traditional mores are still powerful in agriculture rents support a retinue of domestic servants maintained by the rural rich. The rich landlord's riotous living, his unproductive consumption, becomes in this way a source of employment to a number of people, who would otherwise have been on the scrap-heap of the unemployed. This is reminiscent of the Malthusian phenomenon, with its attendant evils of indebted and permanently attached agricultural labourers. If there obtains exploitation, there obtains agitation as well — a grim battle wages, robbing the rural side of its much-vaunted serenity and tranquillity.

Were the top rich in the ten richest countries to accede to a mere five per cent cut in their current consumption levels, the present world poverty problem would be resolved. The percentages in developing countries would, of course, be higher in both cases in the nature of existing circumstances but it appears as if neither through increased saving nor through increased investment would the higher income groups in developing countries be contributing to the elimination of poverty in them. Yield from agricultural income tax is of any moment only in States which raise plantation crops, such as Assam, Kerala, Mysore, Tamil Nadu and West Bengal. Increased reliance placed on indirect taxation has increased the hiatus between the rich and the poor. Increase in public expenditure in the agricultural sector has been a multiple of the increase in direct taxation during the plan period. Land revenue which had been a good source of revenue to the States prior to the mid-1960s degenerated into an insignificant source within a few years partly from reduction and partly from remission but most from neglect. With its decline, imposition as well as realisation of betterment levy, water rates, irrigation cess, etc., became progressively impossible tasks. Today agricultural income offers plenty of scope for camouflaging black money. With untaxed money the capitalist farmers have acquired agricultural farms, vineyards and orchards. For fear of loss of votes no political party in India is in a mood to muster the necessary political will to impose agricultural income tax in those States where it is not in vogue and to tighten up its collection in States where it is already in vogue. Short of taxation of agricultural income the State Governments would be hard pressed for funds to push their plans through.

Those small holders of land who could not eke out their subsistence from the proceeds of their respective farm holdings have either sold or leased out their holdings to others and joined the army of farm labourers or migrated to urban areas in quest of some more remunerative employment there. Casual agricultural workers have leased in tiny plots of land from big landlords and worked partly as sub-tenants and share-croppers. It is for them that the Government has wanted to do most but failed to achieve this goal owing to a multitude of adverse factors, existence of the intermediaries being one of them.

The Green Revolution has articulated the income gap among the rural households. It has benefited commercial production rather than subsistence production and among commercial producers it has benefited big producers more than small. Being essentially a technological movement it has had no appreciation of the contribution that institutional reform could make to its own success. The contemplated increased reliance on the market forces is likely to aggravate inequality because the competitive character of the market forces has been diluted and distorted during the plan period, which has witnessed the growth and spread of monopolies, both private and public, with their regime entrenched and their power extended.

Farm mechanisation has resulted in reduced demand for farm workers and added to rural poverty. If wages have risen, total volume of employment in mechanised farms has fallen. The income effect has, in part, been swamped away by the substitution effect.

Other things remaining the same, supply of farm labour is directly linked with the over-all size of population, while demand for agricultural labour force is influenced by the size of the farm, the system of farming and the degree of technological development. In the rain-fed areas demand for farm labour varies according to the nature and amount of rainfall.

Kuznets has shown that higher population growth and urbanisation-cum-industrialisation in the very rigid economic and social structure of developing countries are the two (or three) major (associative) processes responsible for the widening of income inequality in them. Rapid population growth lowers average per capita income as well as per capita income of the lower income groups since the size of families of the poor is generally larger. It is on the basis of this observed fact that poverty is said to be its own cause, that is, poverty breeds poverty.

Agriculture still remains a shock-absorber in the sense that it absorbs the shocks of additional manpower and as such it is the residual sector — when people do not find jobs in other sectors, they cling, willingly or unwillingly, to agriculture. Agriculture is, by and large, subsistence agriculture in that it accommodates more people than it can absorb in the economic sense. Not only the underemployed, both visible and invisible, but also the unemployed and the utterly unemployable people find shelter in agriculture. The saturation point of population in a subsistence economy is higher than that in a wage economy. Many persons who would have been unemployed and have starved in a wage economy are maintained in disguised unemployment by their relatives as part of a traditional social security system.

The outcome of the abundance of the variable labour factor in relation to the fixed land factor in rural India is the negative marginal product of the former. Of late, some agricultural labour has begun finding place in the non-agricultural occupations in the rural sector itself and this trend is on the increase. If this phase gathers momentum, we should have a large-scale expansion of the industrial sector with surplus agricultural labour finding employment in it. The age-old rigidity in the occupational structure has diminished. Caste is not today the sole determinant of a man's avocation. Decline in the supply of casual labour in agriculture compels better farm labour management.

As part of labour engaged erstwhile in agriculture is being

withdrawn from it to the non-agricultural occupations in the countryside itself, could we infer from this that a capitalist sector is emerging there — capitalist sector in the sense of expansion of wage employment. If the reply is in the negative because of self-employment in the non-agricultural occupations, then agricultural surplus is not being generated in an increased magnitude. There are not increased profits to be reinvested. What has really occurred is the expansion of the subsistence sector both internal and external to agriculture in the rural economy itself. Part of the rural population not absorbed in agriculture is being absorbed in the non-agricultural occupations in the rural economy itself and a sizable proportion of it which is being engaged in the non-agricultural occupations in the rural economy itself more or less at constant real wages is always prepared to go to towns and cities for being employed there at higher wages, provided there is really scope for more employment there. Whatever capital formation has materialised in the rural side has been financed largely by funds coming from outside, being institutional, and one effect of this capital formation has been to drive up real wages. Agriculturists have to compete with the organisers of the rural projects for the supply of labour. Payment of increased wages makes inroads into the agricultural surplus acquired by the individual farmers.

In regions where industrialisation, before or after independence, has been profoundly influenced by the presence in them of minerals of various kinds and in huge numbers and volumes, there too it has been realised ere long that mineral products-based industrialisation calls for not one mineral product but a combination of them, to be used in certain proportions. In other words, minerals must exist in one and the same locality and be available in such a fashion that they could be readily used in those proportions. Moreover, industrialisation, whether it is mineral products-based or not, calls for other facilities like supply of capital, power transport, skilled labour, and a friendly state policy (not, of course, the highly disabling and offsetting Freight Equalisation Scheme which was in force from 1956 to 1992) to exist or be available conveniently in the same locality. Where the preconditions have existed, mining-based industries have grown like mushroom and their units have formed a bee-line in the area and a huge army of workers, chiefly unskilled, drawn from all parts of the country, has found employment there. The mining-cum-industry belt has constituted a sort of enclave or island of development, such that its backwash effect has often overshadowed its spread effect. The industry has become skewed in its structure and the economy lopsided. The proportion of workers employed in the given belt has been a very small fraction of those employed in agriculture so much so that the economy has remained characterically agricultural.

During the period in which the terms of trade have turned against agriculture and in favour of industry, agriculture has paid for industrialisation to that extent and rural poverty has escalated in consequence. The subsidised inflow of inputs and credit and the ever-increasing pumping of public sector outlays in rural areas have been paralleled by the outflow of rural bank deposits. Rural savings have fared better relatively to urban savings.

In particular areas the process of development has proceeded by rendering many people homeless, jobless and rootless. Several construction works have uprooted and evicted a large number of people from their original habitats and forced them to join the ranks of development refugees and hence those of the poor. The compensation paid to them has been inadequate. In the few cases where it has been adequate the social costs of dehabilitation have been extremely high. No sensible rehabilitation programme has so far been evolved. The tribals in a number of places have been pushed further to the margin of subsistence and thereby marginalised. They represent the highly indebted sections. The movement launched in these regions is a struggle of the aggrieved and their sympathisers against the given people's right to resources for survival and against the destruction of their environment. It is questioning the hierarchies/oligarchies which allow the rights of the tribals and semi-aboriginals to be sacrificed at the altar of the interests of other parties and the rights of the rural communities to be sacrificed for the sake of those of the urban ones.

As the supply of cheap full-time domestic labour to the urban middle class families has fallen sharply with the passage of time and the capacity of these families to afford full-time domestic help has, in general, also been drastically reduced under the non-relenting inflationary regime, demand for part-time and contract domestic help has risen, and with it has its supply, provided mainly by the rural families that have migrated to urban areas, combined with their increased participation in the supply of vegetables and fruits, milk from the *khatals*, snacks, household wares (all these are being vended or hawked either physically on the head or on tricycles or *thelas*), plying of rickshaws and tempos, hauling of personal effects from one flat to another, serving in tea-stalls, in the sale and purchase of waste materials, and in scores of other jobs. But a host of factors has for some time past upset this mechanism. To substantiate, the *jhuggies* and *jhonparies*, the roadside tea-stalls, eating houses, shops, etc., are dismantled by the municipal authorities every now and then, and the rural migrants occupying/running them are forced to move elsewhere. Mechanisation of waste management in recent years has deprived many poor people of their only livelihood. Plastic products have dispossessed many poor persons of their only means of survival, that is, making of hand products. It is against this backdrop that there exists no significant difference between the working poor on very low wages because the employment provided is non-viable or unproductive, on the one hand, and the unemployed poor supported by their relations, on the other. Migration to urban areas in excess of job opportunities is at once a symptom and a contributing factor to the development process typical of a developing country like India. Many rural migrants are from the marginalised section, a deficiency which their urban trek is incapable of curing permanently. All that it does is to palliate it for a time.

The visible tip of the iceberg of unemployment in our country is open unemployment which is, oftener than not, coterminus with educated unemployment, which, when viewed in terms of the different levels of education, from the matriculate to the postgraduate and even beyond that, takes after a pyramid or a bell-shaped object. Higher education has over the years become a necessary evil, a drug, so to say, for the educated graduate, on failing to get a job, decides to stay on in the university in order to equip himself with another degree or qualification in the hope that this would repair his academic deficiency. In this he is guilty of self-delusion. For at every level either he has learnt less or has been taught less than the desired norm. Education was supposed to act like yeast to development in developing countries. Instead it has degerated into a veritable drug. One has to go on taking the drug in order just to survive. The teachers who once upon a time were regarded as the toast of society are right now regarded as less than crumbs by the general public. They have in many parts of the country got everything for practically nothing and without facing at any stage competition in its true sense. The moral decadence and the social unrest of today are no less owing to the collapse of the academic system, which is the manufacturer as well as the purveyor of knowledge and character, the two strongest pillars of the human resource. The over-indulgence of the politicians to education for furtherance of their narrow ends has seriously impaired the moral spine of our society.

If 80 to 90 per cent of the current income of any State Government is spent on meeting its establishment costs alone and if of the remaining 10 to 20 per cent, 9 to 16 per cent is dissipated on keeping the 'white elephants' alive, with the residue of one to four per cent the new investment made in the organised or economic and social services sector of the Government, the number of persons employed for the first time would always be very small. Even that small number of jobs which is created would be further monopolised by those sections of society which are at present monopolising them or have so far monopolised them. If there has been growth at the exponential rate anywhere in our society it has been in this area of casteism or sectionalism. In a pragmatic, down-to-earth analysis such non-economic variables are not inconsequential. What people denounced when they were out of power, they did with a vengeance and an aggressiveness when they got into power themselves rather unabashedly — different castes at different times. A social malady like this has existed because it has benefited certain powerful sections of society, and being in administration they have wielded maximum power. The gains have snowballed. It would not be out of place to point out here that the social myths have proved to be the greatest energisers of the masses but most of their paraders have turned to be the worst betrayers of the people's cause.

The degree of inequality has increased because the growth process has led to a trickle-up in favour of the top one-sixth of the income pyramid. Poverty has increased as the lower middle class has been gradually marginalised. Despite the countervailing forces the range of the gap between salaries and wages is still wide. Appropriation of the lion's share of the public sector outlays (including subsidies and easy credit) by the trinity of contractors, bureaucrats and politicians has made inequality worse. At the farm level, 66 per cent of large owner cultivators, 46 per cent of medium owner cultivators and 22 per cent of small owner cultivators have benefited from the institutional supply of inputs and credit and assistance in other forms — the benefit derived has been more or less proportionate to the area of land owned. In so far as the better-off sections have benefited more it has been in their interest that they work for the stability of the government formed by those political parties which have been instrumental in ensuring this.

In the initial years of planning growth came to be measured objectively by growth of industrial output, particularly in the public sector and its rate came to be related with the level of consumption – growth is faster if consumption does not grow at the same rate as does current income but at a rate lower than it or grows slowly, if at all, and if real wages in the export sector are kept down at a low level. As the pace of development speeded up and the public sector investment in industry rose by leaps and bonds, with the majority of the public undertakings running at a loss, the gap between the rich and the poor widened both absolutely and relatively. As the production structure became geared to unequal distribution and the domestic market which subserved largely the higher income groups became entrenched, it became extremely difficult, both economically and politically, to alter it at a later point of time in the direction of greater equality. Inequality was aggravated by growth of technological dualism and growth of the multinationals.

Reduction of inequality of income, wealth and unearned increment is, to a certain extent, closely connected with reduction in poverty. The proponents of equality contend that greater equality is a help rather than a hindrance to the pace of growth of a developing country. Increased equality promotes effective demand. Sectors such as industry which are capable of faster rates of growth are at present constrained by lack of effective demand. Greater equality in land ownership among the farmers can boost agricultural production.

The hard core of the new development strategy is 'Reaching the Poor'. The 'Greater Equality Approach' is directed at the toning up of the Quality of Life of the poorer and weaker sections. The emergence of the Basic Human Needs Approach to Poverty Alleviation has revolutionised the concept of poverty itself: Poverty is no longer an individual household's problem but a broad social problem which public policy must surmount. Poverty persists because of the failure of public policy. It is the lack of political will or commitment which accounts for the failure of public policy.

On the authority of Singer, we can point out that the Basic Human Needs Approach, firstly, does away with the negative concept of reducing or eliminating poverty by substituting in its place the more positive operational concept of satisfying the basic human needs. Secondly, it shifts from a more monetary definition of poverty in terms of income (which does not suit the conditions of many of the really poor in a developing country, who may be susbsistence farmers or producers) to a definition in terms of physical needs which can be defined in concrete material terms. Thirdly, it frees the poverty concept from the stranglehold of traditional thinking which considers the poor themselves responsible for their poverty or finds fault with their government or with both in part. In sum, the approach believes that poverty could be reduced through public investment in favour of the poor and at least a 40 per cent increase in the per capita calorie intake of the poor could bring about a modicum of equality.

The fight against poverty and inequality is intended to be fought by a couple of major weapons: One, *Redistribution with growth* and two, *redistribution with institutional change*. The first is to be achieved through the creation of productive employment opportunities at an increasing rate out of increased income. But this has not been much of a success story. For some time past both the rate of unemployment and the rate of growth have been accelerating in a number of developing countries. In these countries the increase in the number of the employed has fallen short of the increase in the number of poeple of the working age-groups — whereas the former has been governed by expansion in productive capacity, the latter has been determined by the growth rate of population.

There is no denying the fact that if unutilised and underutilised resources were to be brought into full production, the GNP is bound to increase. Normally, a higher rate of employment must be accompained by a higher rate of production. Employment is, as a rule, a cause of increase in national product. Planning should be so devised that, in the first instance, rural labour leaves land but not agriculture and finds employment in agriculture itself, that is, in agriculture-oriented activities in the rural sector itself. In the second instance, rural labour should be in a position to leave agriculture but not the village and find employment in agro-industries located outside towns and cities and near a cluster of villages. In the third instance, rural labour should leave both agriculture and his village and find employment, in the main, in the urban, formal sector, apart from the urban, informal sector. This phase would be coordinate with a sectoral displacement of labour or structural transformation. The assumption central to this three-phase programming of unemployment eradication is recognition of the fact that urban unemployment or urban poverty is an extension or overflow of rural unemployment or rural poverty and hence by maintaining or restoring economic well-being of the people in rural areas urban poverty or urban unemployment can be tackled to an appreciable extent, for a time being.

Construction of infrastructure is not production in and by itself; it is a vital adjunct to production in agriculture and industry. It generates more employment for the given period only, and not for the succeeding periods on a sustained basis. A sizable chunk of the public sector expenditure leaks out from the income stream and goes into the pockets of the triad of contractors, bureaucrats and politicians. The McCords found mismanagement and corruption to be largely responsible for the increase in the numbers of the poor in developing countries in spite of the efforts made to mitigate it. According to them, its remedy lay in rapid agricultural development, imaginative and innovative industrialisation and investment in human resource development. *Factor H* (Human factor or Resource) was the ultimate touchstone of everything. Its quality, its character was the final acid-test of the success or failure of every new device or policy or programme in any economy, be it a free enterprise economy or a totally regimented economy or a socialist pattern of society. Its intractability in most situations rendered planning an uncertain exercise.

In the monitoring of the various poverty-alleviation and employment-generation programmes chalked out by the planners the administrative input has far exceeded proportionally other — scientific, technical and economic — inputs, and the programmes have smacked of over-officialisation with no signs of transfer of the control at any stage to those for whom they were meant. Where people have shown interest in sharing the responsibility, for reasons largely suspect the governmental agencies have refused to part with their power and authority. Progress has been checkmated on account of this.

The vested interests have vehemently opposed the slogan 'Redistribution with Institutional Change'. The 'Land to the Tillers' movement had so far a chequered career. It was scuttled and sabotaged. The higher degree of landlessness has been one significant factor in low agricultural development in developing countries. Agricultural productivity has been higher in the case of farms owned and cultivated by the proprietors themselves. Not the lack of technical and other means of lowering inequality but the lack of political will to achieve it by redistribution of the existing property has been the real stumbling-block. The soft measures have pre-empted the strong ones. Where a holistic solution was the only remedy, piecemeal and vertically compartmentalised ones were hammered out and applied. The structures and processes, the rules and procedures created or adopted have not been in consonance with the dynamics of the social order, already in the melting pot. The mould chosen has not been one that could have accommodated the diverse interest groups. Self-interest has not gone beyond the frontiers of family and caste. People have not been enthused. They have not been convinced, not assured with regard to their right to live and their right to work, and no mass fervour has so far been kindled. Something has gone wrong somewhere at some stage in planning in the last four decades in this country.

The Upshot[2]

The full meaning of the high drama of economic privation of the poorer States in India can be properly appreciated only against the backdrop of their population question, as Myint puts this in a different context. For the net growth rate of an economy is nothing more than its GDP growth rate simultaneously adjusted to its population growth rate.

Viewed against its resource base, the population of a State may be an obstacle to its economic development. Roughly, the percentage of poor population is related with the level of economic development as indicated by per capita income, the resource base as indicated by the net area sown per head and the level of productivity per man and per hectare engaged in cultivation.

Andhra Pradesh, Karnataka, Jammu and Kashmir, Tamil Nadu, Kerala, Uttar Pradesh and Orissa are better placed with regard to the percentages of population below the Poverty Line *vis-a-vis* their per capita SDPs. On the other hand, Punjab, Haryana, Maharashtra, Gujarat, West Bengal, Himachal Pradesh and Assam are worse placed from this standpoint. Of them, the first six States confirm the belief that poverty co-exists with progress. Bihar and Rajasthan have their population percentages below the Poverty Line in perfect accord with their relative positions in per capita SDP.

There is no linear relationship between the rate of growth of SDP and the rate of fall in the percentage of population below the Poverty Line. The two rates vary for the increase as well as the decrease in the rate of growth of SDP, and are not necessarily in one and the same direction.

When the level of economic development is low (as manifest in per capita SDP), population pressure is also very high (as in the case of Bihar and Uttar Pradesh), and *vice versa* (as in the case of Punjab, Haryana and Himachal Pradesh. Maharashtra, Karnataka and Rajasthan revealed an ideal correlation.

Undeniably, higher growth rate of SDP has denoted an improvement in the economic lot of the common man, subject to the proviso that it has exceeded the rate of growth of population but apart from that it has not had any marked general brunt on the number and percentage of the poor in all States.

Population pressure is a real issue in most States, as seen from the point of view of food or aggregate income. Erosion of per capita SDP and the decelerating rate of growth of per capita foodgrains production are evidence of the contention by many authors that the Demultiplier Effect of population growth on income at work in these States in varying degrees. The rate of erosion of per capita SDP has been the highest in the case of Rajasthan and the lowest in that of Tamil Nadu.

Lastly, no other indicator of the lowness of the resource base is as pertinent to our study as is net area sown per cultivator. But productivity (measured per cultivator and per hectare) is, in the final analysis, the hard core of the explanation of inter-State disparities in poverty levels.

NOTES

1. Approved by the National Development Council at its 43rd meeting held in December, 1991 to be adopted in the Eighth Plan (1992-97).
2. See our *The Indian Economy Since 1951: Growth with Imbalances.*

BIBLIOGRAPHY*

Books

Adler, J.H., *Development and Income Distribution*, Washington, 1972.

Agrawal, A.N., *Indian Economy*, Delhi, 1986.

Ahmad, E., *Bihar*, Ranchi, 1965.

Alexander, P.C., *Industrial Estates in India*, Bombay, 1963.

Anjaria, J.J., *Essays in Planning and Growth*, Bombay, 1972.

Asian Development Bank, *Asian Development Outlook*, Washington, 1990

Bairoch, P., *Urban Unemployment in Developing Countries*, Geneva, 1973.

Balakrishna, R., *Regional Planning in India*, Madras, 1946.

Balogh, T., *The Economics of Poverty*, London, 1966.

Bauer, P.T. and Yamey, B.S., *The Economics of Underdeveloped Countries*, Cambridge, 1959.

Bhagwati, J., *The Economics of Underdeveloped Countries*, Verona, 1967.

Bhalla, G.S., and Alagh, Y.K., *Performance of Indian Agriculture*, New Delhi, 1979.

Birmingham, W. and Ford, A.G. (eds.), *Planning and Growth in Rich and Poor Countries*, London, 1966.

Blaug, M., *The Causes of Graduate Unemployment in India*, London, 1969.

—, *Education and the Employment Problem in Developing Countries*, Geneva, 1973.

Bose, A. et al (eds.), *Population in India's Development*, Delhi, 1974.

Bredo, W., *Industrial Estates*, Bombay, 1960.

Chaudhuri, P., *Aspects of Indian Economic Development*, London, 1971.

---

* By and large, in addition to those mentioned in the tables.

—, *The Indian Economy : Poverty and Development*, Delhi, 1978.

Cairncross, A. and Puri, M. (eds.), *Employment, Income Distribution and Development Strategy*, Bristol, 1976.

Coale, A.J. and Hoover, E.M., *Population Growth and Economic Development in Low-Income Countries*, Princeton, 1972.

Connell, J. et al (eds.), *Migration from Rural Areas*, Delhi, 1976.

Connell, J. and Lipton, M., *Assessing Village Labour Situations in Developing Countries*, Delhi, 1977.

Datt, R. and Sundharam, K.P.M., *Indian Economy*, New Delhi, 1989.

Dandekar, V. M. and Rath, R., *Poverty in India*, Bombay, 1971.

Dantwala, M. L., *Poverty in India : Then and Now*, Bombay, 1973.

De Castro, J., *Geography of Hunger*, 1952.

Desai, M., Rudolph, S.H., and Rudra, A., *Agrarian Power and Agricultural Productivity in South Asia*, O.U.P., Delhi, 1984.

Fiegel, F.C. et al, *Agricultural Innovations in Indian Villages*, Hyderabad, 1968.

Fishlow, A. et al, *Rich and Poor Nations in the World Economy*, Ludhiana, 1980.

Fonseca, A.J. (ed.), *Challenge of Poverty in India*, Delhi, 1971.

Gadgil, D.R., *Planning and Economic Policy in India*, Bombay, 1961.

Galbraith, J. K., *The Affluent Society*, Boston, 1956.

Ghatak, S. and Ingersent, K., *Agriculture and Economic Development*, New Delhi, 1984.

Ghosh, R.N., *Agriculture in Economic Development*, New Delhi, 1977.

Guha, *Rural Manpower and Capital Formation in India*, New Delhi, 1969.

Gupta, A.P., *Fiscal Policy for Employment Generation in India*, New Delhi, 1977.

Hajra, S., *Bihar and Punjab: A Study in Regional Economic Disparity*, Economic and Scientific Research Foundation, New Delhi, 1973.

Hanson, A.H., *The Process of Planning*, London, 1966.

Hanumantha Rao, C.H., *Technological Change and Distribution of Gains in Indian Agriculture*, New Delhi, 1975.

—, and Joshi, P.C. (eds.), *Essays in Honour of Professor V.K.R.V. Rao*, New Delhi, 1979.

Haq, M.U., *The Strategy of Economic Planning*, London 1966.

Healey, J.M., *The Development of Social Overhead Capital in India*, London, 1965.

Higgins, B., *Economic Development*, Allahabad, 1963.

Hirschman, A.O., *The Strategy of Economic Development*, New Haven, 1958.
Houlton, J., *Bihar : The Heart of India*, London, 1948.
Huq, M.S., *Education, Manpower and Development in South and South-East Asia*, New York, 1975.
ILO, *Action Against Unemployment*, Geneva, 1950.
ILO, *Employment and Economic Growth*, Geneva, 1964.
ILO, *The World Employment Programme*, Geneva, 1971.
John, P.V., *Some Aspects of the Structure of Indian Agricultural Economy, 1947-48 to 1961-62*, Bombay, 1968.
Khusro, A.M. (ed.), *Readings in Agricultural Development*, Delhi, 1968.
Kaser, M. and Portes, R. (eds.), *Planning and Market Relations*, London, 1971.
Klassen, L.H., *Methods of Selecting Industries for Depressed Areas*, Paris, 1967.
Leipenstein, H., *Economic Backwardness and Economic Growth*, New York, 1960.
Lewis, J.P., *Quiet Crisis in India*, Washington, 1962.
Lewis, W.A., *The Theory of Economic Growth*, London, 1968.
—, *Dynamic Factors in Economic Growth*, Bombay, 1974.
Maddison, A., *Class Structure and Economic Growth*, London, 1979.
Mahajan, V.S., *Studies in Indian Agriculture and Rural Development*, New Delhi, 1986.
Majumdar, N.A., *Problems of Underemployment*, Bombay, 1961.
Malenbaum, W., *Prospects for Indian Development*, London, 1962.
Mandal, G.C., *Studies in the Problem of Growth of Rural Economy*, Calcutta, 1961.
—. et al, *Economics of Rural Change: A Study in East India*, Calcutta, 1974.
Marglin, S.A., *Value and Price in the Labour-Surplus Economy*, Oxford, 1976.
Mazoomdar, A., *Bihar : Problem of Development*, Delhi, July 1990.
Mehta, V.L., *Decentralised Economic Development*, Bombay, 1964.
Meier, G.M. and Baldwin, R.L., *Economic Development*, Bombay, 1964.
—, (ed.), *Leading Issues in Development Economics*, New York, 1966.
Mellor, J.W., *The Economics of Agricultural Development*, Bombay, 1969.

Minhas, B.S., *Planning and the Poor*, Delhi, 1974.

Mishra, S.K. and Puri, U.K., *Indian Economy*, Bombay, 1986.

Mulay, M. and Ray, G.L., *Towards Modernisation*, Delhi, 1975.

Mukherjee, R.K., *The Regional Balance of Man: An Ecological Theory of Population*, Madras, 1938.

—, *Man and His Habitation*, Bombay, 1968.

Mukhopadhyay, S., *Source of Variation in Agricultural Productivity*, New Delhi, 1976.

Myint, H., *Economics of Developing Countries*, London, 1964.

—, *Economic Theory and the Underdeveloped Countries*, 1971.

Myrdal, G., *Rich Lands and Poor*, New York, 1957.

—, *Economic Theory and Underdeveloped Regions*, London, 1957.

—, *Beyond the Welfare State*, London, 1960.

—, *Challenge to Affluence*, London, 1964.

—, *Asian Drama*, London, 1968.

Naiyar, K., *Blossoms in the Dust*, London, 1962.

NCAER, *Techno-Economic Survey of Bihar*, Bombay, 1959.

NCAER, *Perspective Plan of Industrial Development of Bihar 1979-80 to 1988-89*, New Delhi, 1980.

Planning Commission, Government of India, *India's First Five Year Plan*, New Delhi, 1951.

—, *India's Second Five-Year Plan*, New Delhi, 1956.

—, *India's Third Five-Year Plan,* New Delhi, 1961.

—, *India's Annual Plans 1968-69*.

—, *India's Fourth Five-Year Plan*, 1970.

—, *India's Fifth Five-Year Plan*, 1975.

—, *India's Sixth Five-Year Plan*, 1980.

—, *India's Seventh Five-Year Plan*, 1985.

—, *India's Approach to the Eighth Five-Year Plan*, 1990

—, *Report of the Committee of Experts on Unemployment*, New Delhi, 1970.

Prasad, K.N., *Bihar Ke Sadhan, Krishi Aur Udyog*, Ram Narain Lal & Sons, Allahabad, 1954.

—, *Technological Choice Underdevelopmental Planning*, Popular Prakashan, Bombay, 1963.

—, *Economics of A Backward Region in A Backward Economy: A Case Study of Bihar in Relation to other States*, 2 Vol., 1967 and 1968, Scientific Book Agency, Calcutta.

—, *Strategy of Industrial Dispersal and Decentralised Development*, S. Chand & Co., New Delhi and Patna, 1973.

—, *Problems of Economic Development in the Third World*, Sterling Publishers, New Delhi, 1980.

—, *Problems of Indian Economic Development*, Sterling Publishers, New Delhi, 1983.

—, *Studies in Economic Analysis and Policy*, Sterling Publishers, New Delhi, 1984.

—, *Development of Philosophical Thought in Economics (in relation to those in other social sciences)*, Himalaya Publishing House, Bombay, 1985.

—, *Foundations of Modern Economics*, Sterling Publishers, New Delhi, 1986.

—, *Lectures on Micro-economic Theory*, Himalayas Publishing House, Bombay, 1987.

—, *India's Rural Problems*, Concept Publishing Company, New Delhi, 1990.

—, *The Indian Economy Since 1951 : Growth with Imbalances*, Intellectual Book Corner, New Delhi, 1992.

Puttaswamaiah, K., *Unemployment in India : Policy for Manpower*, New Delhi, 1977.

Raj, K.N., *Some Economic Aspects of the Bhakra-Nangal Project*, Bombay, 1960.

Rangnekar, D.K., *Poverty and Capital Development in India*, London, 1962.

Ranis, G. (ed.), *The Gap Between Rich and Poor Nations*, Edinburgh, 1972.

Reddaway, W.B., *The Development of the Indian Economy*, London, 1962.

Ridker, R.G. and Lubbell, H. (eds.), *Employment and Unemployment Problems of the Near East and South East*, New Delhi, 1971.

Rosen, G., *Industrial Change in India*, Bombay, 1959.

Resenstein-Rodan, P.N. (ed.), *Pricing and Fiscal Policies*, London, 1964.

Roy, A., *Planning in India*, Calcutta, 1965.

Schultz, T.W., *Economic Growth and Agriculture*, New York, 1965

Sen, A.K., *Employment, Technology and Development*, Delhi, 1975.

Sen, S.R., *The Strategy for Agricultural Development*, Bombay, 1966.

Singh, A., *Planning for Developing a Backward Economy*, New Delhi, 1989.

Singh, T., *Towards an Integrated Society*, Calcutta, 1969.

Sinha, G., *Food Economics*, Allahabad, 1956.

Sinha, S., *The Bitter Harvest*, New Delhi, 1975.

Sharma, T.R., *Location of Industries in India*, Delhi, 1952.

Shonfield, A., *The Attack on World Poverty*, New York, 1960.

Southworth, H.M. and Johnston, B.F. (eds.), *Agricultural Development and Economic Growth*, New York, 1967.

Srinivasan, T.N. and Bardhan, P.K. (eds.), *Poverty and Income Distribution in India*, Calcutta, 1974.

Stewart, F., *Technology and Underdevelopment*, London, 1977.

Streeten, P. and Lipton, M. (eds.), *The Crisis of Indian Planning*, Bombay, 1968.

Swamy, S., *Indian Economic Planning*, Delhi, 1971.

Thirdwall, A.P., *Growth and Development*, New Delhi, 1972.

Thorner, D. and A., *Land and Labour in India*, Bombay, 1962.

Times of India, *Directory and Year Book*, Bombay, 1984.

Todaro, M.P., *Internal Migration in Developing Countries*, Geneva, 1976.

—, *Economic Development in the Third World*, London, 1985.

Turnhom, D., *The Employment Problem in Less Developed Countries*, Paris, 1971.

United Nations, *Attack on Mass Poverty and Unemployment*, New York, 1972.

Uppal, J.S., *Disguised Unemployment in an Underdeveloped Economy*, Bombay, 1972.

—, (ed.), *India's Economic Problems*, New Delhi, 1987.

Vakil, C.N. and Brahmananda, P.R., *Planning for an Expanding Economy*, Bombay, 1956.

Verghese, B.G., *Design for Tomorrow*, Bombay, 1965.

Warriner, D., *Land Reform in Principle and Practice*, London, 1968.

—, *Land Reform in Principle and Practice*, London, 1969.

Weiner, M., *Sons of the Soil, Migration and Ethnic Conflict in India*, Delhi, 1978.

Weitz, R. (ed.), *Rural Planning in Developing Countries*, London, 1965.

Wilber, C.K. (ed.), *The Political Economy of Development and Underdevelopment*, New York, 1979.

World Bank, *Assault on Poverty*, Washington, 1975.

—, *World Development Report*, Washington, 1990.

Yates, P.L. (ed.), *Employment Policies in Developing Countries*, London 1974.

Articles

Economic and Political Weekly
8.2.1973 (P. K. Bardhan)
15.5.1973 (P. K. Bardhan)
15.8.1976 (K. N. Raj)
6.1.1990 (K. N. Raj)
27.1.1990 (K. Bhardwaj)
10.3.1990 (B. Gopal Krishan Kumar)
7.4.1990 (D. V. S. Sastry and A. K. Nag)
9.6.1990 (M. Govinda Rao)
13.4.1991 (P. Visaria and B. S. Minhas)
1.9.1991 (A. Ghosh)

Economic Times
9.5.1975 (H.S. Bal)
24.12.1986 (K.N. Prasad)
25-26.2.1988 (I.J. Ahluwalia and K. Srinivasan)
20.1.1990 (T.S. Papola)
8.1.1991 (M. Guruswamy and S. Nagpal)
28.3.1991 (P. K. Bhargava)
23.4.1991 (A. Vaidyanathan)
27.9.1991 (N. A. Majumdar and V. D. Lall)
15.10.1991 (S. Jha)

Finance and Development
September 1974 (M. Ahluwalia)

Financial Express
4.3.1991 (J. D. Sethi)
16.6.1991 (N.C. Joshi)

Indian Economic Review
April 1970 (P. K. Bardhan)

International Encyclopaedia of Social Sciences
P. F. Hoselitz
C. Ranis

Journal of Development Studies
1977 Volume (M. Ahluwalia)

New Encyclopaedia Britannica
J.C. L.
H. Myint

Times of India
1.5.1986 (K. N. Prasad)
1.5.1987 (K. N. Prasad)
12.1.1990 (D. D. Monte).
16.7.1990 (C. H. Hanumantha Rao)
26.1.1991 (K. N. Prasad)
1.5.1991 (S. S. Anklesaria Aiyar)
21.5.1991 (D. Khatkhate)
5.8.1991 (D. D. Monte)

INDEX